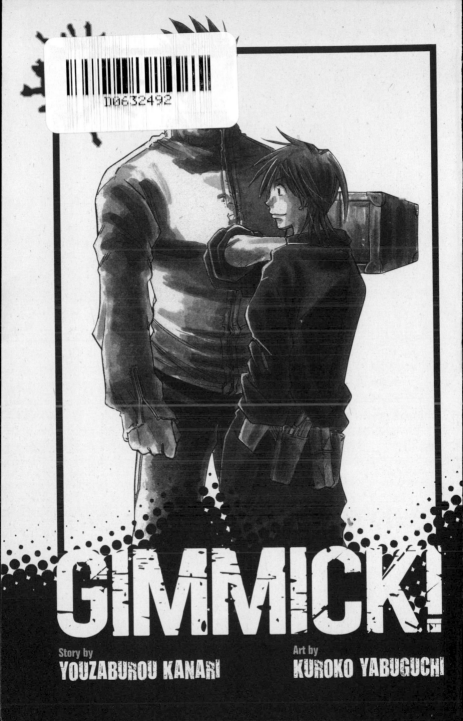

GIMMICK!

Story by
YOUZABUROU KANARI

Art by
KUROKO YABUGUCHI

GIMMICK!

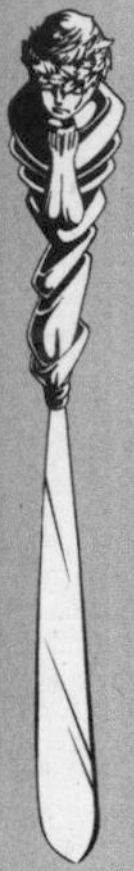

CONTENTS

VOL 6

Scene 47: My Favorite Things (Part 3)

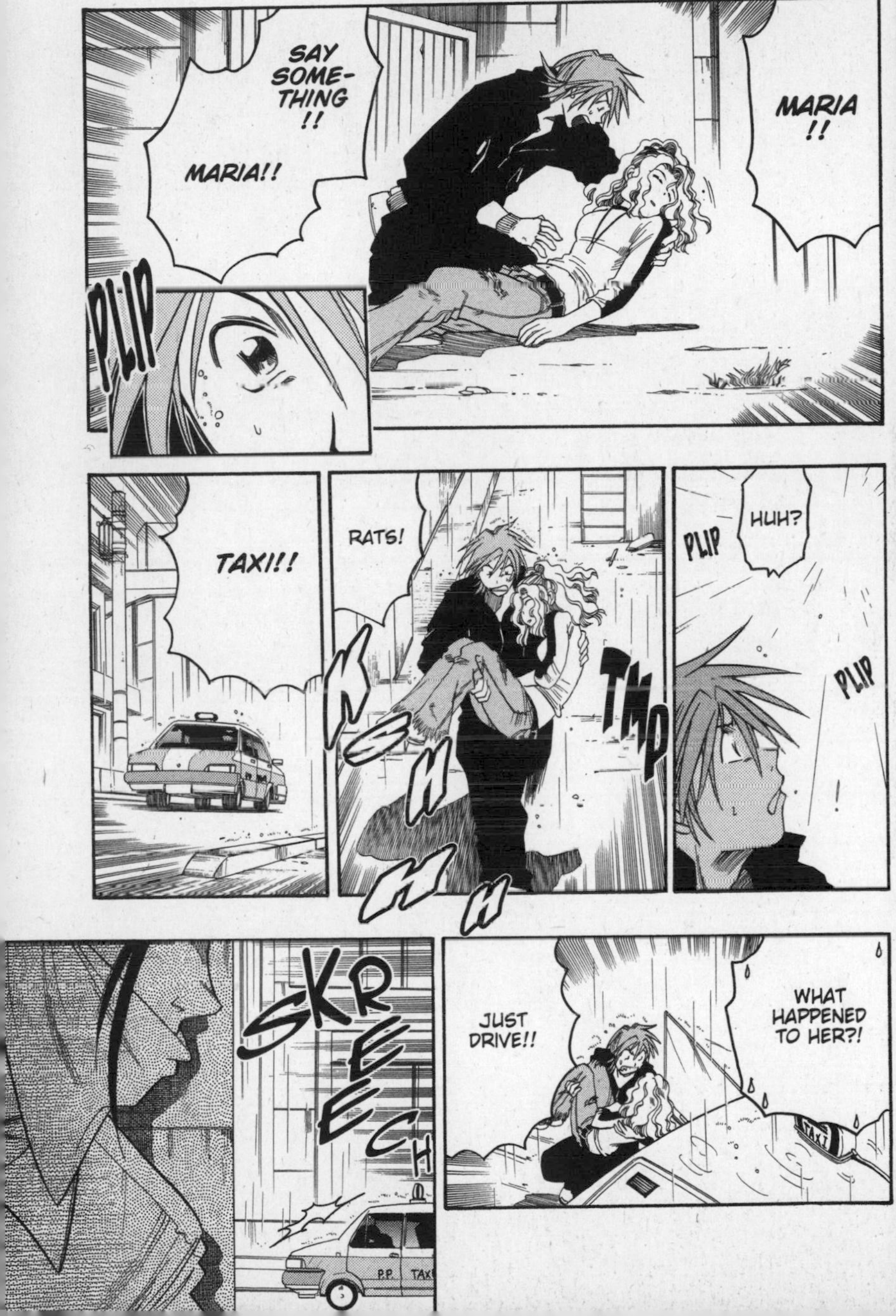
MARIA !!
SAY SOME-THING !!
MARIA!!
PLIP
PLIP
HUH?
PLIP
RATS!
TMP
TAXI!!
WHAT HAPPENED TO HER?!
JUST DRIVE!!
SKREEECH
TAXI
P.P. TAX

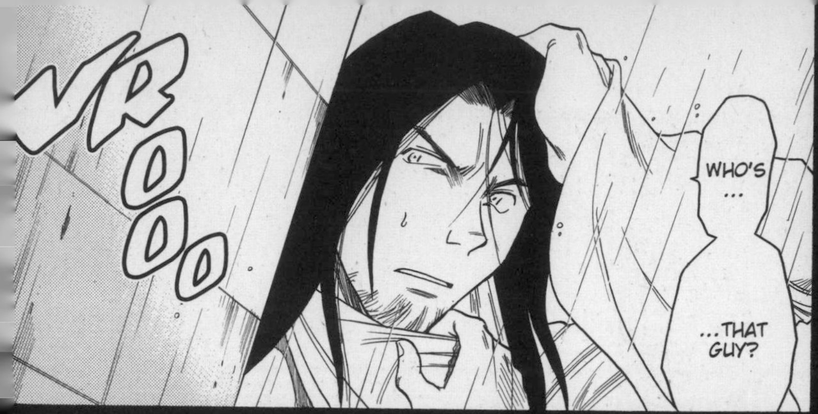
WHO'S ...
...THAT GUY?
VROOOO

Scene 47: My Favorite Things (Part 3)

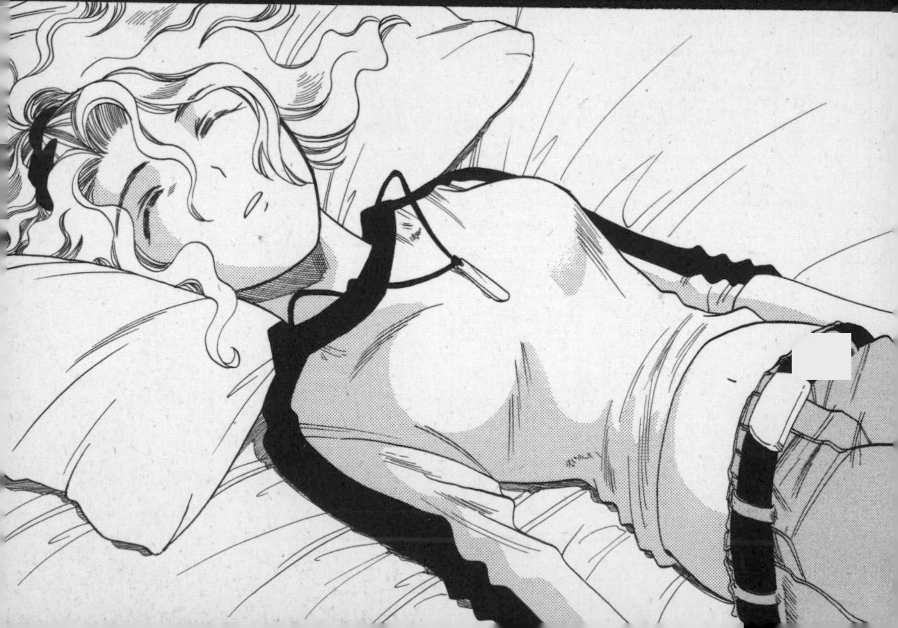

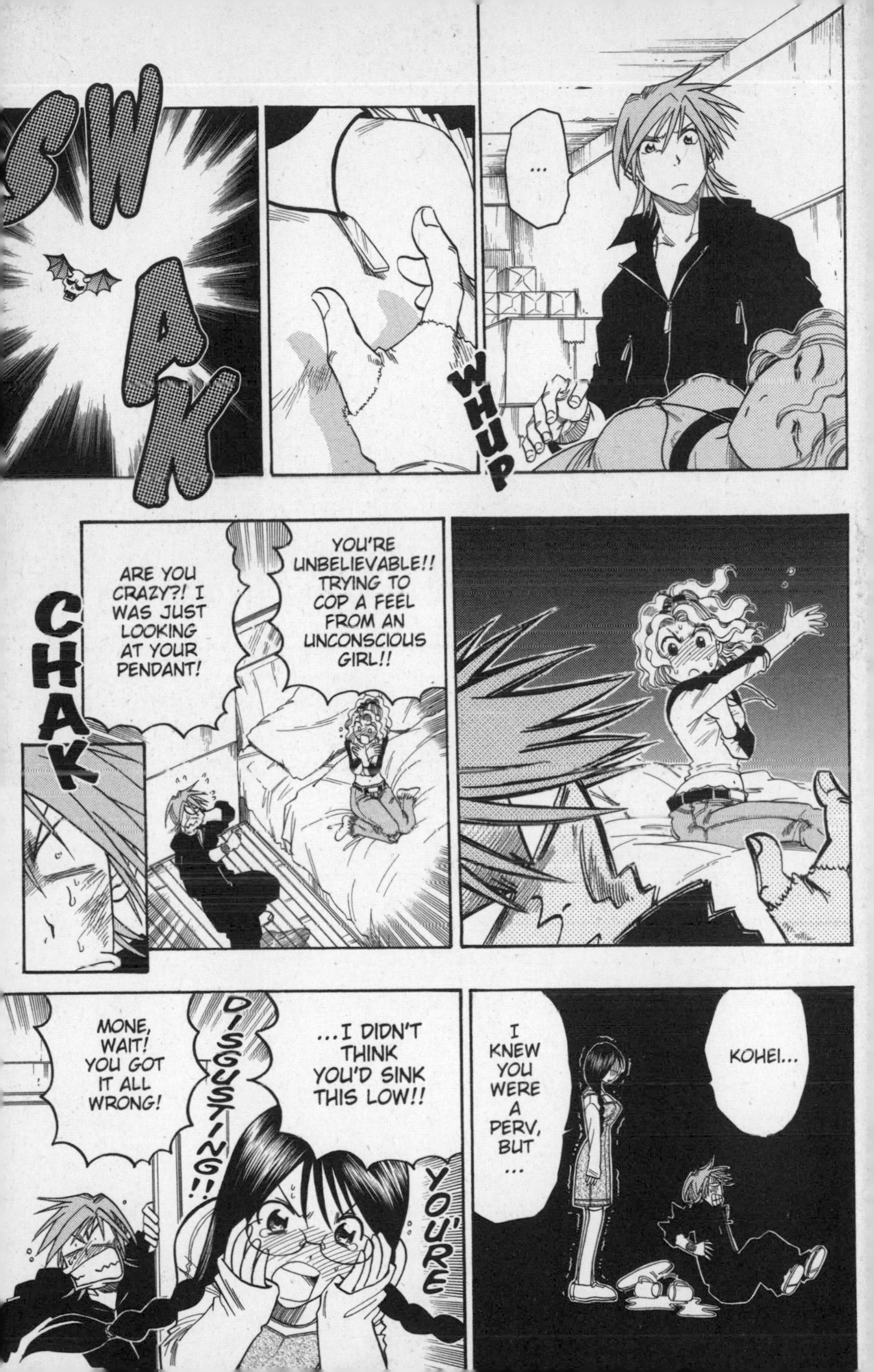
...
WHUP
SWAK
YOU'RE UNBELIEVABLE!! TRYING TO COP A FEEL FROM AN UNCONSCIOUS GIRL!!
ARE YOU CRAZY?! I WAS JUST LOOKING AT YOUR PENDANT!
CHAK
KOHEI...
I KNEW YOU WERE A PERV, BUT...
YOU'RE
DISGUSTING!!
...I DIDN'T THINK YOU'D SINK THIS LOW!!
MONE, WAIT! YOU GOT IT ALL WRONG!

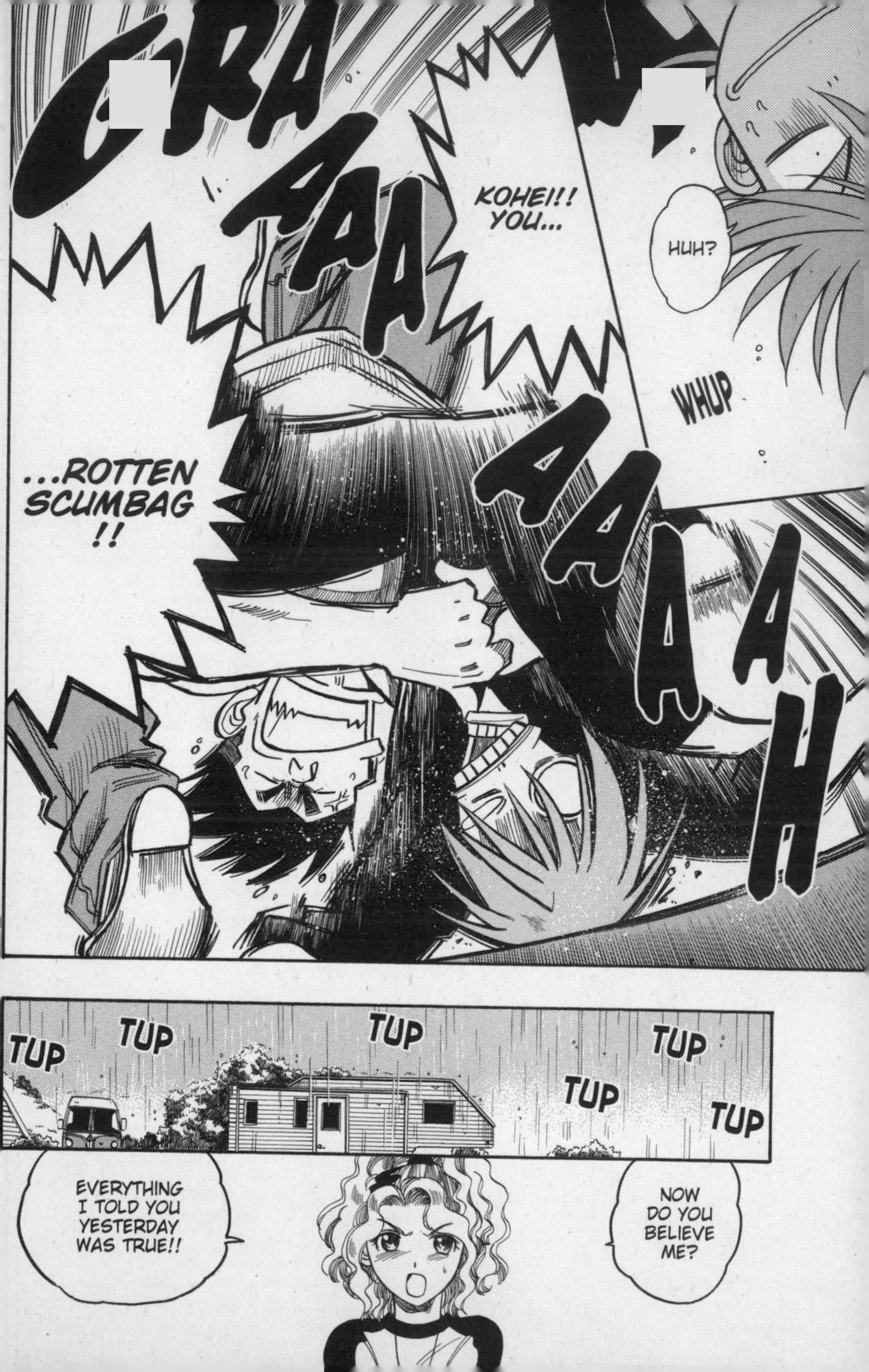
HUH?
WHUP
GRAAAAAAAAAAH
KOHEI!! YOU...
...ROTTEN SCUMBAG!!
TUP
TUP
TUP
TUP
TUP
TUP
NOW DO YOU BELIEVE ME?
EVERYTHING I TOLD YOU YESTERDAY WAS TRUE!!

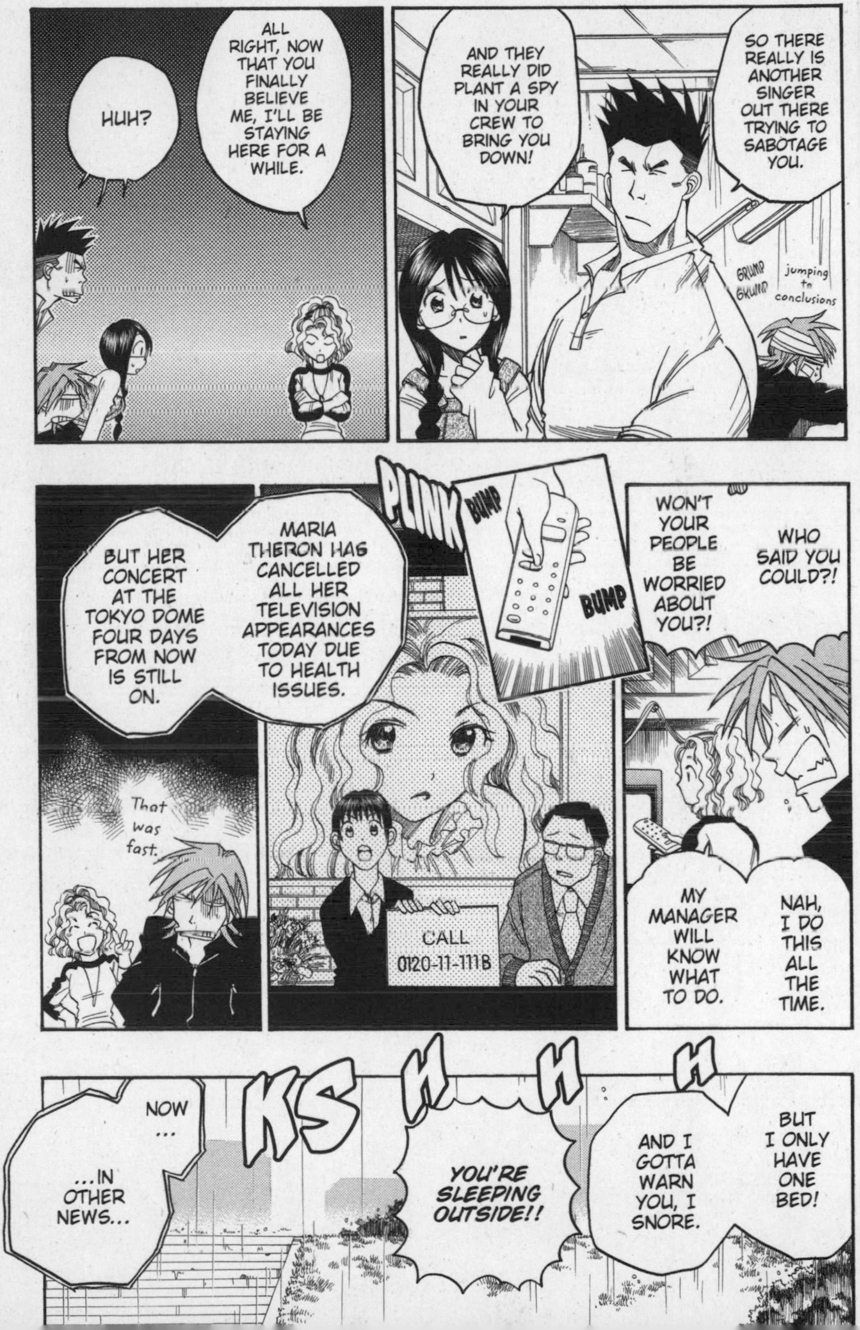
SO THERE REALLY IS ANOTHER SINGER OUT THERE TRYING TO SABOTAGE YOU.
AND THEY REALLY DID PLANT A SPY IN YOUR CREW TO BRING YOU DOWN!
GRUMP GRUMP
jumping to conclusions
ALL RIGHT, NOW THAT YOU FINALLY BELIEVE ME, I'LL BE STAYING HERE FOR A WHILE.
HUH?
WHO SAID YOU COULD?!
WON'T YOUR PEOPLE BE WORRIED ABOUT YOU?!
NAH, I DO THIS ALL THE TIME.
MY MANAGER WILL KNOW WHAT TO DO.
PLINK
BUMP
BUMP
MARIA THERON HAS CANCELLED ALL HER TELEVISION APPEARANCES TODAY DUE TO HEALTH ISSUES.
BUT HER CONCERT AT THE TOKYO DOME FOUR DAYS FROM NOW IS STILL ON.
CALL 0120-11-111B
That was fast.
BUT I ONLY HAVE ONE BED!
AND I GOTTA WARN YOU, I SNORE.
KSHHH
YOU'RE SLEEPING OUTSIDE!!
NOW...
...IN OTHER NEWS...

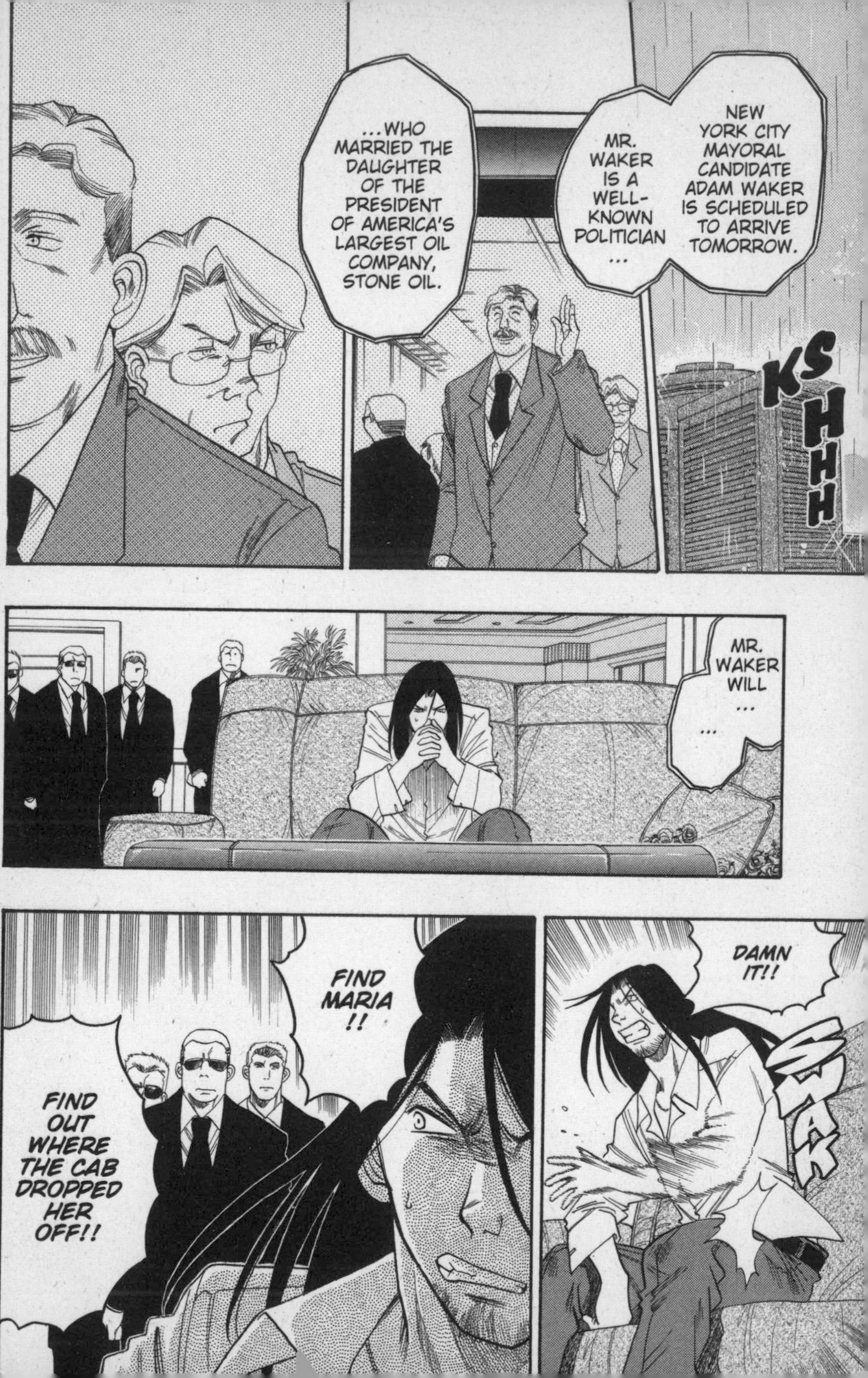
NEW YORK CITY MAYORAL CANDIDATE ADAM WAKER IS SCHEDULED TO ARRIVE TOMORROW.
KSHHH
MR. WAKER IS A WELL-KNOWN POLITICIAN ...
...WHO MARRIED THE DAUGHTER OF THE PRESIDENT OF AMERICA'S LARGEST OIL COMPANY, STONE OIL.
MR. WAKER WILL ... ...
DAMN IT!!
SWAK
FIND MARIA !!
FIND OUT WHERE THE CAB DROPPED HER OFF!!

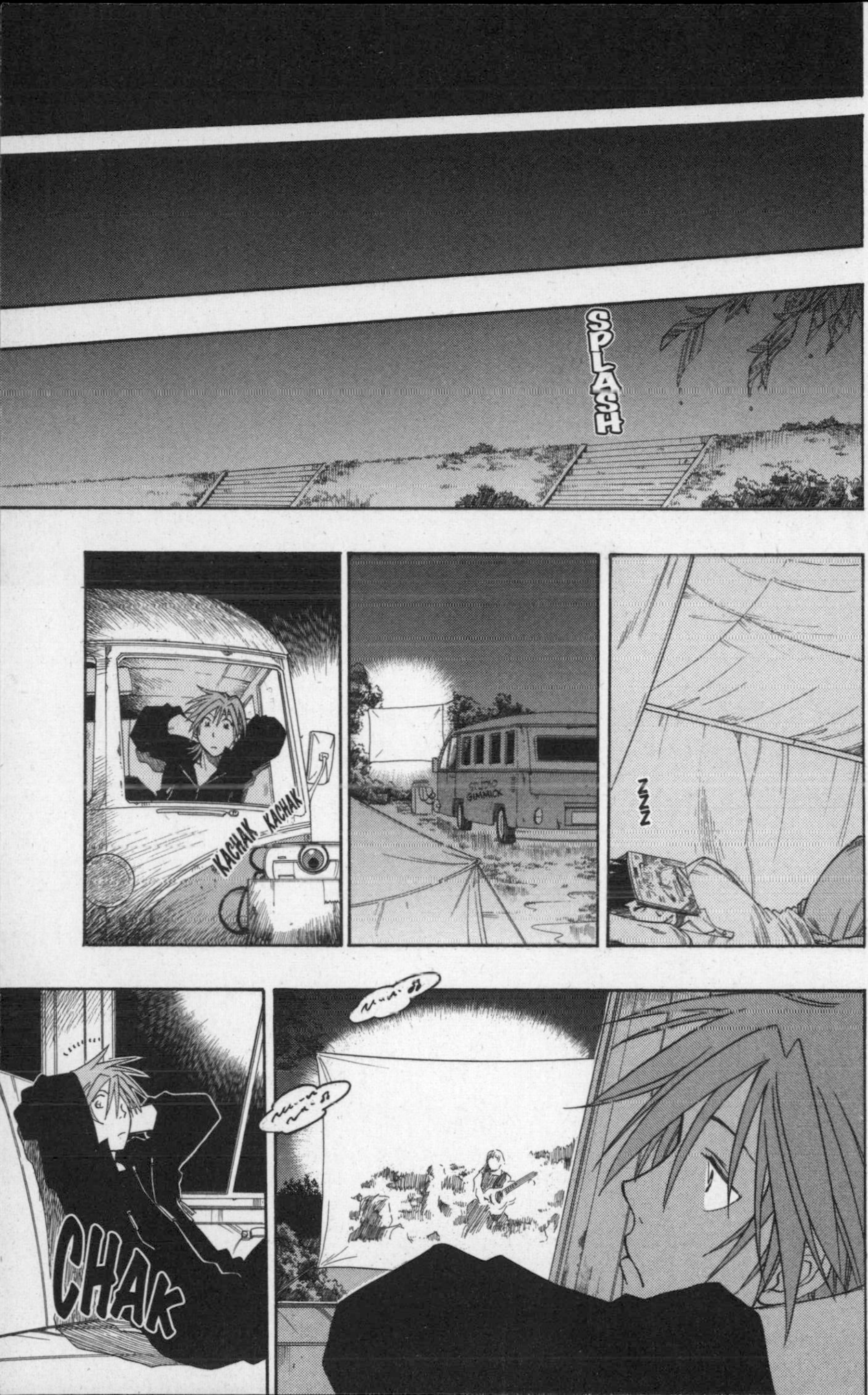
SPLASH
ZZZ
STUDIO GIMMICK
KACHAK KACHAK
CHAK

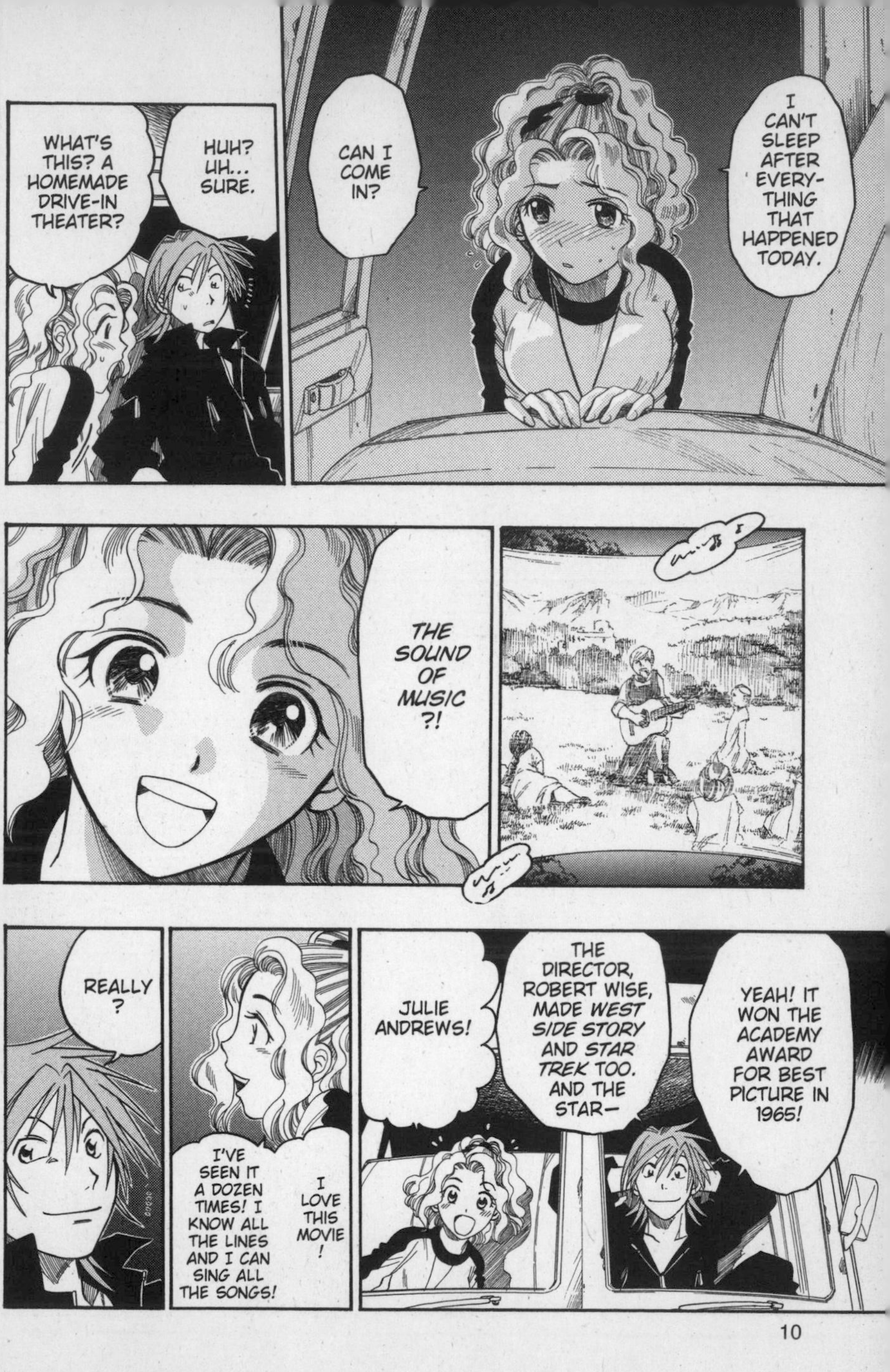
I CAN'T SLEEP AFTER EVERY-THING THAT HAPPENED TODAY.
CAN I COME IN?
HUH? UH... SURE.
WHAT'S THIS? A HOMEMADE DRIVE-IN THEATER?
THE SOUND OF MUSIC ?!
YEAH! IT WON THE ACADEMY AWARD FOR BEST PICTURE IN 1965!
THE DIRECTOR, ROBERT WISE, MADE *WEST SIDE STORY* AND *STAR TREK* TOO. AND THE STAR—
JULIE ANDREWS!
I LOVE THIS MOVIE!
I'VE SEEN IT A DOZEN TIMES! I KNOW ALL THE LINES AND I CAN SING ALL THE SONGS!
REALLY ?

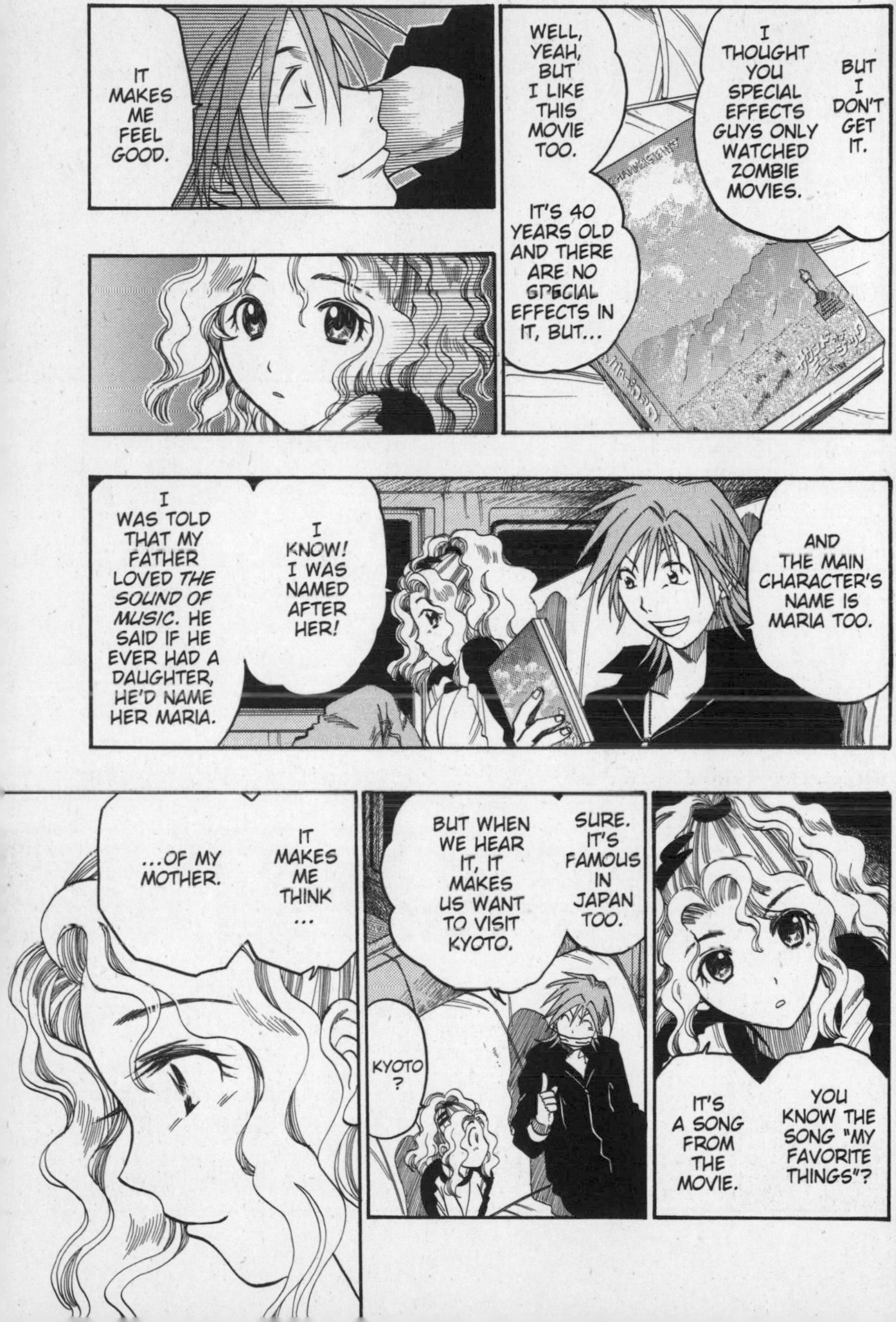
BUT I DON'T GET IT.
I THOUGHT YOU SPECIAL EFFECTS GUYS ONLY WATCHED ZOMBIE MOVIES.
WELL, YEAH, BUT I LIKE THIS MOVIE TOO.
IT'S 40 YEARS OLD AND THERE ARE NO SPECIAL EFFECTS IN IT, BUT...
IT MAKES ME FEEL GOOD.
AND THE MAIN CHARACTER'S NAME IS MARIA TOO.
I KNOW! I WAS NAMED AFTER HER!
I WAS TOLD THAT MY FATHER LOVED *THE SOUND OF MUSIC*. HE SAID IF HE EVER HAD A DAUGHTER, HE'D NAME HER MARIA.
YOU KNOW THE SONG "MY FAVORITE THINGS"?
IT'S A SONG FROM THE MOVIE.
SURE. IT'S FAMOUS IN JAPAN TOO.
BUT WHEN WE HEAR IT, IT MAKES US WANT TO VISIT KYOTO.
KYOTO?
IT MAKES ME THINK...
...OF MY MOTHER.

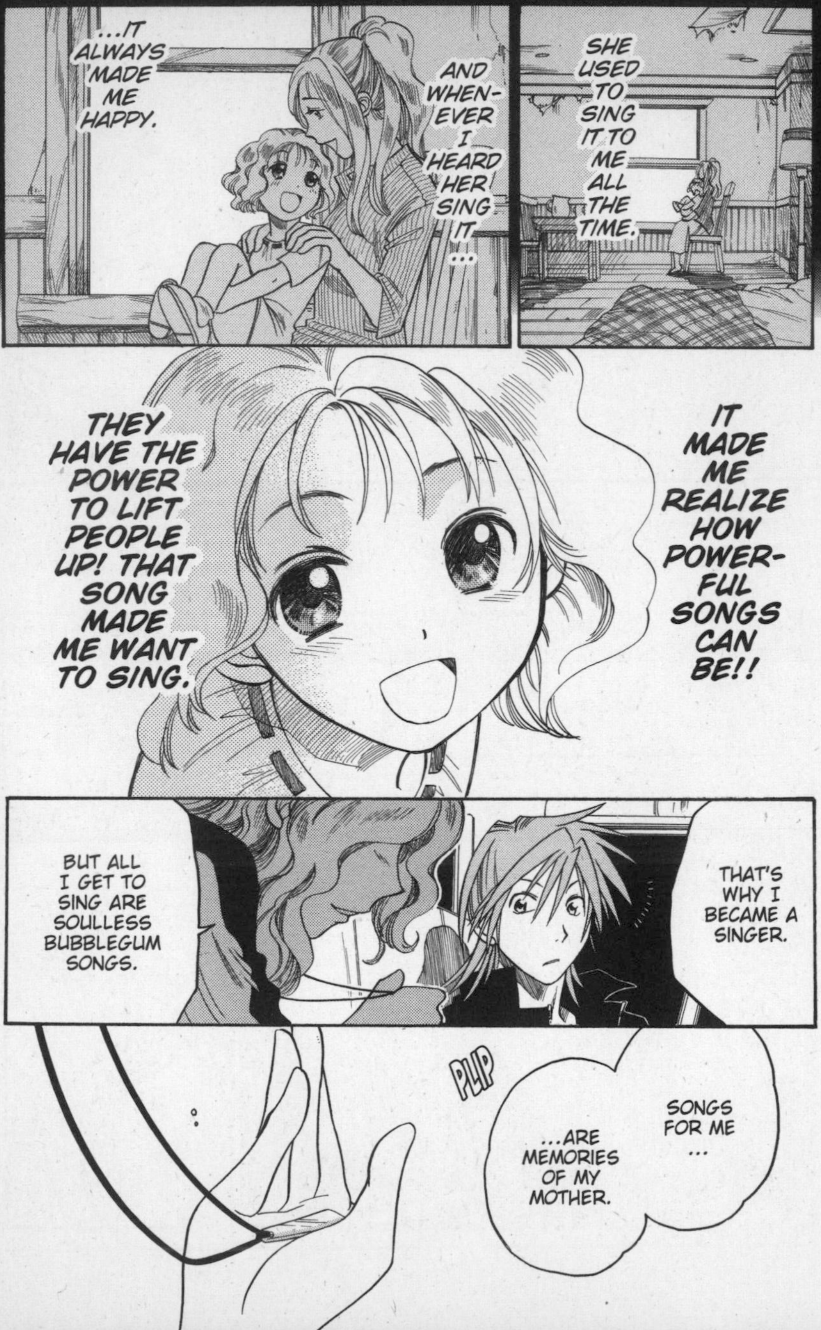
SHE USED TO SING IT TO ME ALL THE TIME.
AND WHEN-EVER I HEARD HER SING IT ...
...IT ALWAYS MADE ME HAPPY.
IT MADE ME REALIZE HOW POWER-FUL SONGS CAN BE!!
THEY HAVE THE POWER TO LIFT PEOPLE UP! THAT SONG MADE ME WANT TO SING.
THAT'S WHY I BECAME A SINGER.
BUT ALL I GET TO SING ARE SOULLESS BUBBLEGUM SONGS.
PLIP
SONGS FOR ME ...
...ARE MEMORIES OF MY MOTHER.

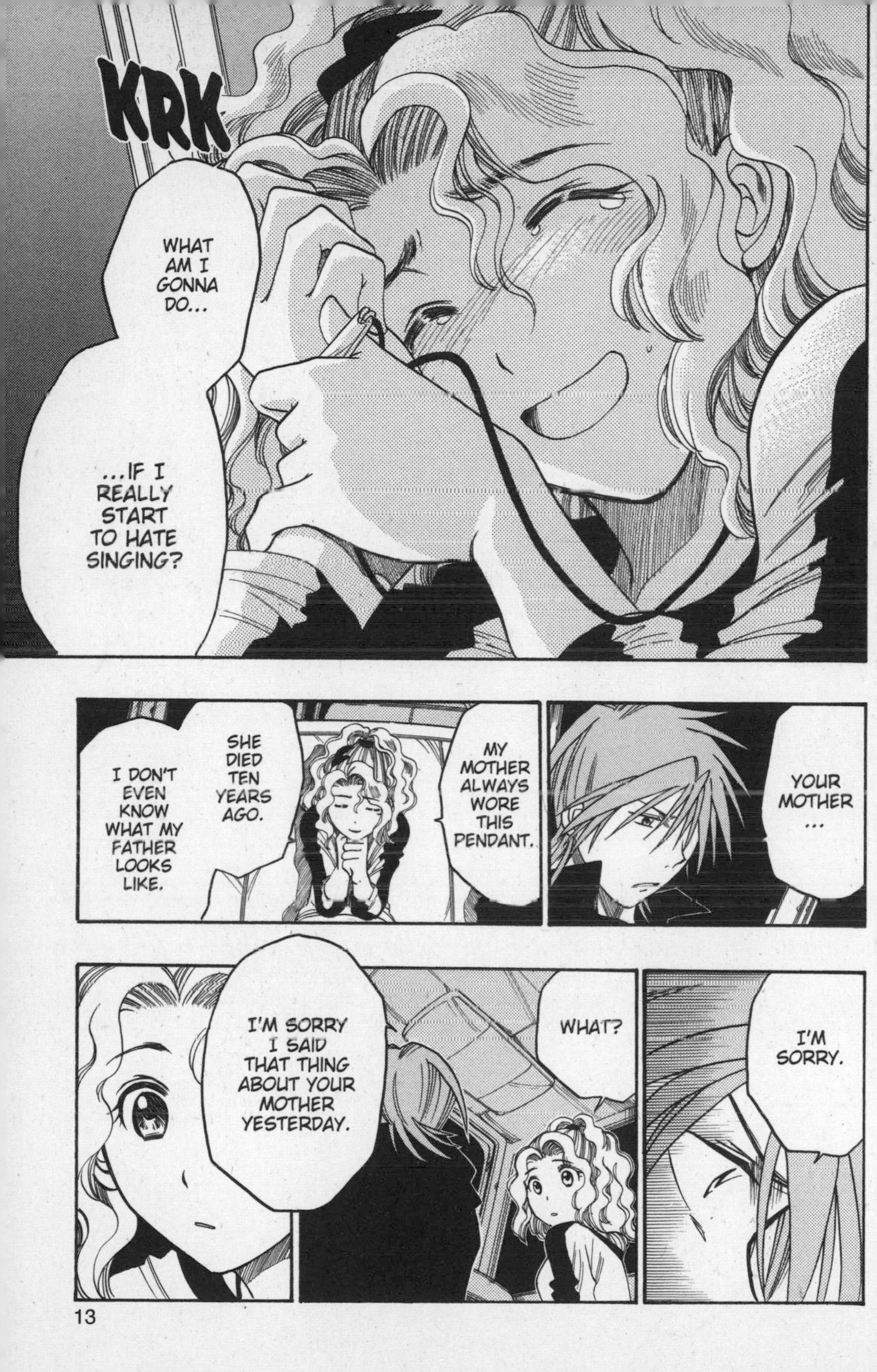
KRK
WHAT AM I GONNA DO...
...IF I REALLY START TO HATE SINGING?
YOUR MOTHER ...
MY MOTHER ALWAYS WORE THIS PENDANT.
SHE DIED TEN YEARS AGO.
I DON'T EVEN KNOW WHAT MY FATHER LOOKS LIKE.
I'M SORRY.
WHAT?
I'M SORRY I SAID THAT THING ABOUT YOUR MOTHER YESTERDAY.

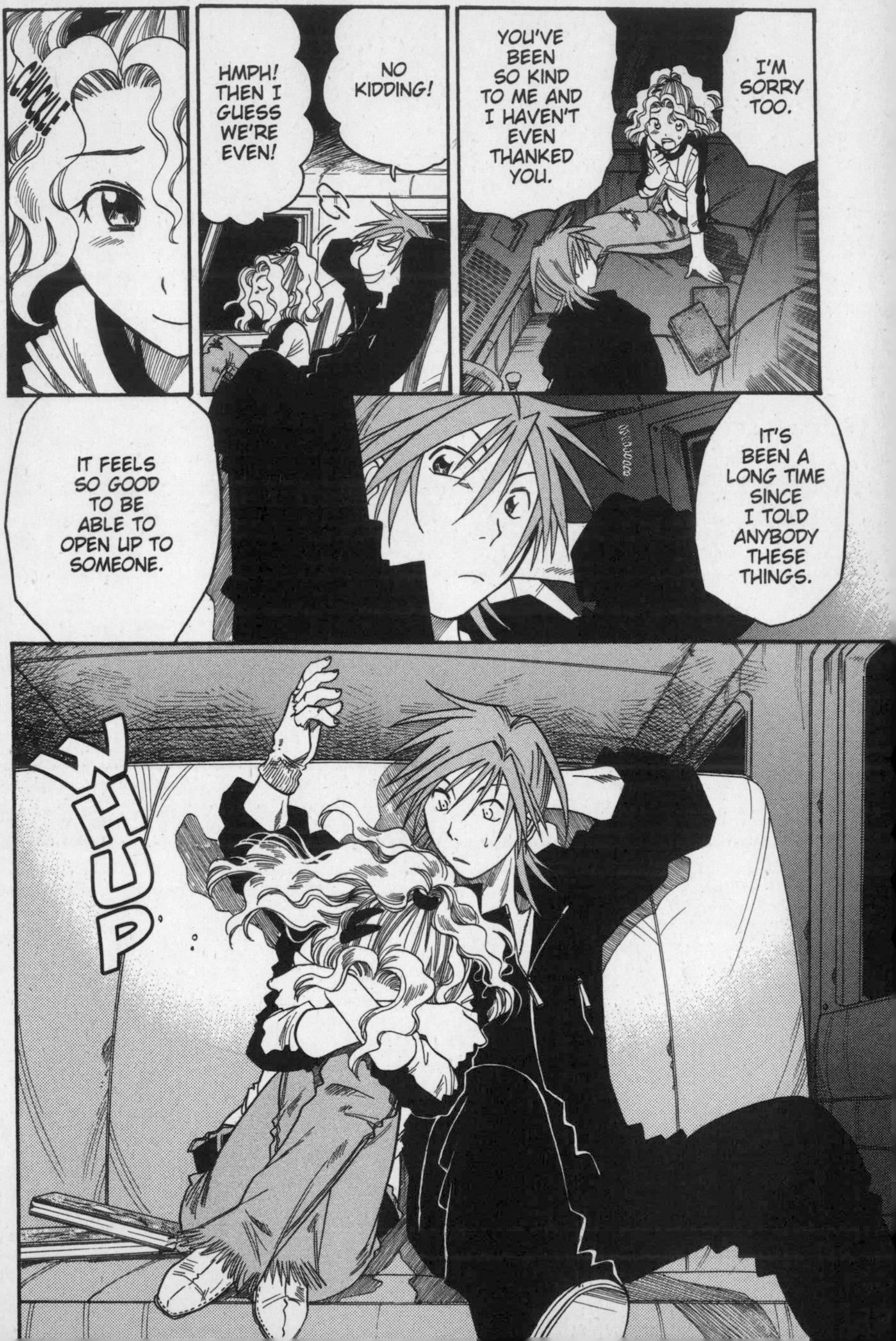
I'M SORRY TOO.
YOU'VE BEEN SO KIND TO ME AND I HAVEN'T EVEN THANKED YOU.
NO KIDDING!
HMPH! THEN I GUESS WE'RE EVEN!
CHUCKLE
IT'S BEEN A LONG TIME SINCE I TOLD ANYBODY THESE THINGS.
IT FEELS SO GOOD TO BE ABLE TO OPEN UP TO SOMEONE.
WHUP

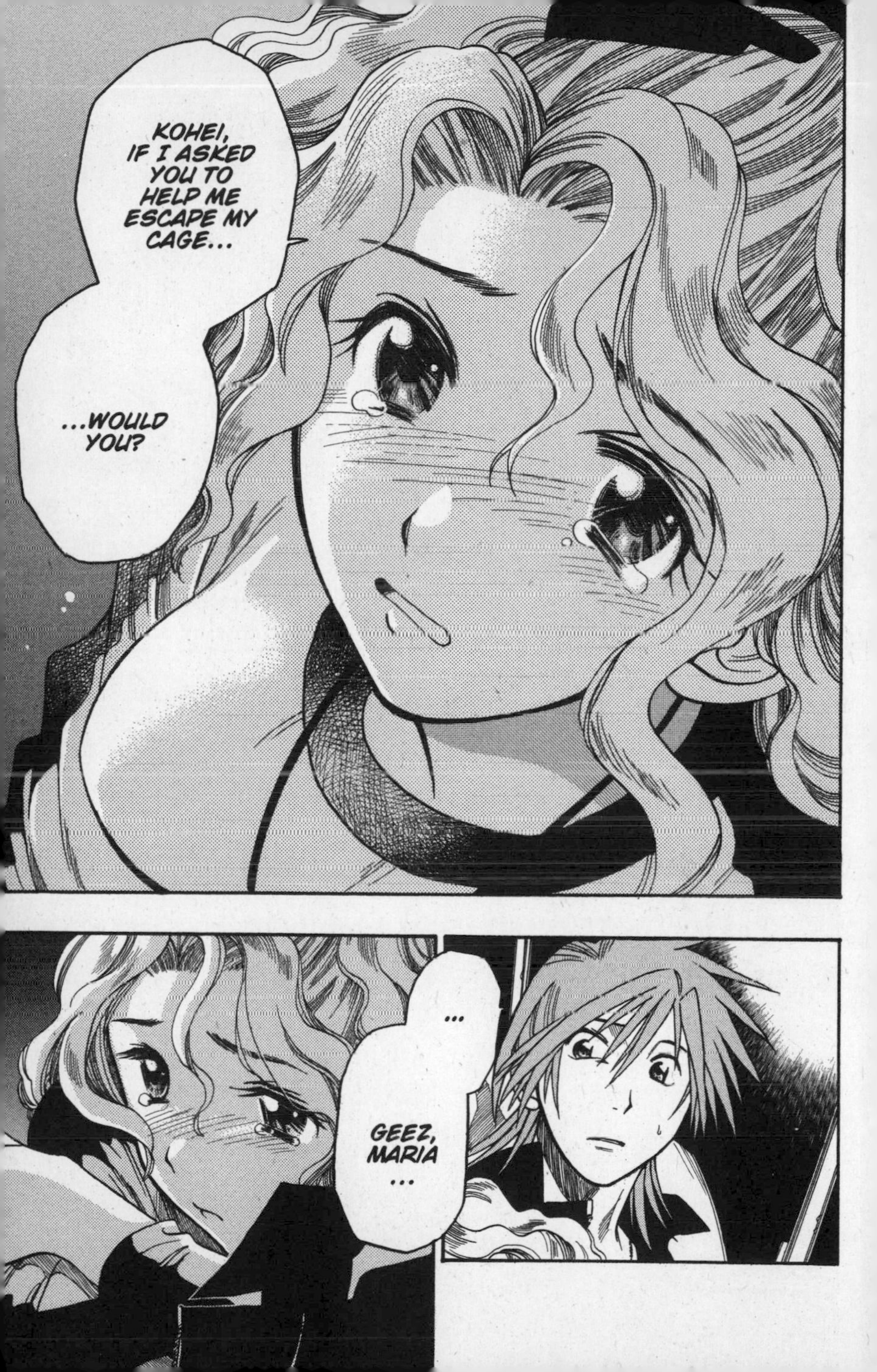
KOHEI, IF I ASKED YOU TO HELP ME ESCAPE MY CAGE...
...WOULD YOU?
...
GEEZ, MARIA ...

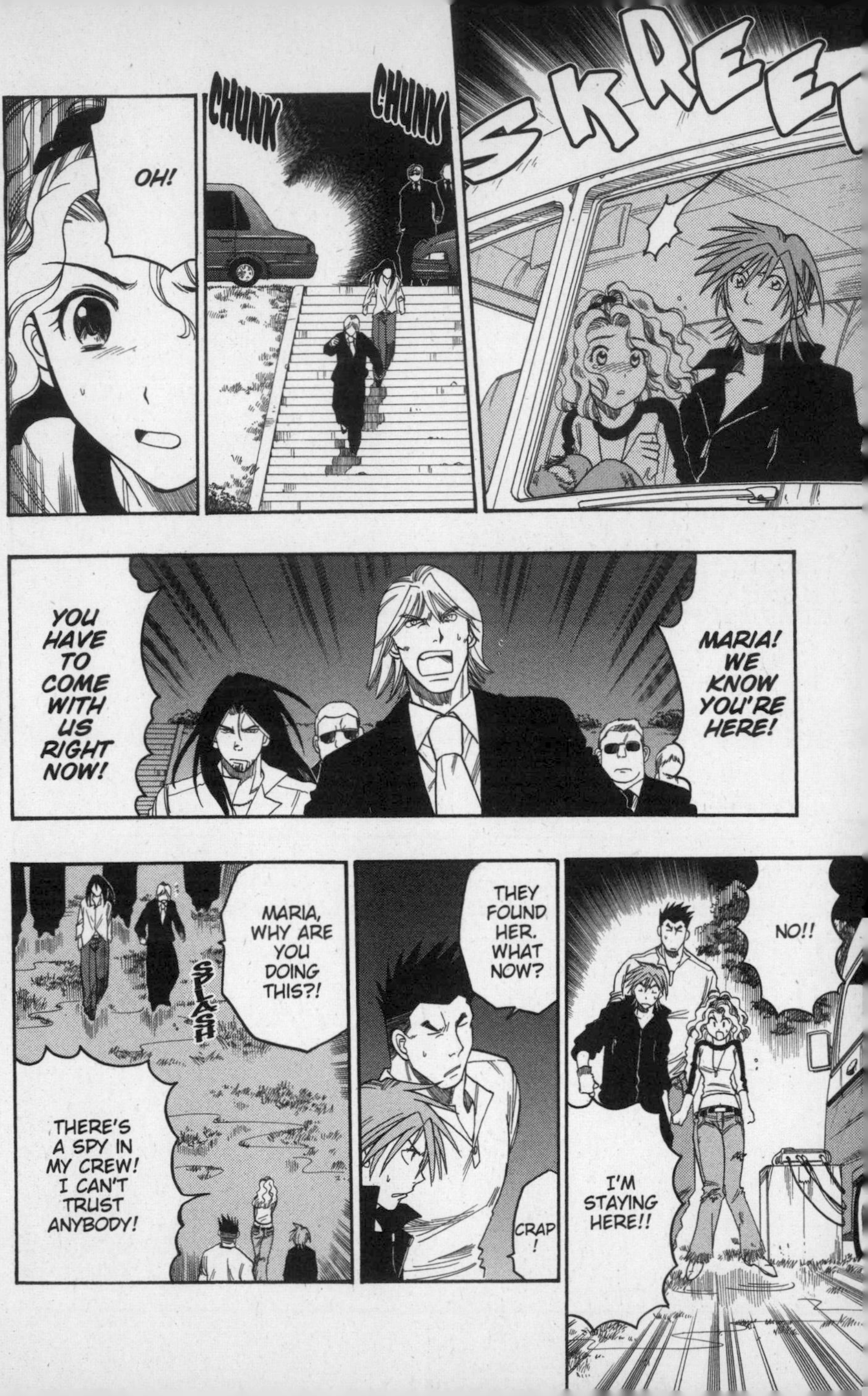
SKREE
CHUNK
CHUNK
OH!
MARIA! WE KNOW YOU'RE HERE!
YOU HAVE TO COME WITH US RIGHT NOW!
NO!!
I'M STAYING HERE!!
THEY FOUND HER. WHAT NOW?
CRAP!
MARIA, WHY ARE YOU DOING THIS?!
SPLASH
THERE'S A SPY IN MY CREW! I CAN'T TRUST ANYBODY!

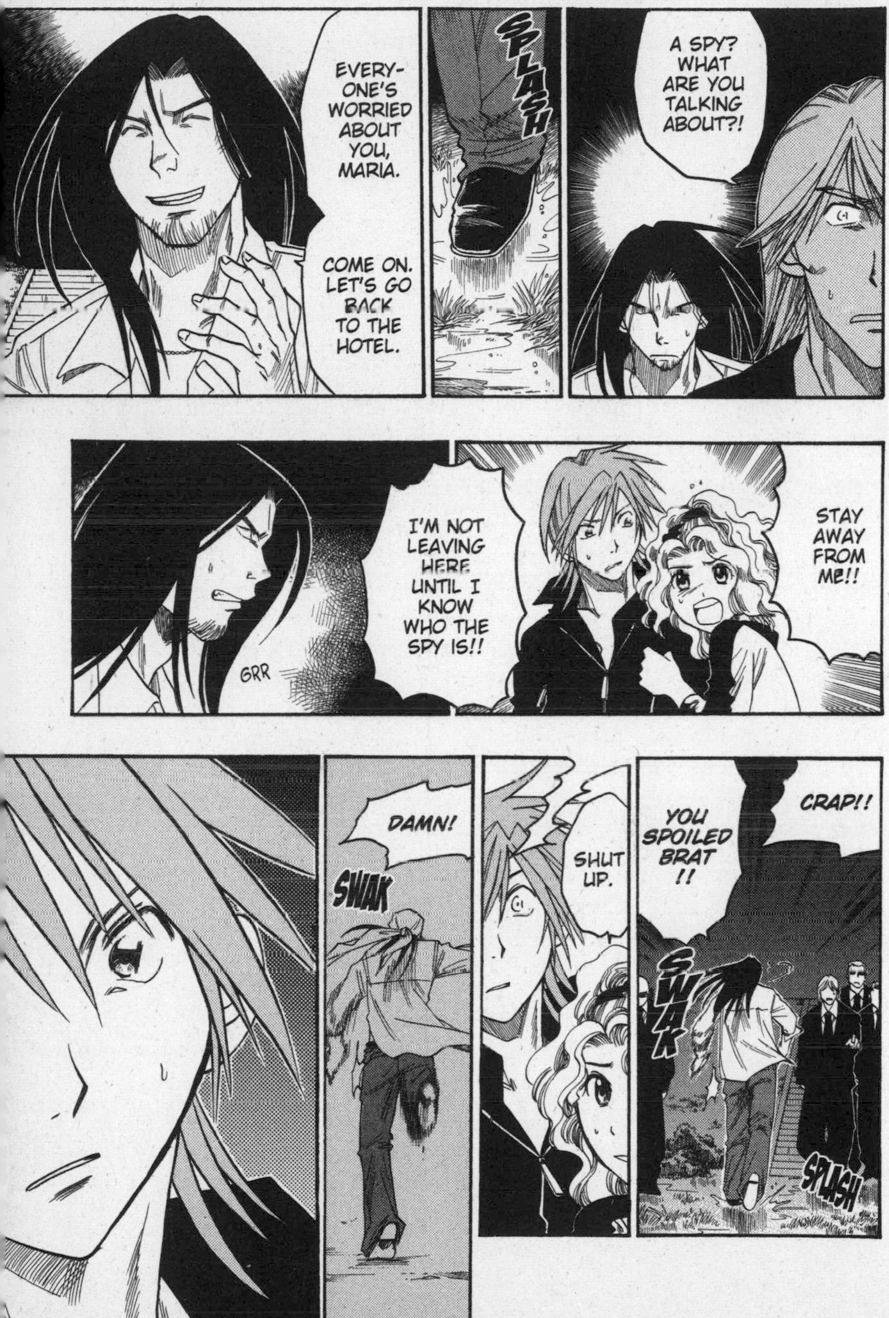
A SPY? WHAT ARE YOU TALKING ABOUT?!
SPLASH
EVERY-ONE'S WORRIED ABOUT YOU, MARIA.
COME ON. LET'S GO BACK TO THE HOTEL.
STAY AWAY FROM ME!!
I'M NOT LEAVING HERE UNTIL I KNOW WHO THE SPY IS!!
GRR
CRAP!!
YOU SPOILED BRAT!!
SWAK
SPLASH
SHUT UP.
DAMN!
SWAK

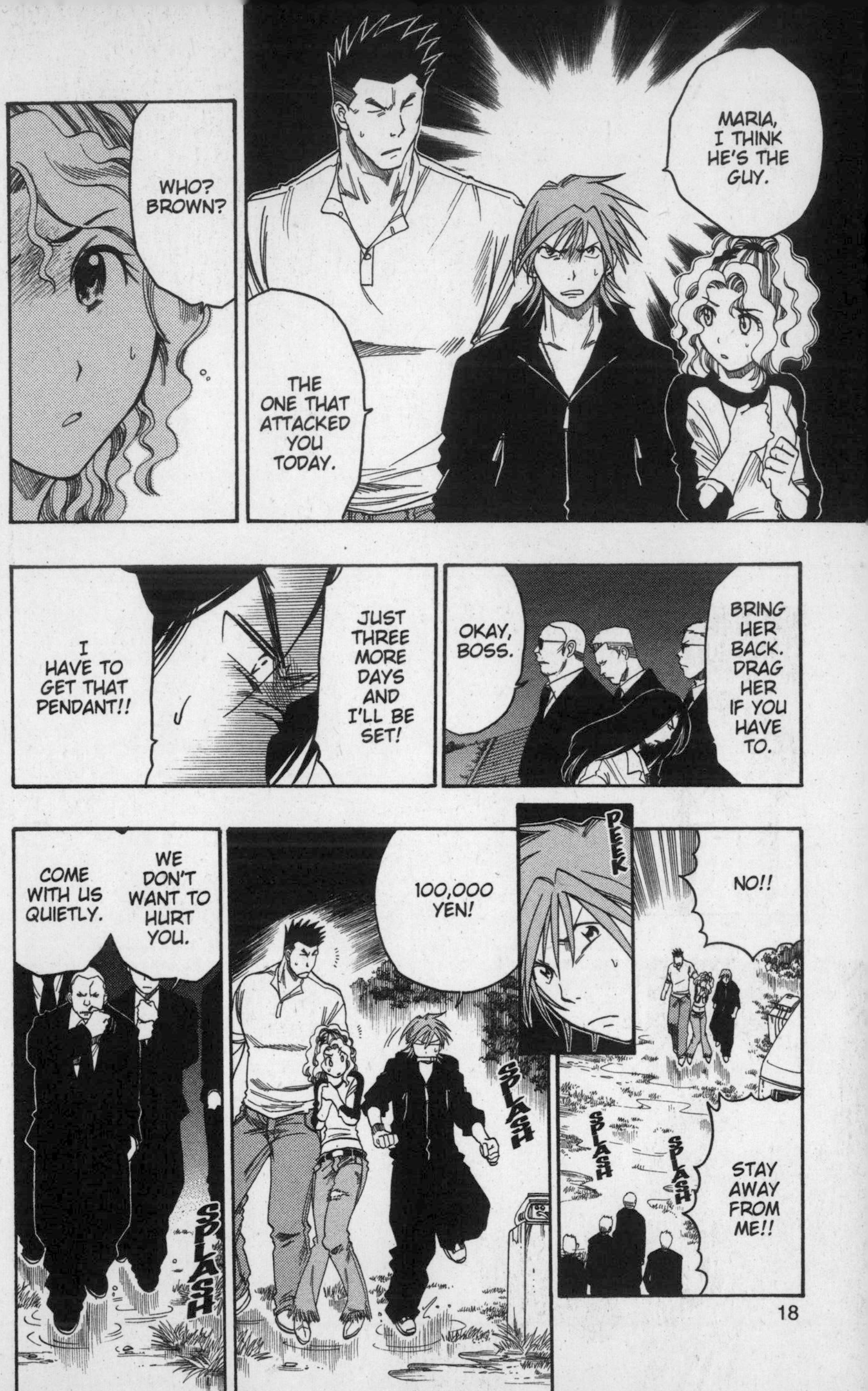
MARIA, I THINK HE'S THE GUY.
THE ONE THAT ATTACKED YOU TODAY.
WHO? BROWN?
BRING HER BACK. DRAG HER IF YOU HAVE TO.
OKAY, BOSS.
JUST THREE MORE DAYS AND I'LL BE SET!
I HAVE TO GET THAT PENDANT!!
PEEK
NO!!
SPLASH
SPLASH
STAY AWAY FROM ME!!
100,000 YEN!
SPLASH
WE DON'T WANT TO HURT YOU.
COME WITH US QUIETLY.
SPLASH

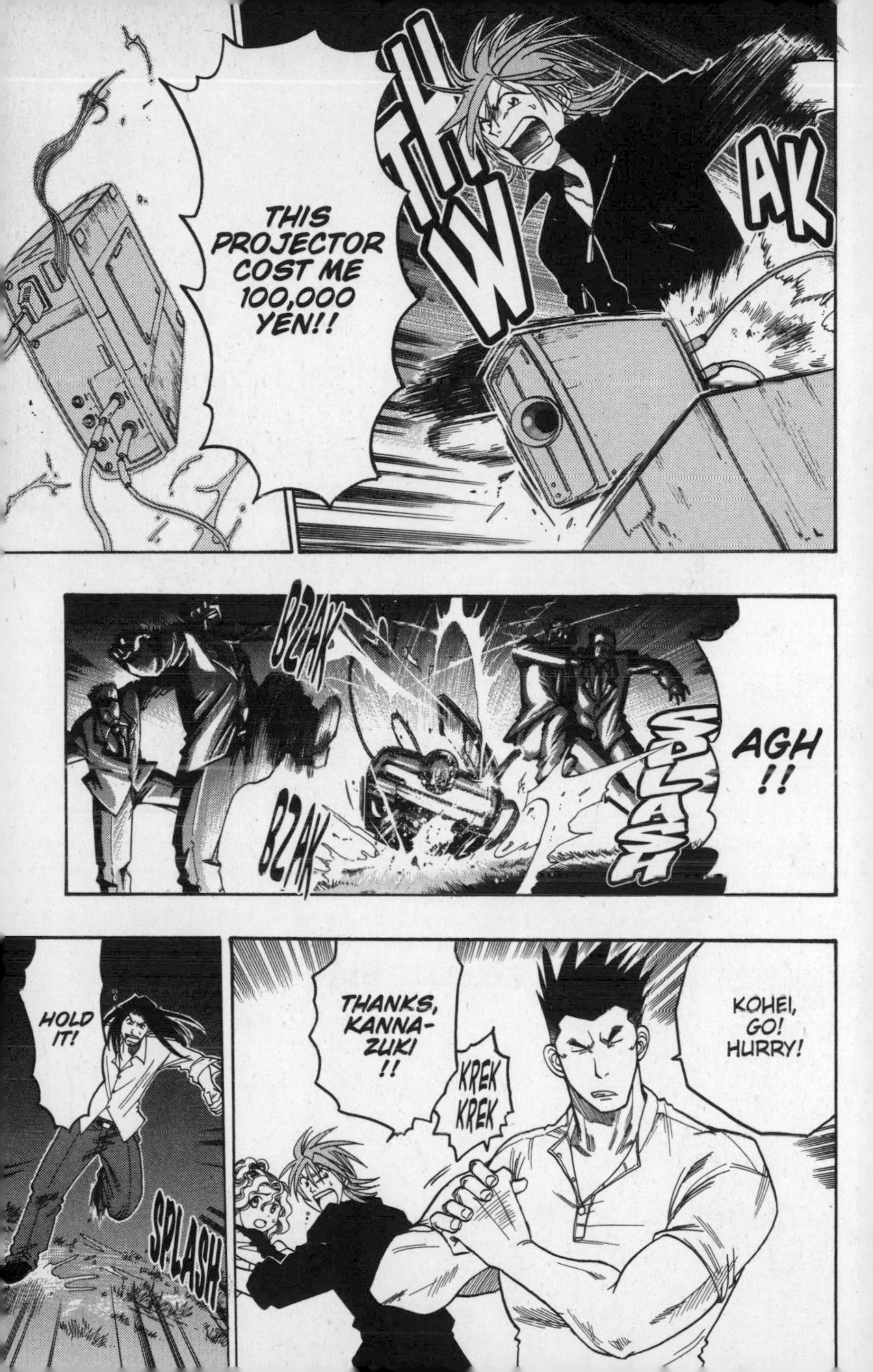
THWAK
THIS PROJECTOR COST ME 100,000 YEN!!
AGH!!
SPLASH
BZAK
BZAK
KOHEI, GO! HURRY!
KREK KREK
THANKS, KANNAZUKI!!
HOLD IT!
SPLASH

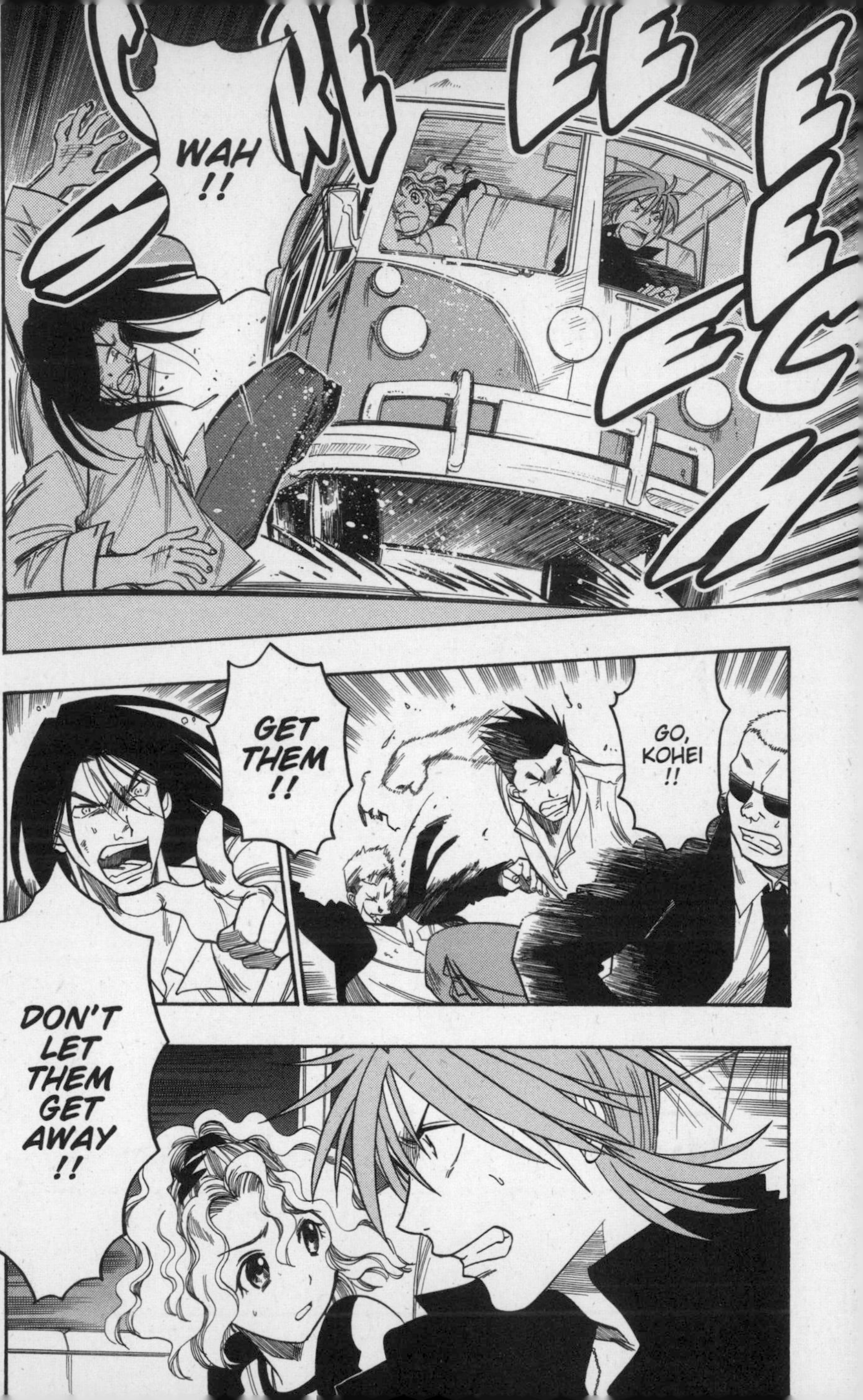
WAH!!
GO, KOHEI!!
GET THEM!!
DON'T LET THEM GET AWAY!!

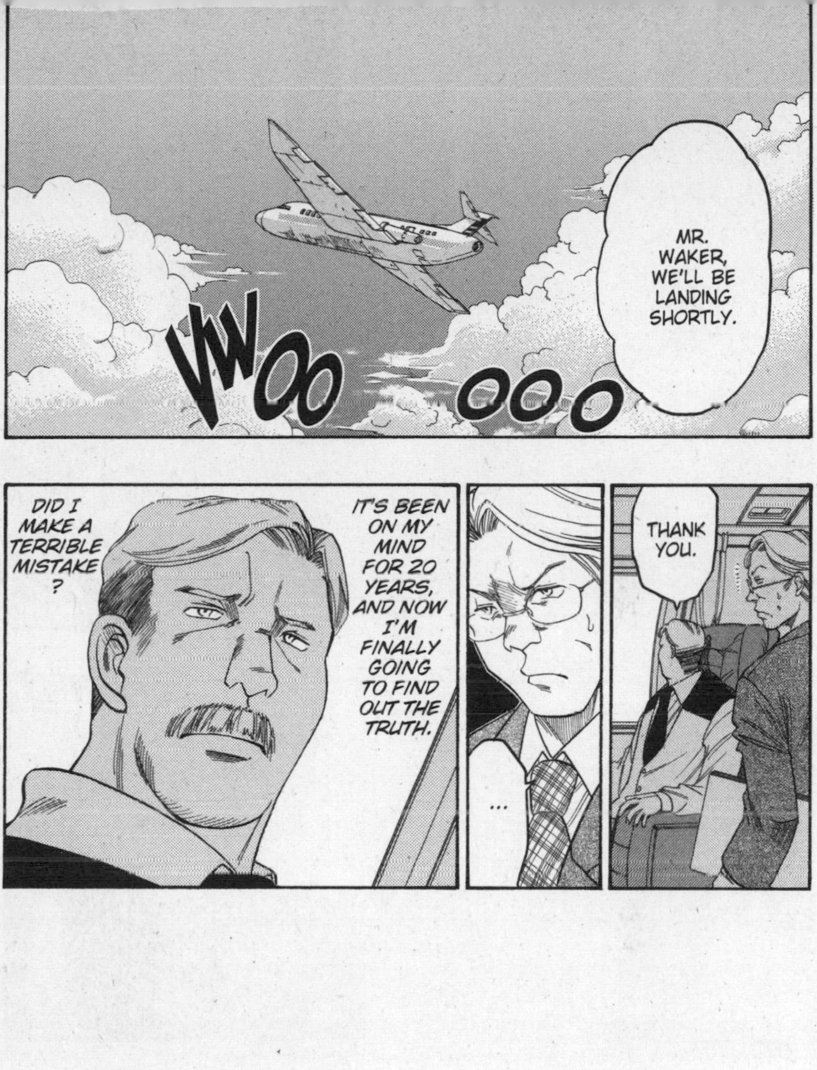
VVWOOOOOO
MR. WAKER, WE'LL BE LANDING SHORTLY.
THANK YOU.
...
IT'S BEEN ON MY MIND FOR 20 YEARS, AND NOW I'M FINALLY GOING TO FIND OUT THE TRUTH.
DID I MAKE A TERRIBLE MISTAKE?

Scene 48: My Favorite Things (Part 4)

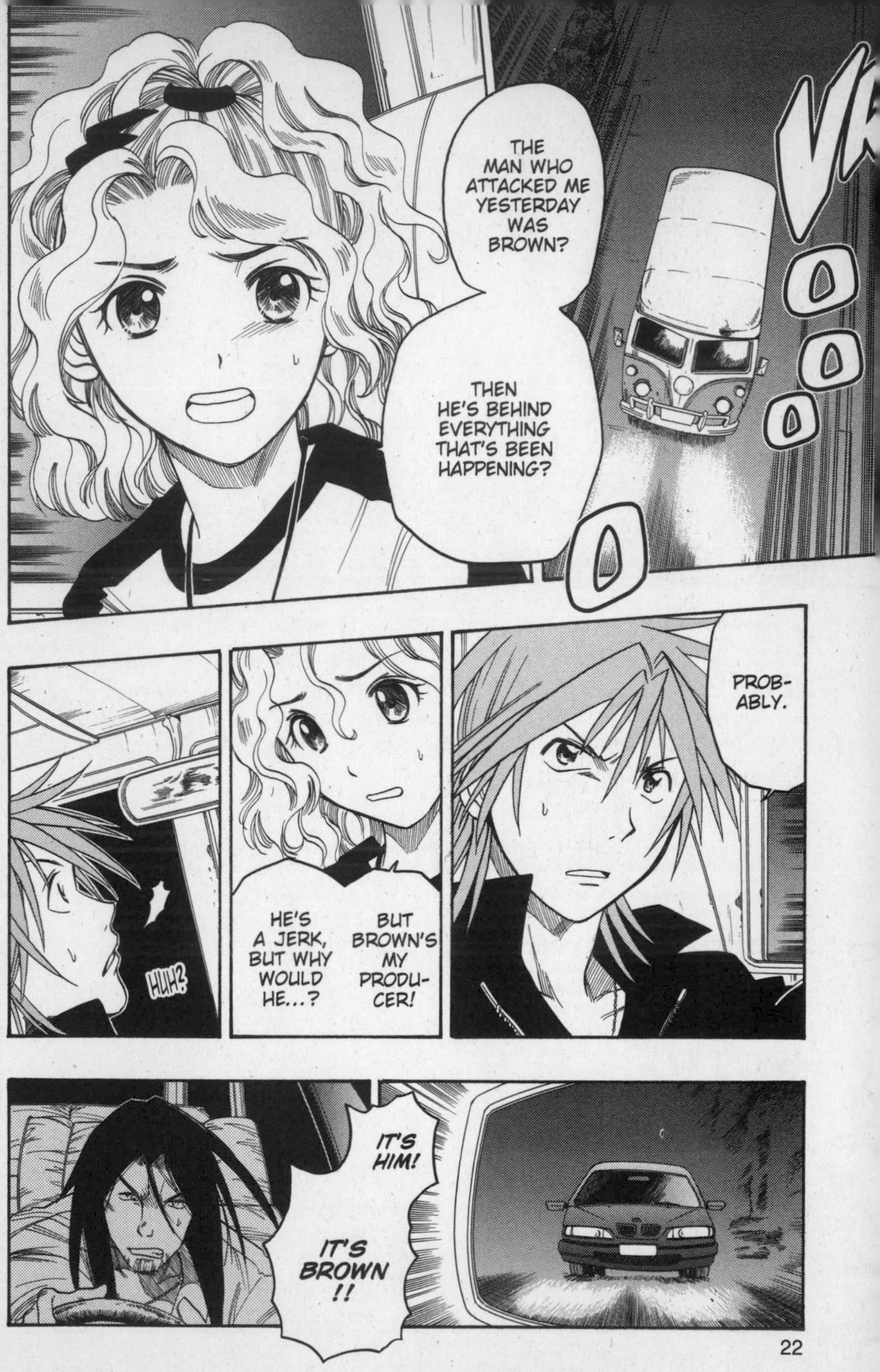
VROOO
THE MAN WHO ATTACKED ME YESTERDAY WAS BROWN?
THEN HE'S BEHIND EVERYTHING THAT'S BEEN HAPPENING?
O
PROB-ABLY.
BUT BROWN'S MY PRODU-CER!
HE'S A JERK, BUT WHY WOULD HE...?
HUH?
IT'S HIM!
IT'S BROWN!!

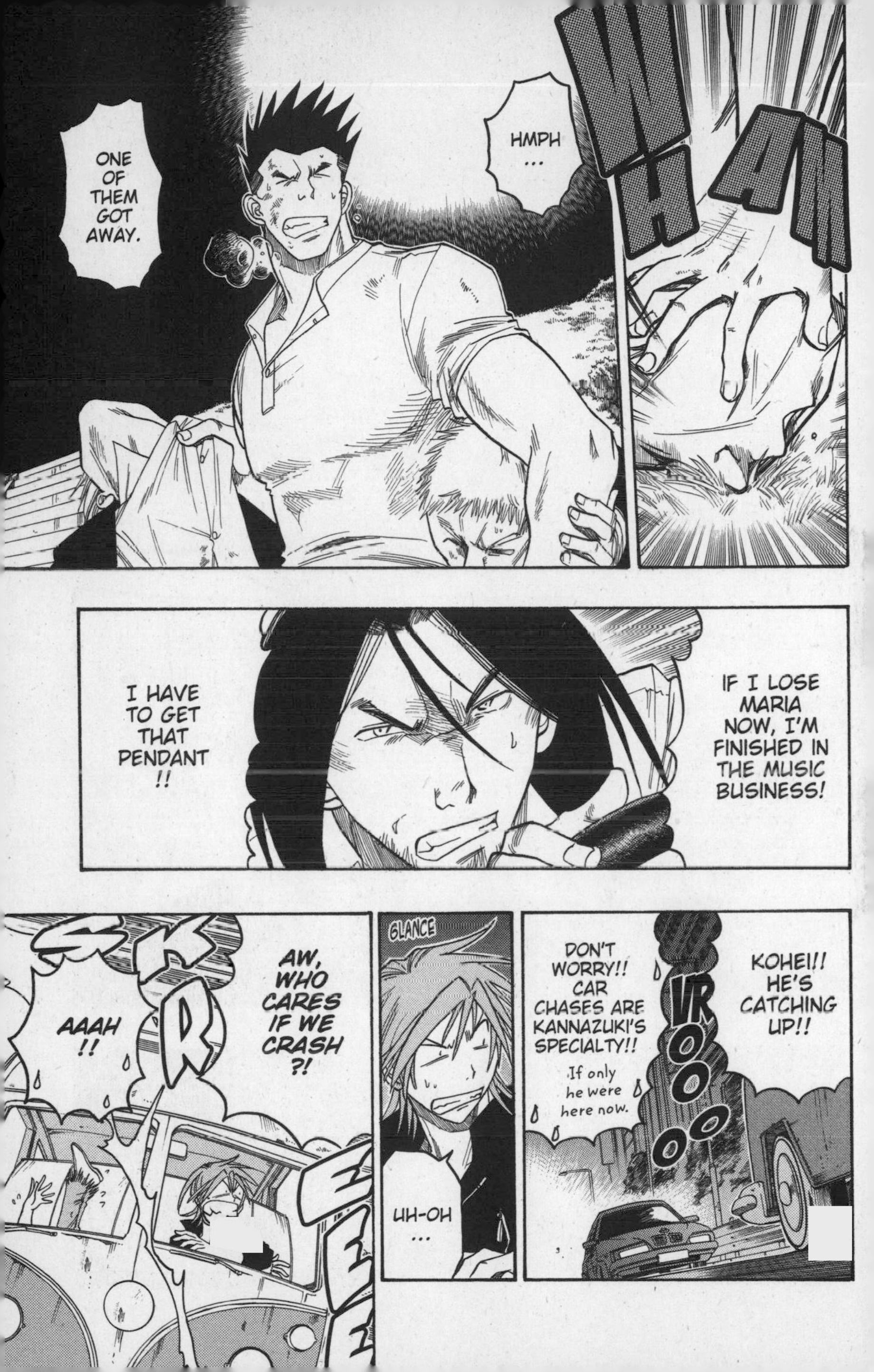
WHAM
HMPH ...
ONE OF THEM GOT AWAY.
IF I LOSE MARIA NOW, I'M FINISHED IN THE MUSIC BUSINESS!
I HAVE TO GET THAT PENDANT !!
KOHEI!!! HE'S CATCHING UP!!
VROOOOOO
DON'T WORRY!! CAR CHASES ARE KANNAZUKI'S SPECIALTY!!
If only he were here now.
GLANCE
UH-OH ...
AW, WHO CARES IF WE CRASH ?!
AAAH !!

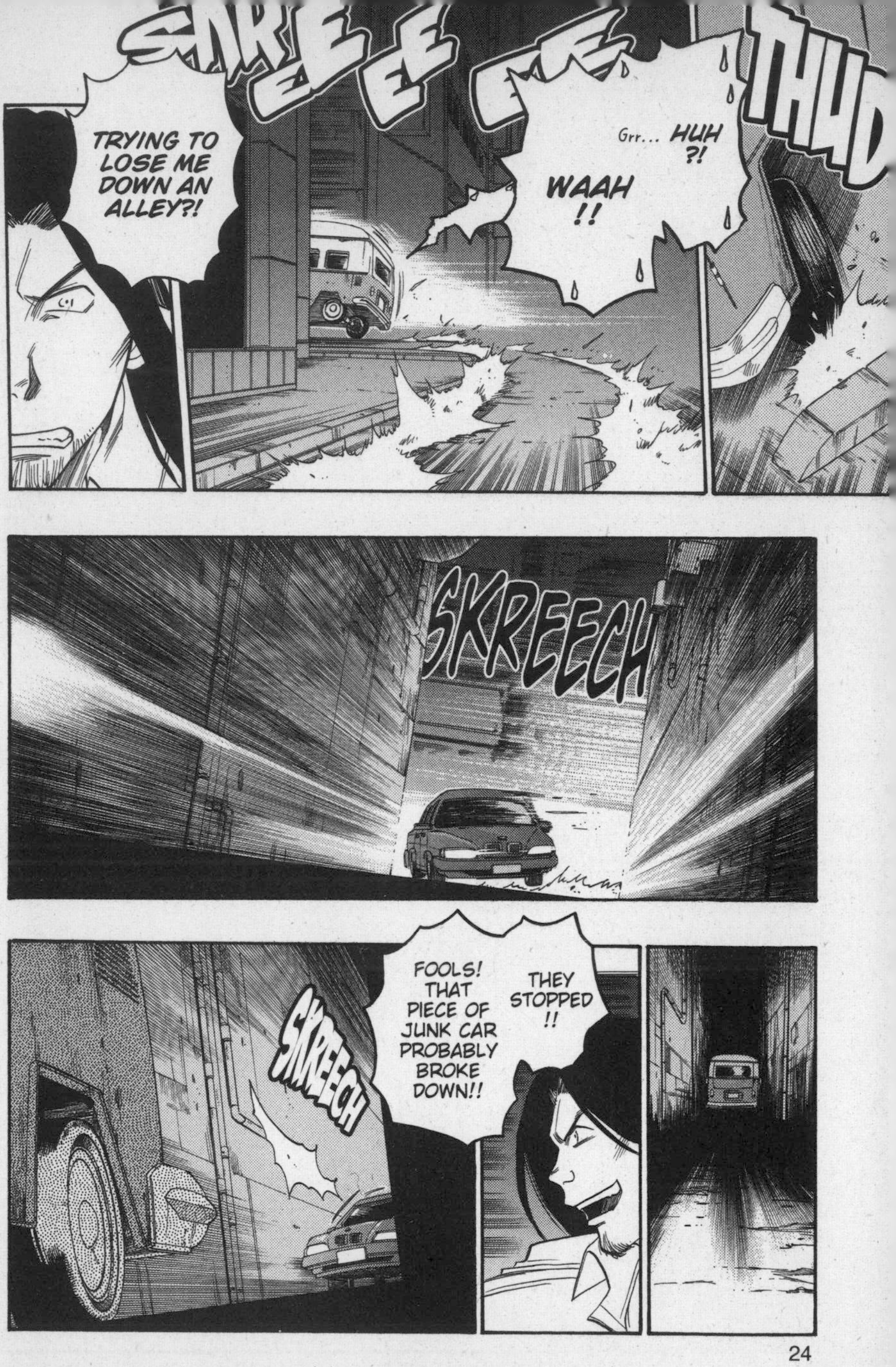
THUD
Grr... HUH ?!
WAAH !!
TRYING TO LOSE ME DOWN AN ALLEY?!
SKREECH
THEY STOPPED !!
FOOLS! THAT PIECE OF JUNK CAR PROBABLY BROKE DOWN!!
SKREECH

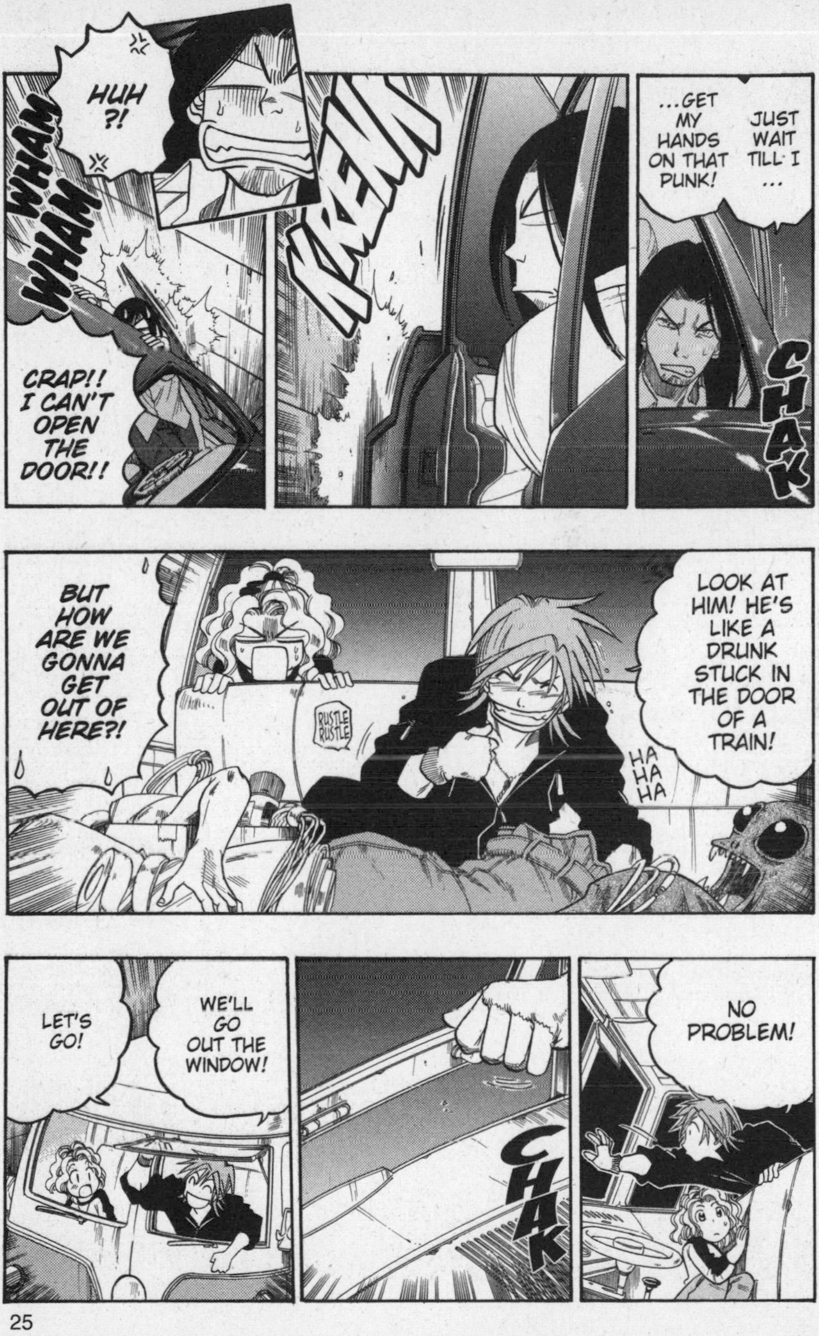
JUST WAIT TILL I ...
...GET MY HANDS ON THAT PUNK!
CHAK
HUH ?!
WHAM WHAM
CRAP!! I CAN'T OPEN THE DOOR!!
LOOK AT HIM! HE'S LIKE A DRUNK STUCK IN THE DOOR OF A TRAIN!
HA HA HA
RUSTLE RUSTLE
BUT HOW ARE WE GONNA GET OUT OF HERE?!
NO PROBLEM!
CHAK
WE'LL GO OUT THE WINDOW!
LET'S GO!

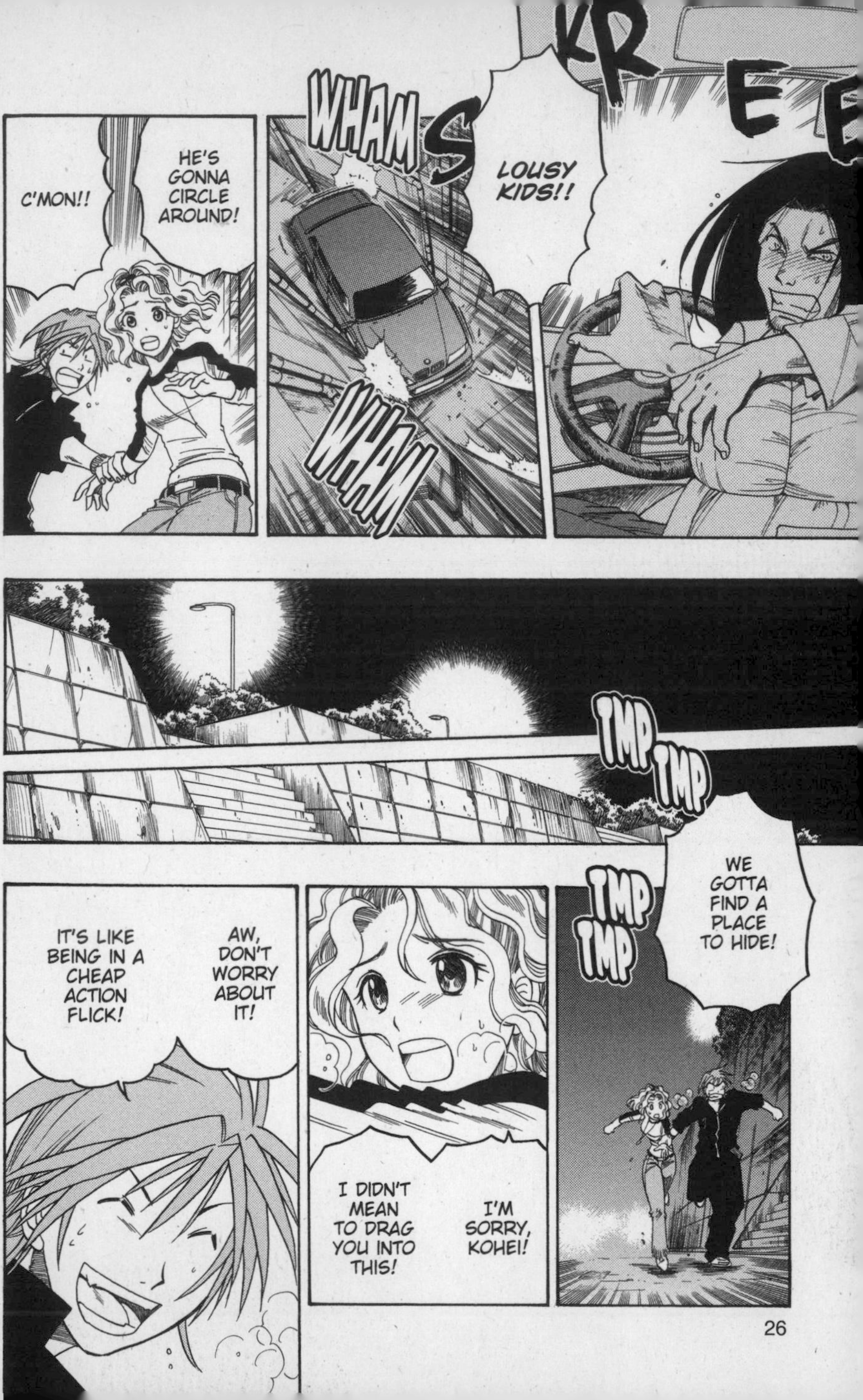
KREE
LOUSY KIDS!!
WHAM
S
WHAM
HE'S GONNA CIRCLE AROUND!
C'MON!!
TMP TMP
WE GOTTA FIND A PLACE TO HIDE!
TMP TMP
I'M SORRY, KOHEI!
I DIDN'T MEAN TO DRAG YOU INTO THIS!
AW, DON'T WORRY ABOUT IT!
IT'S LIKE BEING IN A CHEAP ACTION FLICK!

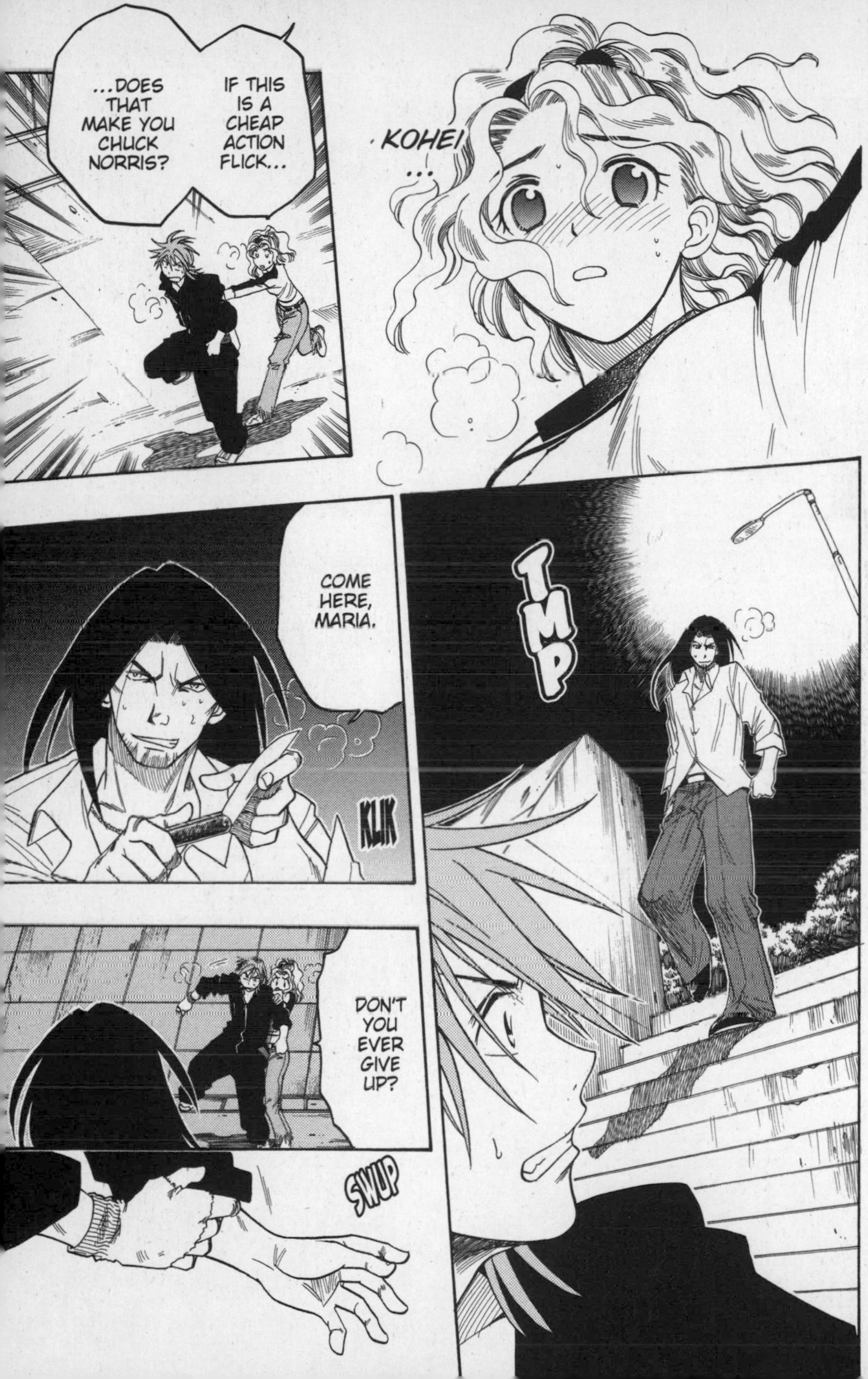
KOHEI ...
IF THIS IS A CHEAP ACTION FLICK...
...DOES THAT MAKE YOU CHUCK NORRIS?
TMP
COME HERE, MARIA.
KLIK
DON'T YOU EVER GIVE UP?
SWUP

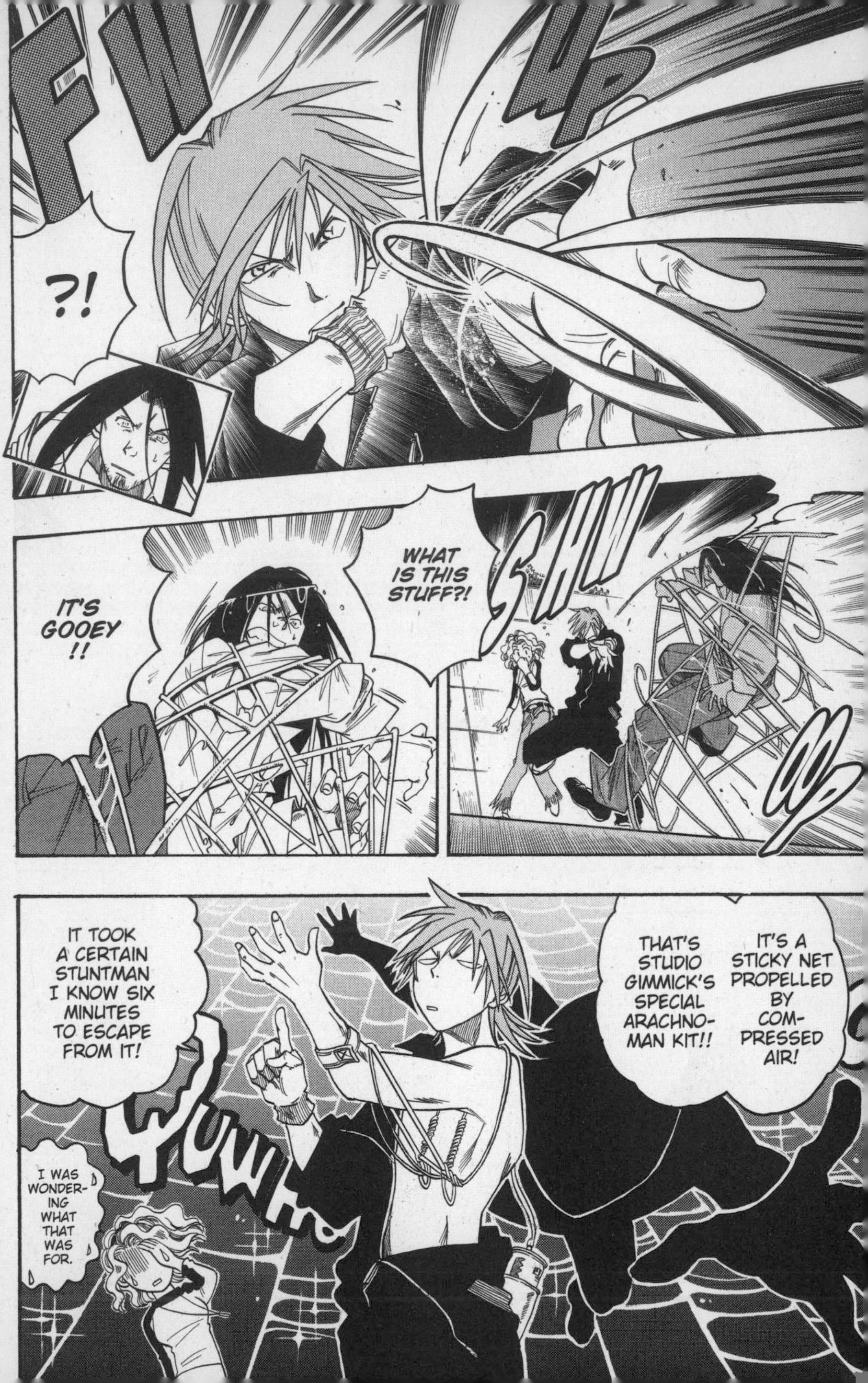
?!
WHAT IS THIS STUFF?!
IT'S GOOEY!!
IT'S A STICKY NET PROPELLED BY COM-PRESSED AIR!
THAT'S STUDIO GIMMICK'S SPECIAL ARACHNO-MAN KIT!!
IT TOOK A CERTAIN STUNTMAN I KNOW SIX MINUTES TO ESCAPE FROM IT!
I WAS WONDER-ING WHAT THAT WAS FOR.

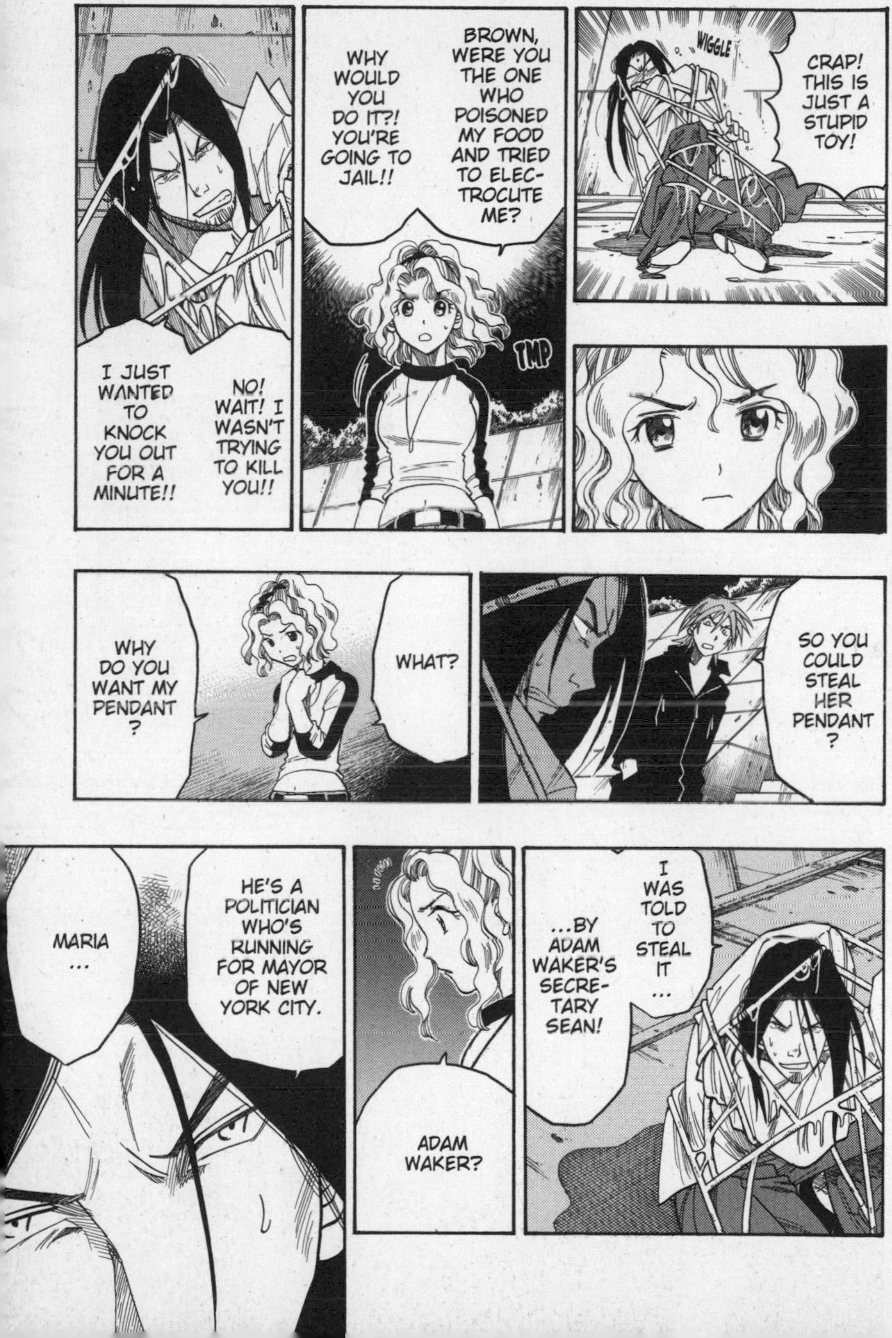
WIGGLE
CRAP! THIS IS JUST A STUPID TOY!
BROWN, WERE YOU THE ONE WHO POISONED MY FOOD AND TRIED TO ELEC-TROCUTE ME?
WHY WOULD YOU DO IT?! YOU'RE GOING TO JAIL!!
TMP
NO! WAIT! I WASN'T TRYING TO KILL YOU!!
I JUST WANTED TO KNOCK YOU OUT FOR A MINUTE!!
SO YOU COULD STEAL HER PENDANT?
WHAT?
WHY DO YOU WANT MY PENDANT?
I WAS TOLD TO STEAL IT...
...BY ADAM WAKER'S SECRE-TARY SEAN!
ADAM WAKER?
HE'S A POLITICIAN WHO'S RUNNING FOR MAYOR OF NEW YORK CITY.
MARIA...

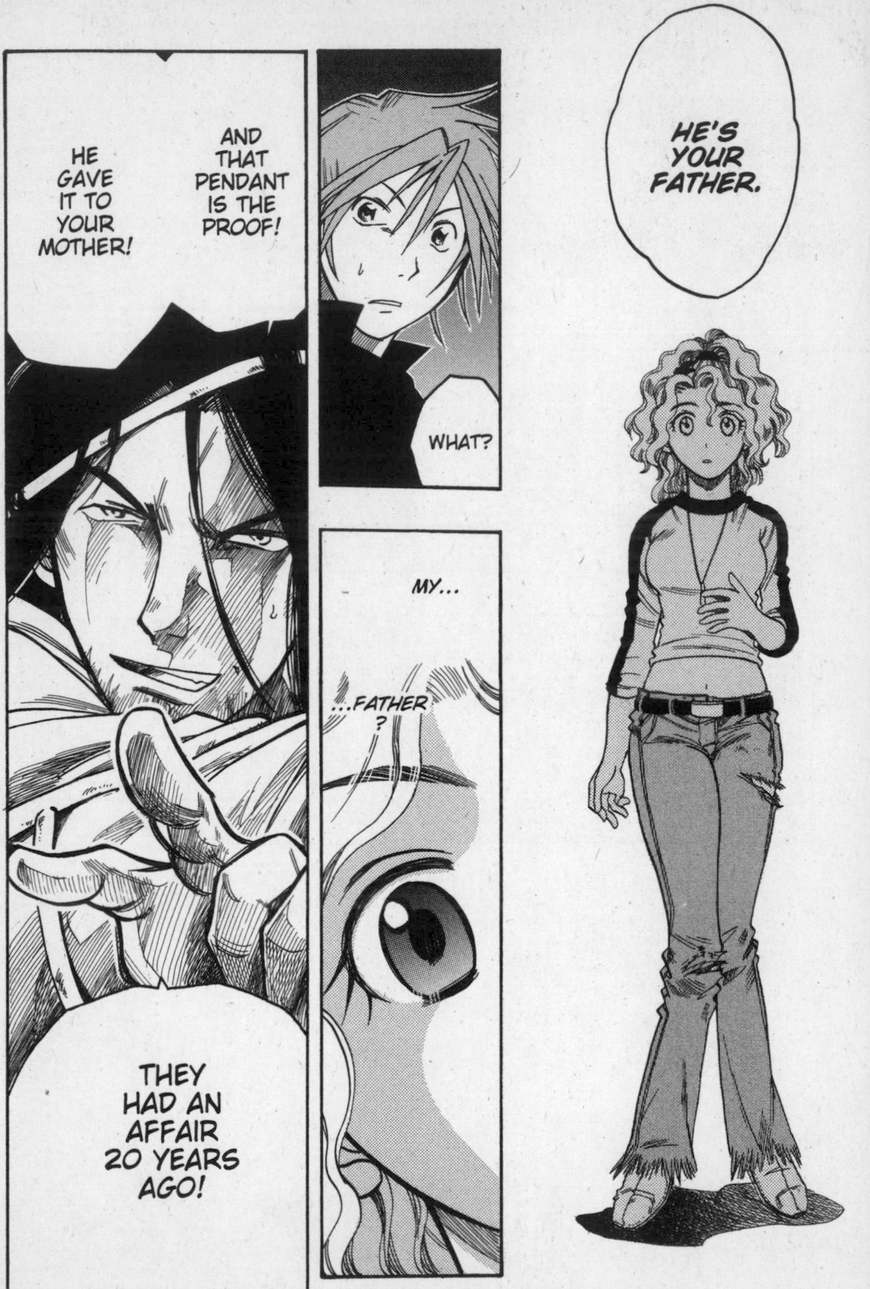
HE'S YOUR FATHER.
WHAT?
MY...
...FATHER?
AND THAT PENDANT IS THE PROOF!
HE GAVE IT TO YOUR MOTHER!
THEY HAD AN AFFAIR 20 YEARS AGO!

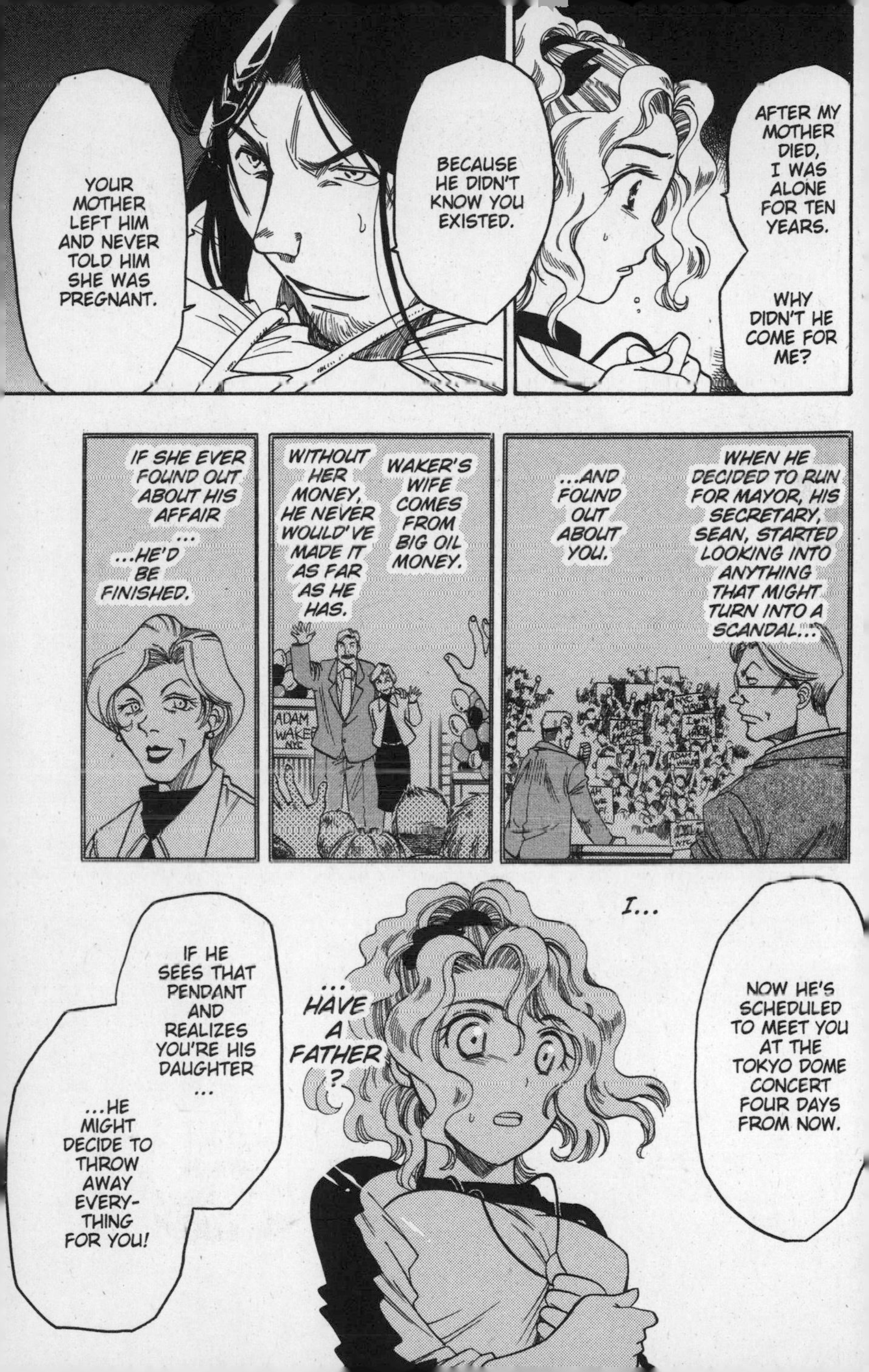
AFTER MY MOTHER DIED, I WAS ALONE FOR TEN YEARS.
WHY DIDN'T HE COME FOR ME?
BECAUSE HE DIDN'T KNOW YOU EXISTED.
YOUR MOTHER LEFT HIM AND NEVER TOLD HIM SHE WAS PREGNANT.
WHEN HE DECIDED TO RUN FOR MAYOR, HIS SECRETARY, SEAN, STARTED LOOKING INTO ANYTHING THAT MIGHT TURN INTO A SCANDAL...
...AND FOUND OUT ABOUT YOU.
WAKER'S WIFE COMES FROM BIG OIL MONEY.
WITHOUT HER MONEY, HE NEVER WOULD'VE MADE IT AS FAR AS HE HAS.
IF SHE EVER FOUND OUT ABOUT HIS AFFAIR ...
...HE'D BE FINISHED.
NOW HE'S SCHEDULED TO MEET YOU AT THE TOKYO DOME CONCERT FOUR DAYS FROM NOW.
I...
...HAVE A FATHER?
IF HE SEES THAT PENDANT AND REALIZES YOU'RE HIS DAUGHTER ...
...HE MIGHT DECIDE TO THROW AWAY EVERY-THING FOR YOU!

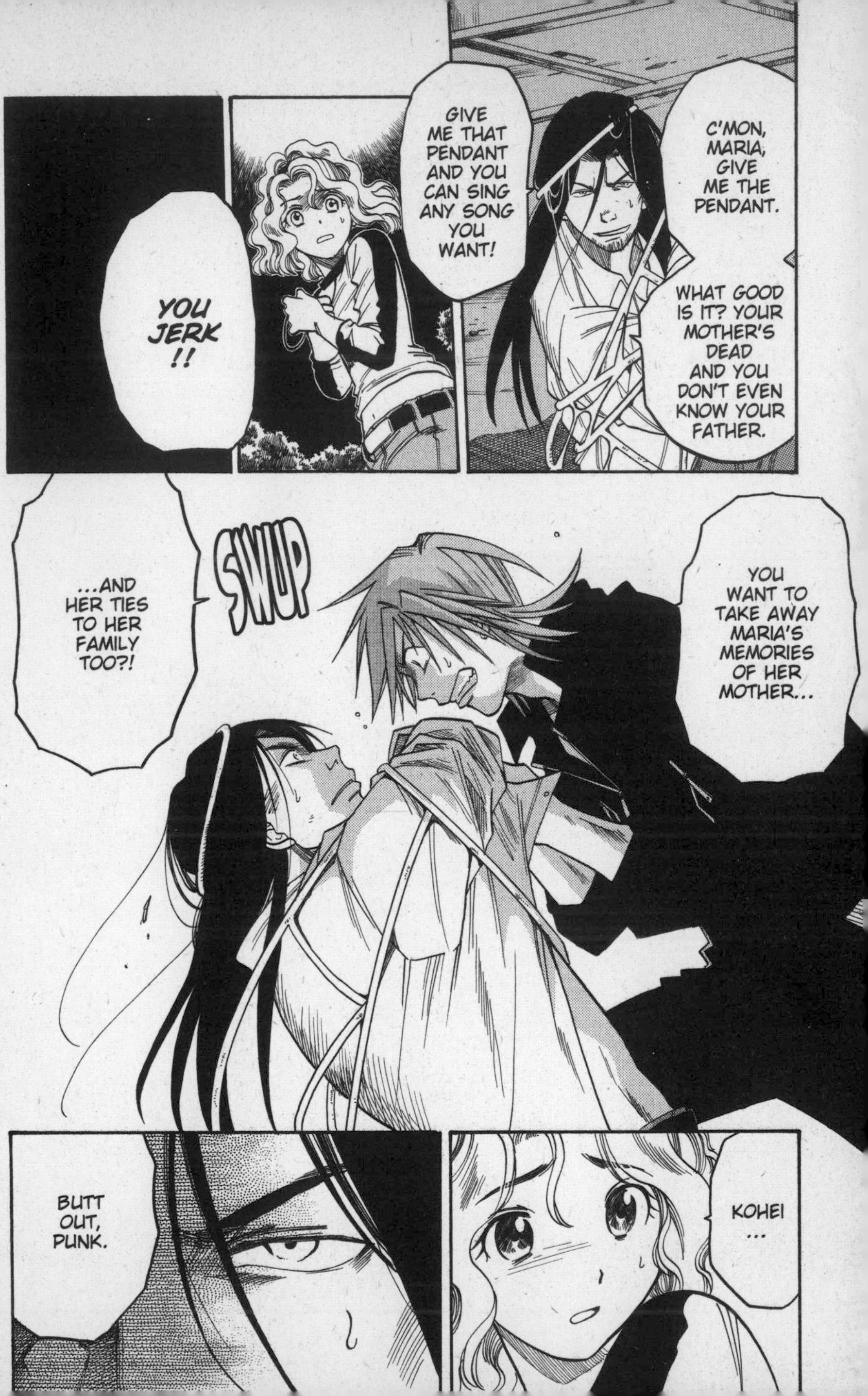
C'MON, MARIA, GIVE ME THE PENDANT.
WHAT GOOD IS IT? YOUR MOTHER'S DEAD AND YOU DON'T EVEN KNOW YOUR FATHER.
GIVE ME THAT PENDANT AND YOU CAN SING ANY SONG YOU WANT!
YOU JERK !!
YOU WANT TO TAKE AWAY MARIA'S MEMORIES OF HER MOTHER...
SWUP
...AND HER TIES TO HER FAMILY TOO?!
KOHEI ...
BUTT OUT, PUNK.

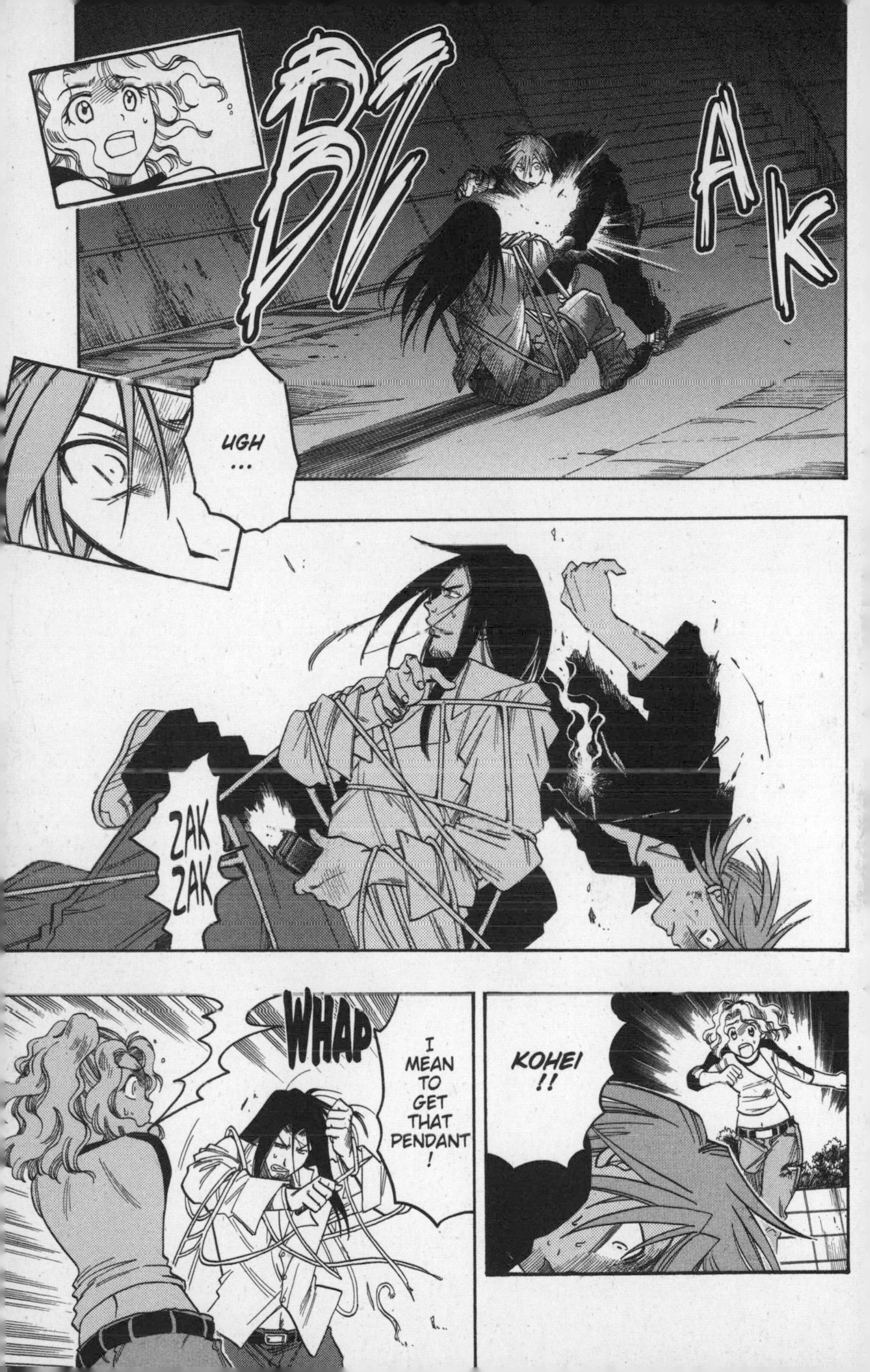
BAK
UGH ...
ZAK ZAK
KOHEI !!
WHAP
I MEAN TO GET THAT PENDANT !

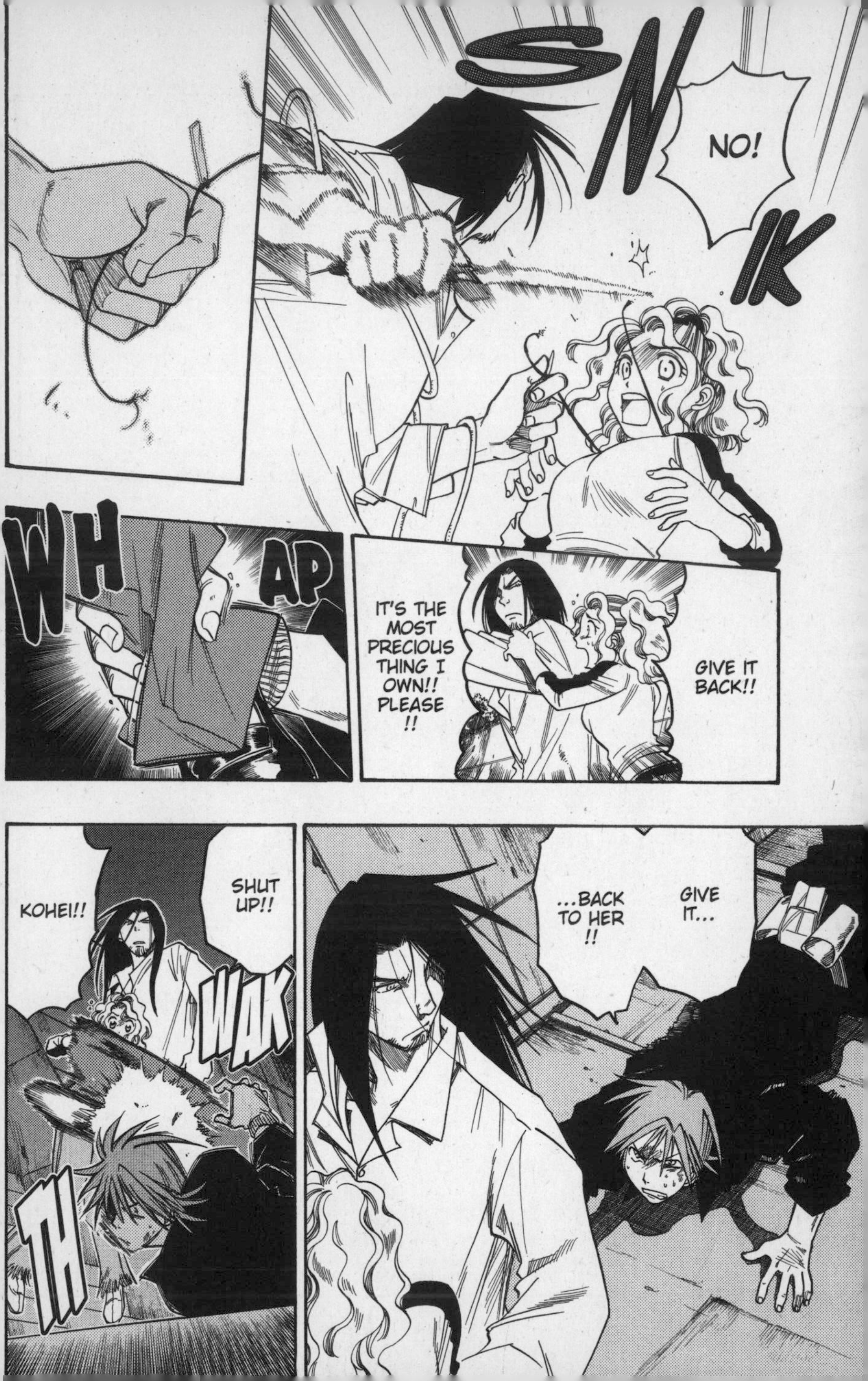
SNIK
NO!
GIVE IT BACK!!
IT'S THE MOST PRECIOUS THING I OWN!! PLEASE!!
WHAP
GIVE IT...
...BACK TO HER!!
SHUT UP!!
KOHEI!!
WAK
TH

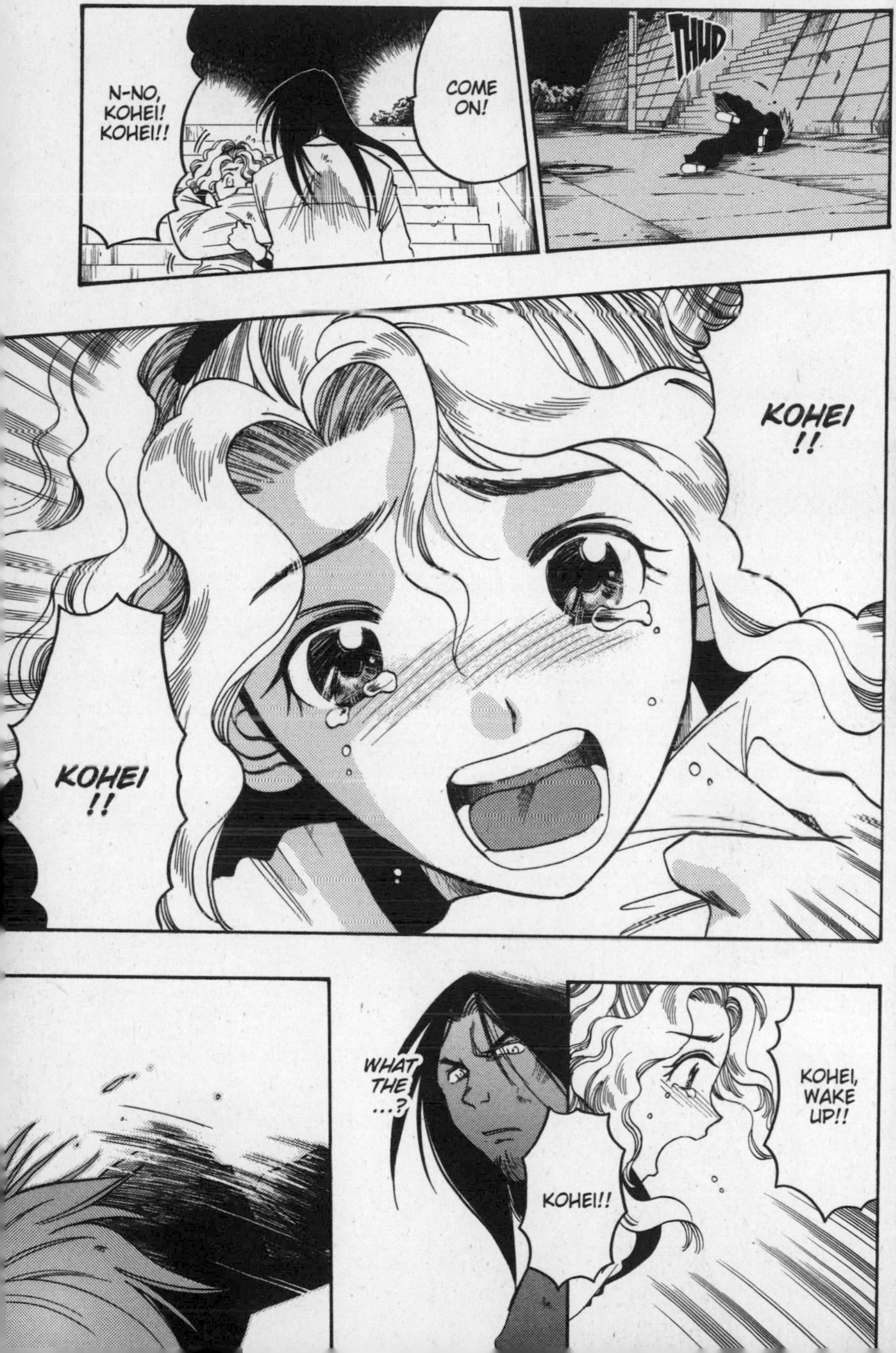
THUD
COME ON!
N-NO, KOHEI! KOHEI!!
KOHEI !!
KOHEI !!
KOHEI, WAKE UP!!
KOHEI!!
WHAT THE ...?

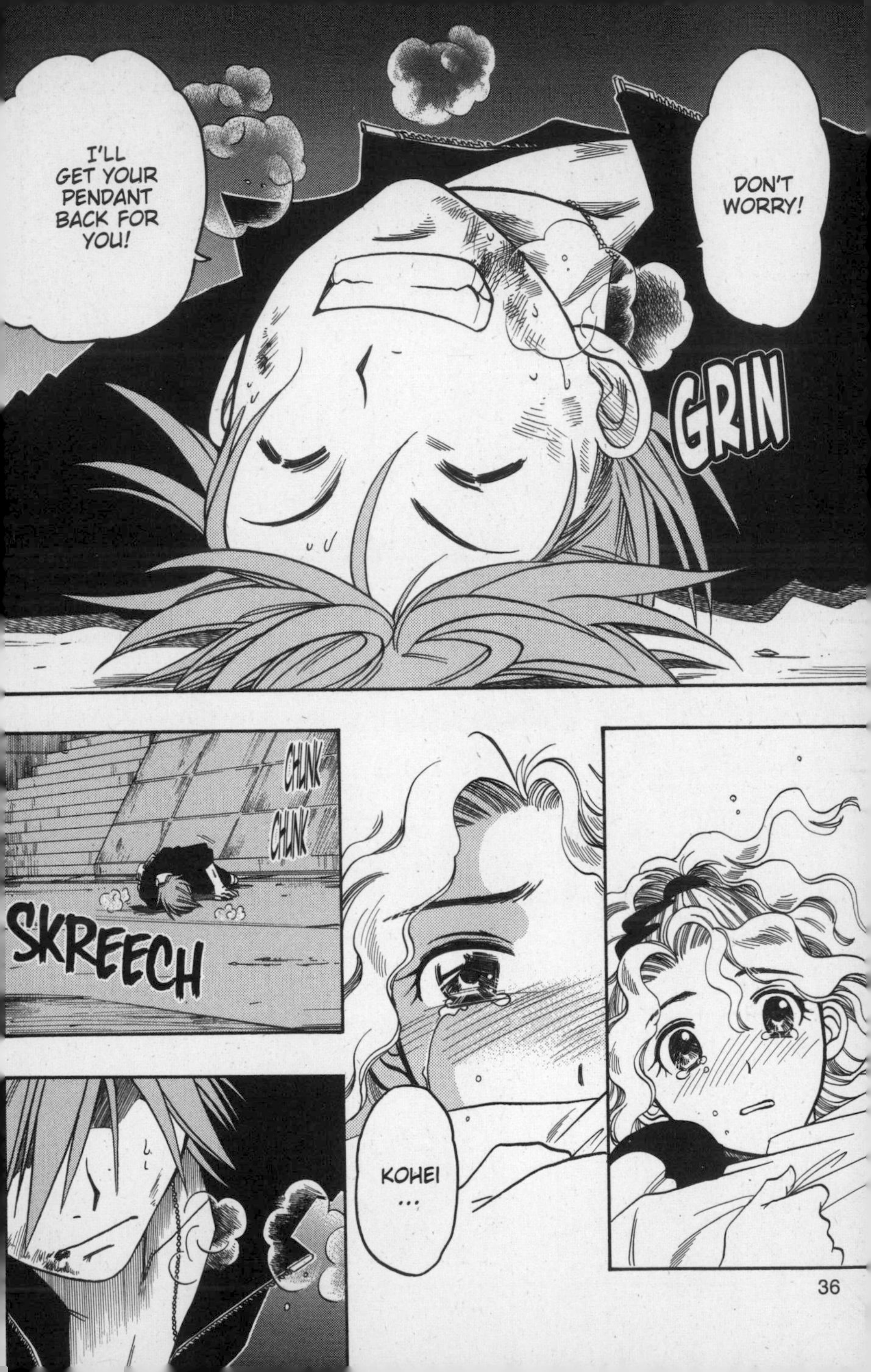

DON'T WORRY!
I'LL GET YOUR PENDANT BACK FOR YOU!
GRIN
KOHEI ...
CHUNK
CHUNK
SKREECH

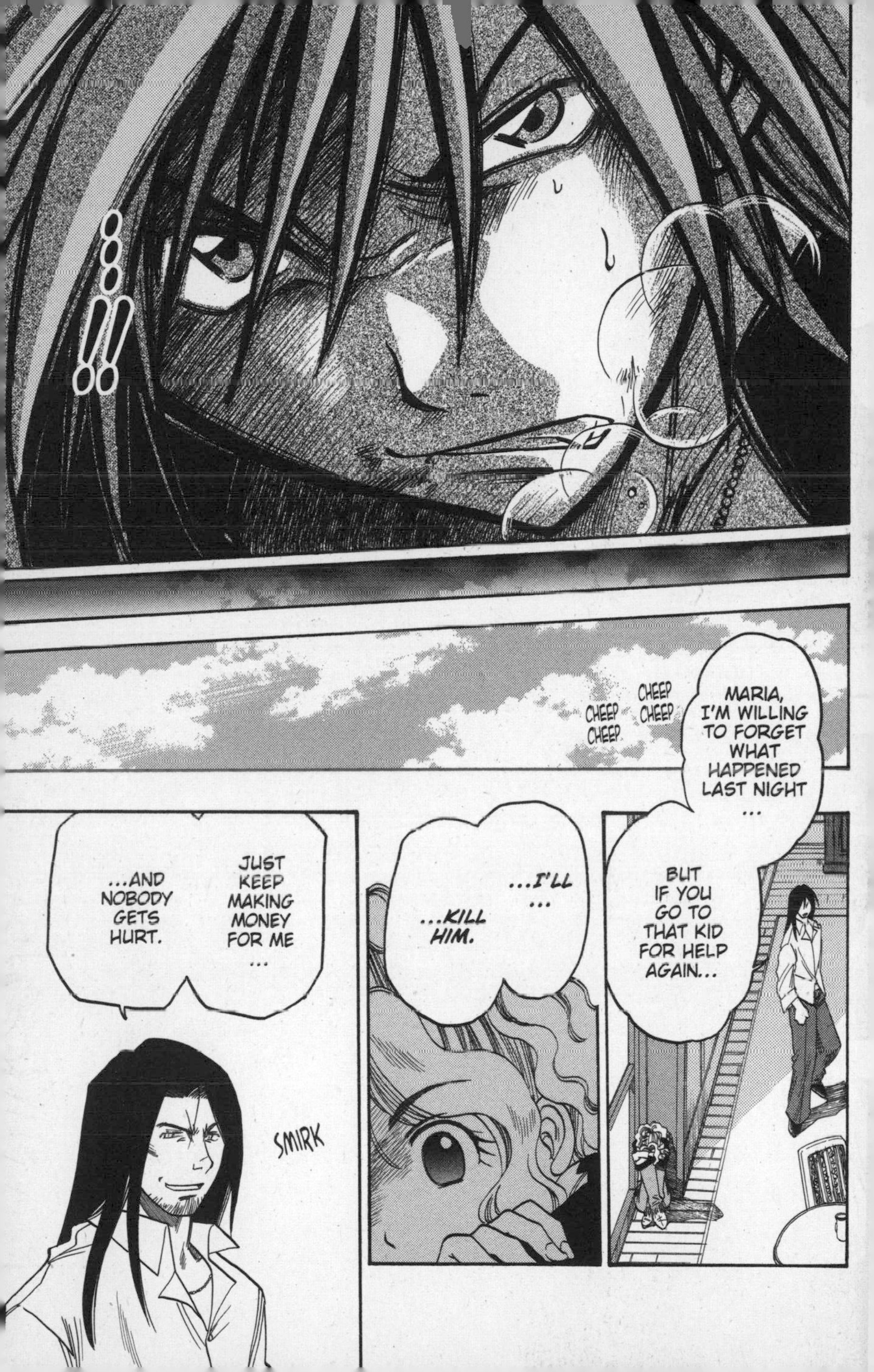
...!!
MARIA, I'M WILLING TO FORGET WHAT HAPPENED LAST NIGHT ...
CHEEP CHEEP
CHEEP CHEEP
BUT IF YOU GO TO THAT KID FOR HELP AGAIN...
...I'LL ...
...KILL HIM.
JUST KEEP MAKING MONEY FOR ME ...
...AND NOBODY GETS HURT.
SMIRK

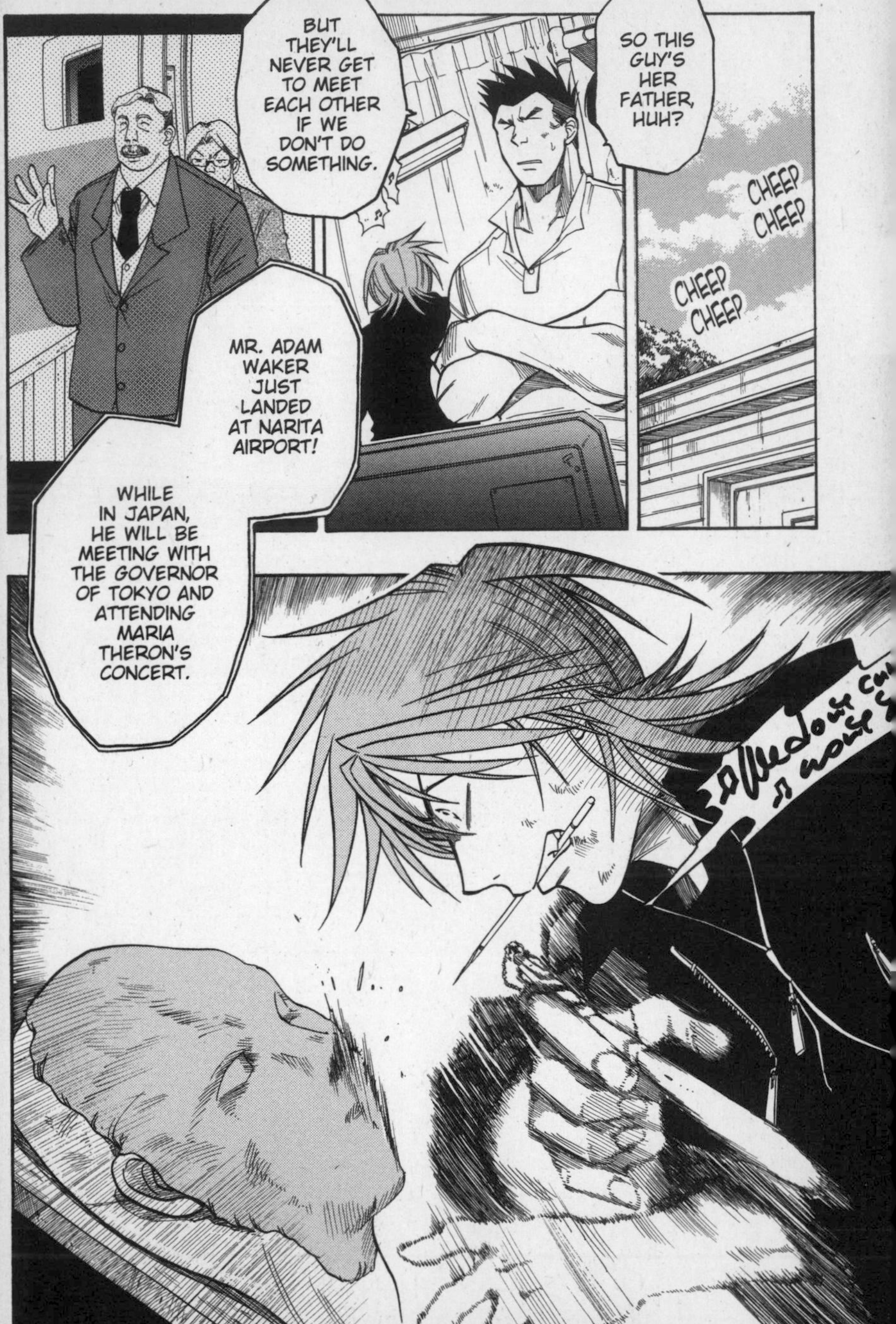
CHEEP CHEEP
CHEEP CHEEP
SO THIS GUY'S HER FATHER, HUH?
BUT THEY'LL NEVER GET TO MEET EACH OTHER IF WE DON'T DO SOMETHING.
MR. ADAM WAKER JUST LANDED AT NARITA AIRPORT!
WHILE IN JAPAN, HE WILL BE MEETING WITH THE GOVERNOR OF TOKYO AND ATTENDING MARIA THERON'S CONCERT.

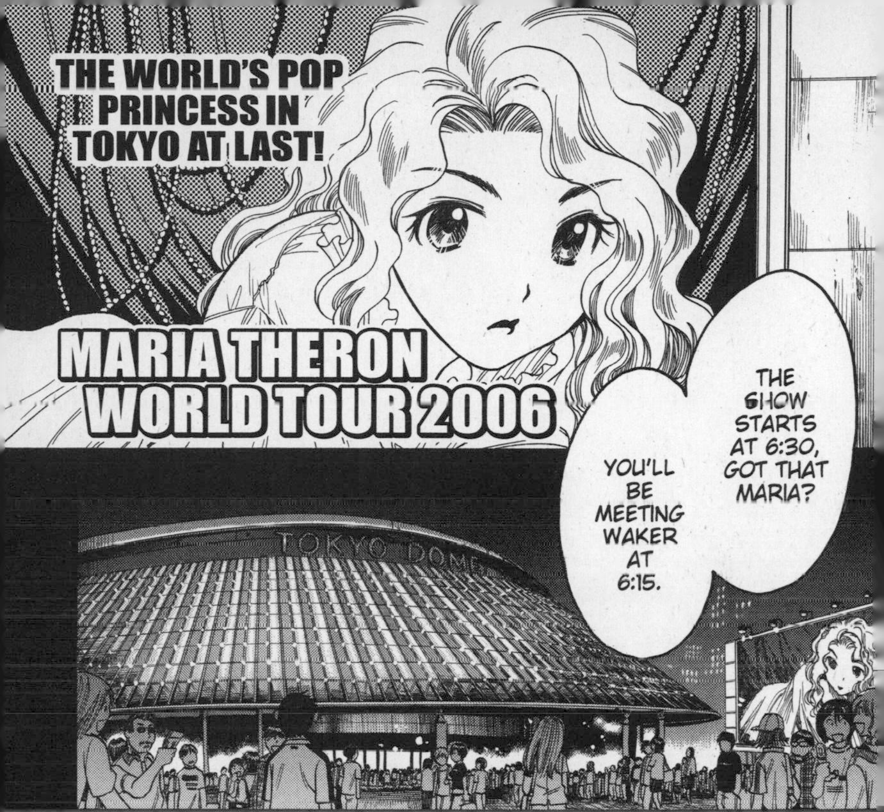
THE WORLD'S POP PRINCESS IN TOKYO AT LAST!
MARIA THERON WORLD TOUR 2006
THE SHOW STARTS AT 6:30, GOT THAT MARIA?
YOU'LL BE MEETING WAKER AT 6:15.
TOKYO DOME

Scene 49: My Favorite Things (Part 5)

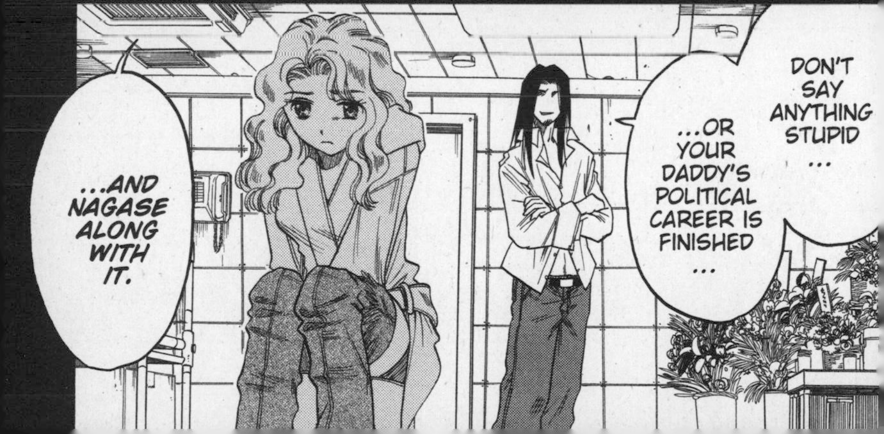
DON'T SAY ANYTHING STUPID ...
...OR YOUR DADDY'S POLITICAL CAREER IS FINISHED ...
...AND NAGASE ALONG WITH IT.

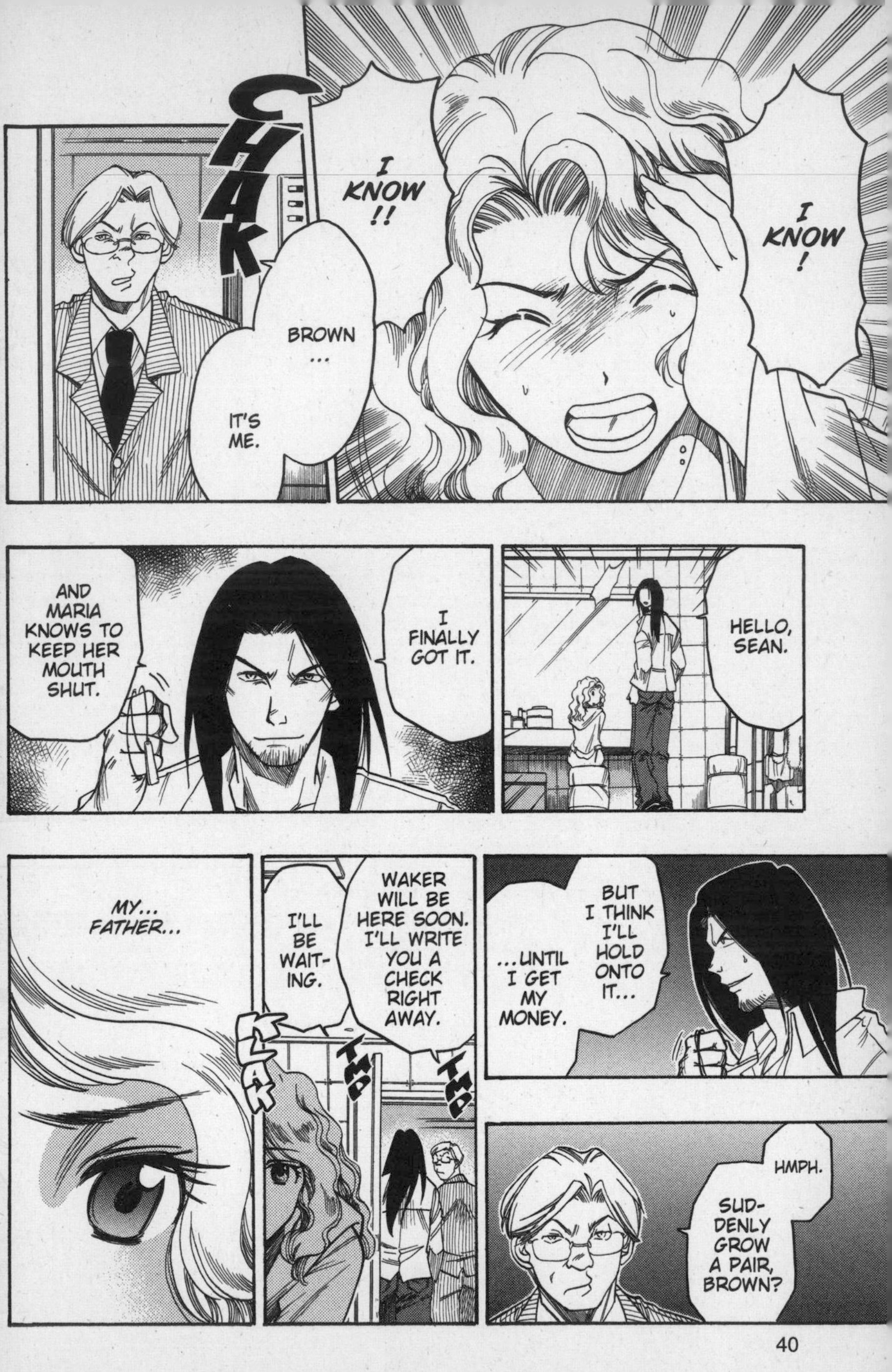
I KNOW!
I KNOW!!
CHAK
BROWN... IT'S ME.
HELLO, SEAN.
I FINALLY GOT IT.
AND MARIA KNOWS TO KEEP HER MOUTH SHUT.
BUT I THINK I'LL HOLD ONTO IT...
...UNTIL I GET MY MONEY.
HMPH.
SUD-DENLY GROW A PAIR, BROWN?
WAKER WILL BE HERE SOON. I'LL WRITE YOU A CHECK RIGHT AWAY.
I'LL BE WAIT-ING.
TMP
TMP
KLAK
MY... FATHER...

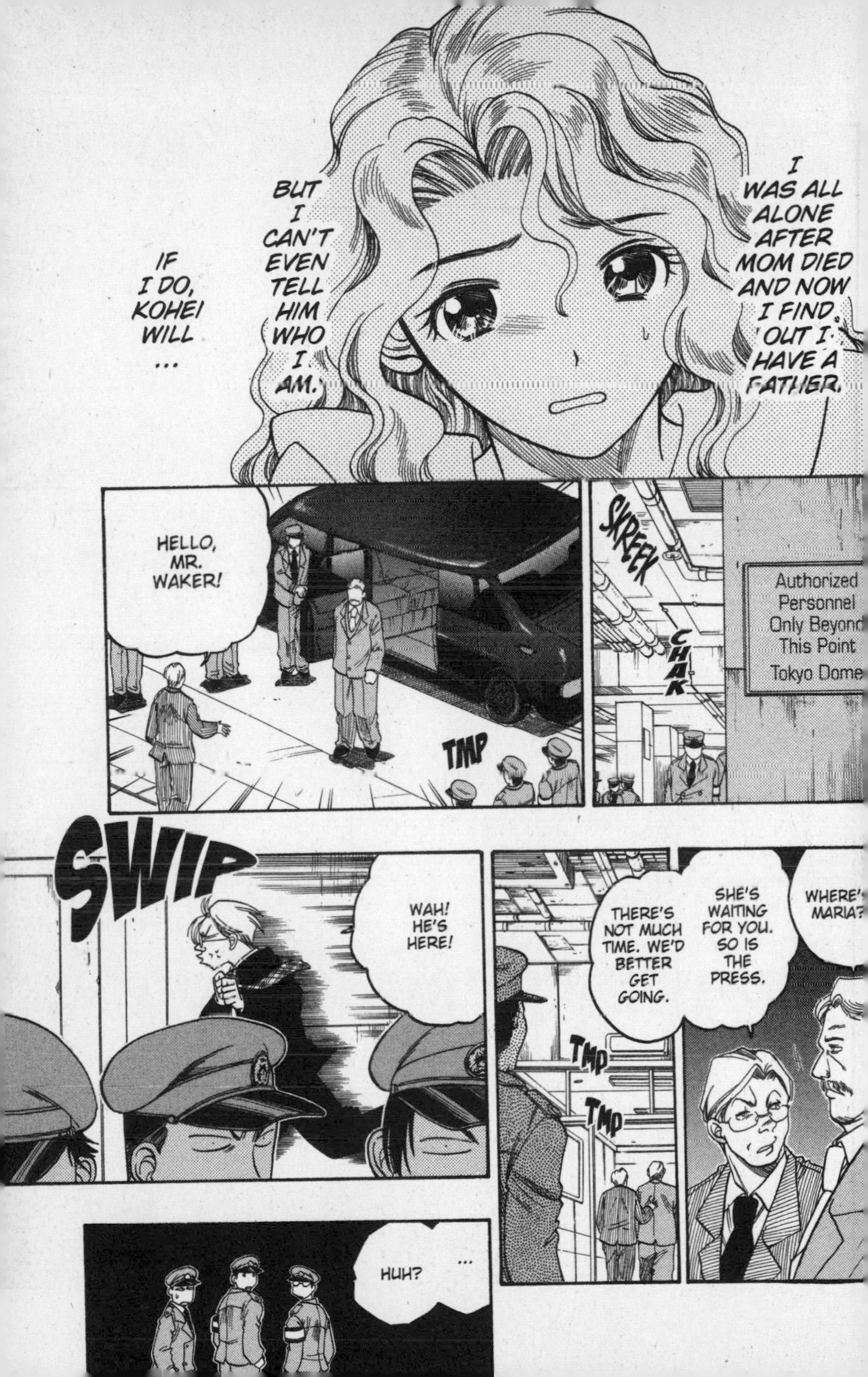
I WAS ALL ALONE AFTER MOM DIED AND NOW I FIND OUT I HAVE A FATHER.
BUT I CAN'T EVEN TELL HIM WHO I AM.
IF I DO, KOHEI WILL ...
SKREEK
CHAK
Authorized Personnel Only Beyond This Point Tokyo Dome
TMP
HELLO, MR. WAKER!
WHERE'S MARIA?
SHE'S WAITING FOR YOU. SO IS THE PRESS.
THERE'S NOT MUCH TIME. WE'D BETTER GET GOING.
TMP
TMP
SWIP
WAH! HE'S HERE!
...
HUH?

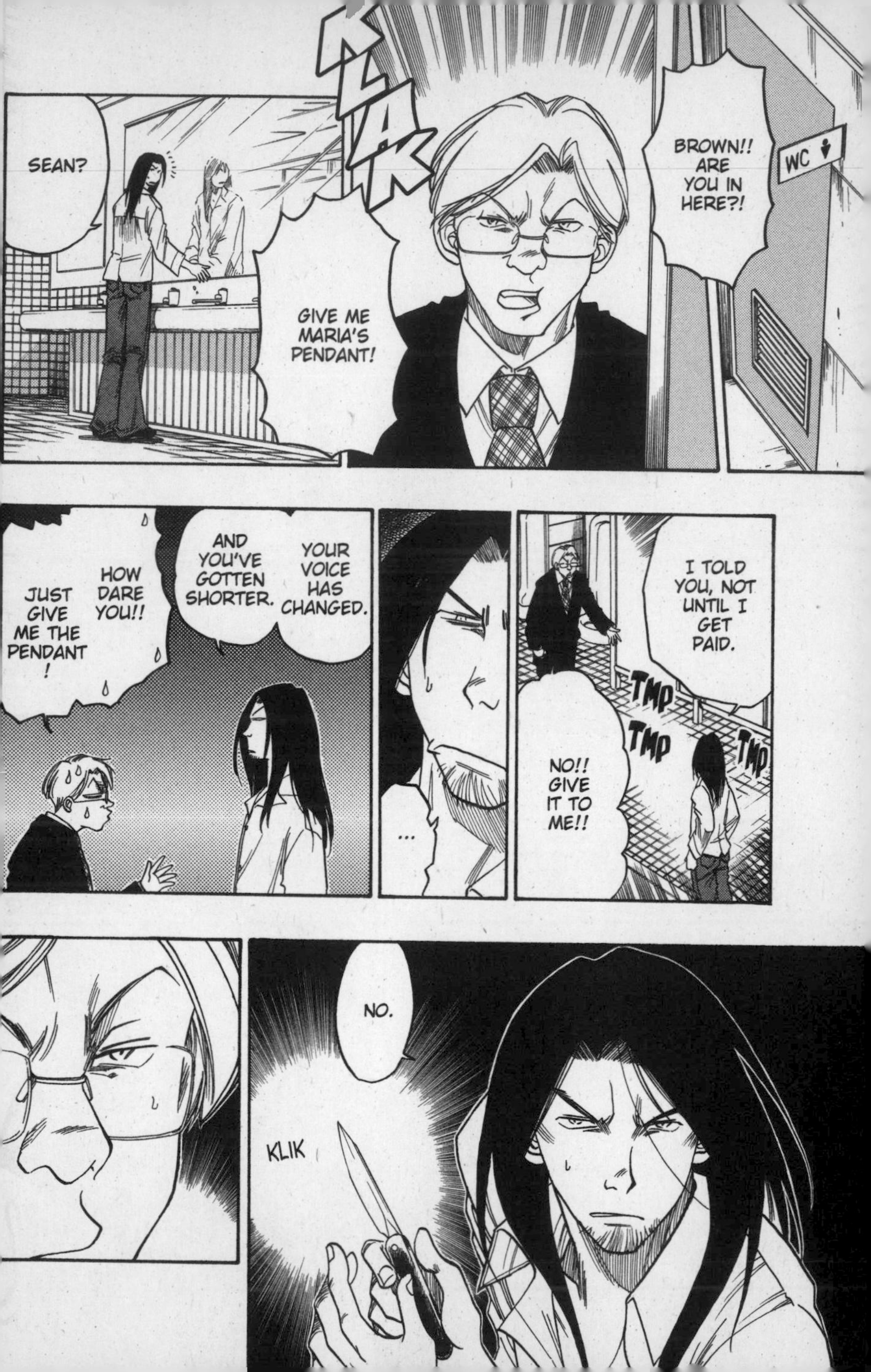
KLAK
WC
BROWN!! ARE YOU IN HERE?!
GIVE ME MARIA'S PENDANT!
SEAN?
I TOLD YOU, NOT UNTIL I GET PAID.
TMP
TMP
TMP
NO!! GIVE IT TO ME!!
...
YOUR VOICE HAS CHANGED.
AND YOU'VE GOTTEN SHORTER.
HOW DARE YOU!!
JUST GIVE ME THE PENDANT!
NO.
KLIK

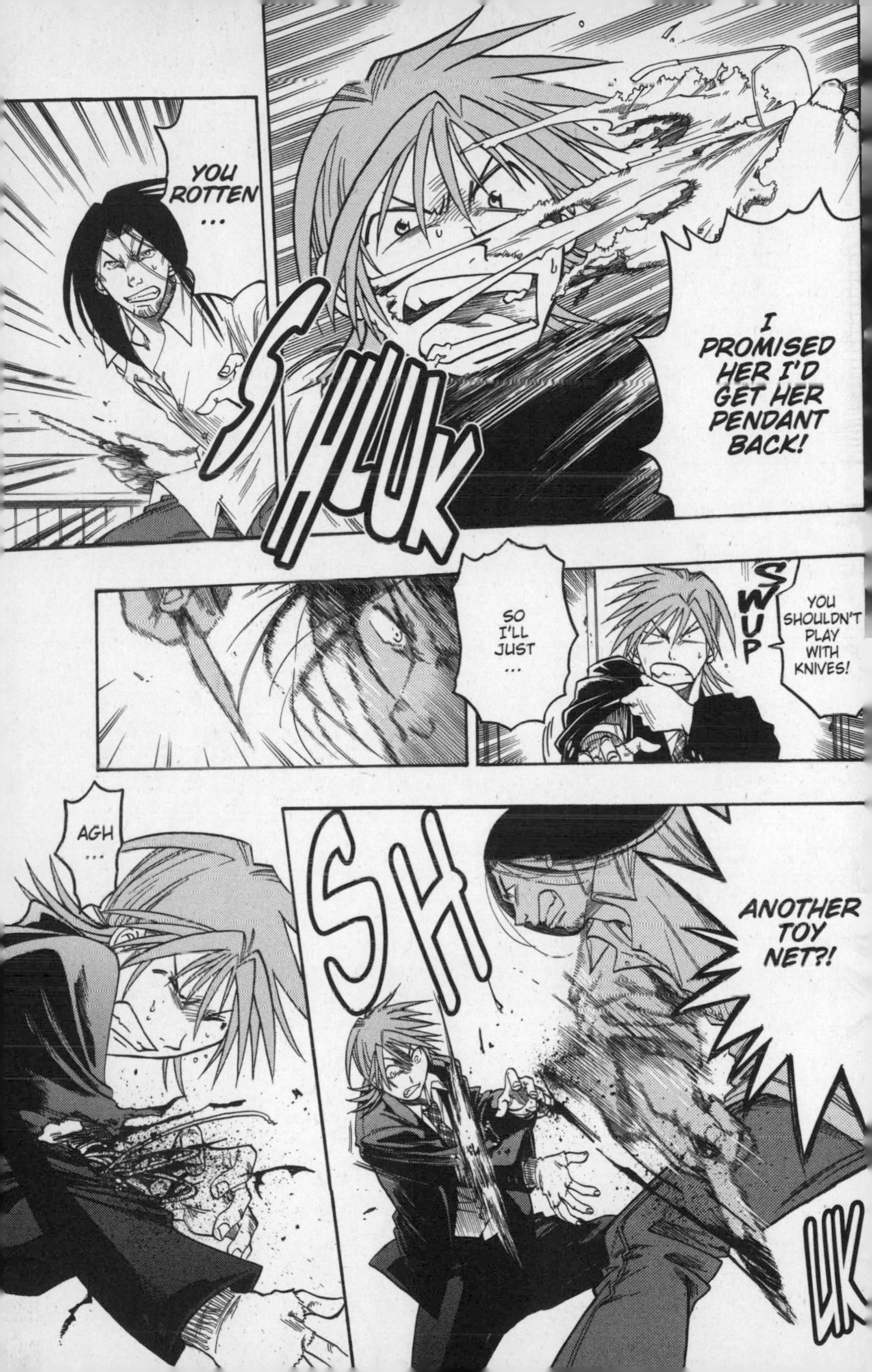
I PROMISED HER I'D GET HER PENDANT BACK!
SHLUK
YOU ROTTEN ...
YOU SHOULDN'T PLAY WITH KNIVES!
SWUP
SO I'LL JUST ...
ANOTHER TOY NET?!
SH
UK
AGH ...

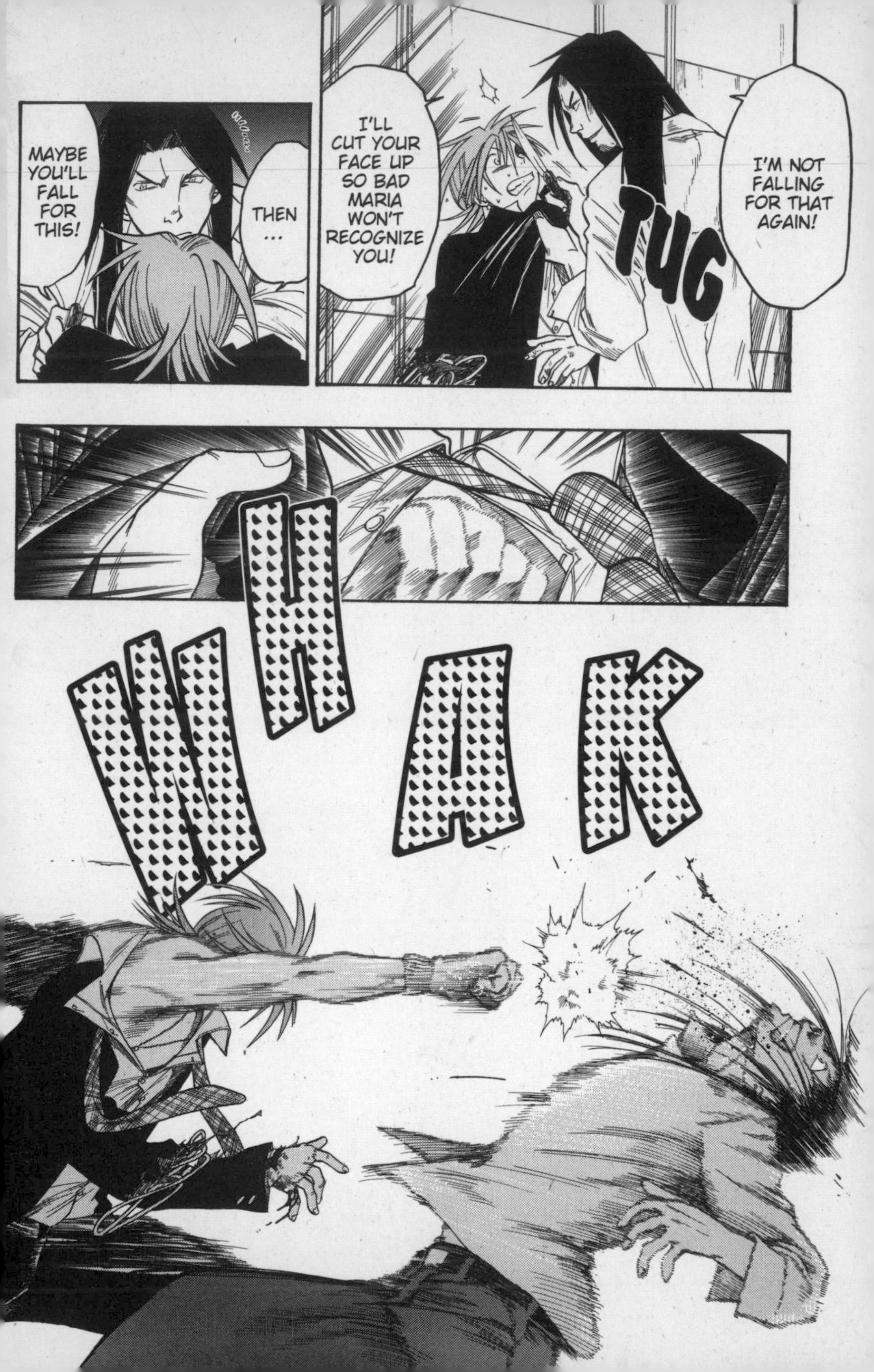
I'M NOT FALLING FOR THAT AGAIN!
TUG
I'LL CUT YOUR FACE UP SO BAD MARIA WON'T RECOGNIZE YOU!
THEN ...
MAYBE YOU'LL FALL FOR THIS!
WHAK

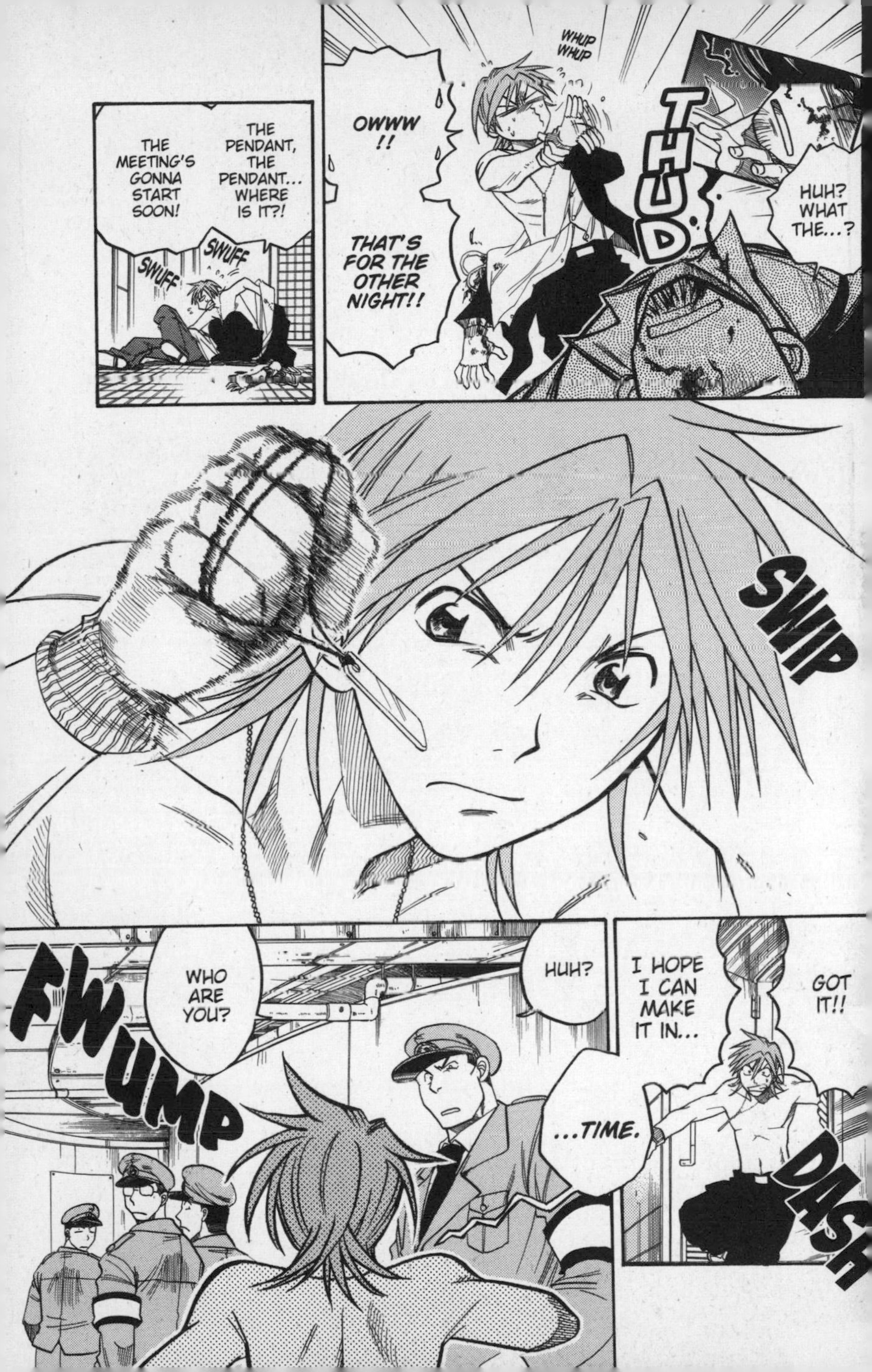
HUH? WHAT THE...?
THUD
WHUP WHUP
OWWW!!
THAT'S FOR THE OTHER NIGHT!!
THE PENDANT, THE PENDANT... WHERE IS IT?!
THE MEETING'S GONNA START SOON!
SWUFF
SWUFF
SWIP
GOT IT!!
I HOPE I CAN MAKE IT IN...
DASH
...TIME.
HUH?
WHO ARE YOU?
FWUMP

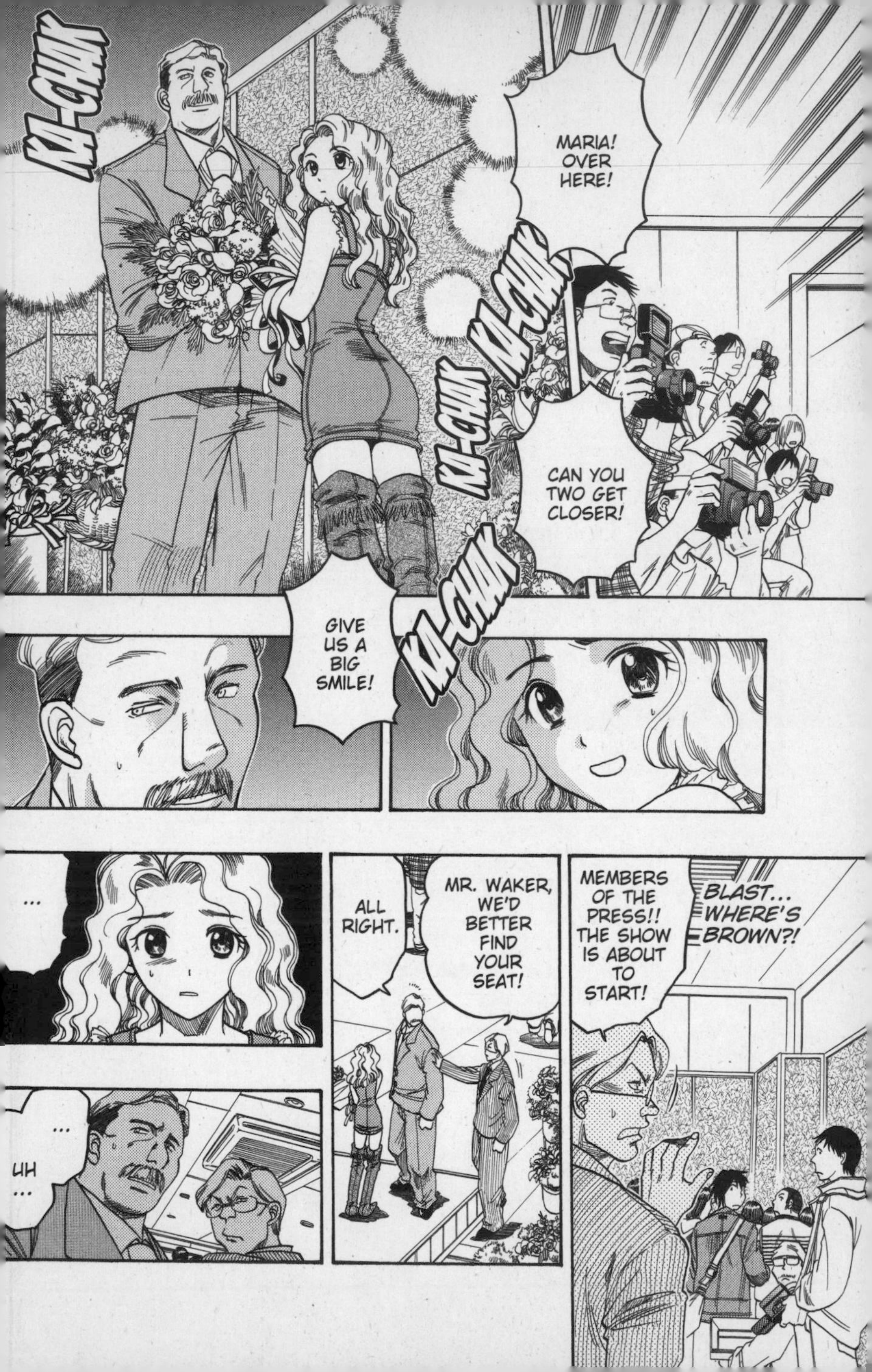
MARIA! OVER HERE!
KA-CHAK
KA-CHAK
CAN YOU TWO GET CLOSER!
KA-CHAK
KA-CHAK
KA-CHAK
GIVE US A BIG SMILE!
BLAST... WHERE'S BROWN?!
MEMBERS OF THE PRESS!! THE SHOW IS ABOUT TO START!
MR. WAKER, WE'D BETTER FIND YOUR SEAT!
ALL RIGHT.
...
...
UH ...

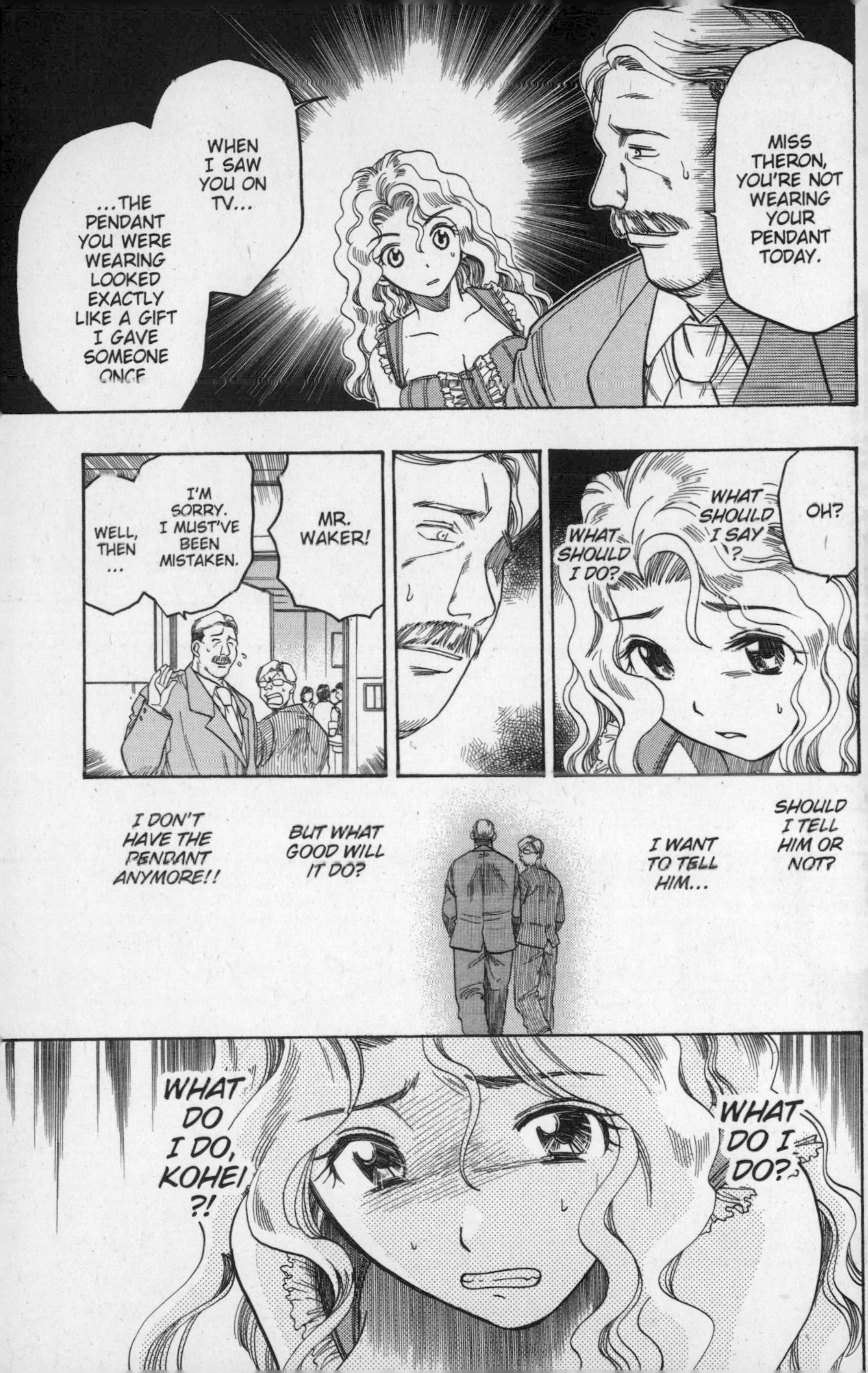
MISS THERON, YOU'RE NOT WEARING YOUR PENDANT TODAY.
WHEN I SAW YOU ON TV...
...THE PENDANT YOU WERE WEARING LOOKED EXACTLY LIKE A GIFT I GAVE SOMEONE ONCE
OH?
WHAT SHOULD I SAY?
WHAT SHOULD I DO?
MR. WAKER!
I'M SORRY. I MUST'VE BEEN MISTAKEN.
WELL, THEN ...
SHOULD I TELL HIM OR NOT?
I WANT TO TELL HIM...
BUT WHAT GOOD WILL IT DO?
I DON'T HAVE THE PENDANT ANYMORE!!
WHAT DO I DO?
WHAT DO I DO, KOHEI?!

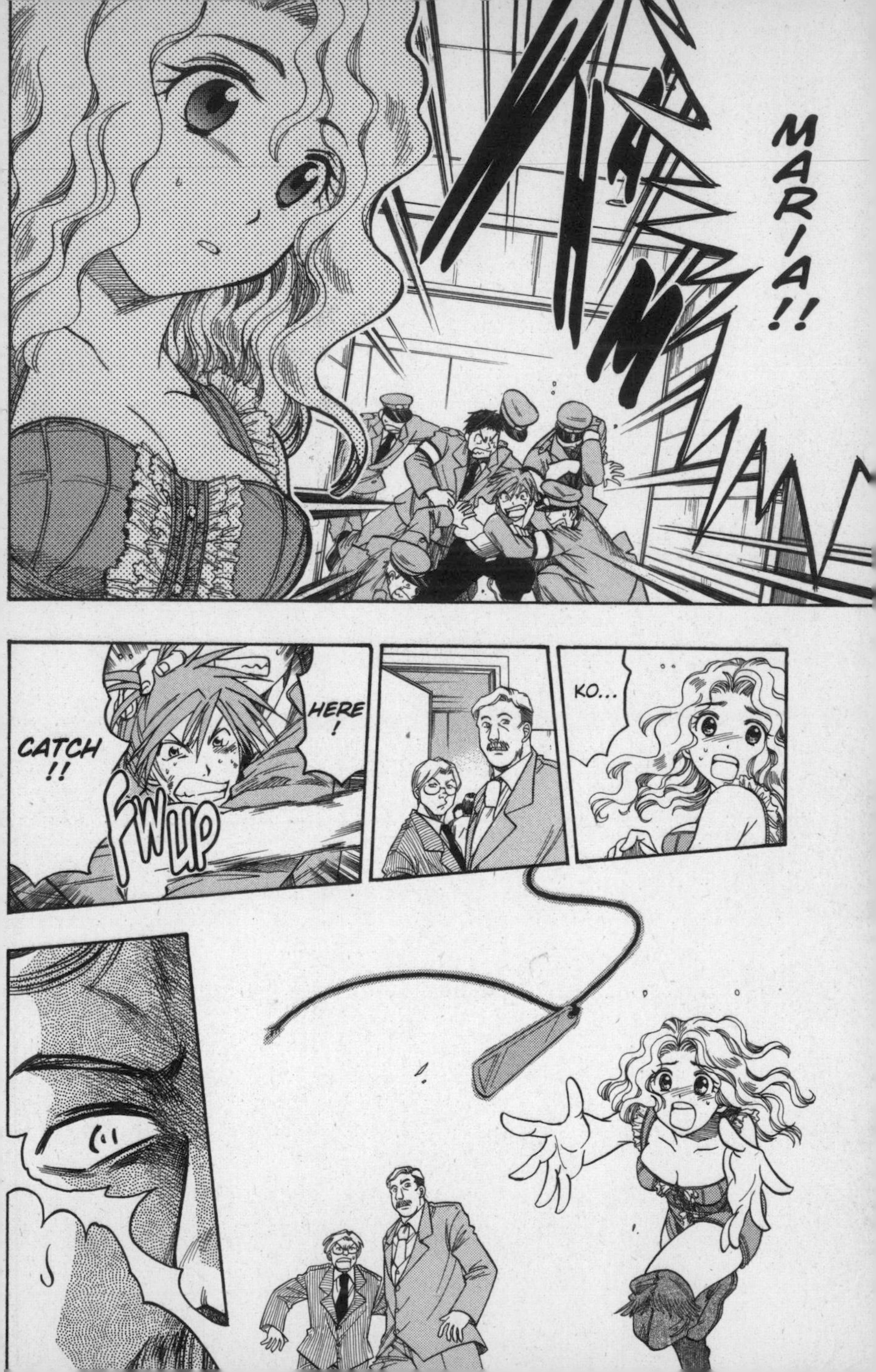
MARIA!!
KO...
HERE!
CATCH!!
FWUP

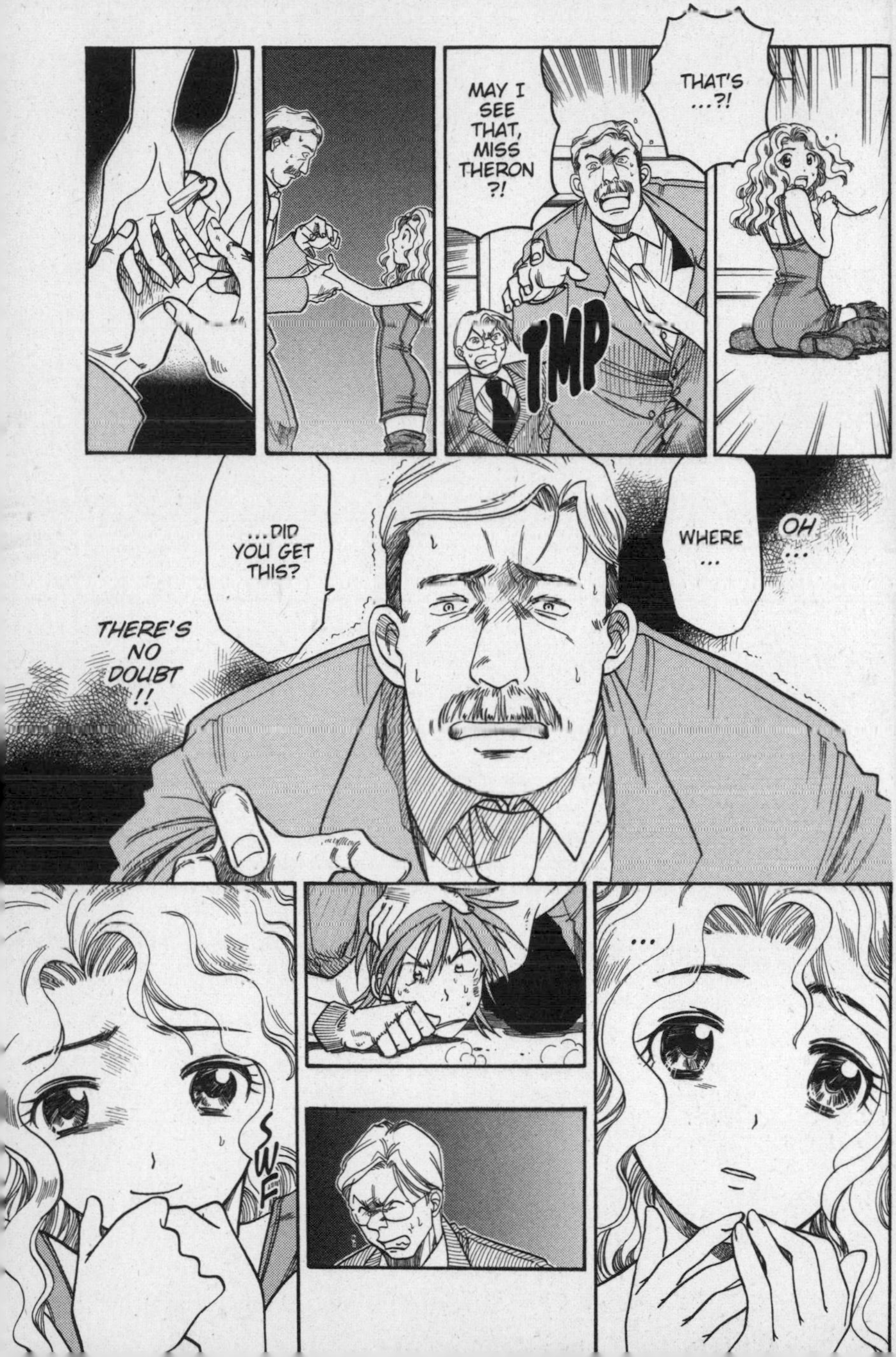
THAT'S ...?!
MAY I SEE THAT, MISS THERON ?!
TMP
OH ...
WHERE ...
...DID YOU GET THIS?
THERE'S NO DOUBT !!
...
SWF

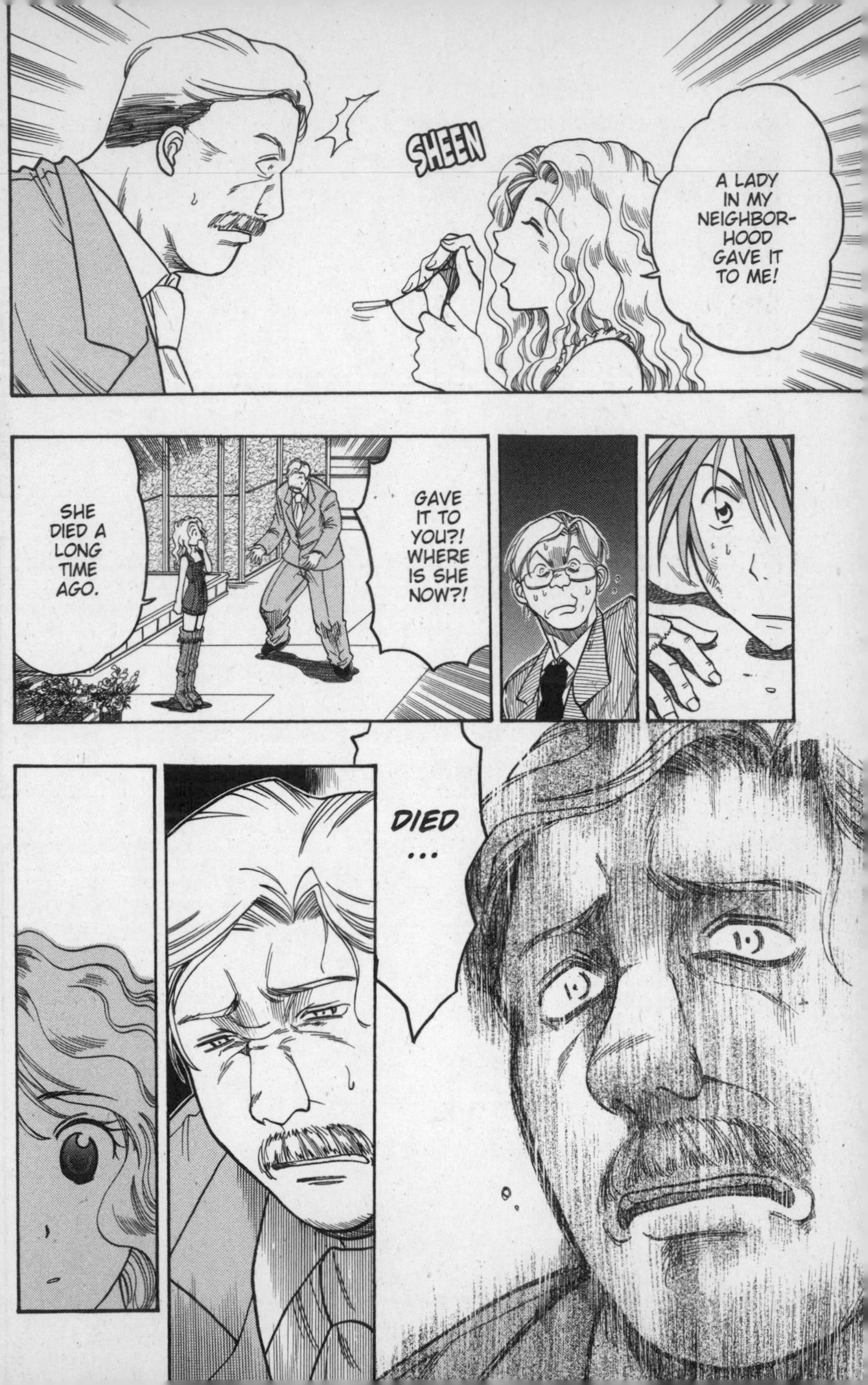
A LADY IN MY NEIGHBOR-HOOD GAVE IT TO ME!
SHEEN
GAVE IT TO YOU?! WHERE IS SHE NOW?!
SHE DIED A LONG TIME AGO.
DIED ...

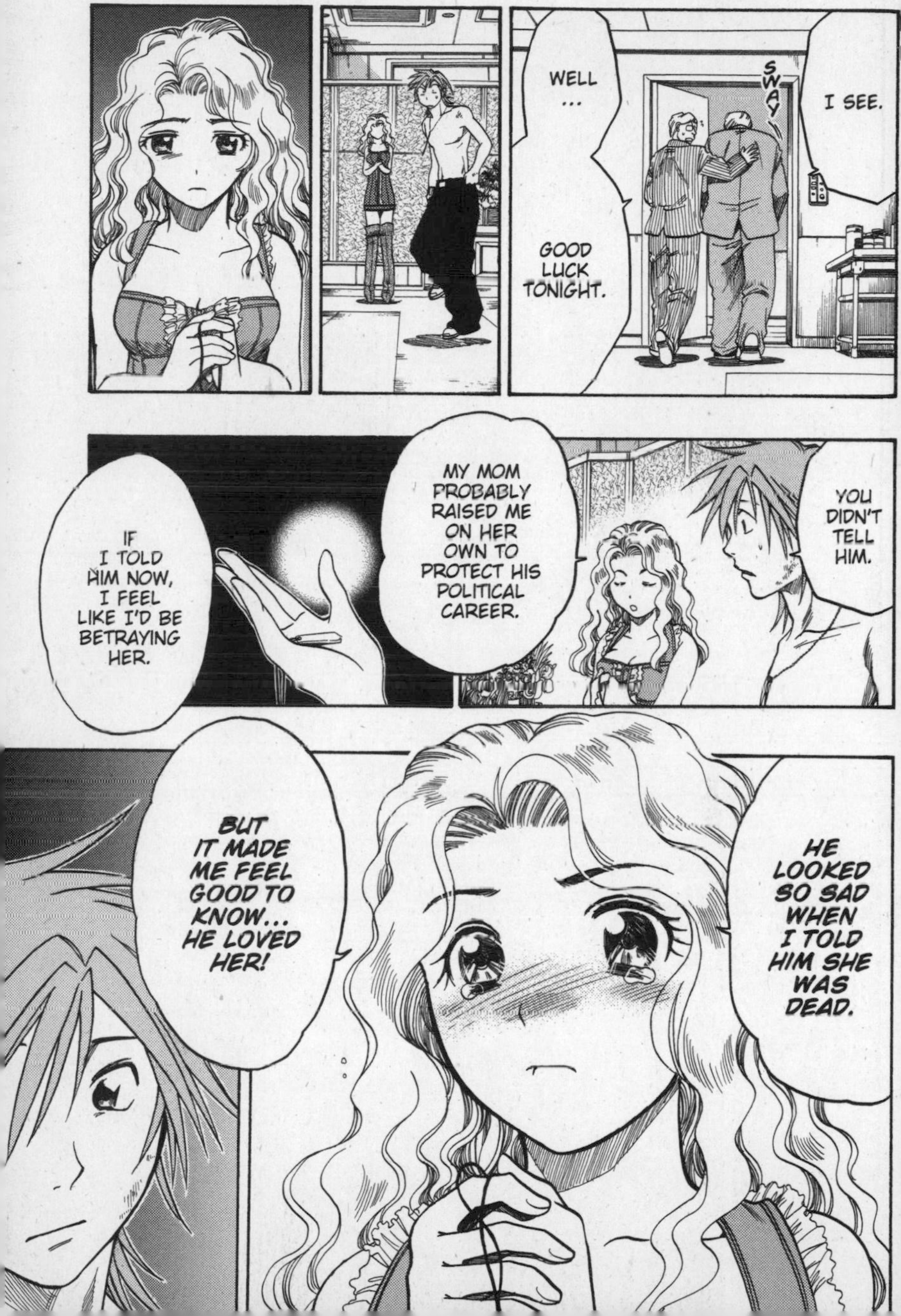
I SEE.
SWAY
WELL ...
GOOD LUCK TONIGHT.
YOU DIDN'T TELL HIM.
MY MOM PROBABLY RAISED ME ON HER OWN TO PROTECT HIS POLITICAL CAREER.
IF I TOLD HIM NOW, I FEEL LIKE I'D BE BETRAYING HER.
HE LOOKED SO SAD WHEN I TOLD HIM SHE WAS DEAD.
BUT IT MADE ME FEEL GOOD TO KNOW... HE LOVED HER!

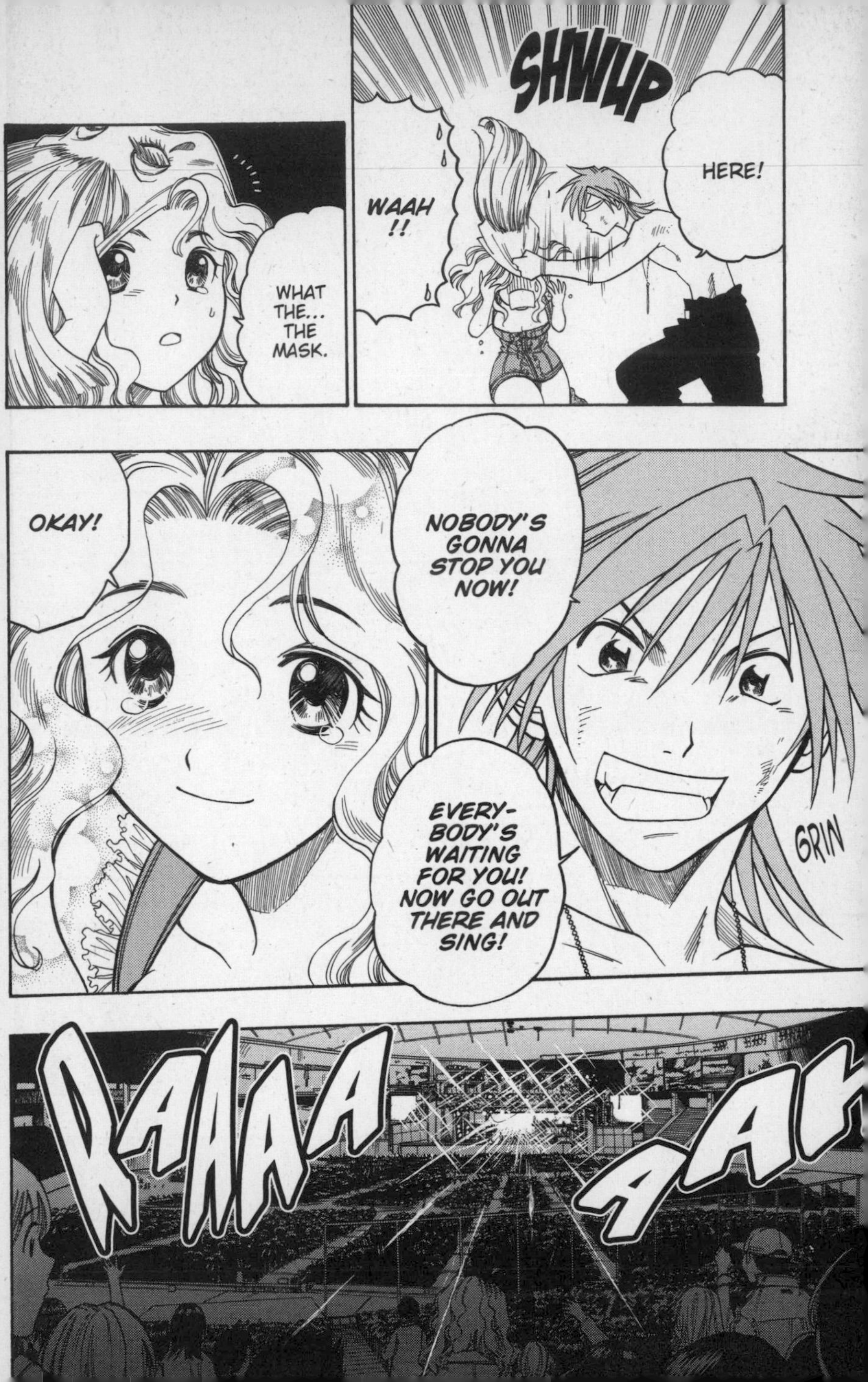
SHWUP
HERE!
WAAH!!
WHAT THE... THE MASK.
NOBODY'S GONNA STOP YOU NOW!
EVERY-BODY'S WAITING FOR YOU! NOW GO OUT THERE AND SING!
GRIN
OKAY!
RAAAA-AAA

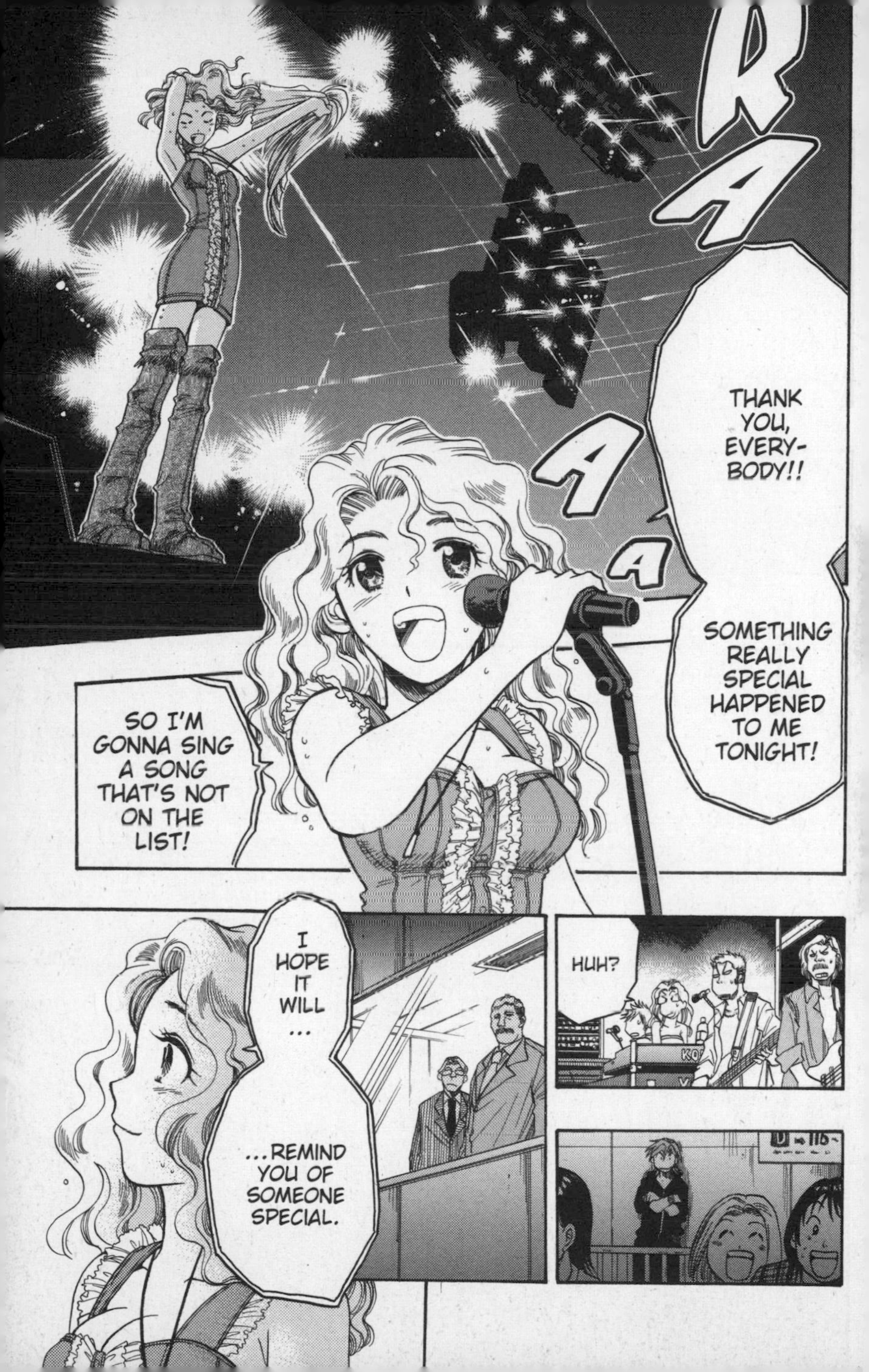
RAAA
THANK YOU, EVERYBODY!!
SOMETHING REALLY SPECIAL HAPPENED TO ME TONIGHT!
SO I'M GONNA SING A SONG THAT'S NOT ON THE LIST!
HUH?
I HOPE IT WILL ...
...REMIND YOU OF SOMEONE SPECIAL.

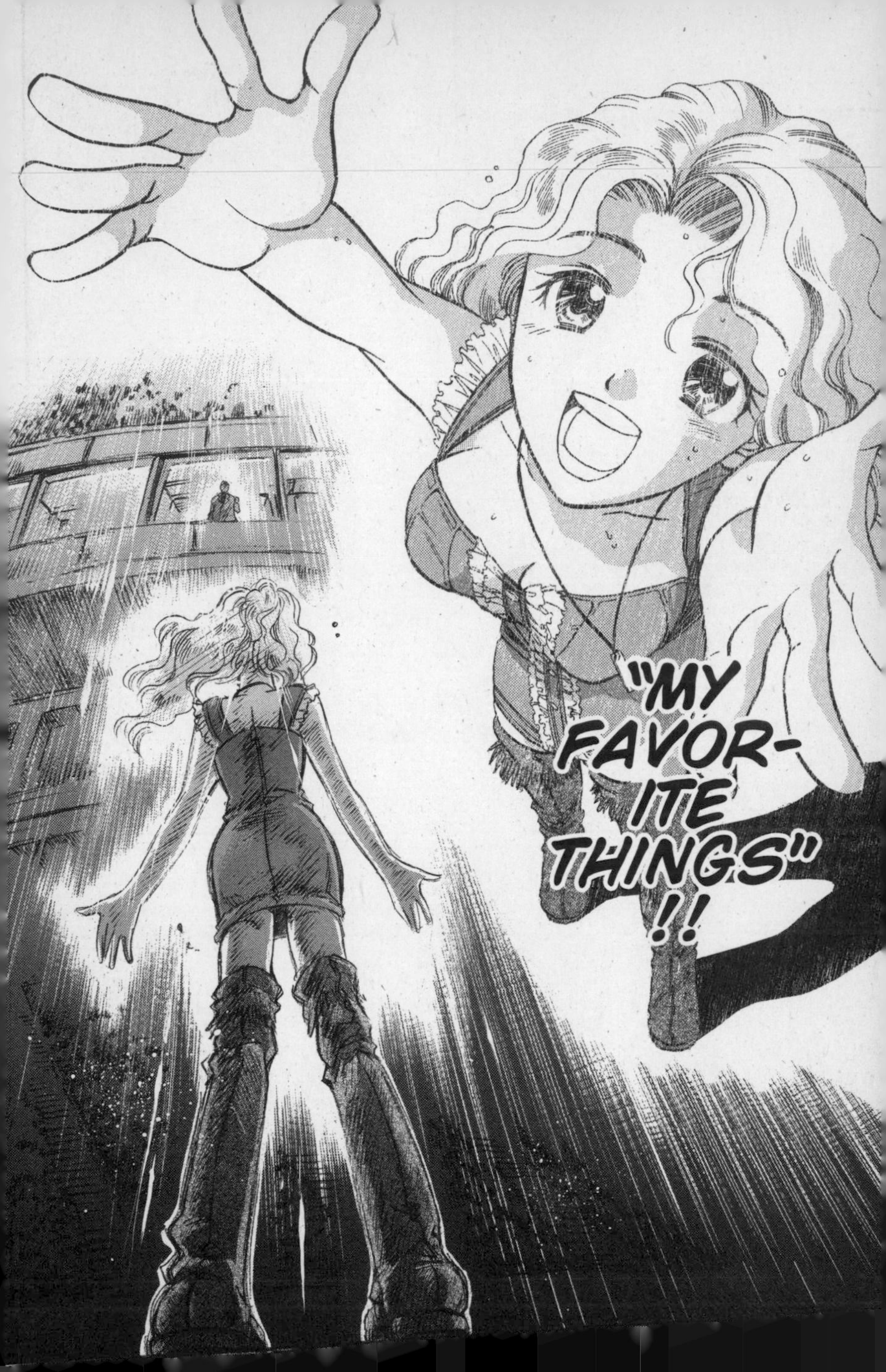
"MY FAVOR-ITE THINGS"!!

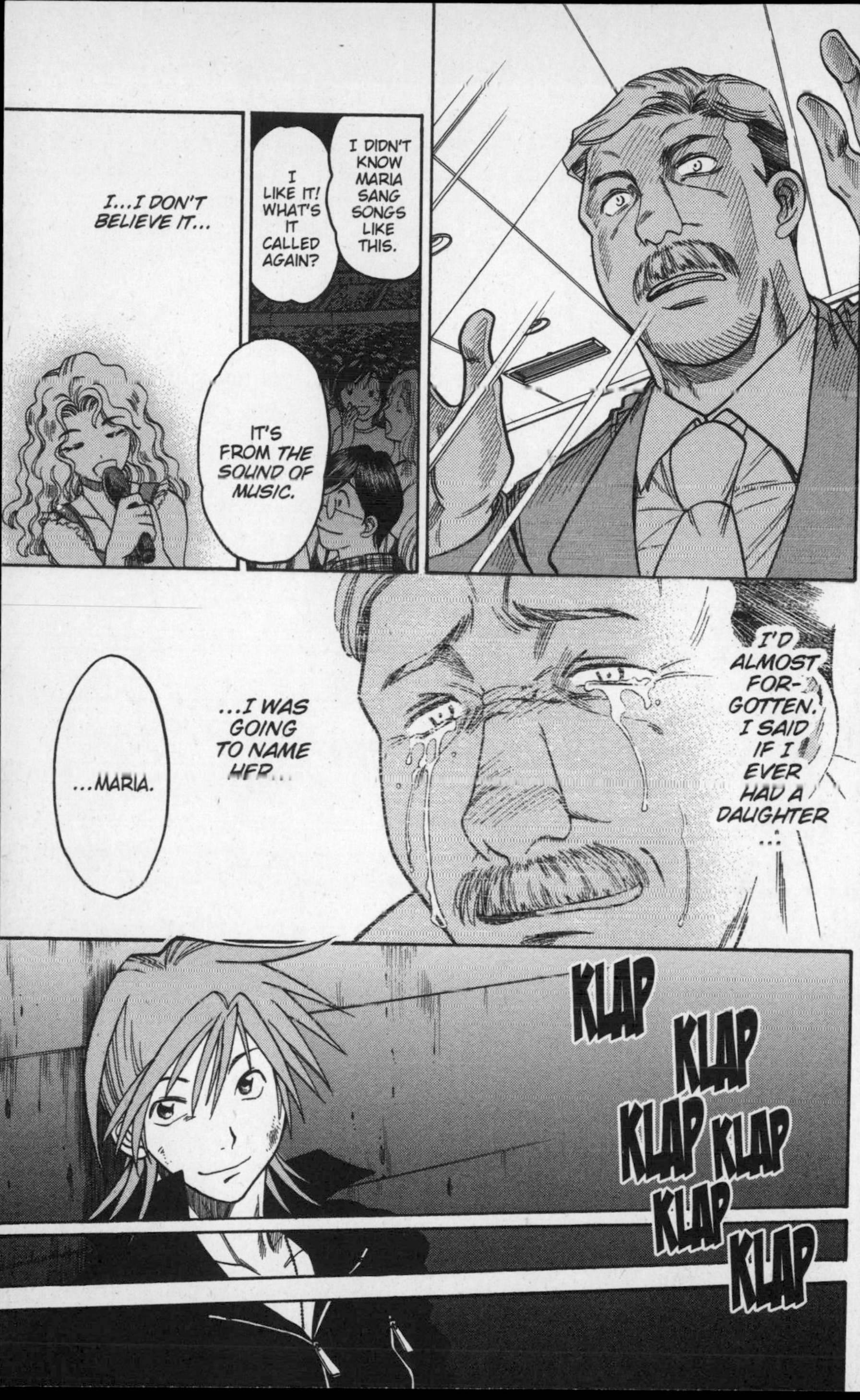
I DIDN'T KNOW MARIA SANG SONGS LIKE THIS.
I LIKE IT! WHAT'S IT CALLED AGAIN?
IT'S FROM THE SOUND OF MUSIC.
I...I DON'T BELIEVE IT...
I'D ALMOST FOR-GOTTEN. I SAID IF I EVER HAD A DAUGHTER...
...I WAS GOING TO NAME HER...
...MARIA.
KLAP
KLAP
KLAP KLAP
KLAP
KLAP

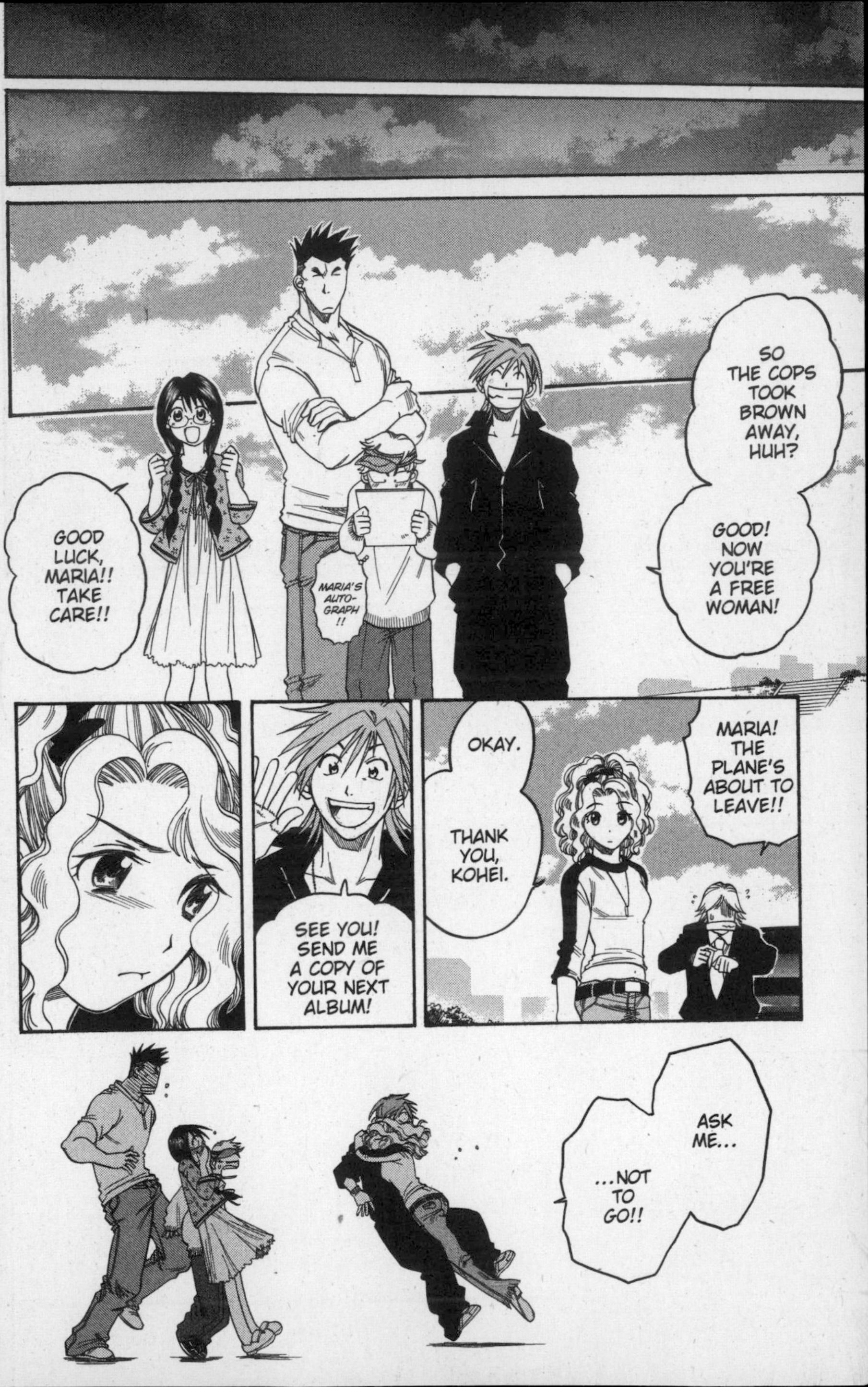
SO THE COPS TOOK BROWN AWAY, HUH?
GOOD! NOW YOU'RE A FREE WOMAN!
MARIA'S AUTO-GRAPH!!
GOOD LUCK, MARIA!! TAKE CARE!!
MARIA! THE PLANE'S ABOUT TO LEAVE!!
OKAY.
THANK YOU, KOHEI.
SEE YOU! SEND ME A COPY OF YOUR NEXT ALBUM!
ASK ME...
...NOT TO GO!!

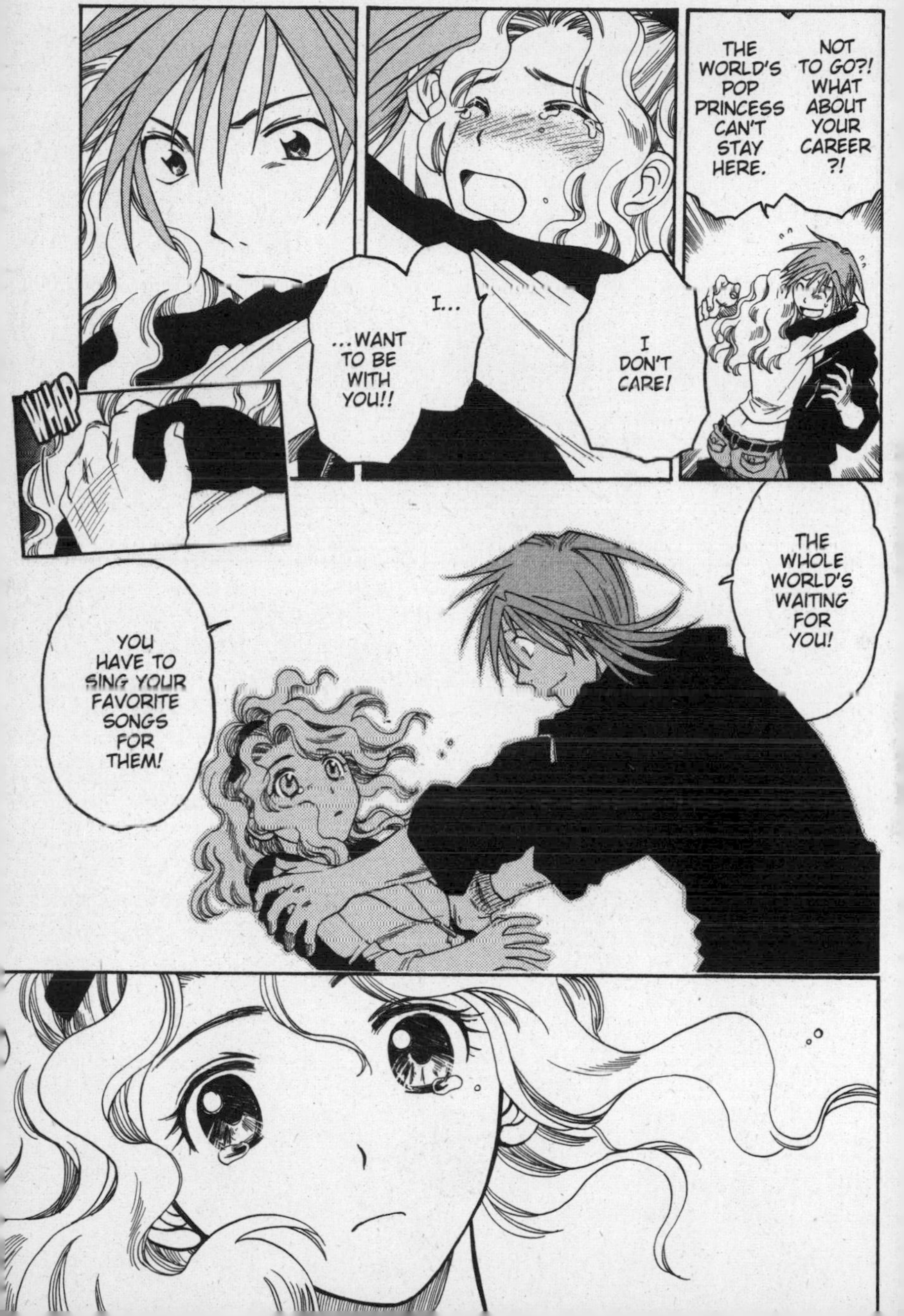
NOT TO GO?! WHAT ABOUT YOUR CAREER ?!
THE WORLD'S POP PRINCESS CAN'T STAY HERE.
I DON'T CARE!
I...
...WANT TO BE WITH YOU!!
WHAP
THE WHOLE WORLD'S WAITING FOR YOU!
YOU HAVE TO SING YOUR FAVORITE SONGS FOR THEM!

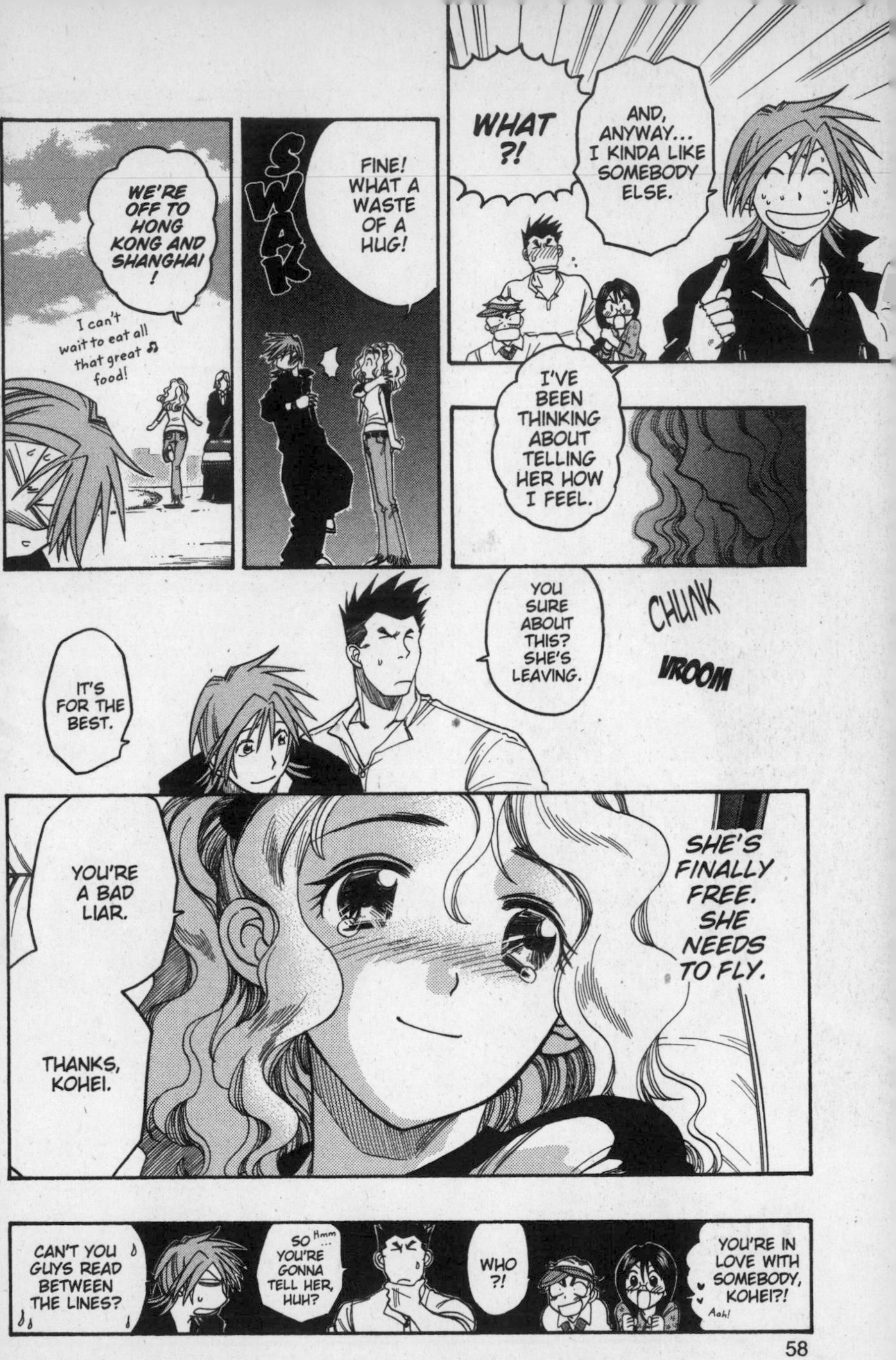
AND, ANYWAY... I KINDA LIKE SOMEBODY ELSE.
WHAT ?!
I'VE BEEN THINKING ABOUT TELLING HER HOW I FEEL.
SWAK
FINE! WHAT A WASTE OF A HUG!
WE'RE OFF TO HONG KONG AND SHANGHAI!
I can't wait to eat all that great ♫ food!
CHUNK
VROOM
YOU SURE ABOUT THIS? SHE'S LEAVING.
IT'S FOR THE BEST.
SHE'S FINALLY FREE. SHE NEEDS TO FLY.
YOU'RE A BAD LIAR.
THANKS, KOHEI.
YOU'RE IN LOVE WITH SOMEBODY, KOHEI?!
Aah!
WHO ?!
Hmm...
SO YOU'RE GONNA TELL HER, HUH?
CAN'T YOU GUYS READ BETWEEN THE LINES?

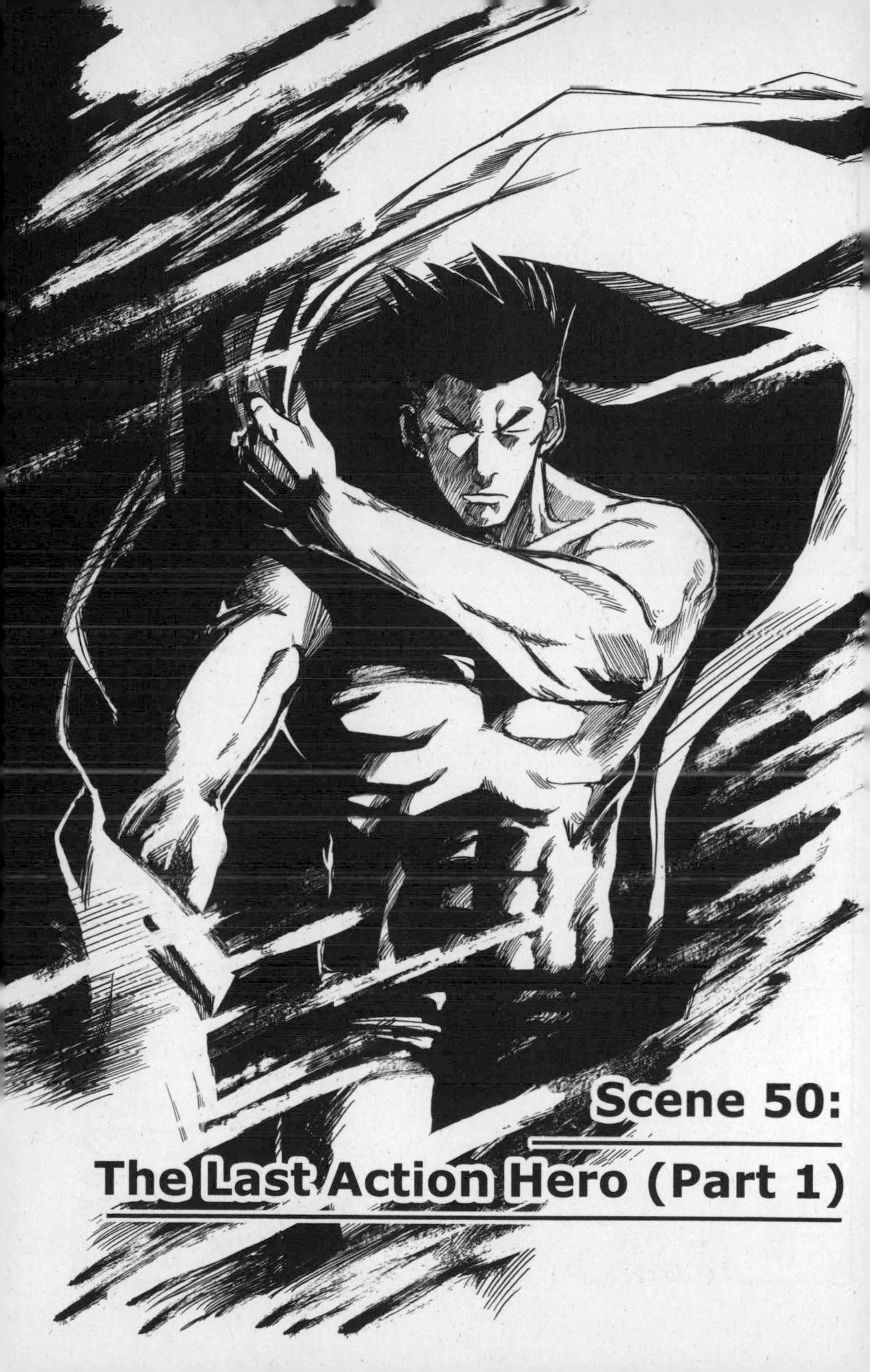
Scene 50:
The Last Action Hero (Part 1)

GIMMICK!

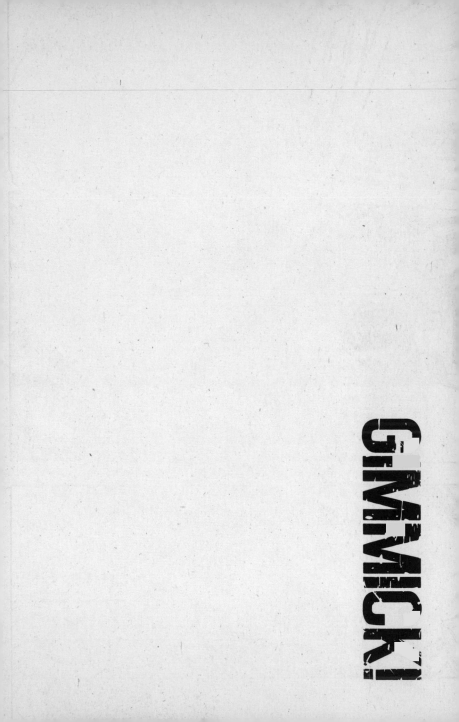

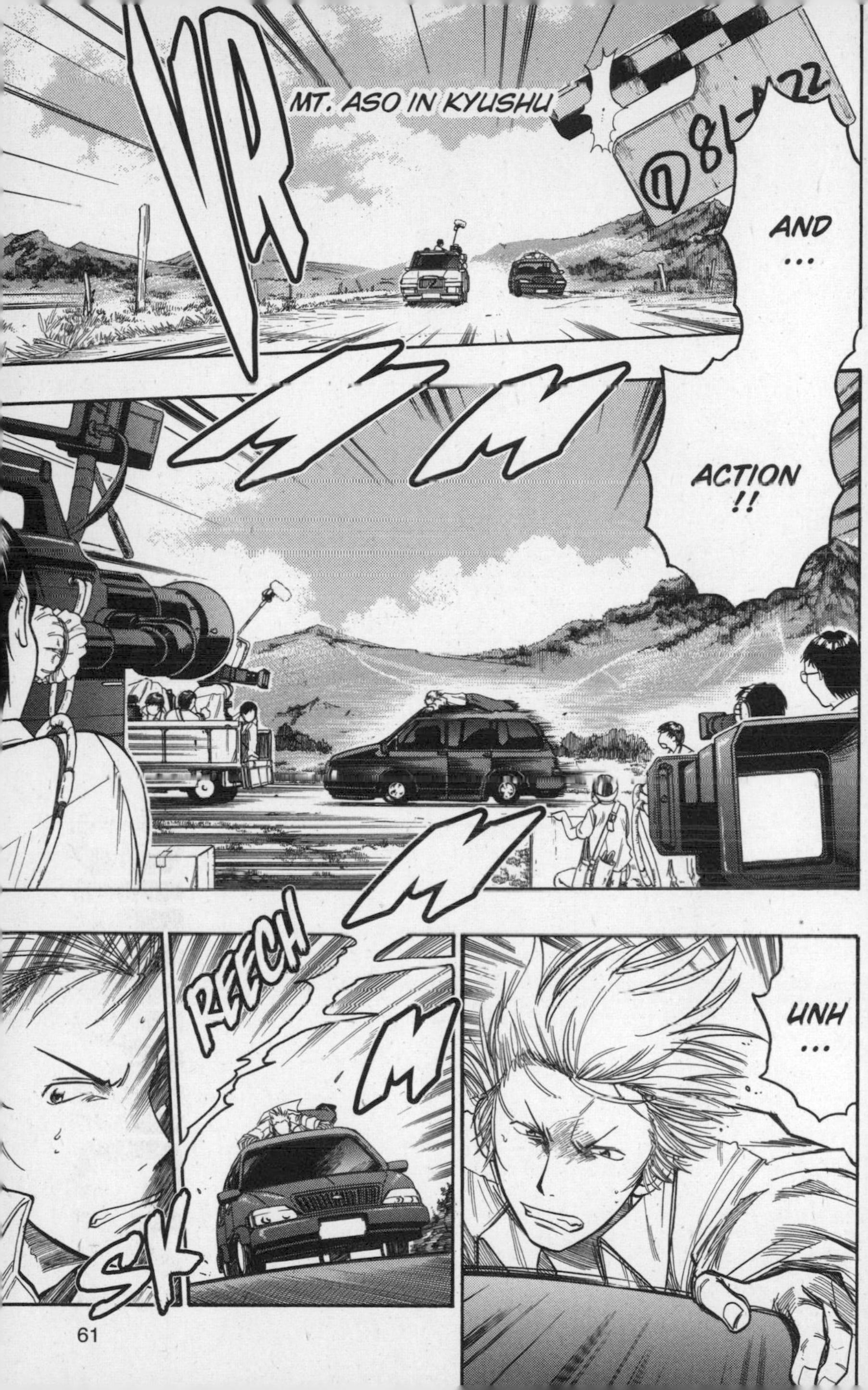
AND ...
MT. ASO IN KYUSHU
VR
MM
ACTION !!
M
UNH ...
REECH
M
SK

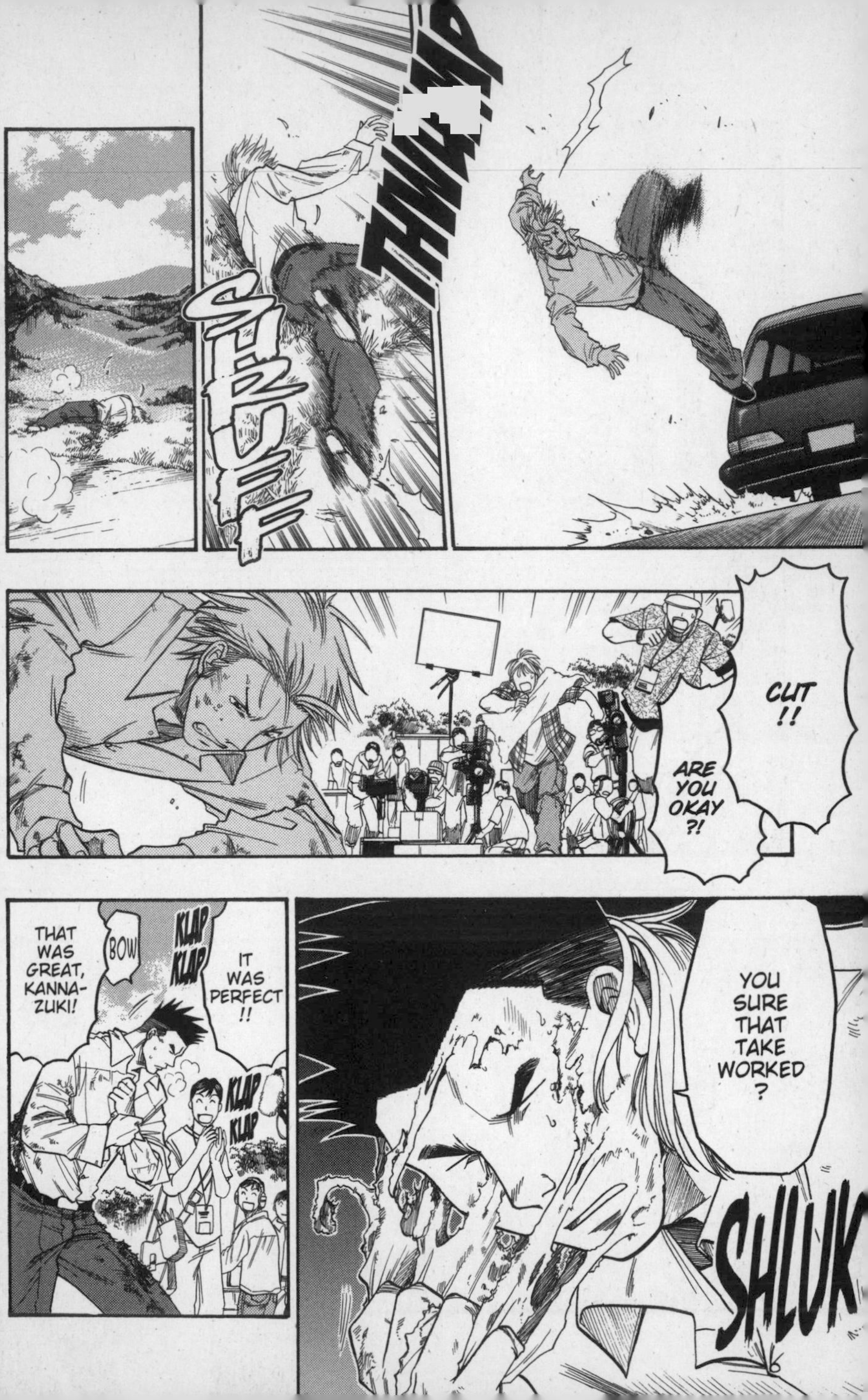
CUT!!
ARE YOU OKAY?!
YOU SURE THAT TAKE WORKED?
SHLUK
KLAP KLAP
IT WAS PERFECT!!
BOW
THAT WAS GREAT, KANNAZUKI!
KLAP KLAP

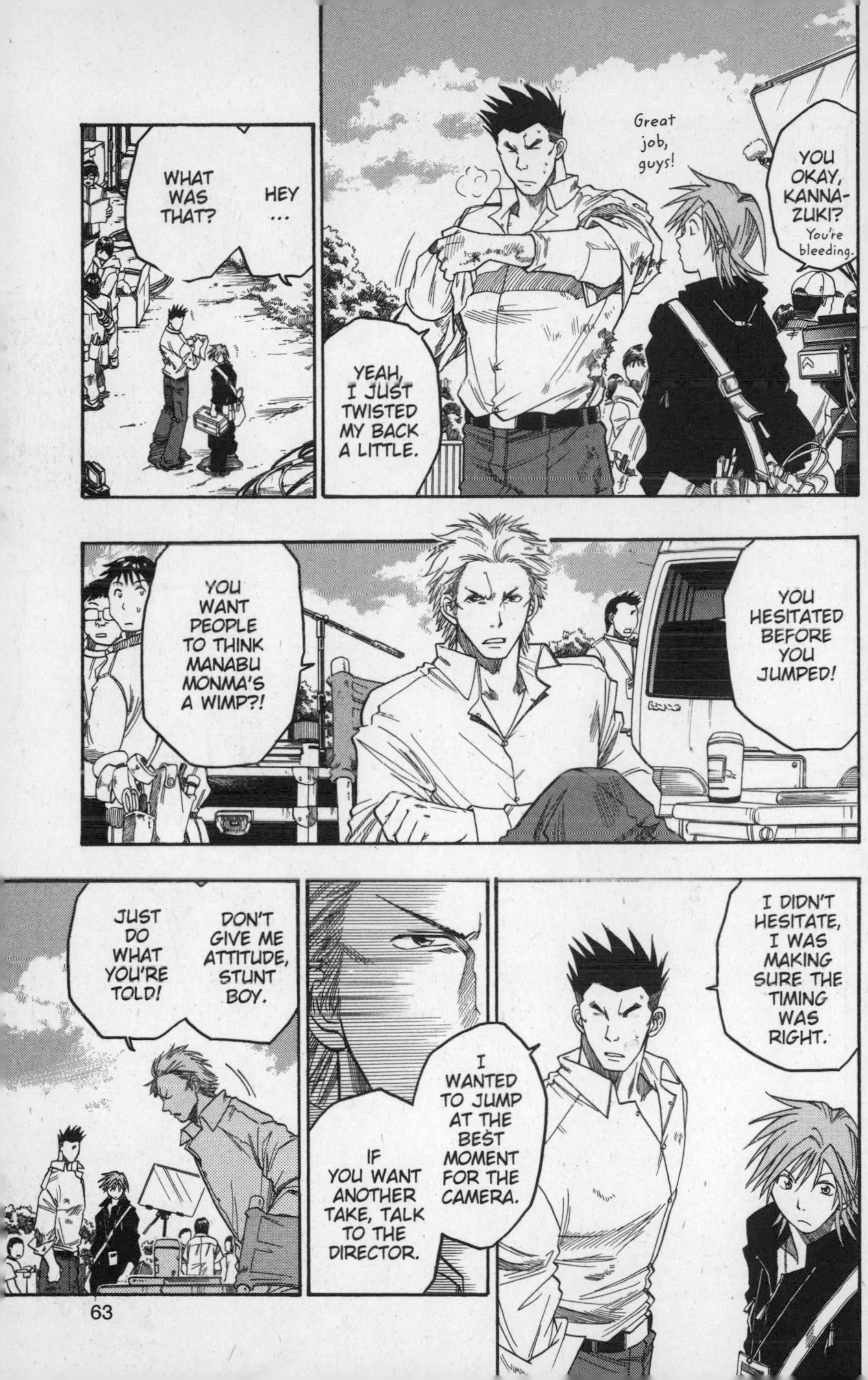
YOU OKAY, KANNA-ZUKI? You're bleeding.
Great job, guys!
YEAH, I JUST TWISTED MY BACK A LITTLE.
HEY ...
WHAT WAS THAT?
YOU HESITATED BEFORE YOU JUMPED!
YOU WANT PEOPLE TO THINK MANABU MONMA'S A WIMP?!
I DIDN'T HESITATE, I WAS MAKING SURE THE TIMING WAS RIGHT.
I WANTED TO JUMP AT THE BEST MOMENT FOR THE CAMERA.
IF YOU WANT ANOTHER TAKE, TALK TO THE DIRECTOR.
DON'T GIVE ME ATTITUDE, STUNT BOY.
JUST DO WHAT YOU'RE TOLD!

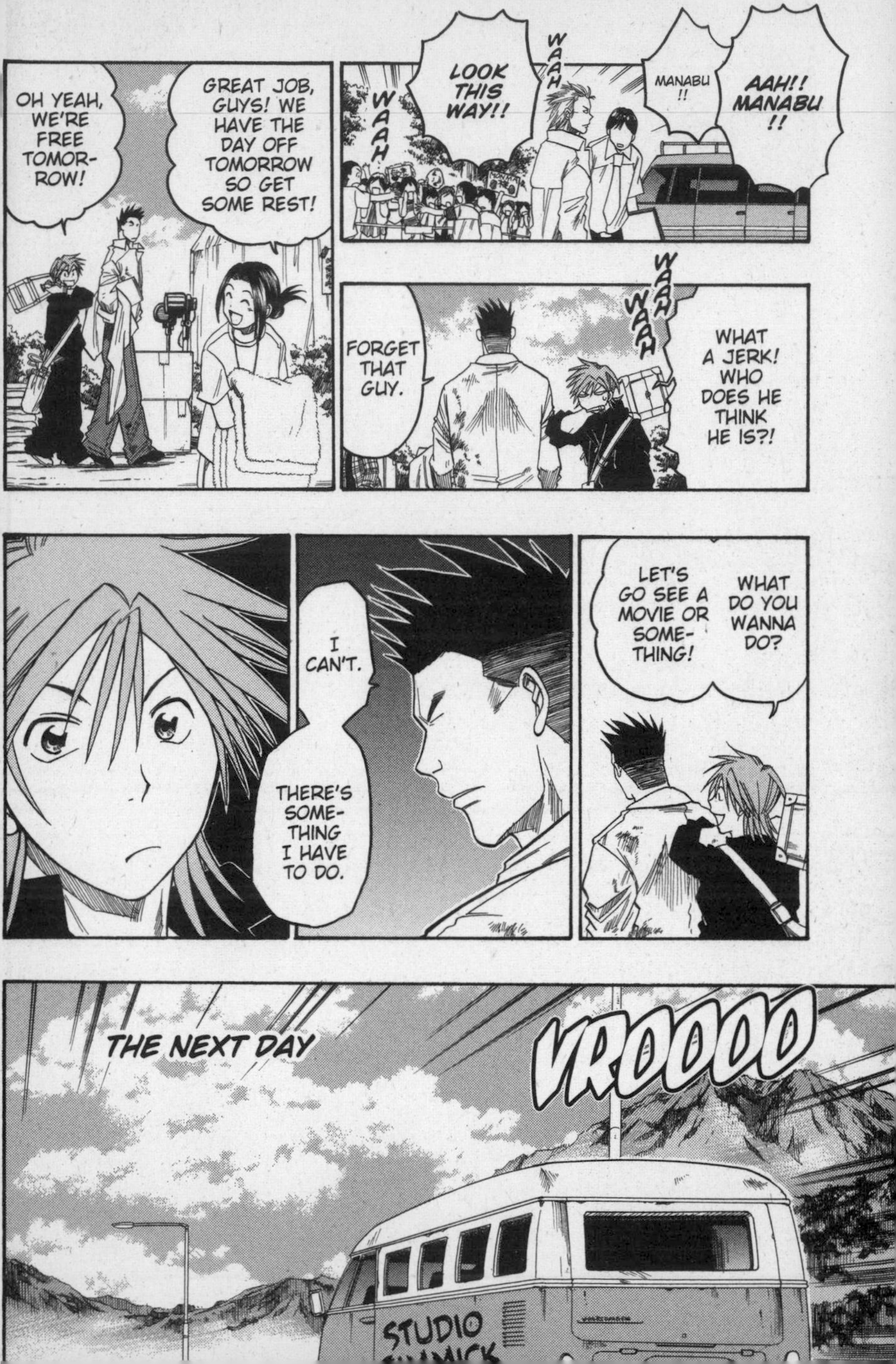

AAH!! MANABU!!
MANABU!!
WAAAH
LOOK THIS WAY!!
WAAAH
WAAAH
WAAAH
WHAT A JERK! WHO DOES HE THINK HE IS?!
FORGET THAT GUY.
GREAT JOB, GUYS! WE HAVE THE DAY OFF TOMORROW SO GET SOME REST!
OH YEAH, WE'RE FREE TOMORROW!
WHAT DO YOU WANNA DO?
LET'S GO SEE A MOVIE OR SOMETHING!
I CAN'T.
THERE'S SOMETHING I HAVE TO DO.
VROOOO
THE NEXT DAY
STUDIO

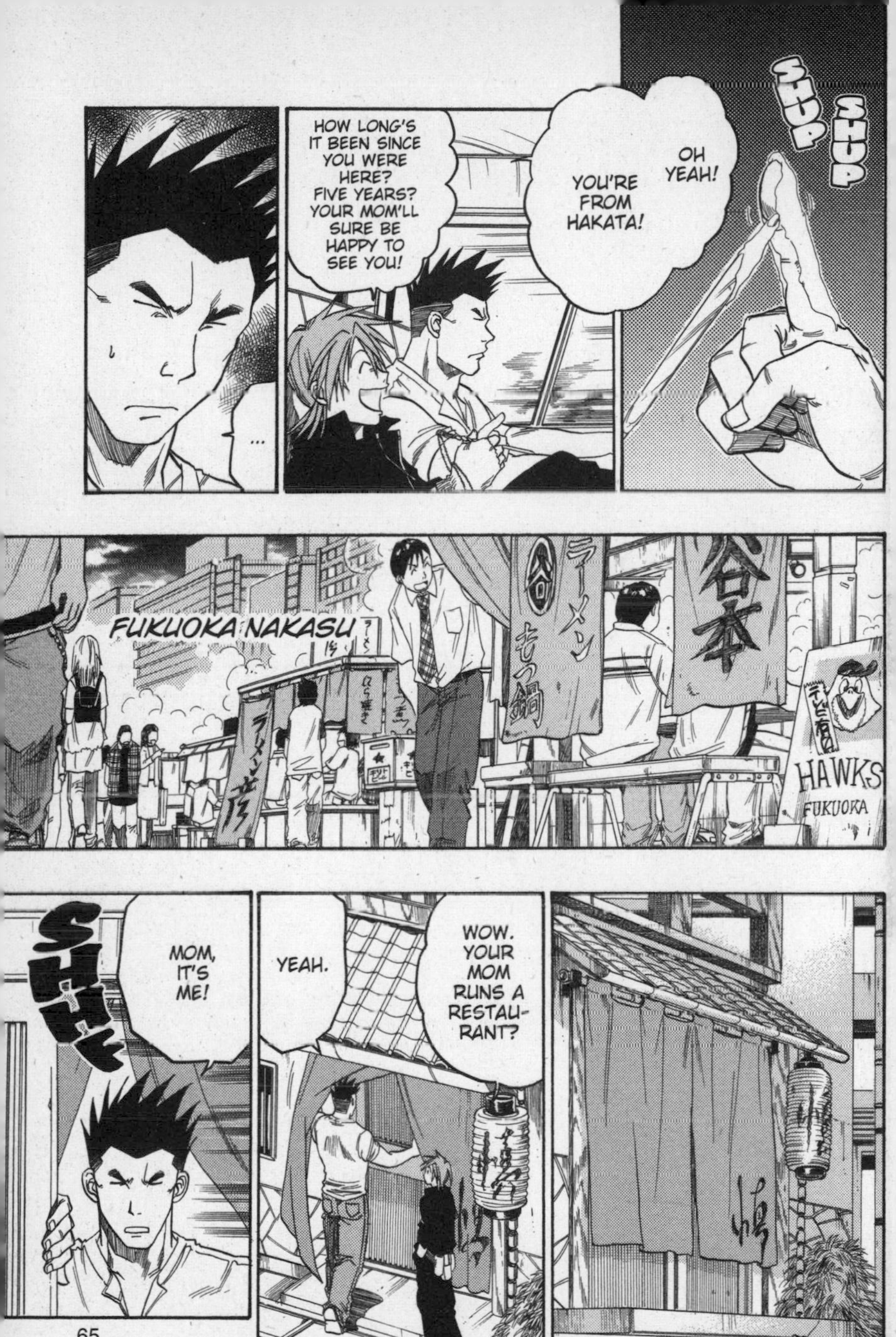
SHUP SHUP
OH YEAH!
YOU'RE FROM HAKATA!
HOW LONG'S IT BEEN SINCE YOU WERE HERE? FIVE YEARS? YOUR MOM'LL SURE BE HAPPY TO SEE YOU!
...
FUKUOKA NAKASU
HAWKS
FUKUOKA
WOW. YOUR MOM RUNS A RESTAU-RANT?
YEAH.
MOM, IT'S ME!

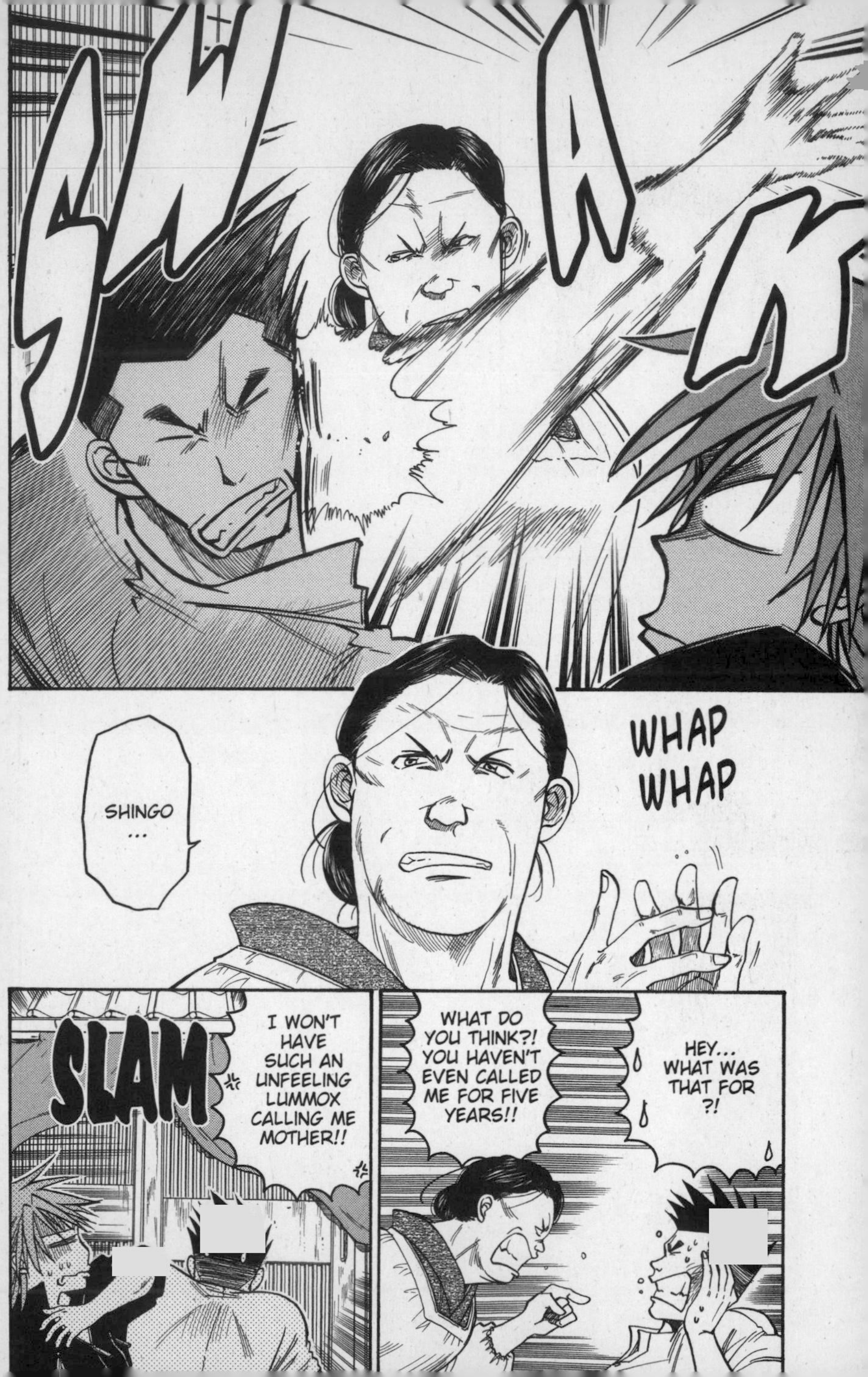
WHAP WHAP
SHINGO ...
HEY... WHAT WAS THAT FOR ?!
WHAT DO YOU THINK?! YOU HAVEN'T EVEN CALLED ME FOR FIVE YEARS!!
I WON'T HAVE SUCH AN UNFEELING LUMMOX CALLING ME MOTHER!!
SLAM

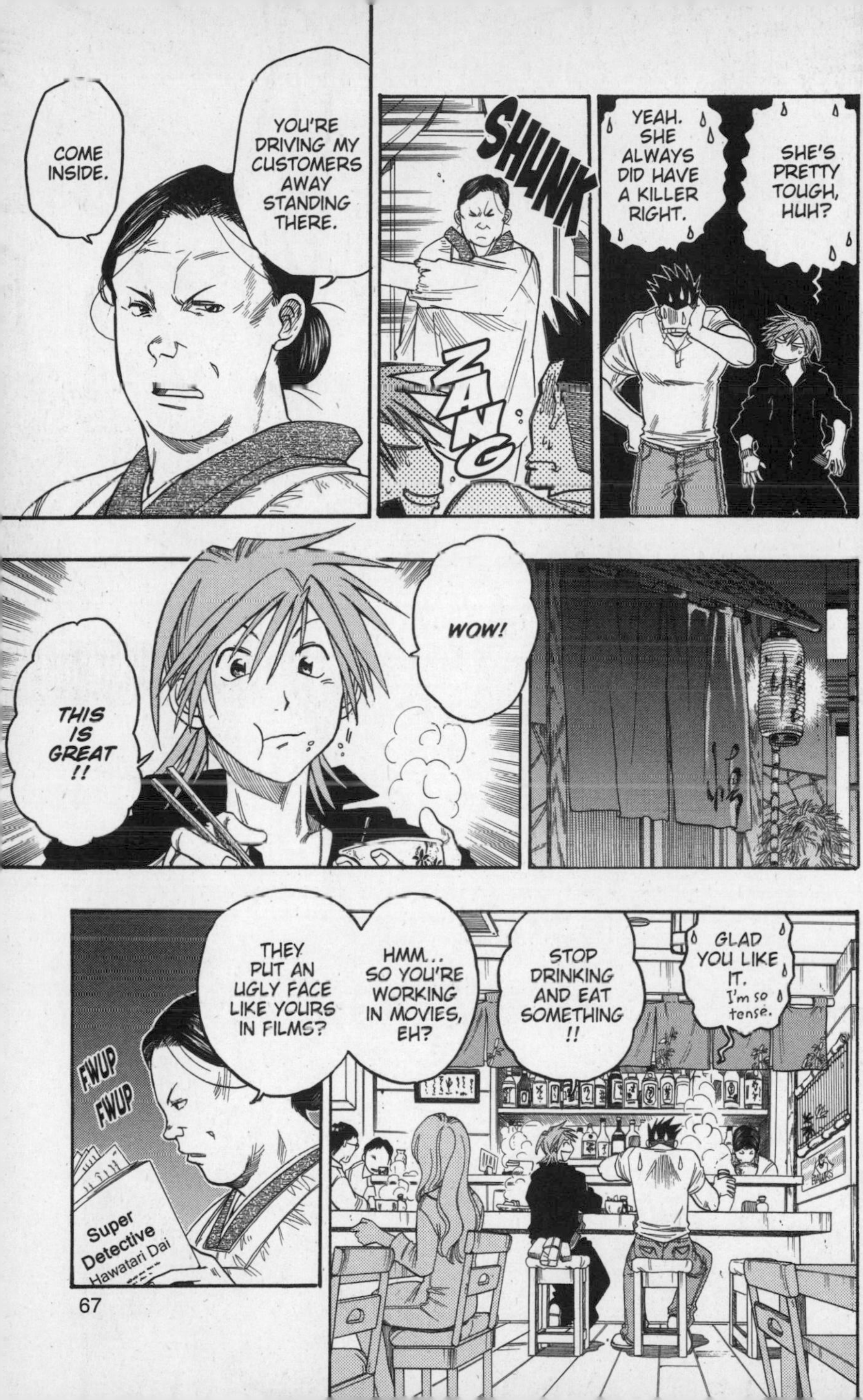
SHE'S PRETTY TOUGH, HUH?
YEAH. SHE ALWAYS DID HAVE A KILLER RIGHT.
SHUNK
ZANG
YOU'RE DRIVING MY CUSTOMERS AWAY STANDING THERE.
COME INSIDE.
WOW!
THIS IS GREAT!!
GLAD YOU LIKE IT.
I'm so tense.
STOP DRINKING AND EAT SOMETHING!!
HMM... SO YOU'RE WORKING IN MOVIES, EH?
THEY PUT AN UGLY FACE LIKE YOURS IN FILMS?
FWUP FWUP
Super Detective Hawatari Dai

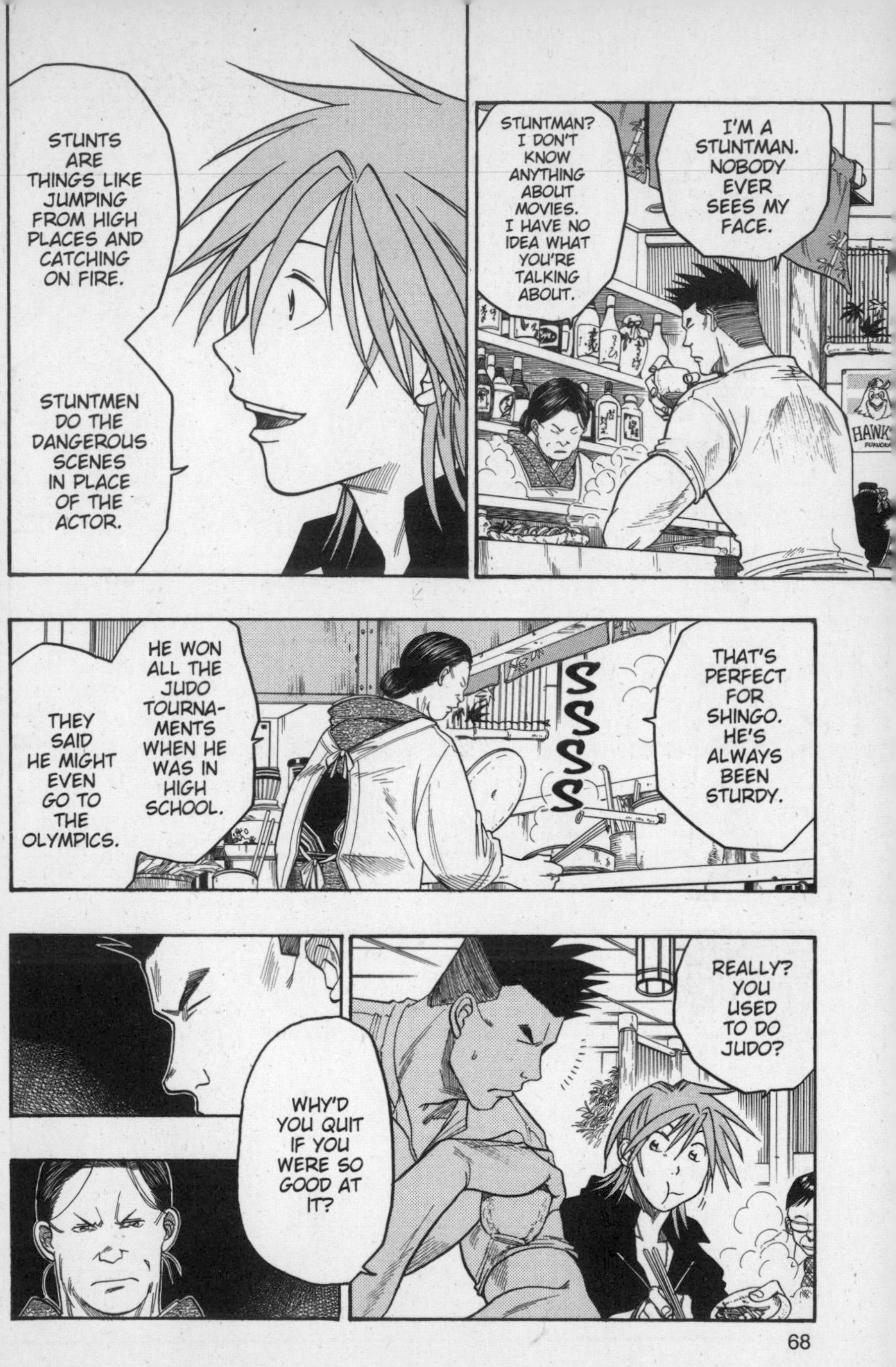
I'M A STUNTMAN. NOBODY EVER SEES MY FACE.
STUNTMAN? I DON'T KNOW ANYTHING ABOUT MOVIES. I HAVE NO IDEA WHAT YOU'RE TALKING ABOUT.
STUNTS ARE THINGS LIKE JUMPING FROM HIGH PLACES AND CATCHING ON FIRE.
STUNTMEN DO THE DANGEROUS SCENES IN PLACE OF THE ACTOR.
THAT'S PERFECT FOR SHINGO. HE'S ALWAYS BEEN STURDY.
SSSS
HE WON ALL THE JUDO TOURNAMENTS WHEN HE WAS IN HIGH SCHOOL.
THEY SAID HE MIGHT EVEN GO TO THE OLYMPICS.
REALLY? YOU USED TO DO JUDO?
WHY'D YOU QUIT IF YOU WERE SO GOOD AT IT?

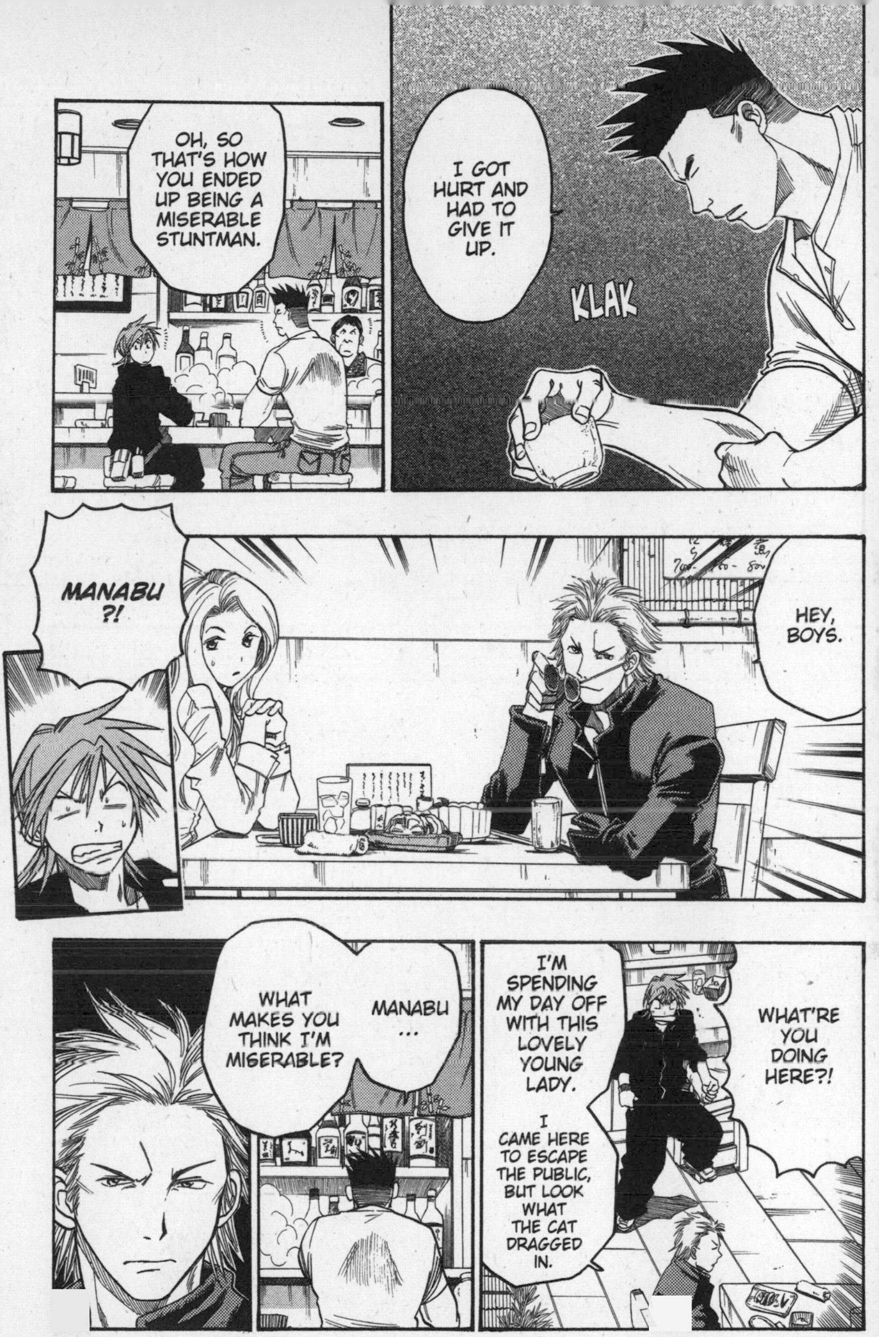
I GOT HURT AND HAD TO GIVE IT UP.
KLAK
OH, SO THAT'S HOW YOU ENDED UP BEING A MISERABLE STUNTMAN.
HEY, BOYS.
MANABU ?!
WHAT'RE YOU DOING HERE?!
I'M SPENDING MY DAY OFF WITH THIS LOVELY YOUNG LADY.
I CAME HERE TO ESCAPE THE PUBLIC, BUT LOOK WHAT THE CAT DRAGGED IN.
MANABU ...
WHAT MAKES YOU THINK I'M MISERABLE?

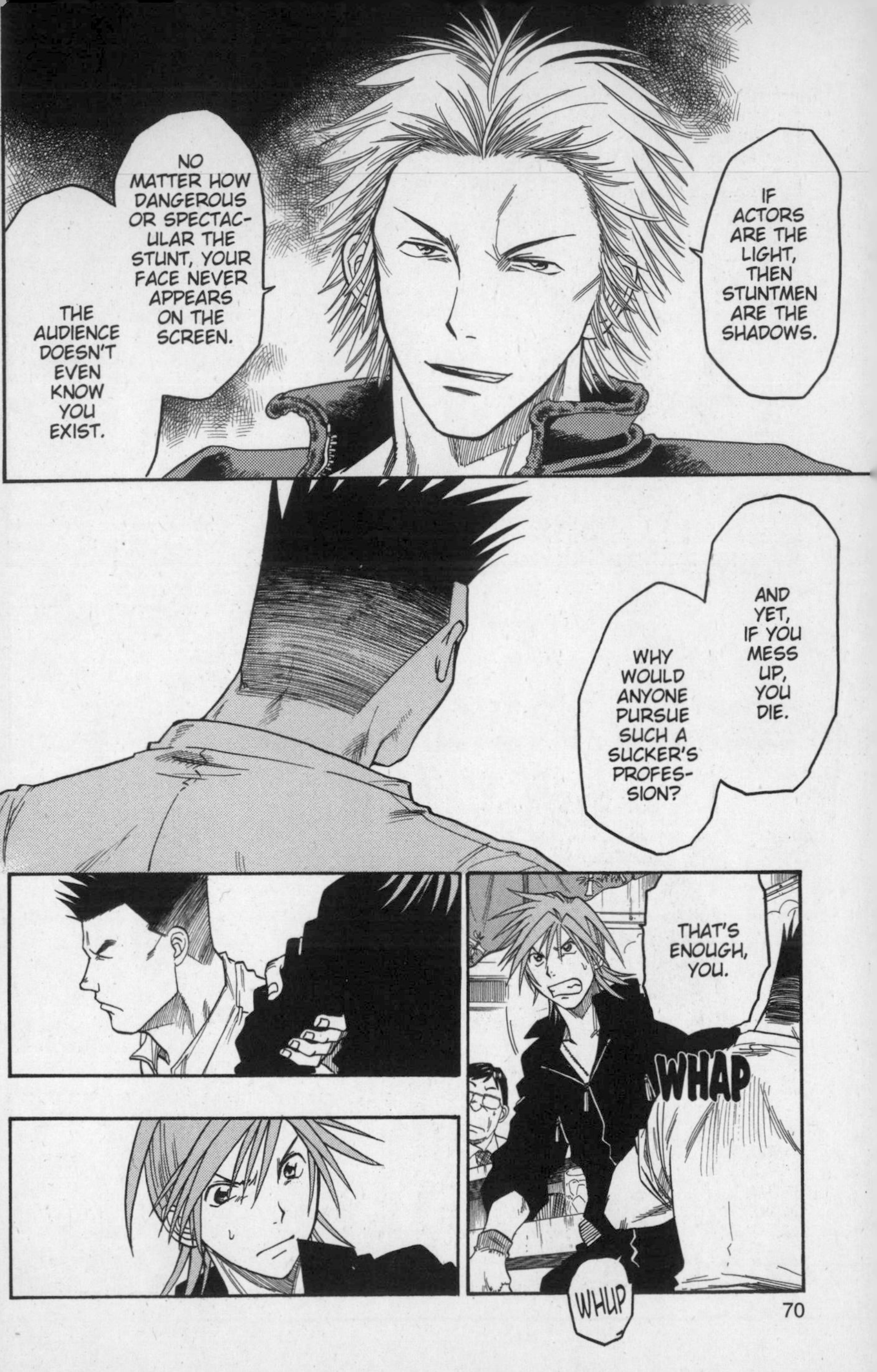
IF ACTORS ARE THE LIGHT, THEN STUNTMEN ARE THE SHADOWS.
NO MATTER HOW DANGEROUS OR SPECTACULAR THE STUNT, YOUR FACE NEVER APPEARS ON THE SCREEN.
THE AUDIENCE DOESN'T EVEN KNOW YOU EXIST.
AND YET, IF YOU MESS UP, YOU DIE.
WHY WOULD ANYONE PURSUE SUCH A SUCKER'S PROFESSION?
THAT'S ENOUGH, YOU.
WHAP
WHUP

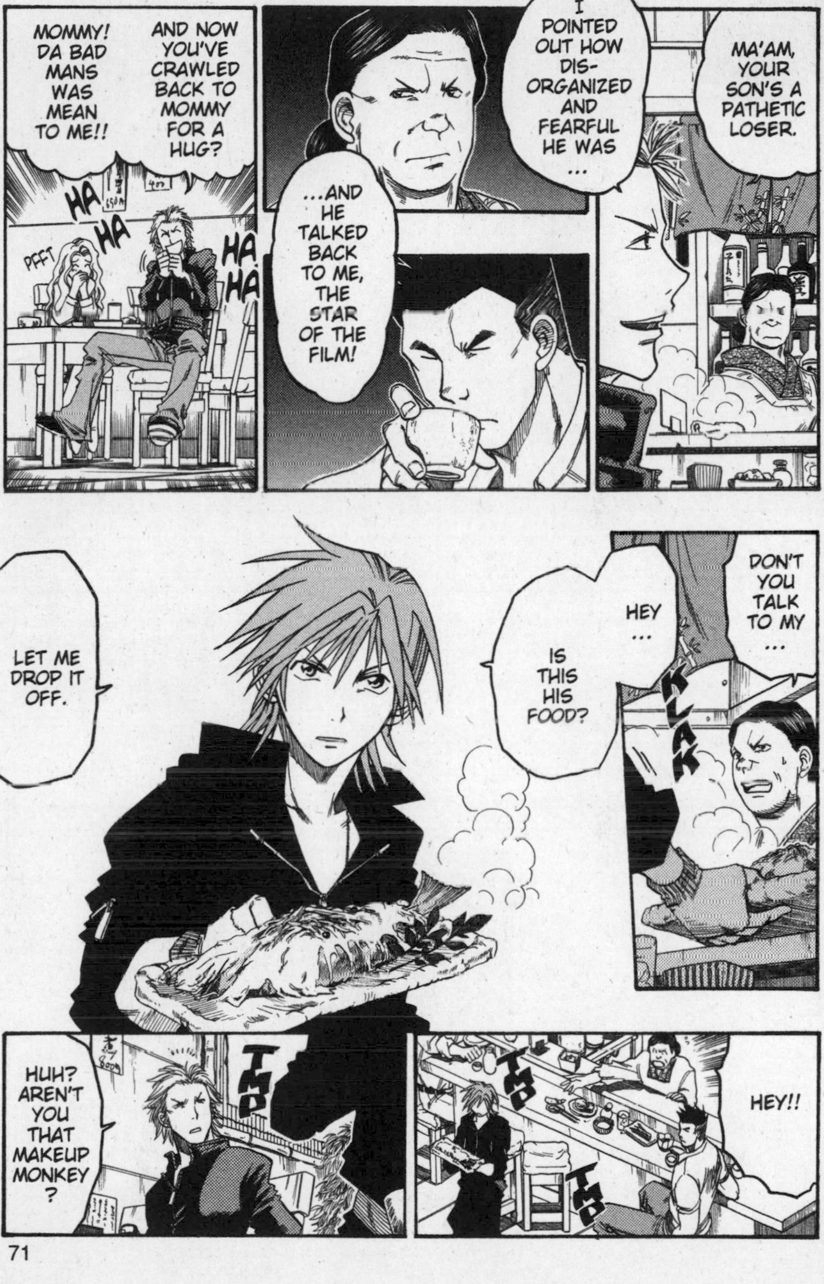
MA'AM, YOUR SON'S A PATHETIC LOSER.
I POINTED OUT HOW DIS-ORGANIZED AND FEARFUL HE WAS ...
...AND HE TALKED BACK TO ME, THE STAR OF THE FILM!
AND NOW YOU'VE CRAWLED BACK TO MOMMY FOR A HUG?
MOMMY! DA BAD MANS WAS MEAN TO ME!!
HA HA
HA HA
PFFT
DON'T YOU TALK TO MY ...
KLAK
HEY ...
IS THIS HIS FOOD?
LET ME DROP IT OFF.
HEY!!
TMP
TMP
TMP
HUH? AREN'T YOU THAT MAKEUP MONKEY?

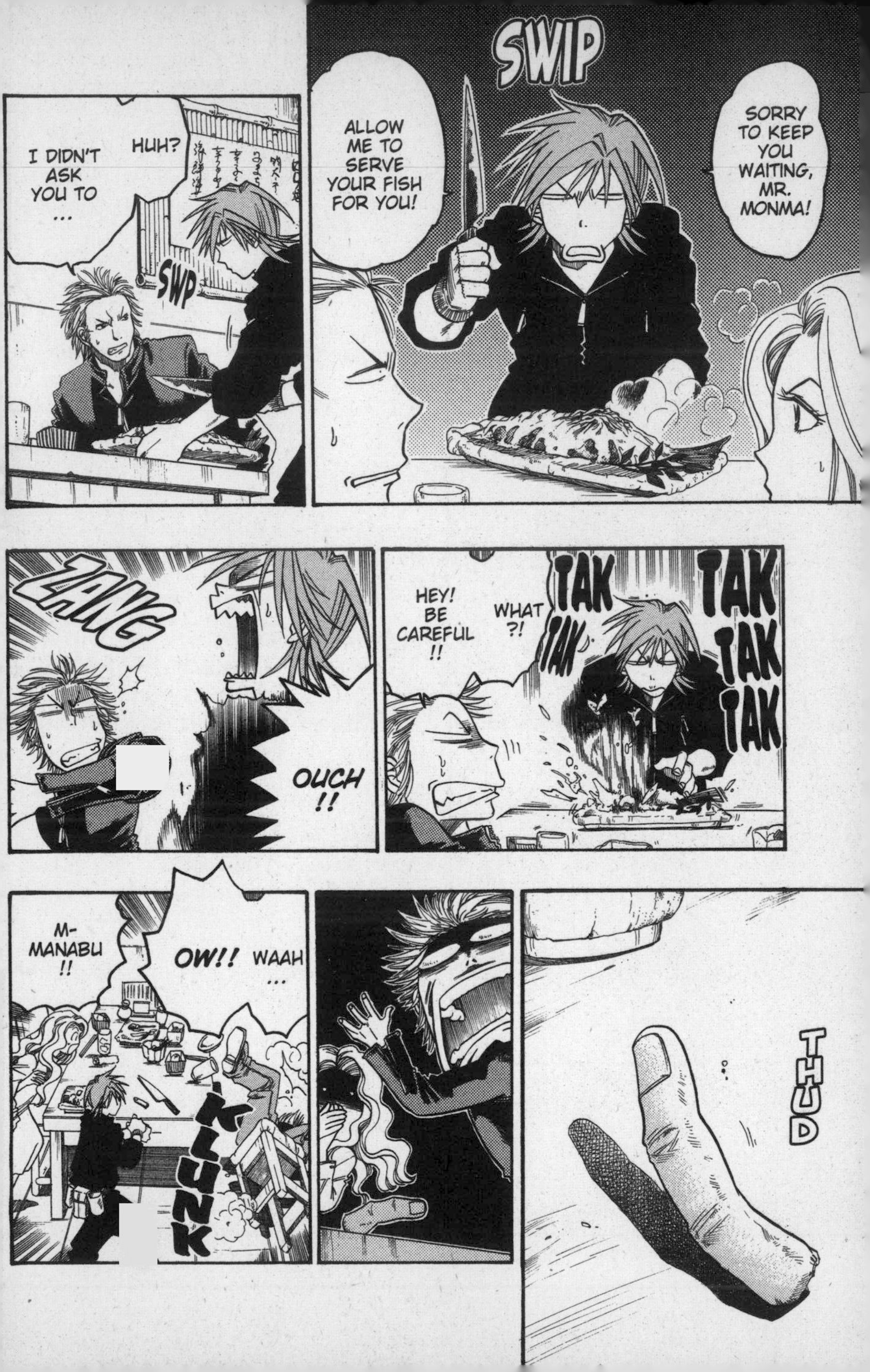
SWIP
SORRY TO KEEP YOU WAITING, MR. MONMA!
ALLOW ME TO SERVE YOUR FISH FOR YOU!
HUH?
SWP
I DIDN'T ASK YOU TO ...
TAK TAK TAK TAK TAK TAK
WHAT ?!
HEY! BE CAREFUL!!
ZANG
OUCH!!
THUD
OW!! WAAH ...
M-MANABU!!
KLUNK

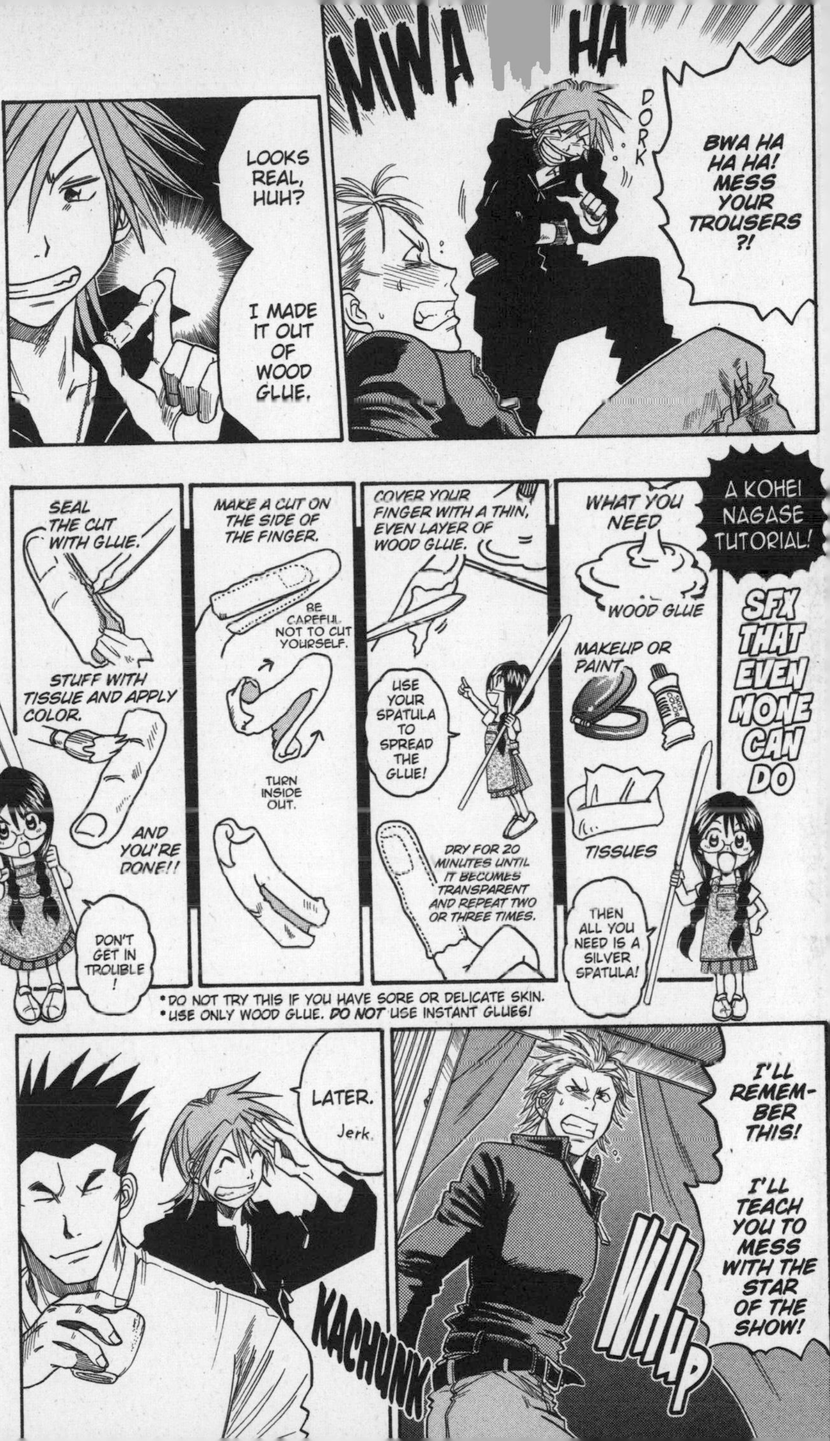
MWA HA
DORK
BWA HA HA HA! MESS YOUR TROUSERS ?!
LOOKS REAL, HUH?
I MADE IT OUT OF WOOD GLUE.
A KOHEI NAGASE TUTORIAL!
SFX THAT EVEN MONE CAN DO
WHAT YOU NEED
WOOD GLUE
MAKEUP OR PAINT
TISSUES
THEN ALL YOU NEED IS A SILVER SPATULA!
COVER YOUR FINGER WITH A THIN, EVEN LAYER OF WOOD GLUE.
USE YOUR SPATULA TO SPREAD THE GLUE!
DRY FOR 20 MINUTES UNTIL IT BECOMES TRANSPARENT AND REPEAT TWO OR THREE TIMES.
MAKE A CUT ON THE SIDE OF THE FINGER.
BE CAREFUL NOT TO CUT YOURSELF.
TURN INSIDE OUT.
SEAL THE CUT WITH GLUE.
STUFF WITH TISSUE AND APPLY COLOR.
AND YOU'RE DONE!!
DON'T GET IN TROUBLE!
*DO NOT TRY THIS IF YOU HAVE SORE OR DELICATE SKIN.
*USE ONLY WOOD GLUE. DO NOT USE INSTANT GLUES!
I'LL REMEMBER THIS!
I'LL TEACH YOU TO MESS WITH THE STAR OF THE SHOW!
WHUP
LATER.
Jerk.
KACHUNK

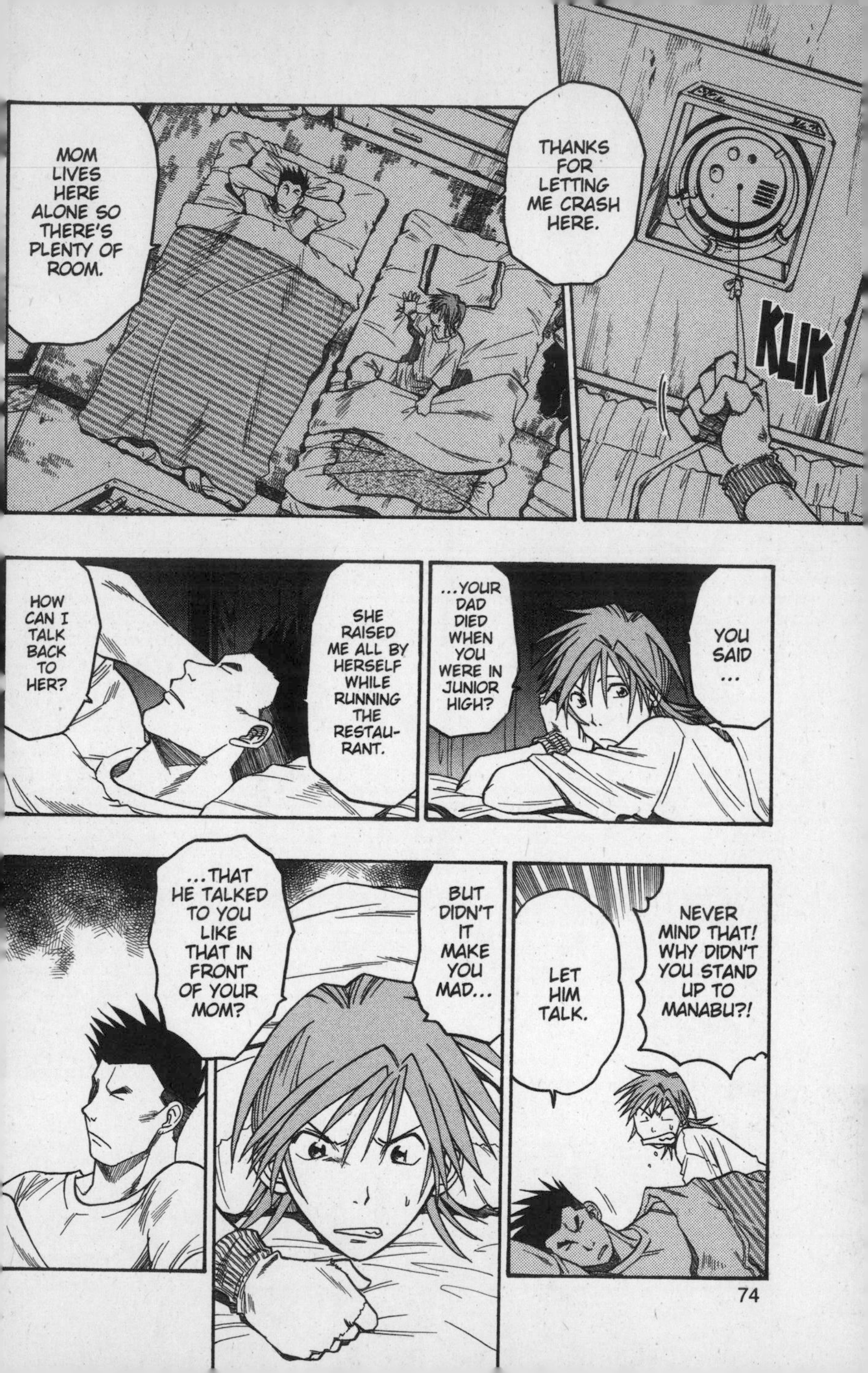
THANKS FOR LETTING ME CRASH HERE.
KLIK
MOM LIVES HERE ALONE SO THERE'S PLENTY OF ROOM.
YOU SAID ...
...YOUR DAD DIED WHEN YOU WERE IN JUNIOR HIGH?
SHE RAISED ME ALL BY HERSELF WHILE RUNNING THE RESTAU-RANT.
HOW CAN I TALK BACK TO HER?
NEVER MIND THAT! WHY DIDN'T YOU STAND UP TO MANABU?!
LET HIM TALK.
BUT DIDN'T IT MAKE YOU MAD...
...THAT HE TALKED TO YOU LIKE THAT IN FRONT OF YOUR MOM?

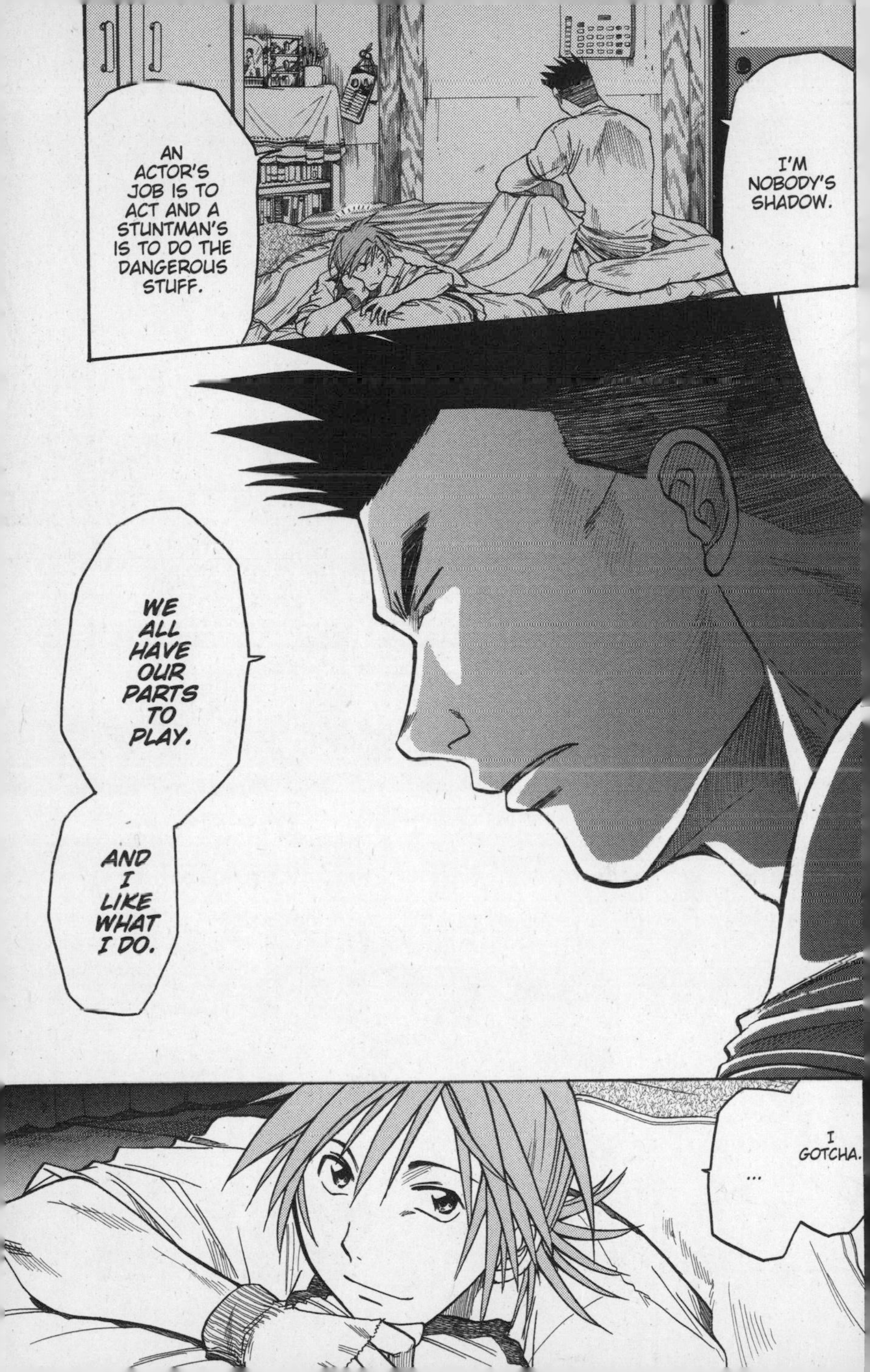
I'M NOBODY'S SHADOW.
AN ACTOR'S JOB IS TO ACT AND A STUNTMAN'S IS TO DO THE DANGEROUS STUFF.
WE ALL HAVE OUR PARTS TO PLAY.
AND I LIKE WHAT I DO.
I GOTCHA.
...

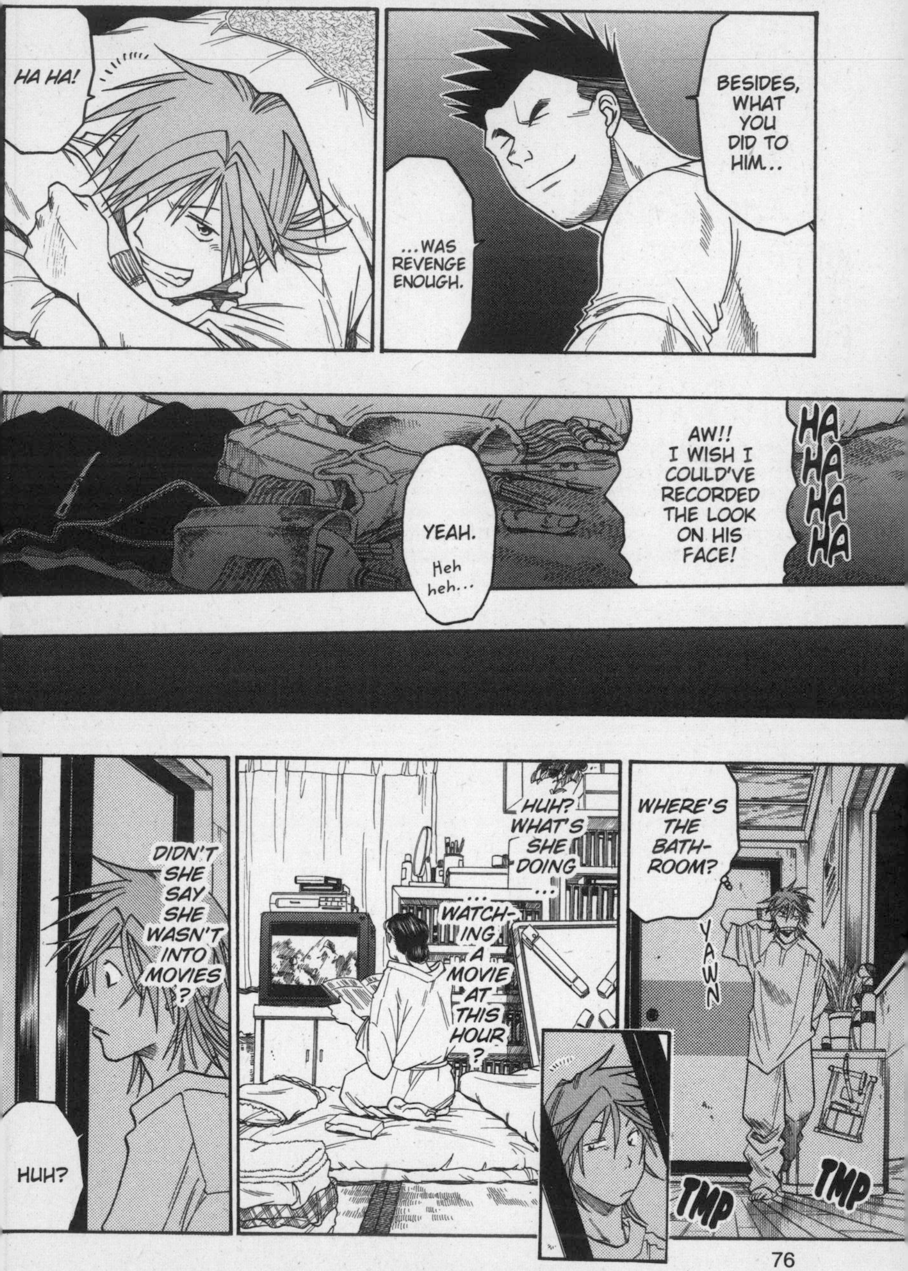
BESIDES, WHAT YOU DID TO HIM...
...WAS REVENGE ENOUGH.
HA HA!
HA HA HA HA
AW!! I WISH I COULD'VE RECORDED THE LOOK ON HIS FACE!
YEAH.
Heh heh...
WHERE'S THE BATH-ROOM?
YAWN
TMP
TMP
HUH? WHAT'S SHE DOING...
...WATCHING A MOVIE AT THIS HOUR?
DIDN'T SHE SAY SHE WASN'T INTO MOVIES?
HUH?

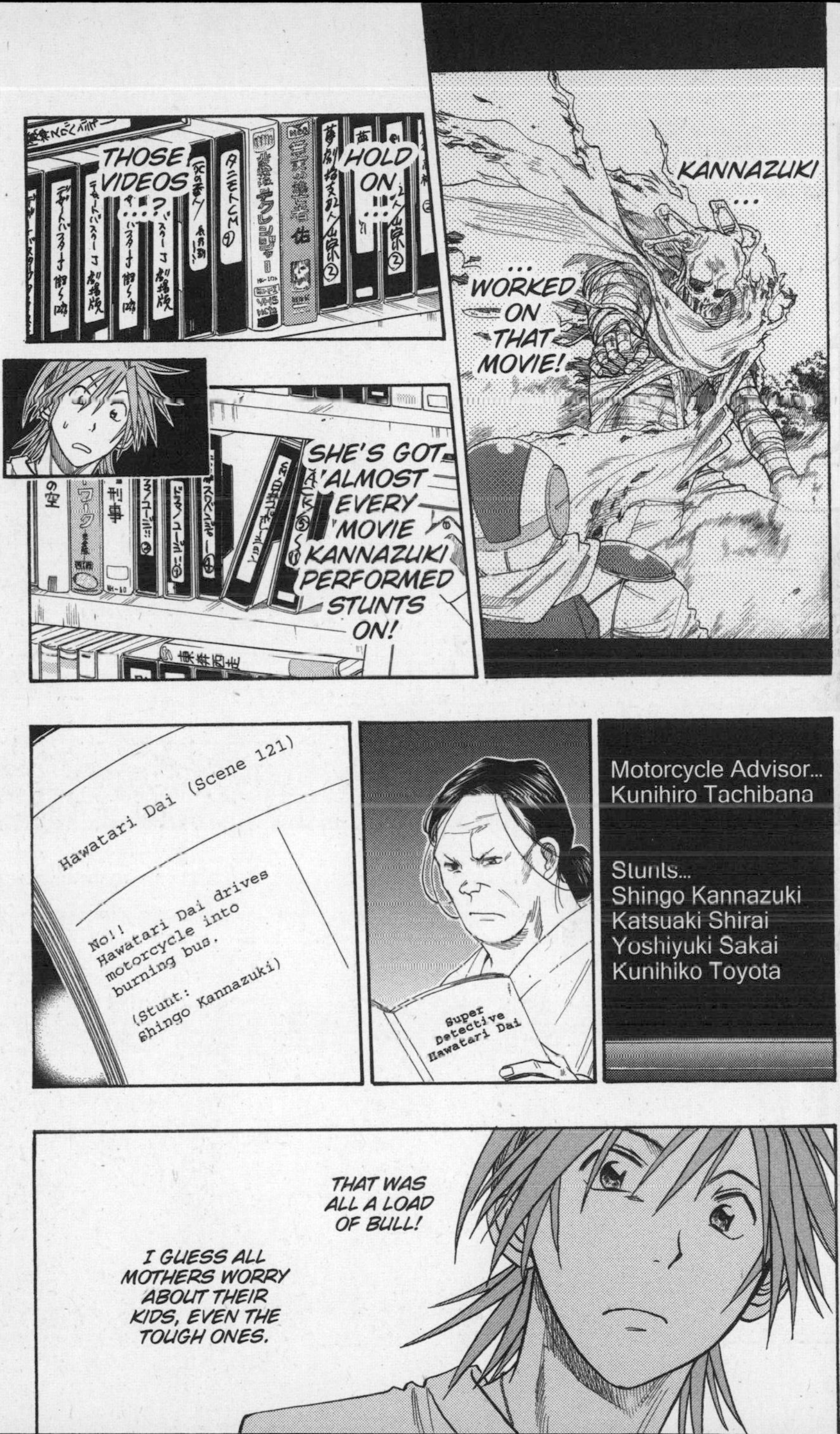
KANNAZUKI ...
... WORKED ON THAT MOVIE!
HOLD ON ...!!
THOSE VIDEOS ...?
SHE'S GOT ALMOST EVERY MOVIE KANNAZUKI PERFORMED STUNTS ON!
Motorcycle Advisor...
Kunihiro Tachibana
Stunts...
Shingo Kannazuki
Katsuaki Shirai
Yoshiyuki Sakai
Kunihiko Toyota
Super Detective Hawatari Dai
Hawatari Dai (Scene 121)
No!! Hawatari Dai drives motorcycle into burning bus.
(Stunt: Shingo Kannazuki)
THAT WAS ALL A LOAD OF BULL!
I GUESS ALL MOTHERS WORRY ABOUT THEIR KIDS, EVEN THE TOUGH ONES.

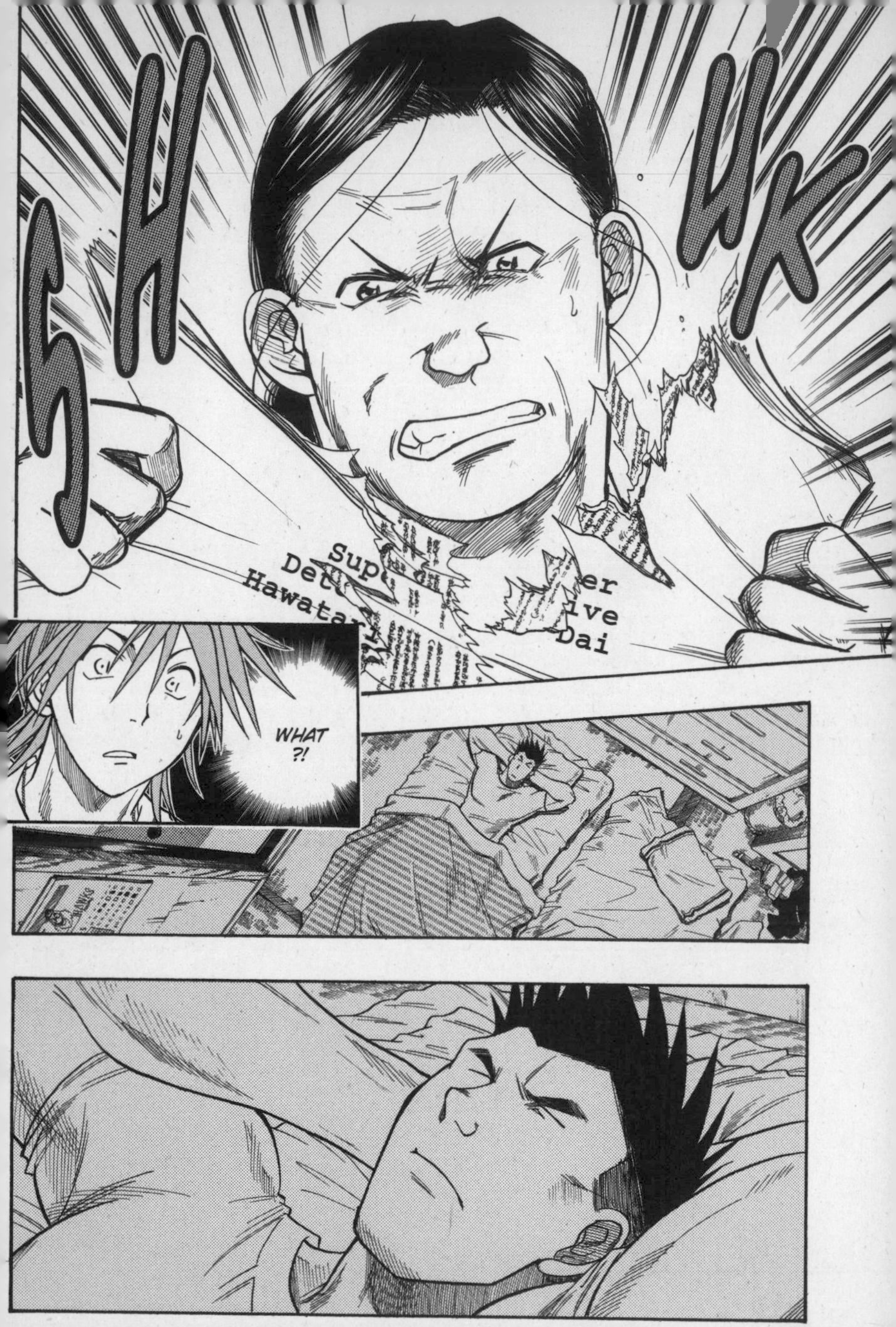
SH
UK
Supe er
Det ive
Hawatari Dai
WHAT ?!

Scene 51:
The Last Action Hero (Part 2)

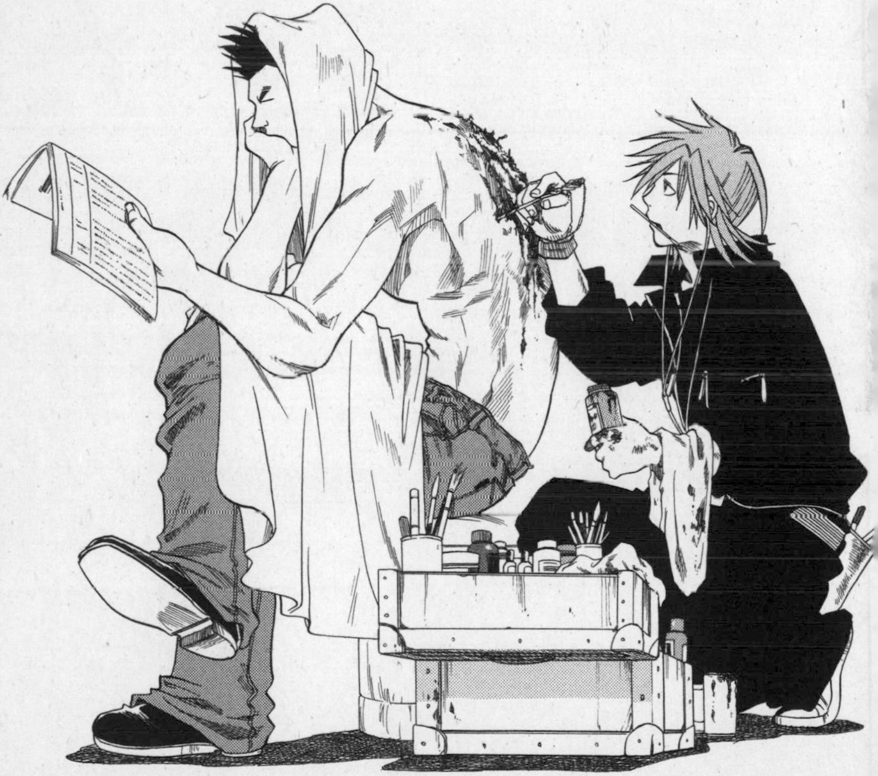

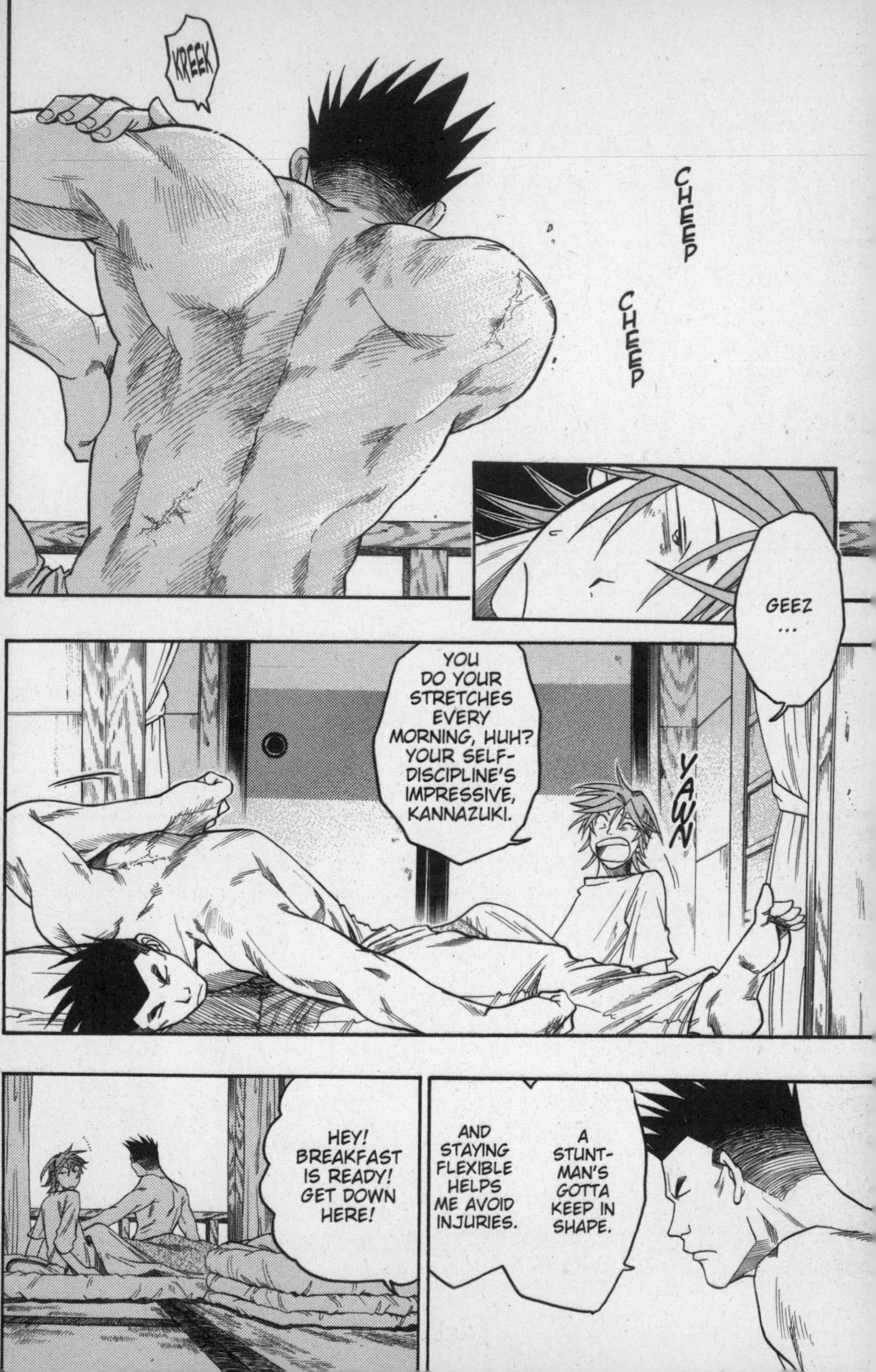
KREEK
CHEEP
CHEEP
GEEZ ...
YOU DO YOUR STRETCHES EVERY MORNING, HUH? YOUR SELF-DISCIPLINE'S IMPRESSIVE, KANNAZUKI.
YAWN
A STUNT-MAN'S GOTTA KEEP IN SHAPE.
AND STAYING FLEXIBLE HELPS ME AVOID INJURIES.
HEY! BREAKFAST IS READY! GET DOWN HERE!

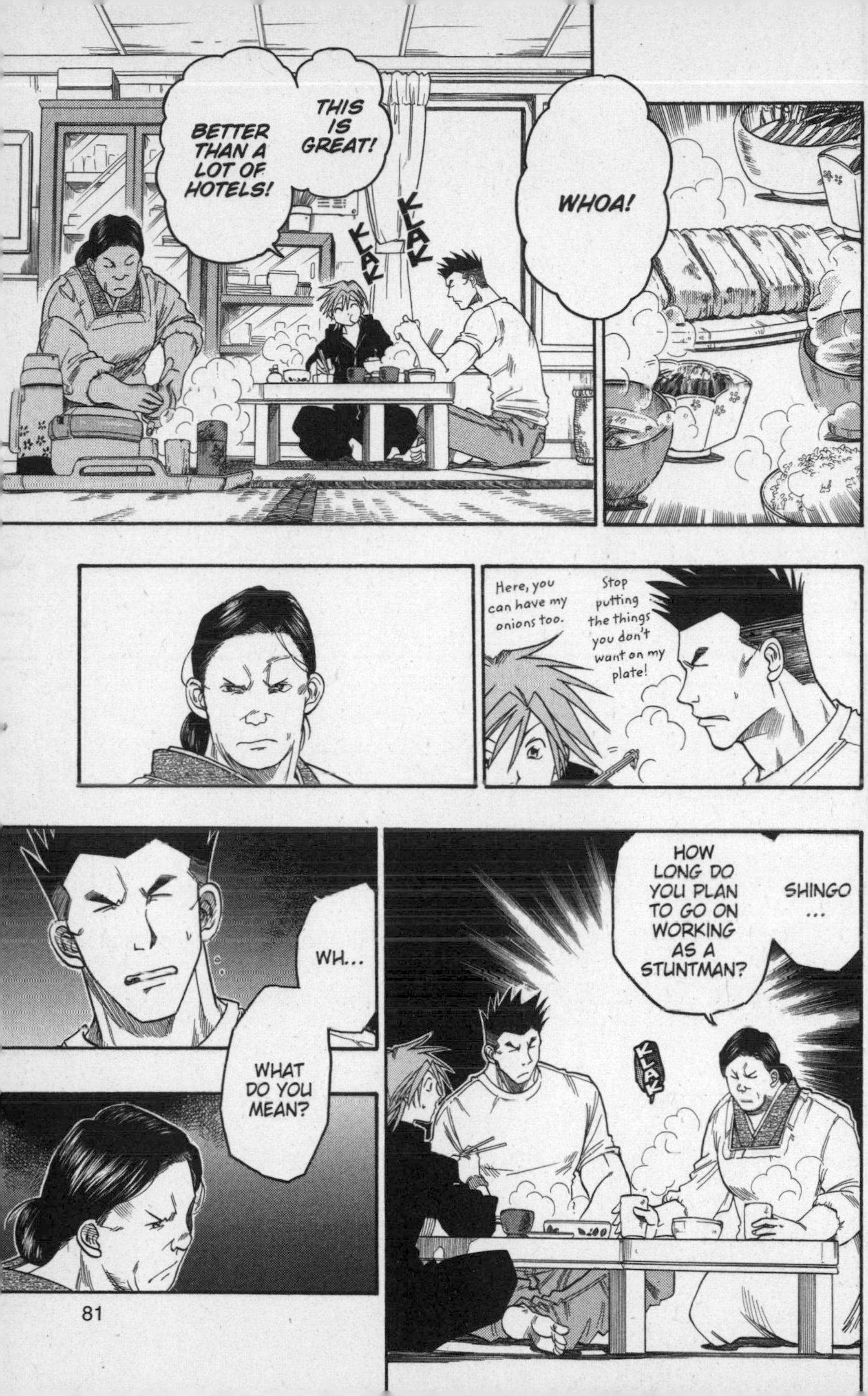
WHOA!
THIS IS GREAT!
BETTER THAN A LOT OF HOTELS!
KLAK
KLAK
Stop putting the things you don't want on my plate!
Here, you can have my onions too.
SHINGO ...
HOW LONG DO YOU PLAN TO GO ON WORKING AS A STUNTMAN?
KLAK
WH...
WHAT DO YOU MEAN?

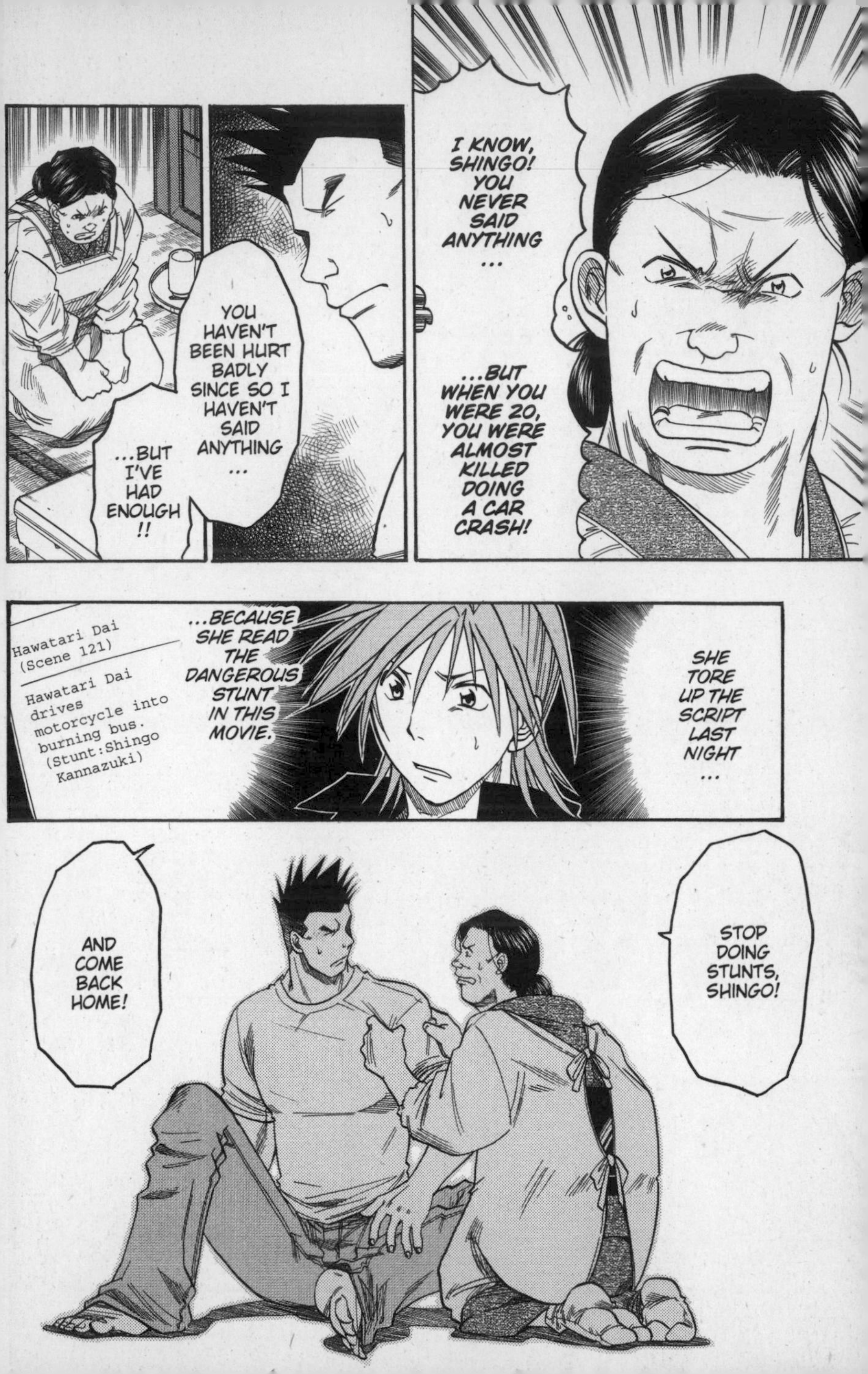
I KNOW, SHINGO! YOU NEVER SAID ANYTHING...
...BUT WHEN YOU WERE 20, YOU WERE ALMOST KILLED DOING A CAR CRASH!
YOU HAVEN'T BEEN HURT BADLY SINCE SO I HAVEN'T SAID ANYTHING...
...BUT I'VE HAD ENOUGH!!
SHE TORE UP THE SCRIPT LAST NIGHT...
...BECAUSE SHE READ THE DANGEROUS STUNT IN THIS MOVIE.
Hawatari Dai (Scene 121)
Hawatari Dai drives motorcycle into burning bus. (Stunt:Shingo Kannazuki)
STOP DOING STUNTS, SHINGO!
AND COME BACK HOME!

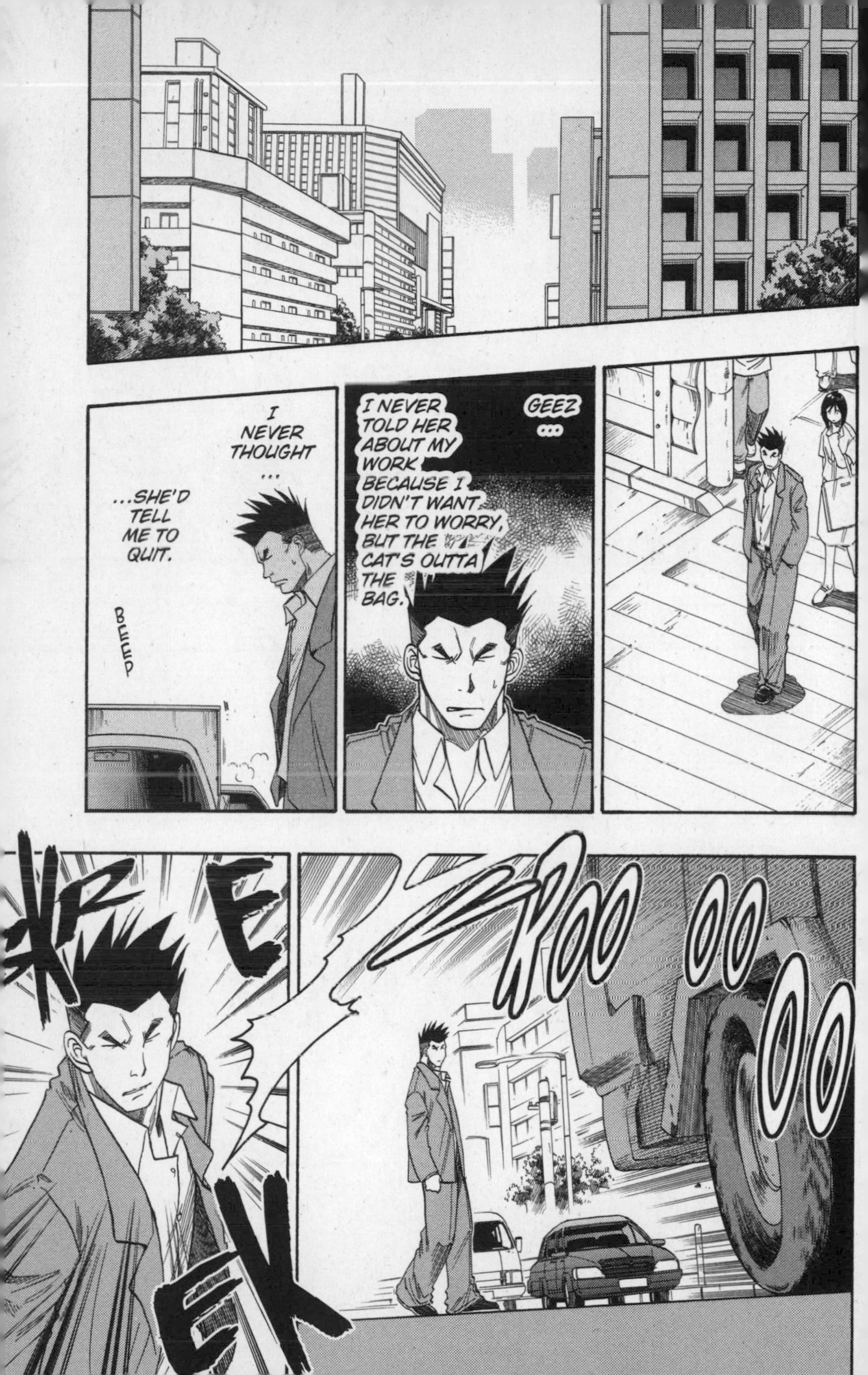
GEEZ...
I NEVER TOLD HER ABOUT MY WORK BECAUSE I DIDN'T WANT HER TO WORRY, BUT THE CAT'S OUTTA THE BAG.
I NEVER THOUGHT...
...SHE'D TELL ME TO QUIT.
BEEEP
VROOOOOO
SKREEK

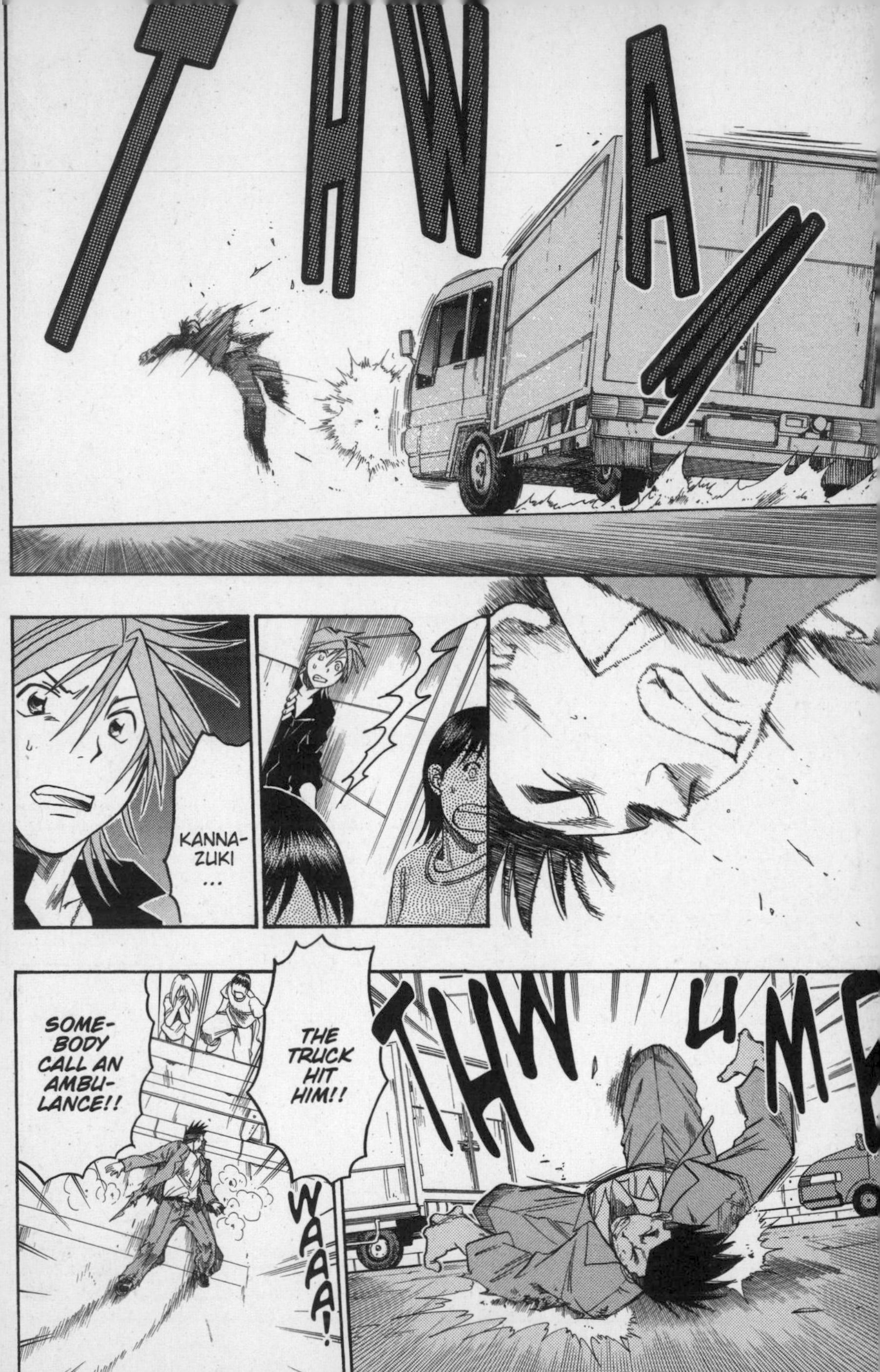
THWAM
KANNA-ZUKI ...
THWUM
WAAA!
THE TRUCK HIT HIM!!
SOME-BODY CALL AN AMBU-LANCE!!

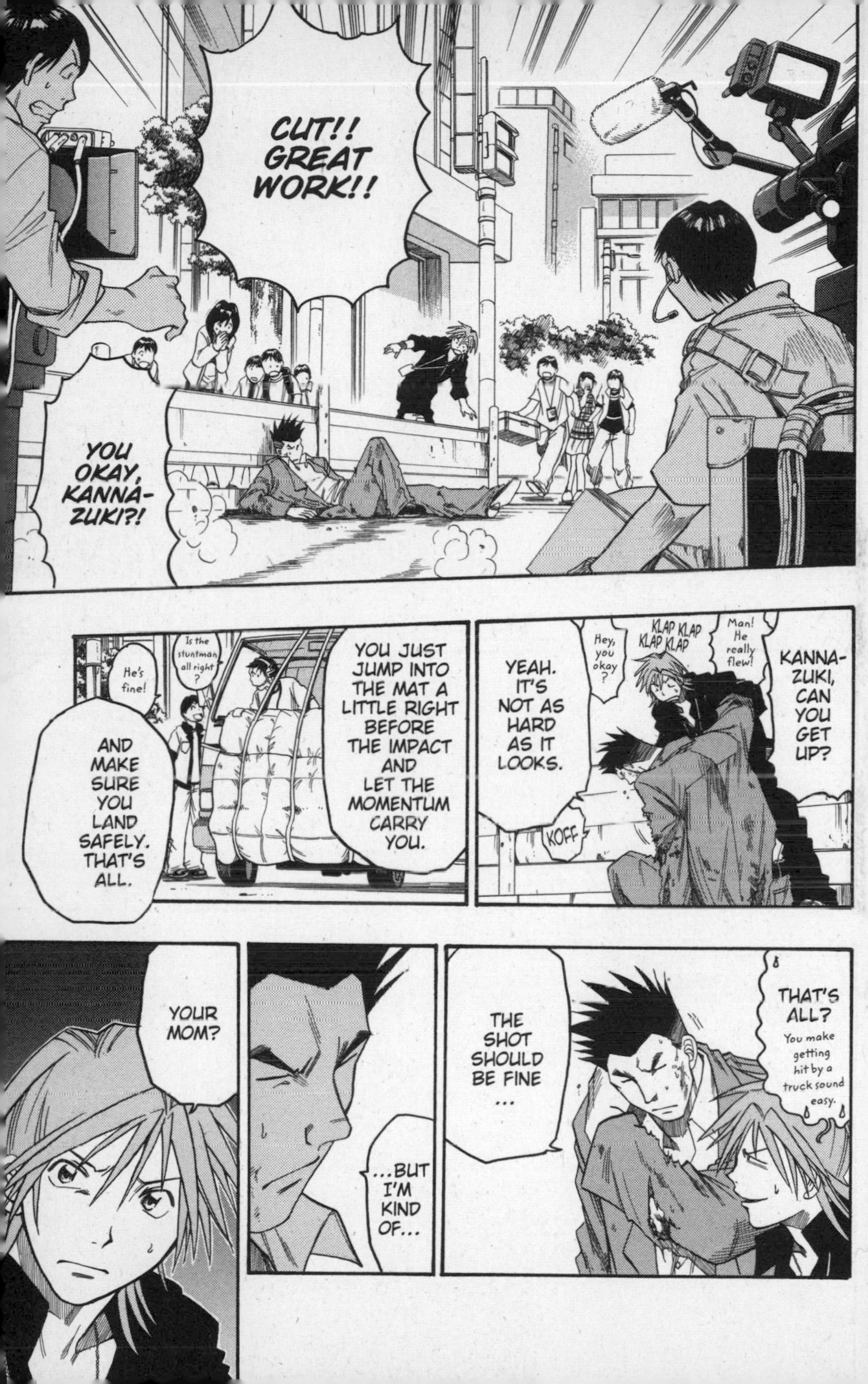
CUT!! GREAT WORK!!
YOU OKAY, KANNA-ZUKI?!
KANNA-ZUKI, CAN YOU GET UP?
Man! He really flew!
KLAP KLAP KLAP KLAP
Hey, you okay?
YEAH. IT'S NOT AS HARD AS IT LOOKS.
KOFF
YOU JUST JUMP INTO THE MAT A LITTLE RIGHT BEFORE THE IMPACT AND LET THE MOMENTUM CARRY YOU.
Is the stuntman all right?
He's fine!
AND MAKE SURE YOU LAND SAFELY. THAT'S ALL.
THAT'S ALL?
You make getting hit by a truck sound easy.
THE SHOT SHOULD BE FINE ...
...BUT I'M KIND OF...
YOUR MOM?

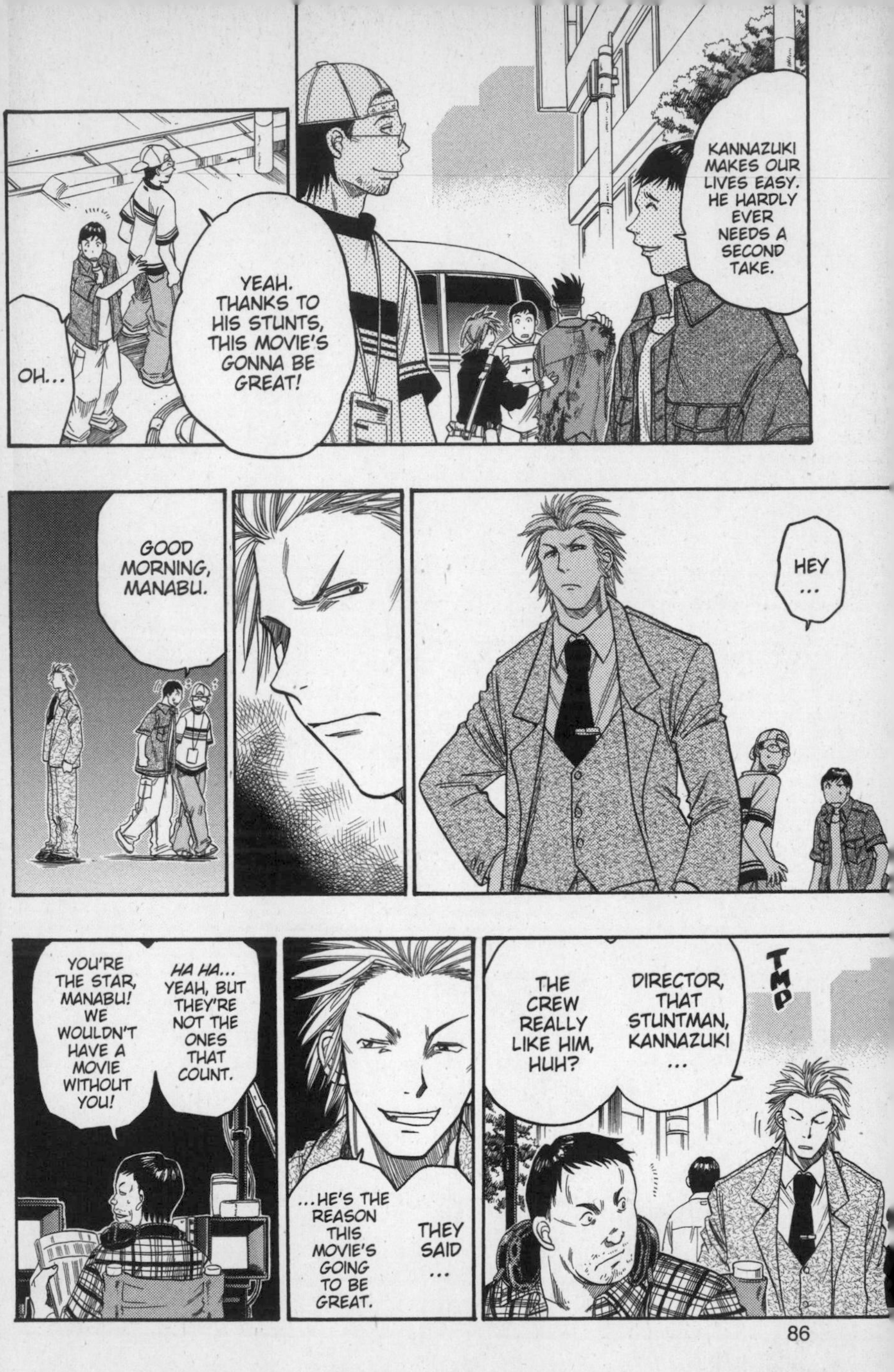
KANNAZUKI MAKES OUR LIVES EASY. HE HARDLY EVER NEEDS A SECOND TAKE.
YEAH. THANKS TO HIS STUNTS, THIS MOVIE'S GONNA BE GREAT!
OH...
HEY ...
GOOD MORNING, MANABU.
TMP
DIRECTOR, THAT STUNTMAN, KANNAZUKI ...
THE CREW REALLY LIKE HIM, HUH?
THEY SAID ...
...HE'S THE REASON THIS MOVIE'S GOING TO BE GREAT.
HA HA... YEAH, BUT THEY'RE NOT THE ONES THAT COUNT.
YOU'RE THE STAR, MANABU! WE WOULDN'T HAVE A MOVIE WITHOUT YOU!

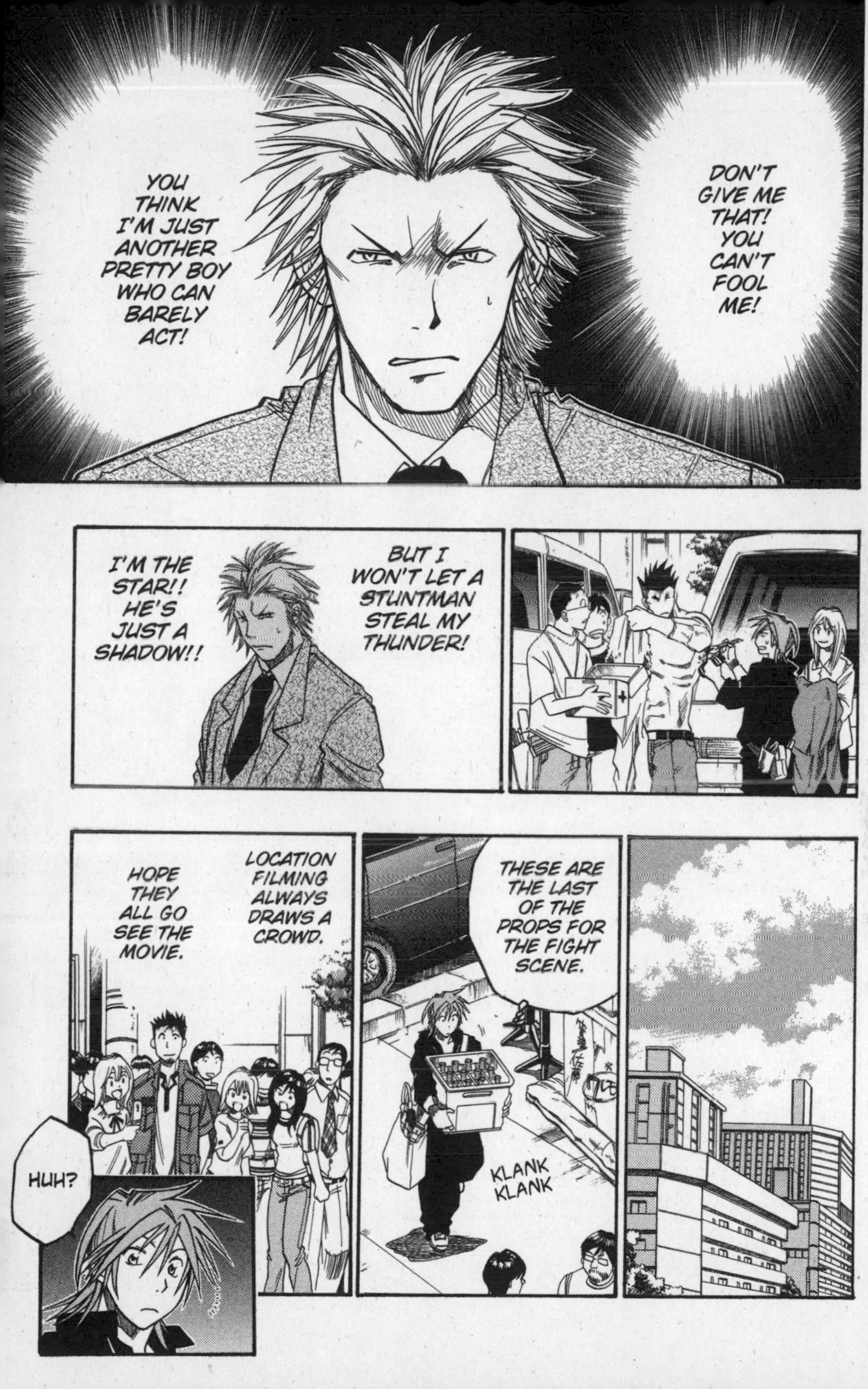
DON'T GIVE ME THAT! YOU CAN'T FOOL ME!
YOU THINK I'M JUST ANOTHER PRETTY BOY WHO CAN BARELY ACT!
BUT I WON'T LET A STUNTMAN STEAL MY THUNDER!
I'M THE STAR!! HE'S JUST A SHADOW!!
THESE ARE THE LAST OF THE PROPS FOR THE FIGHT SCENE.
KLANK KLANK
LOCATION FILMING ALWAYS DRAWS A CROWD.
HOPE THEY ALL GO SEE THE MOVIE.
HUH?

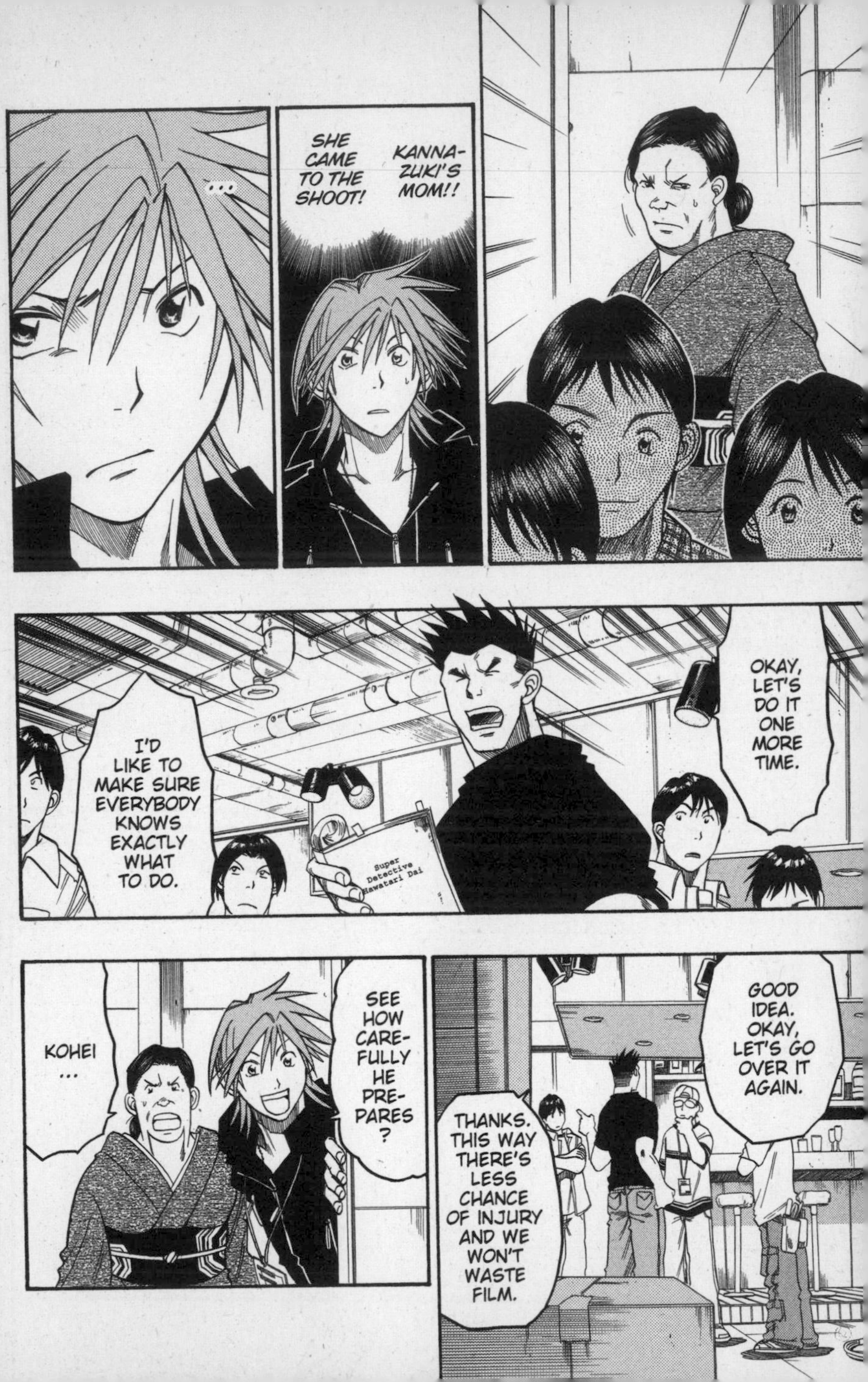
KANNA-ZUKI'S MOM!!
SHE CAME TO THE SHOOT!
...
OKAY, LET'S DO IT ONE MORE TIME.
I'D LIKE TO MAKE SURE EVERYBODY KNOWS EXACTLY WHAT TO DO.
Super Detective Hawatari Dai
GOOD IDEA. OKAY, LET'S GO OVER IT AGAIN.
THANKS. THIS WAY THERE'S LESS CHANCE OF INJURY AND WE WON'T WASTE FILM.
SEE HOW CAREFULLY HE PREPARES?
KOHEI ...

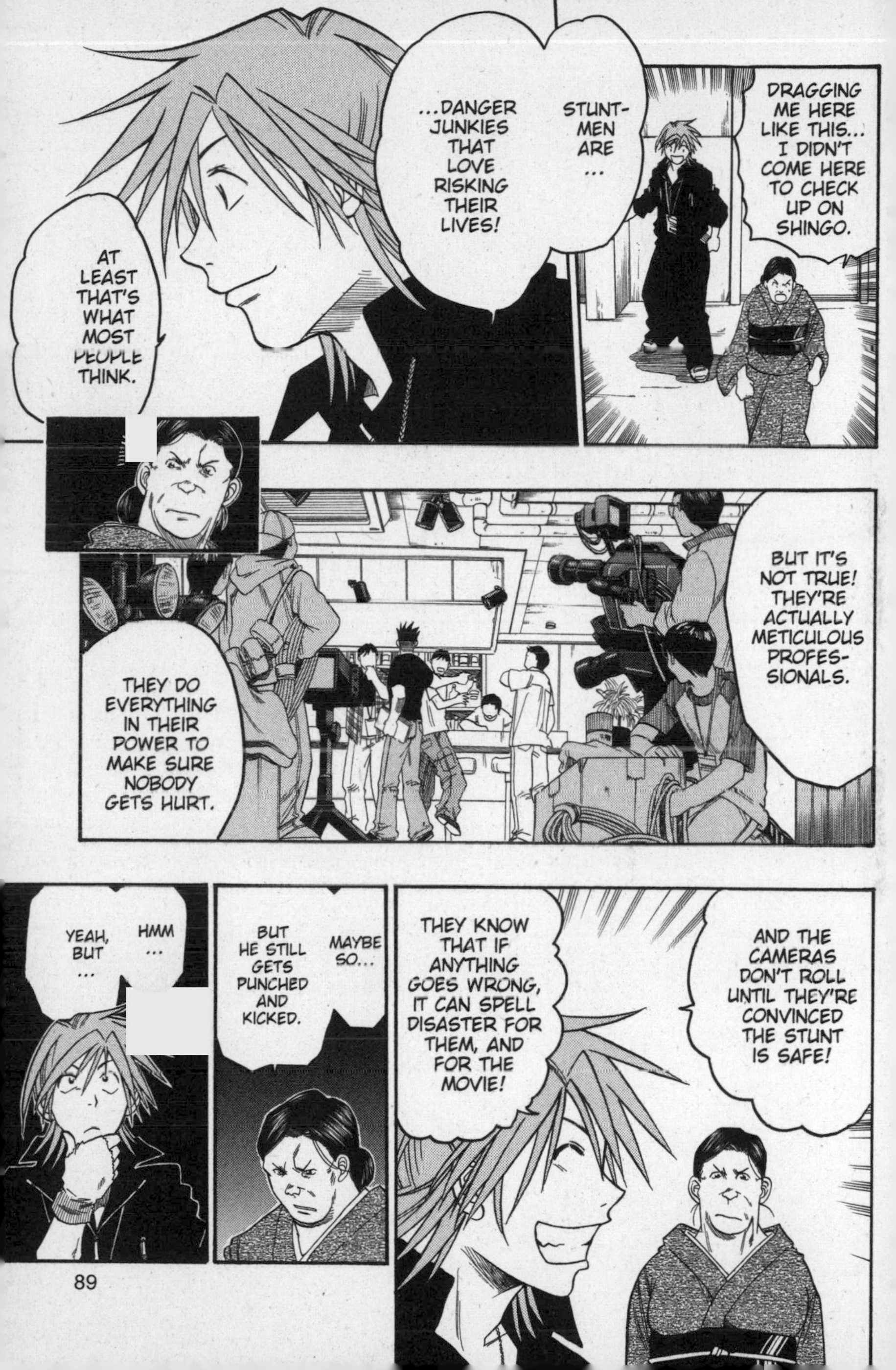
DRAGGING ME HERE LIKE THIS... I DIDN'T COME HERE TO CHECK UP ON SHINGO.
STUNT-MEN ARE ...
...DANGER JUNKIES THAT LOVE RISKING THEIR LIVES!
AT LEAST THAT'S WHAT MOST PEOPLE THINK.
BUT IT'S NOT TRUE! THEY'RE ACTUALLY METICULOUS PROFES-SIONALS.
THEY DO EVERYTHING IN THEIR POWER TO MAKE SURE NOBODY GETS HURT.
AND THE CAMERAS DON'T ROLL UNTIL THEY'RE CONVINCED THE STUNT IS SAFE!
THEY KNOW THAT IF ANYTHING GOES WRONG, IT CAN SPELL DISASTER FOR THEM, AND FOR THE MOVIE!
MAYBE SO...
BUT HE STILL GETS PUNCHED AND KICKED.
HMM ...
YEAH, BUT ...

*Polymer—a polymerized organic compound.

IT BREAKS EASILY.

AND THE FRAGMENTS WON'T CUT YOU.

And it doesn't hurt.

It shatters into tiny pieces.

(OLD STYLE) SUGAR GLASS
POLYMER CAST INTO THE SHAPE OF A BOTTLE

WHEN A BOTTLE IS BROKEN OVER SOMEONE'S HEAD IN A MOVIE...

...THAT BOTTLE IS MADE OF A MATERIAL MUCH LIGHTER AND EASIER TO BREAK THAN REAL GLASS.

(NEW STYLE) DUMMY GLASS POLYMER
SOFTEN IN WARM PLACES, MAKING THEM DIFFICULT TO HANDLE.

*Balsa wood—a very soft lightweight wood.

WHEN YOU FALL ON A BALSA DESK, IT GETS CRUSHED AND COMPRESSES LIKE A CUSHION TO ABSORB THE IMPACT.

This doesn't hurt either.

BALSA WOOD IS SOFT AND FLEXIBLE AND IS USED TO MAKE MODELS.

WHEN MATS WON'T WORK BECAUSE OF CAMERA ANGLES, THEY USE FURNITURE MADE OF BALSA WOOD INSTEAD.

THEY PUT MATS ON THE GROUND IN BRAWL SCENES WHERE PEOPLE GET KNOCKED DOWN.

...in scenes where people fall down.

They use mats...

EXPLOSION + COVERING IN FLAMES + JUMP FROM HEIGHT: 1,200,000 YEN *

ENGULFED IN FLAMES: 800,000 YEN *

RUN OVER BY CAR: 750,000 YEN *

A STUNTMAN'S FEES VARY ACCORDING TO THE NATURE OF THE STUNT.

THE GREATER THE DANGER OR DIFFICULTY, THE HIGHER THE PAY.

WH AM

* about $11,250

* about $7,500   * about $7,000

90

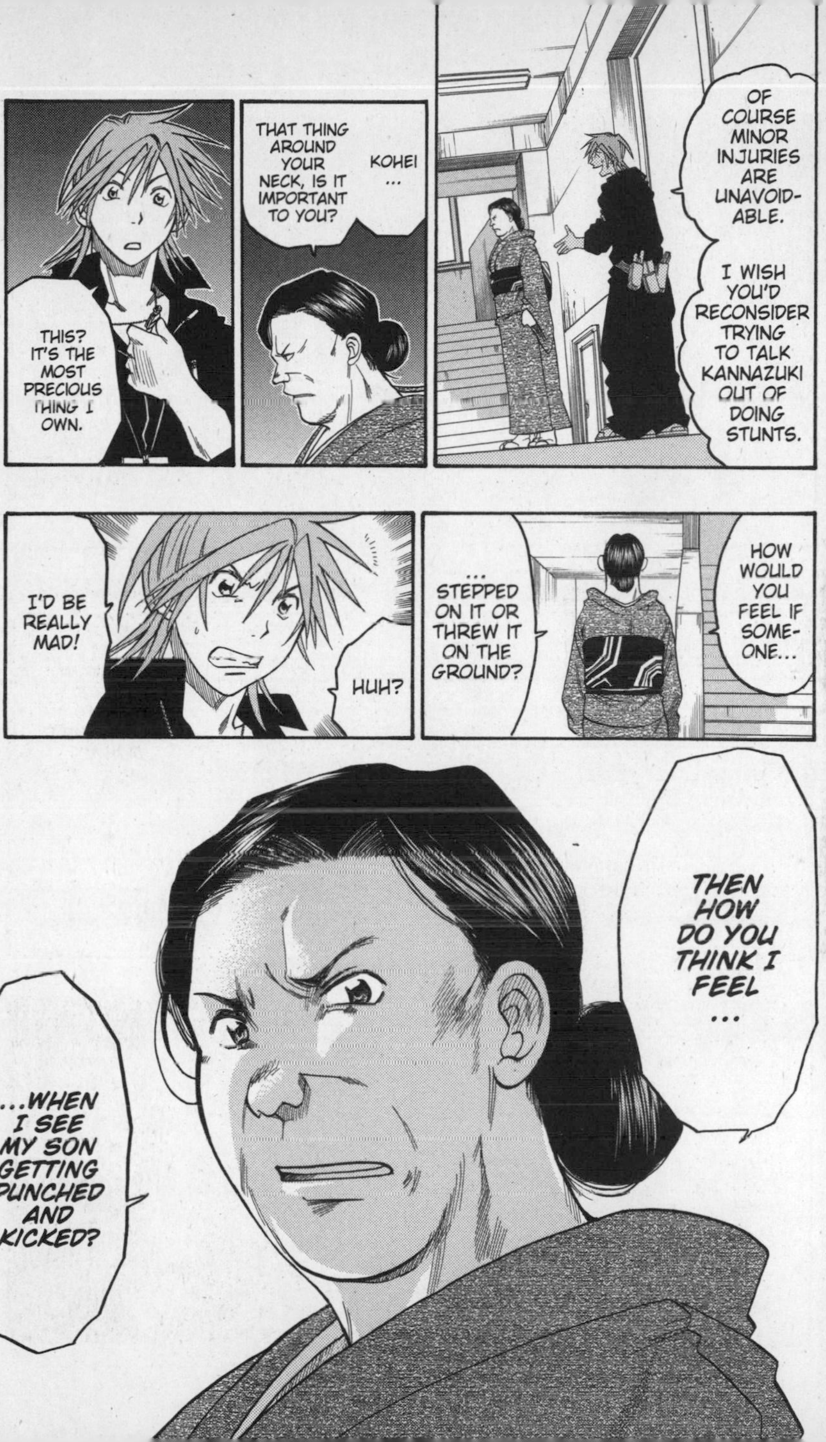
OF COURSE MINOR INJURIES ARE UNAVOIDABLE.
I WISH YOU'D RECONSIDER TRYING TO TALK KANNAZUKI OUT OF DOING STUNTS.
KOHEI ...
THAT THING AROUND YOUR NECK, IS IT IMPORTANT TO YOU?
THIS? IT'S THE MOST PRECIOUS THING I OWN.
HOW WOULD YOU FEEL IF SOMEONE...
...STEPPED ON IT OR THREW IT ON THE GROUND?
HUH?
I'D BE REALLY MAD!
THEN HOW DO YOU THINK I FEEL ...
...WHEN I SEE MY SON GETTING PUNCHED AND KICKED?

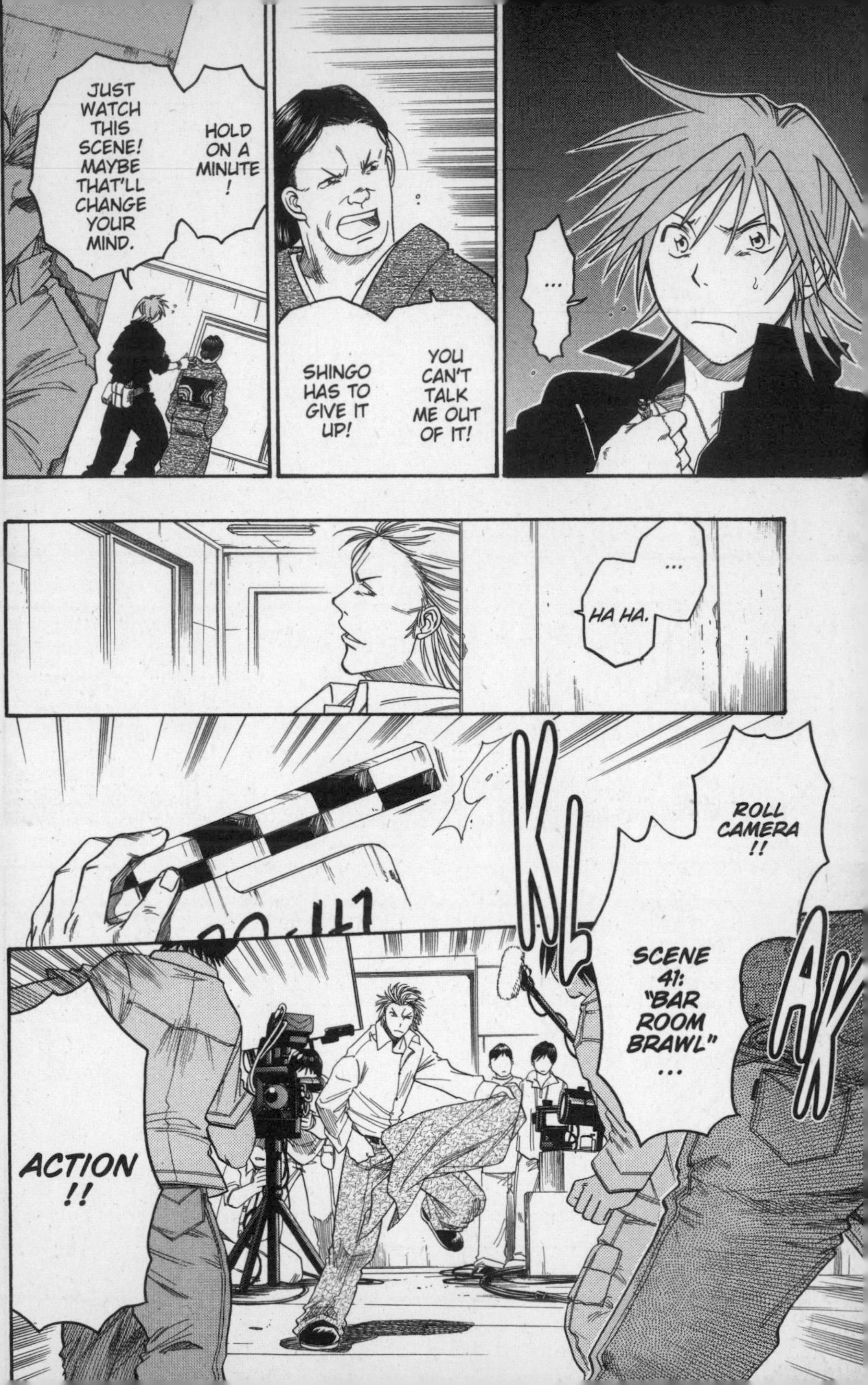
...
YOU CAN'T TALK ME OUT OF IT!
SHINGO HAS TO GIVE IT UP!
HOLD ON A MINUTE!
JUST WATCH THIS SCENE! MAYBE THAT'LL CHANGE YOUR MIND.
... HA HA.
ROLL CAMERA!!
KLAK
SCENE 41: "BAR ROOM BRAWL" ...
ACTION!!

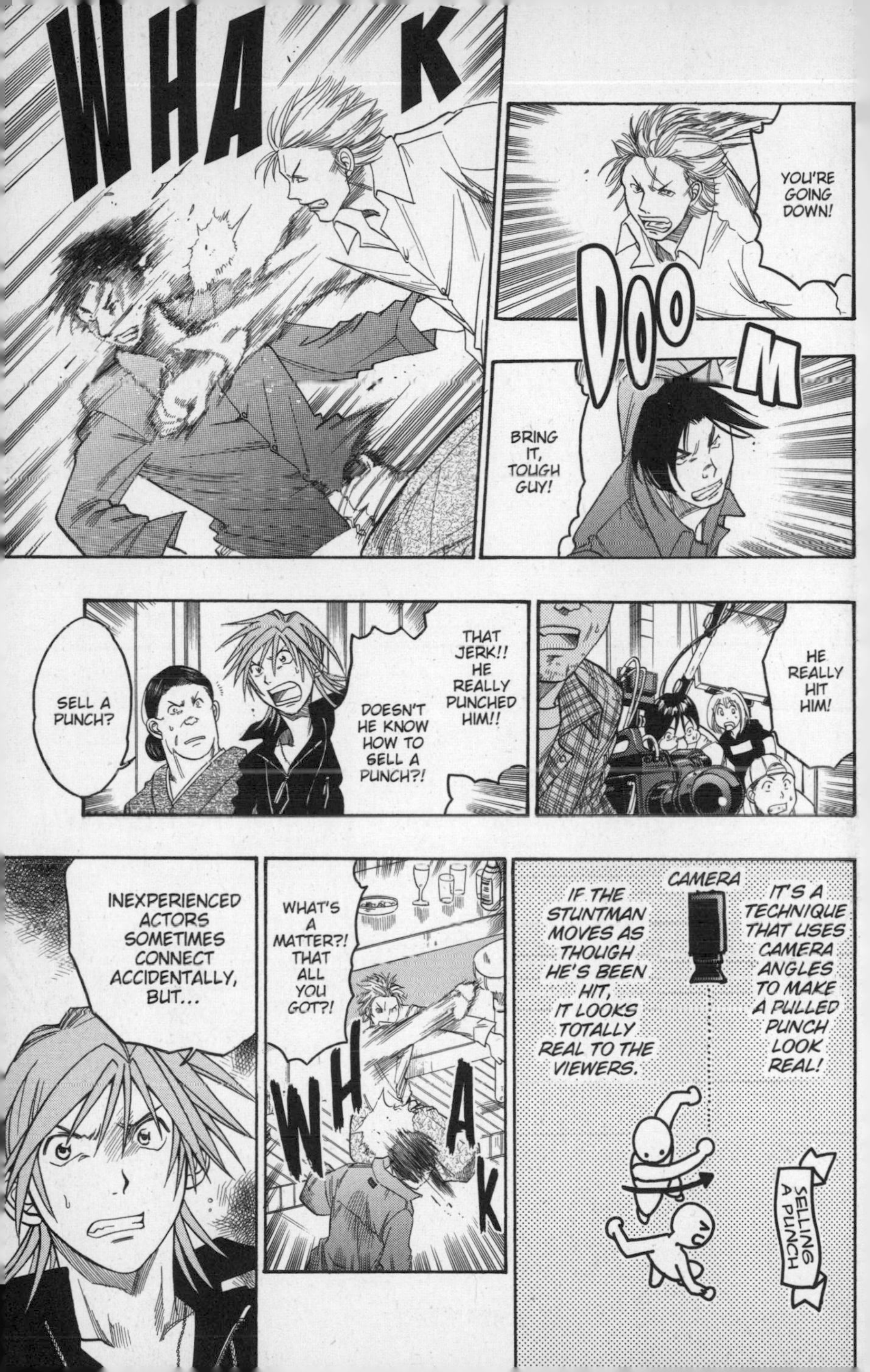

YOU'RE GOING DOWN!
DOOM
BRING IT, TOUGH GUY!
WHAK
HE REALLY HIT HIM!
THAT JERK!! HE REALLY PUNCHED HIM!!
DOESN'T HE KNOW HOW TO SELL A PUNCH?!
SELL A PUNCH?
IT'S A TECHNIQUE THAT USES CAMERA ANGLES TO MAKE A PULLED PUNCH LOOK REAL!
CAMERA
IF THE STUNTMAN MOVES AS THOUGH HE'S BEEN HIT, IT LOOKS TOTALLY REAL TO THE VIEWERS.
SELLING A PUNCH
WHAT'S A MATTER?! THAT ALL YOU GOT?!
WHAK
INEXPERIENCED ACTORS SOMETIMES CONNECT ACCIDENTALLY, BUT...

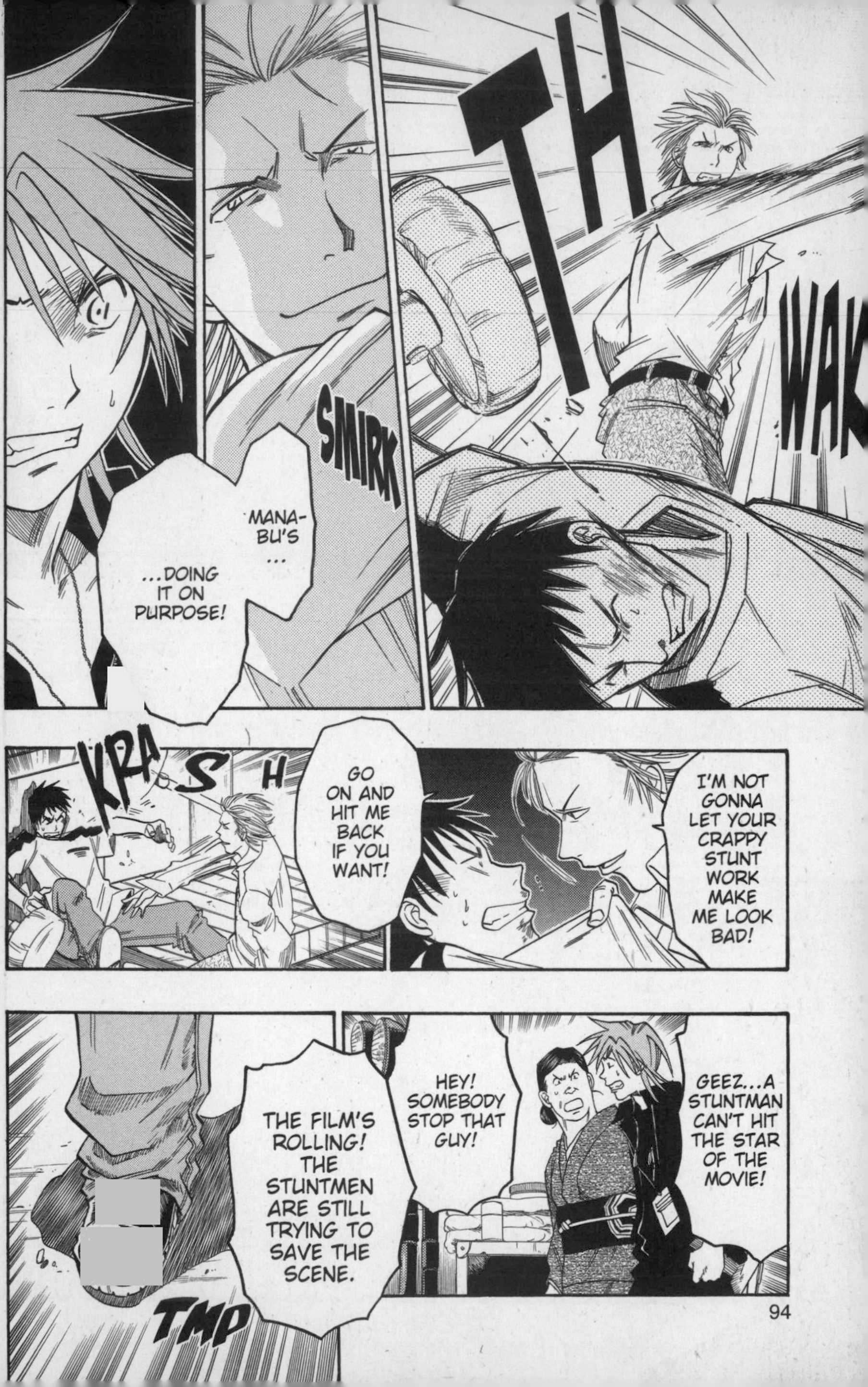
TH
WAK
...
SMIRK
MANA-BU'S ...
...DOING IT ON PURPOSE!
I'M NOT GONNA LET YOUR CRAPPY STUNT WORK MAKE ME LOOK BAD!
GO ON AND HIT ME BACK IF YOU WANT!
KRASH
GEEZ...A STUNTMAN CAN'T HIT THE STAR OF THE MOVIE!
HEY! SOMEBODY STOP THAT GUY!
THE FILM'S ROLLING! THE STUNTMEN ARE STILL TRYING TO SAVE THE SCENE.
TMP

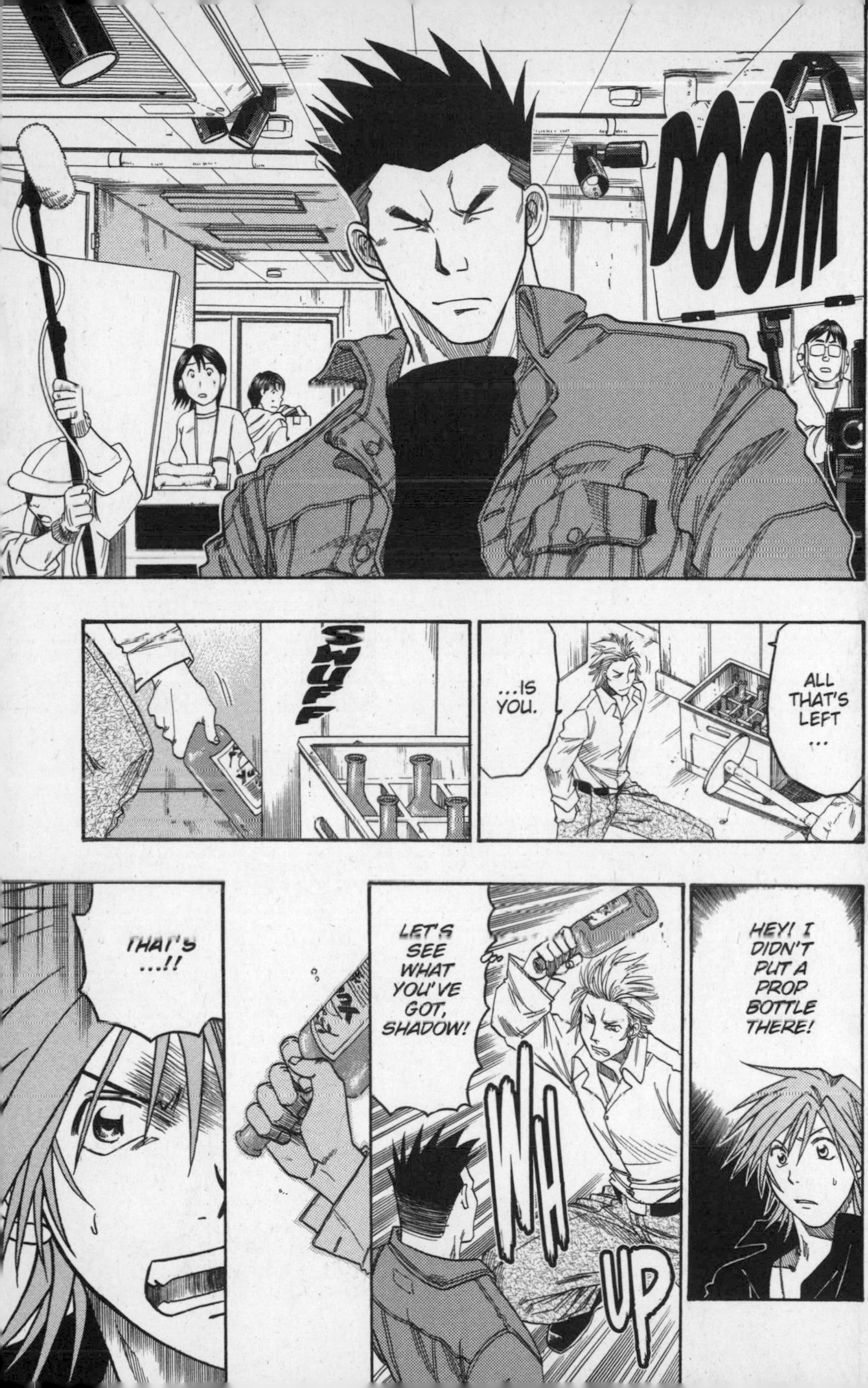
DOOM
ALL THAT'S LEFT ...
...IS YOU.
SWUFF
HEY! I DIDN'T PUT A PROP BOTTLE THERE!
LET'S SEE WHAT YOU'VE GOT, SHADOW!
WHUP
THAT'S ...!!

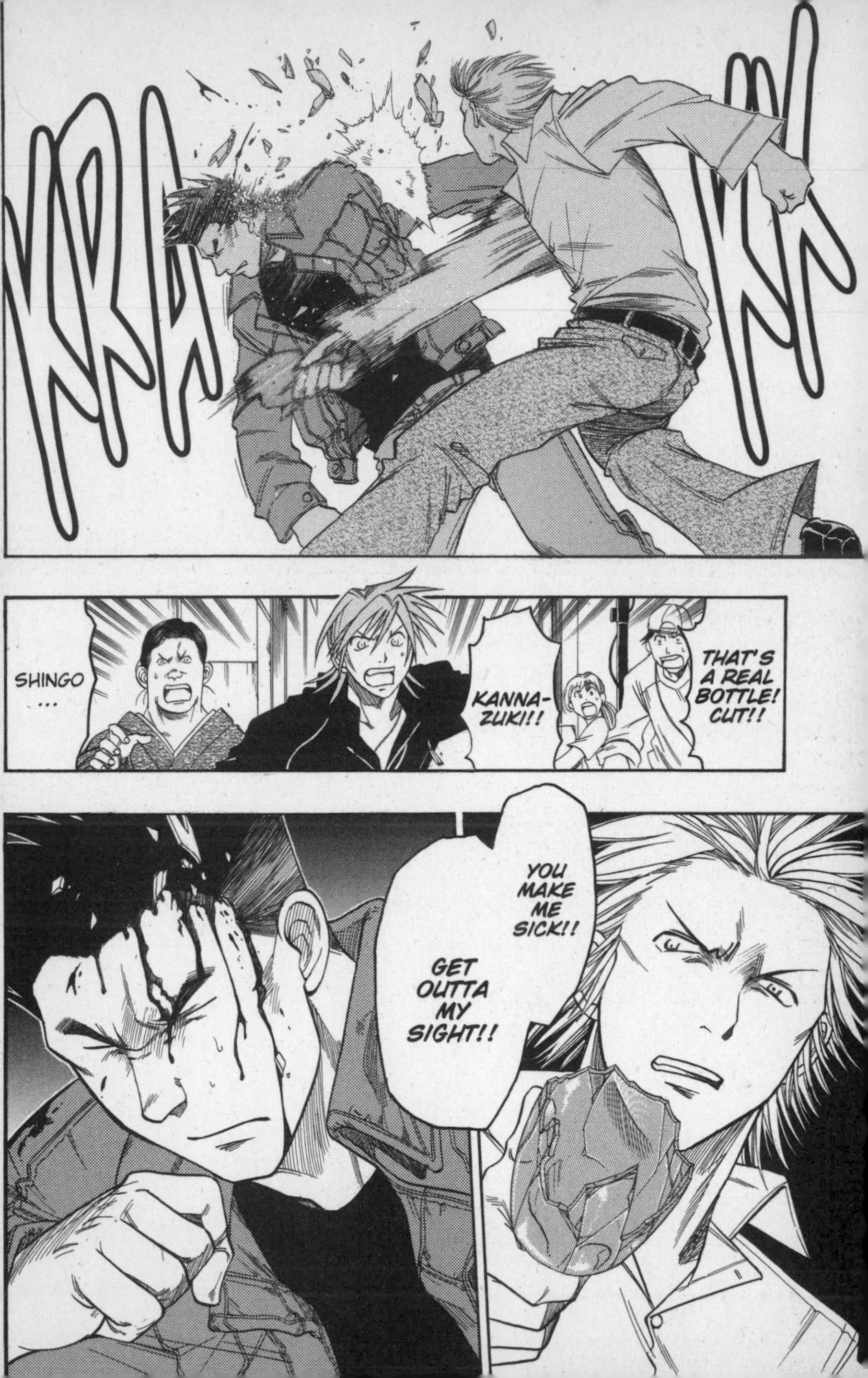
THAT'S A REAL BOTTLE! CUT!!
KANNA-ZUKI!!
SHINGO ...
YOU MAKE ME SICK!!
GET OUTTA MY SIGHT!!

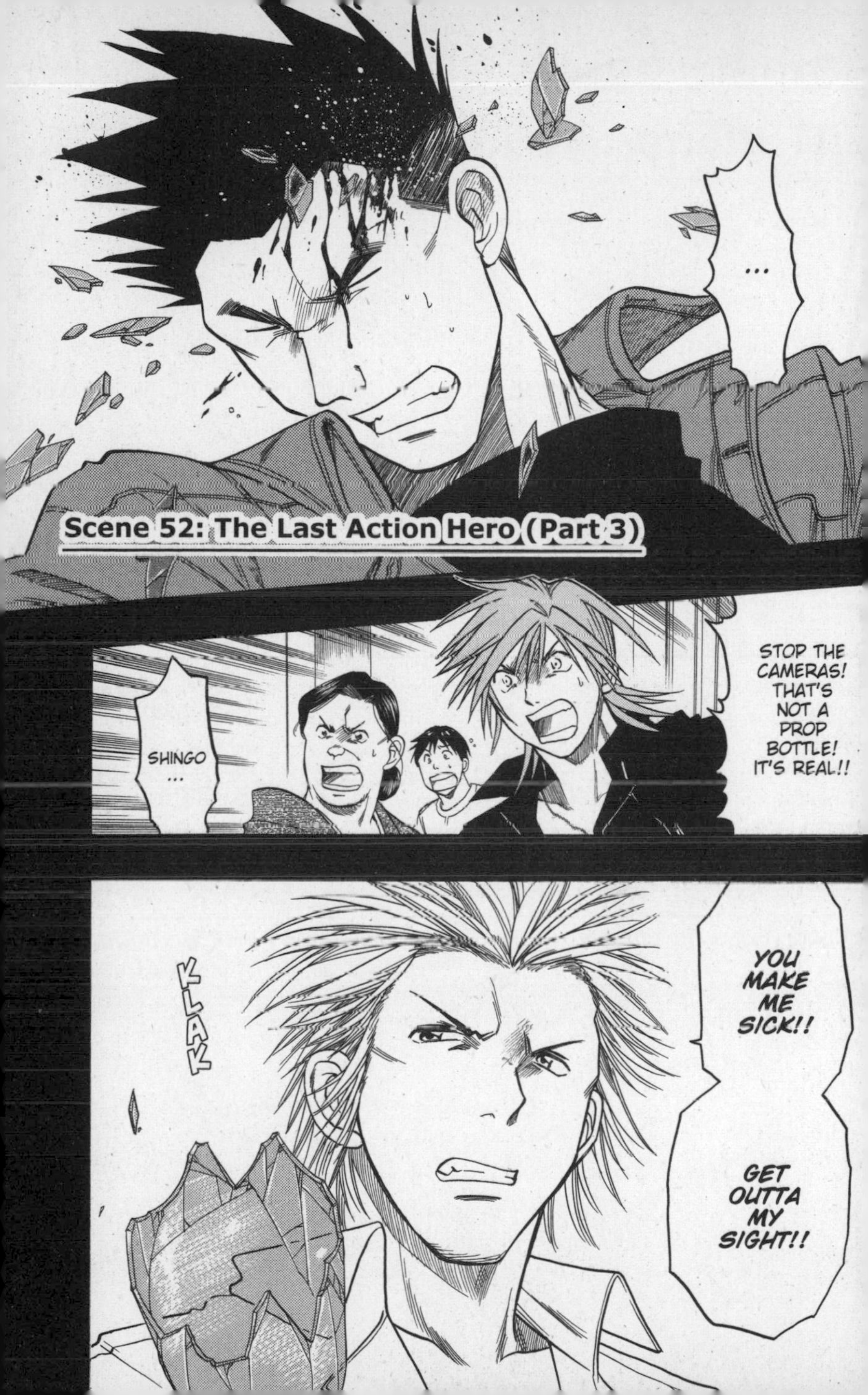
...
Scene 52: The Last Action Hero (Part 3)
STOP THE CAMERAS! THAT'S NOT A PROP BOTTLE! IT'S REAL!!
SHINGO ...
YOU MAKE ME SICK!!
GET OUTTA MY SIGHT!!
KLAK

Scene 52:
The Last Action Hero (Part 3)

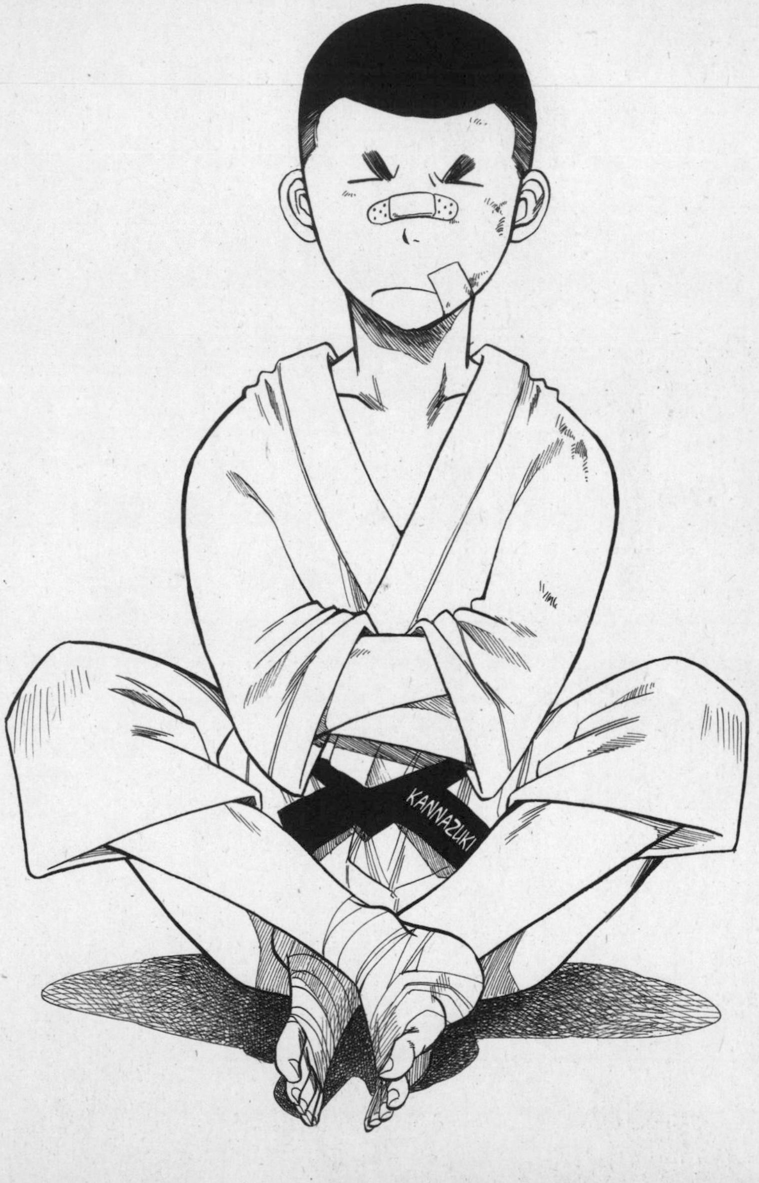
KANNAZUKI

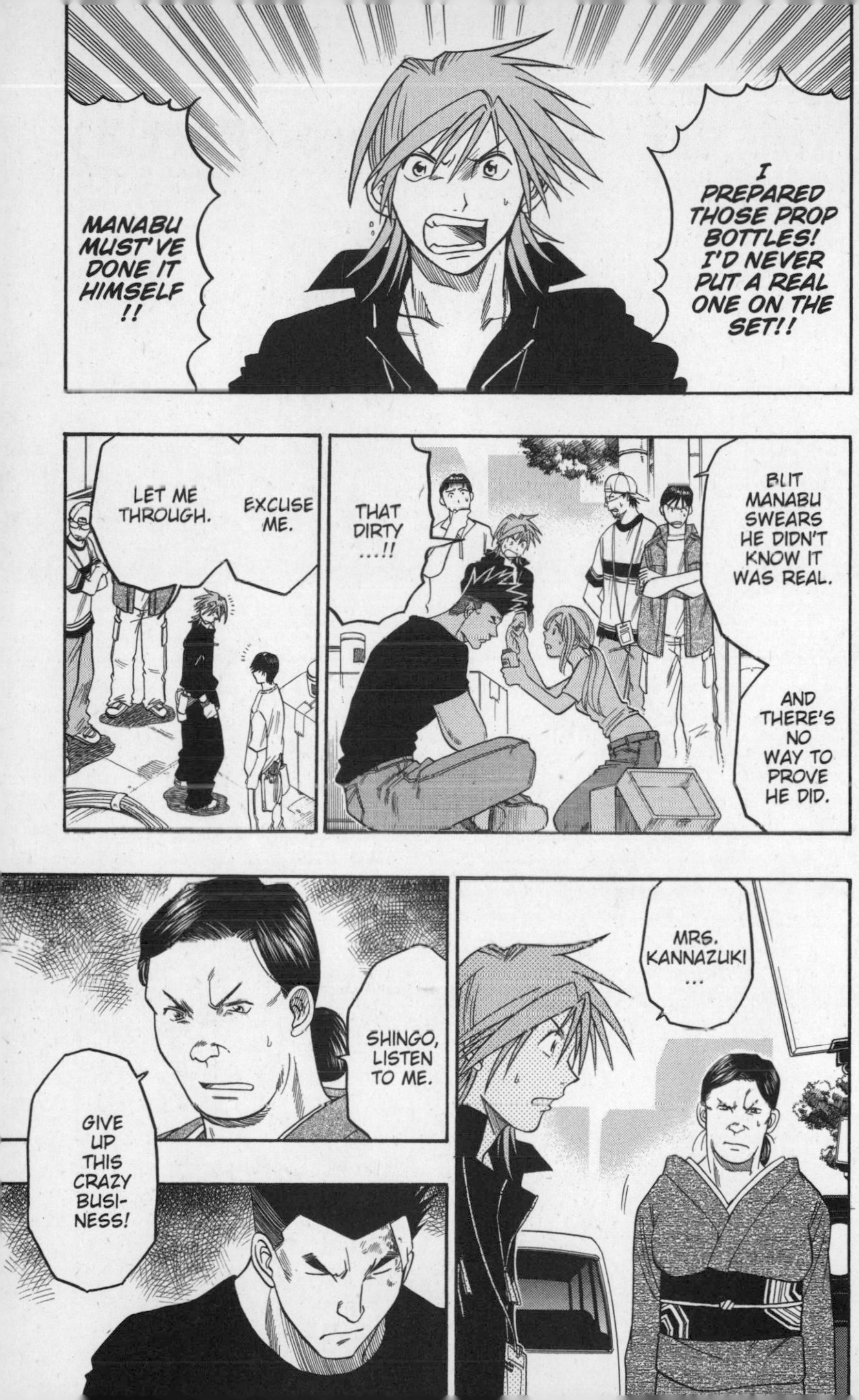
I PREPARED THOSE PROP BOTTLES! I'D NEVER PUT A REAL ONE ON THE SET!!
MANABU MUST'VE DONE IT HIMSELF!!
BUT MANABU SWEARS HE DIDN'T KNOW IT WAS REAL.
AND THERE'S NO WAY TO PROVE HE DID.
THAT DIRTY ...!!
EXCUSE ME.
LET ME THROUGH.
MRS. KANNAZUKI ...
SHINGO, LISTEN TO ME.
GIVE UP THIS CRAZY BUSINESS!

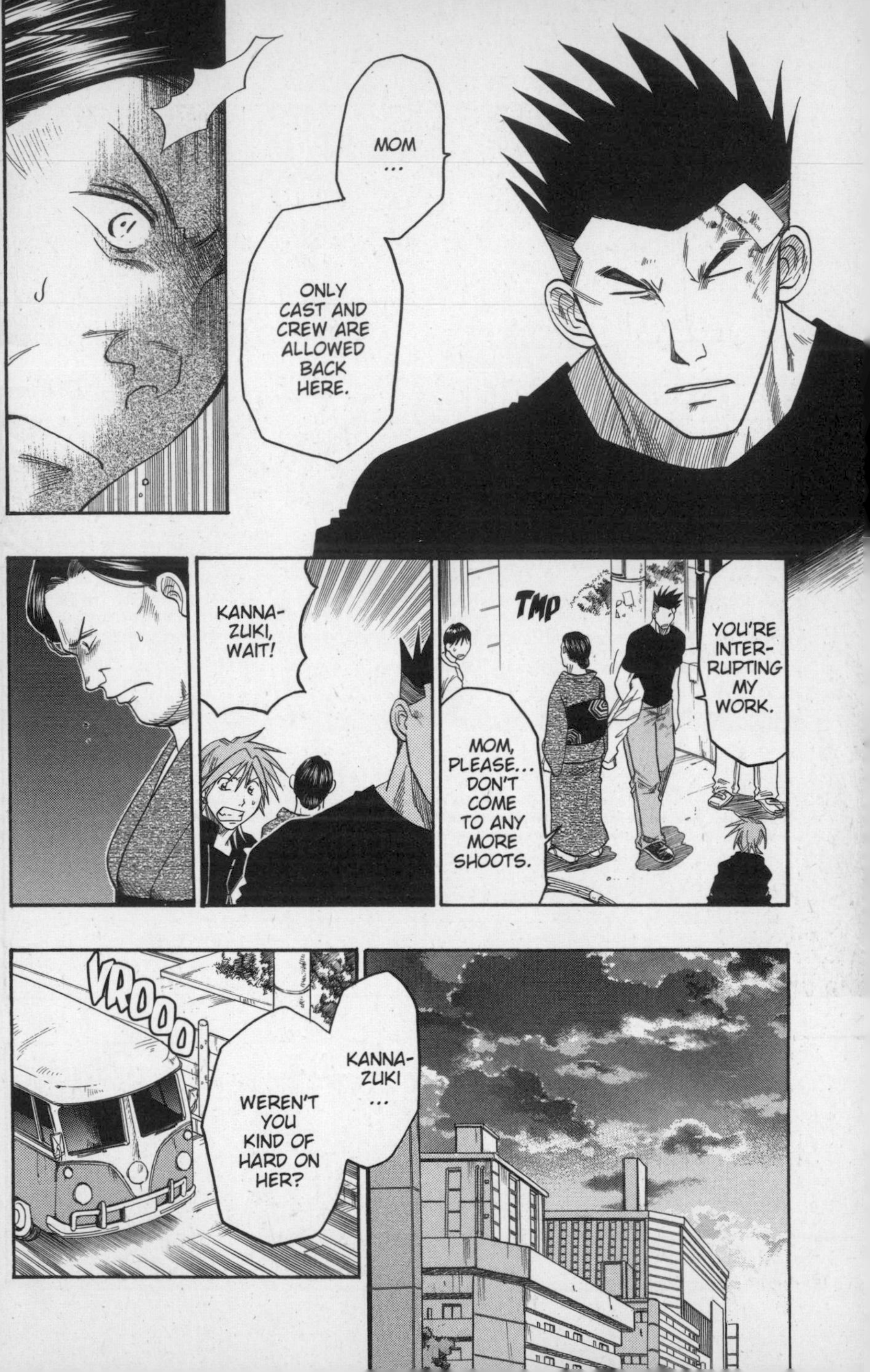
MOM...
ONLY CAST AND CREW ARE ALLOWED BACK HERE.
YOU'RE INTERRUPTING MY WORK.
TMP
MOM, PLEASE... DON'T COME TO ANY MORE SHOOTS.
KANNAZUKI, WAIT!
KANNAZUKI...
WEREN'T YOU KIND OF HARD ON HER?
VROOO

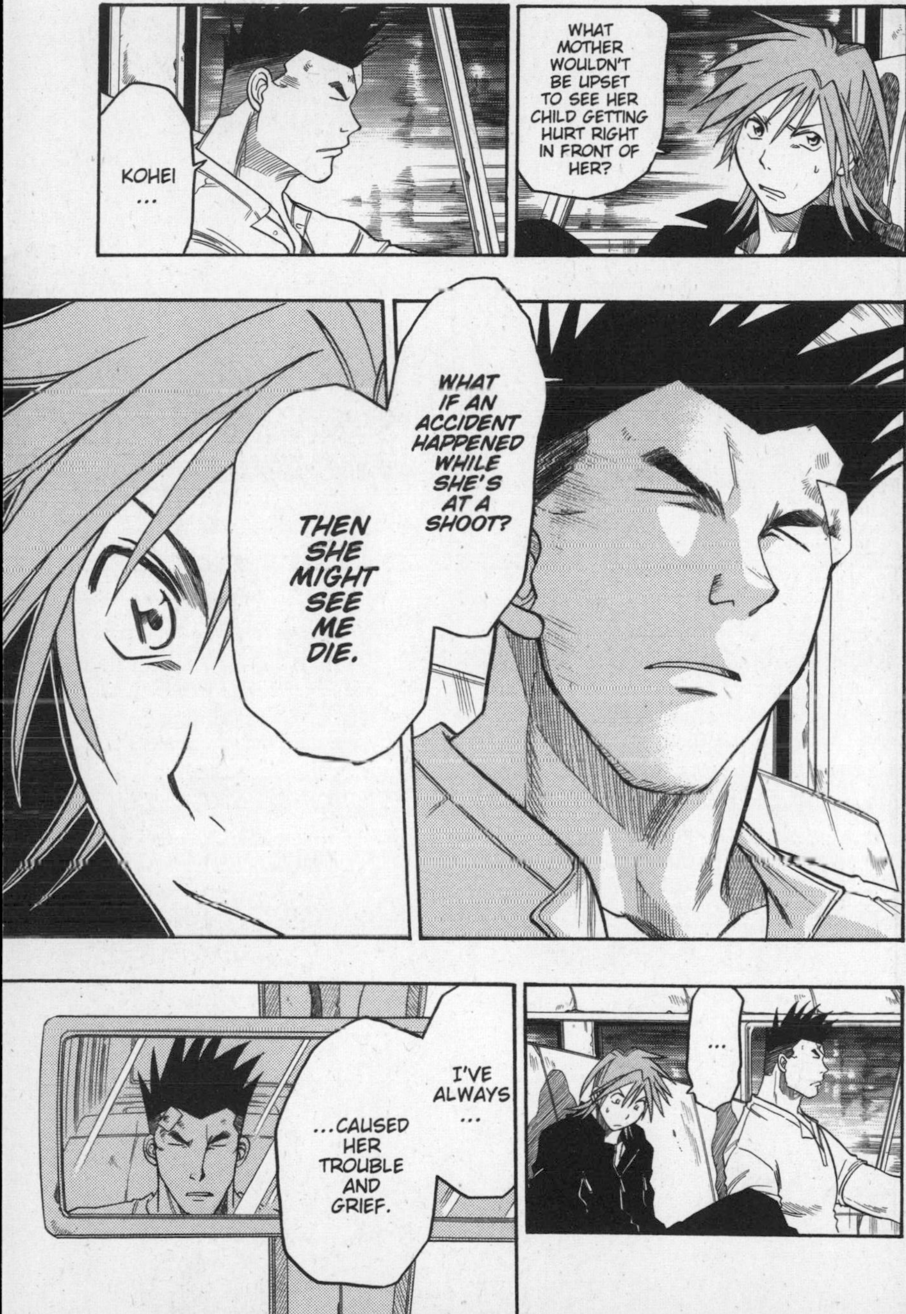
WHAT MOTHER WOULDN'T BE UPSET TO SEE HER CHILD GETTING HURT RIGHT IN FRONT OF HER?
KOHEI ...
WHAT IF AN ACCIDENT HAPPENED WHILE SHE'S AT A SHOOT?
THEN SHE MIGHT SEE ME DIE.
...
I'VE ALWAYS ...
...CAUSED HER TROUBLE AND GRIEF.

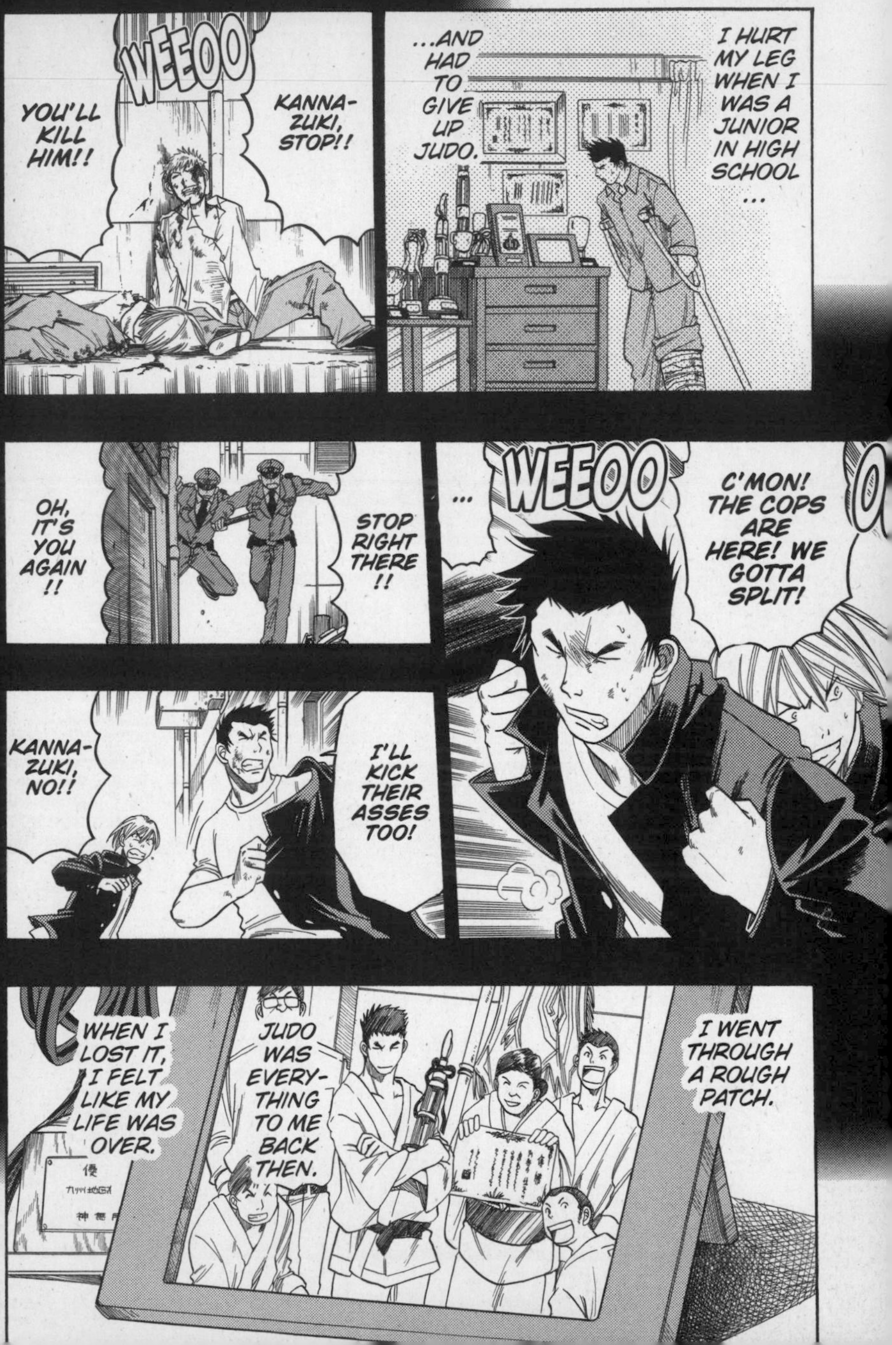
I HURT MY LEG WHEN I WAS A JUNIOR IN HIGH SCHOOL ...
...AND HAD TO GIVE UP JUDO.
WEEOO
KANNA-ZUKI, STOP!!
YOU'LL KILL HIM!!
WEEOO
C'MON! THE COPS ARE HERE! WE GOTTA SPLIT!
...
STOP RIGHT THERE!!
OH, IT'S YOU AGAIN!!
I'LL KICK THEIR ASSES TOO!
KANNA-ZUKI, NO!!
I WENT THROUGH A ROUGH PATCH.
JUDO WAS EVERY-THING TO ME BACK THEN.
WHEN I LOST IT, I FELT LIKE MY LIFE WAS OVER.

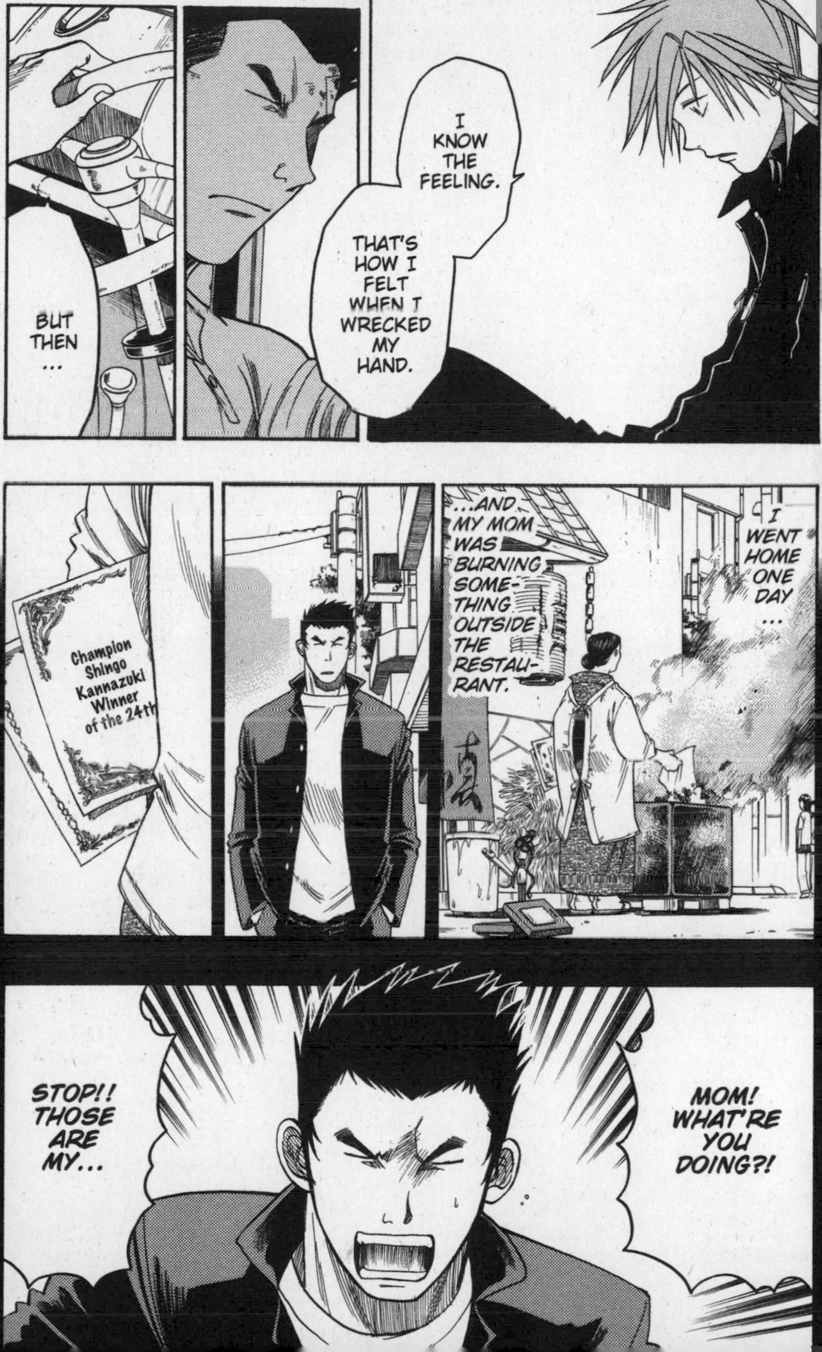
I KNOW THE FEELING.
THAT'S HOW I FELT WHEN I WRECKED MY HAND.
BUT THEN ...
I WENT HOME ONE DAY ...
...AND MY MOM WAS BURNING SOME-THING OUTSIDE THE RESTAU-RANT.
Champion Shingo Kannazuki Winner of the 24th
MOM! WHAT'RE YOU DOING?!
STOP!! THOSE ARE MY...

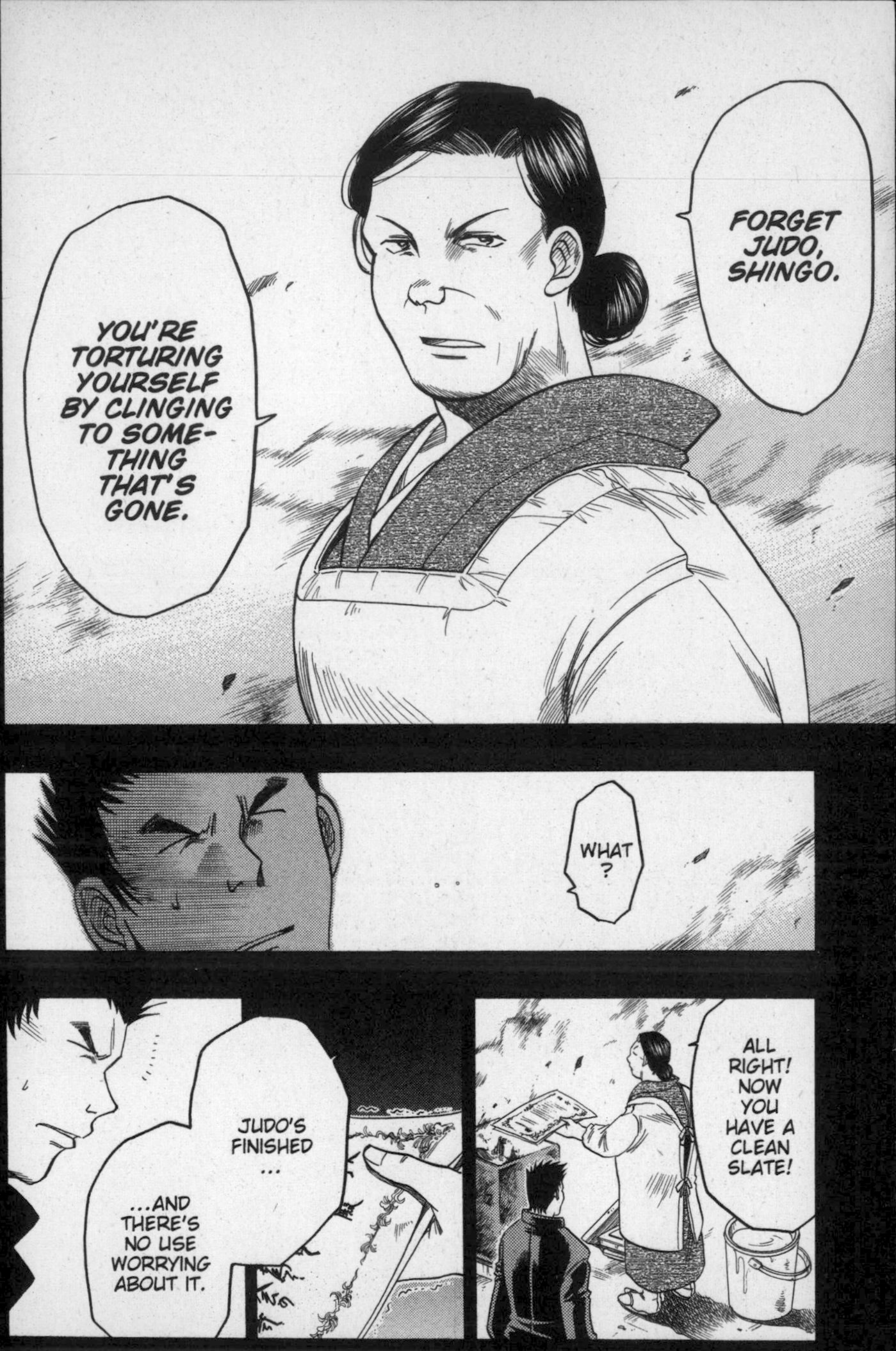
FORGET JUDO, SHINGO.
YOU'RE TORTURING YOURSELF BY CLINGING TO SOME-THING THAT'S GONE.
WHAT ?
ALL RIGHT! NOW YOU HAVE A CLEAN SLATE!
JUDO'S FINISHED ...
...AND THERE'S NO USE WORRYING ABOUT IT.

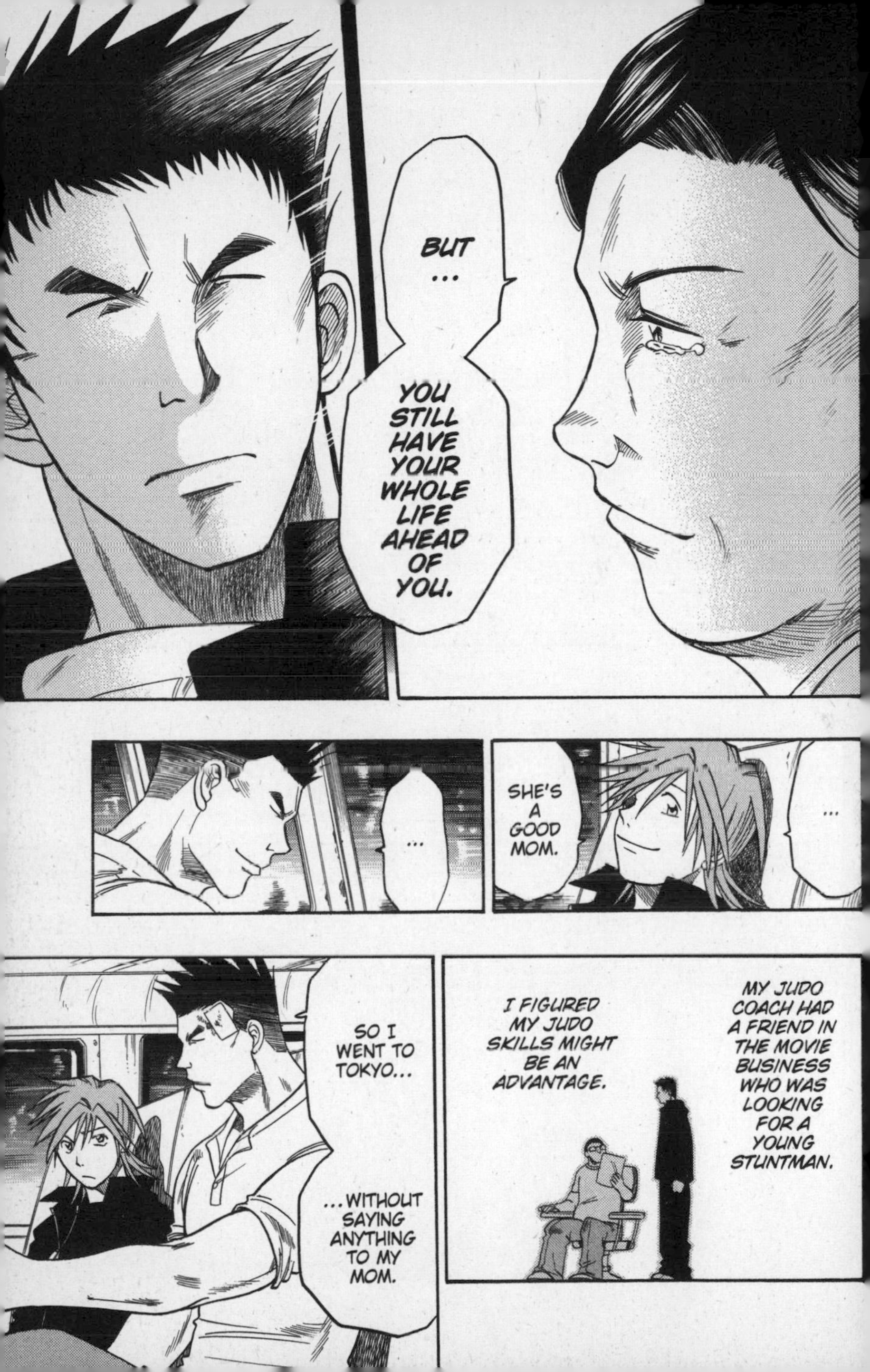
BUT ...
YOU STILL HAVE YOUR WHOLE LIFE AHEAD OF YOU.
...
SHE'S A GOOD MOM.
...
MY JUDO COACH HAD A FRIEND IN THE MOVIE BUSINESS WHO WAS LOOKING FOR A YOUNG STUNTMAN.
I FIGURED MY JUDO SKILLS MIGHT BE AN ADVANTAGE.
SO I WENT TO TOKYO...
...WITHOUT SAYING ANYTHING TO MY MOM.

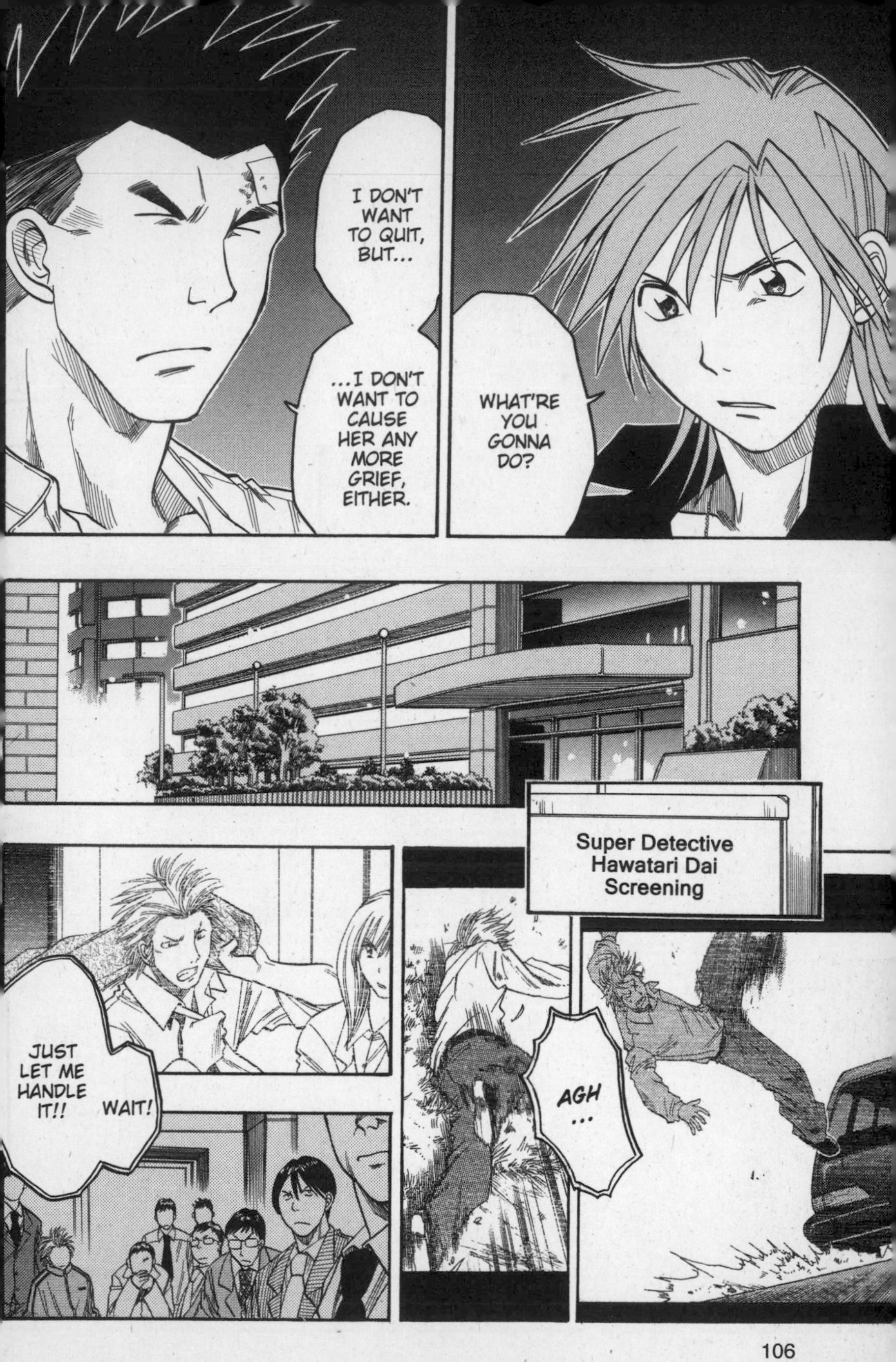
WHAT'RE YOU GONNA DO?
I DON'T WANT TO QUIT, BUT...
...I DON'T WANT TO CAUSE HER ANY MORE GRIEF, EITHER.
Super Detective Hawatari Dai Screening
AGH ...
JUST LET ME HANDLE IT!!
WAIT!

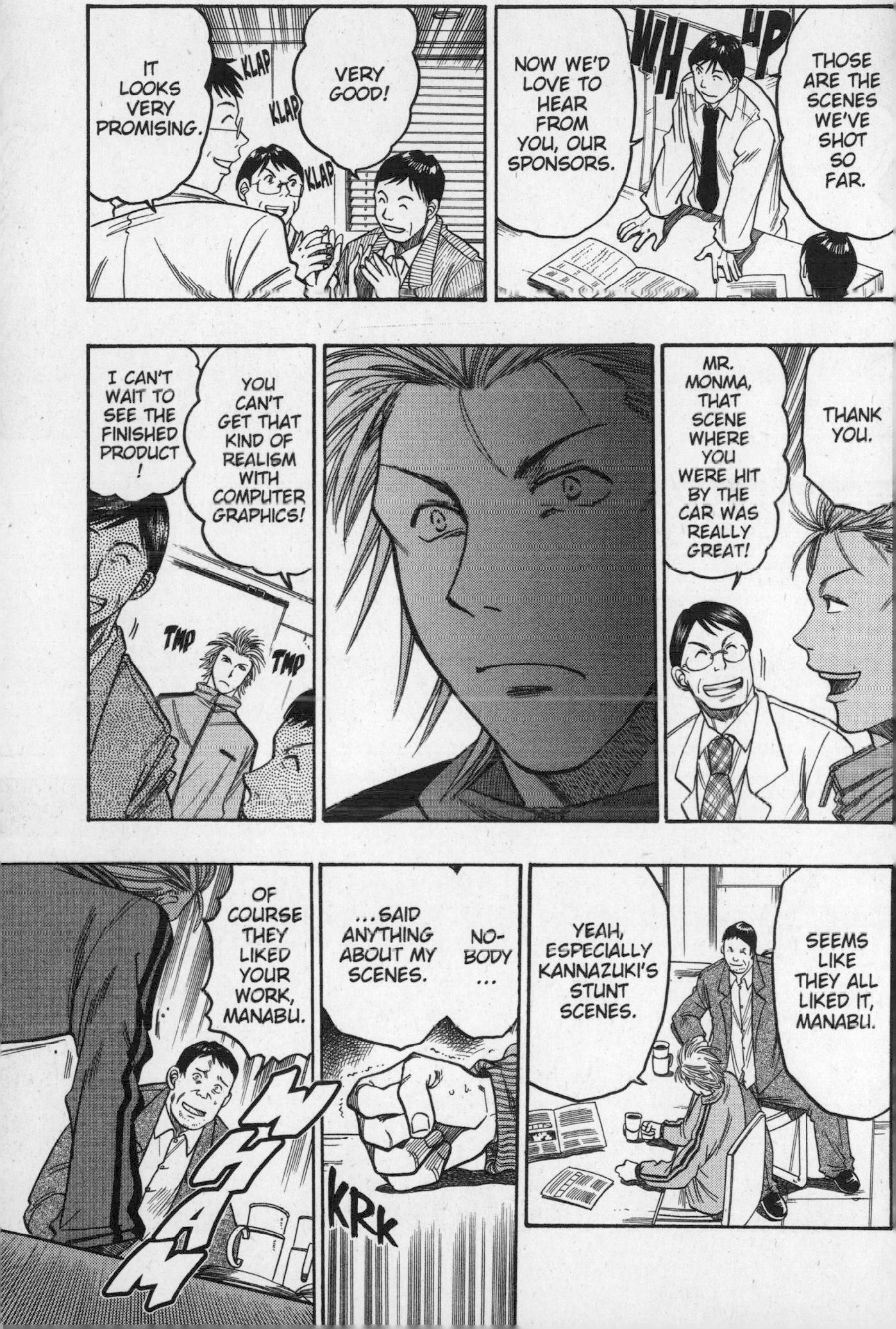
WHUP
THOSE ARE THE SCENES WE'VE SHOT SO FAR.
NOW WE'D LOVE TO HEAR FROM YOU, OUR SPONSORS.
VERY GOOD!
KLAP
KLAP
KLAP
IT LOOKS VERY PROMISING.
THANK YOU.
MR. MONMA, THAT SCENE WHERE YOU WERE HIT BY THE CAR WAS REALLY GREAT!
YOU CAN'T GET THAT KIND OF REALISM WITH COMPUTER GRAPHICS!
I CAN'T WAIT TO SEE THE FINISHED PRODUCT!
TMP
TMP
SEEMS LIKE THEY ALL LIKED IT, MANABU.
YEAH, ESPECIALLY KANNAZUKI'S STUNT SCENES.
NO-BODY...
...SAID ANYTHING ABOUT MY SCENES.
KRK
OF COURSE THEY LIKED YOUR WORK, MANABU.
WHAM

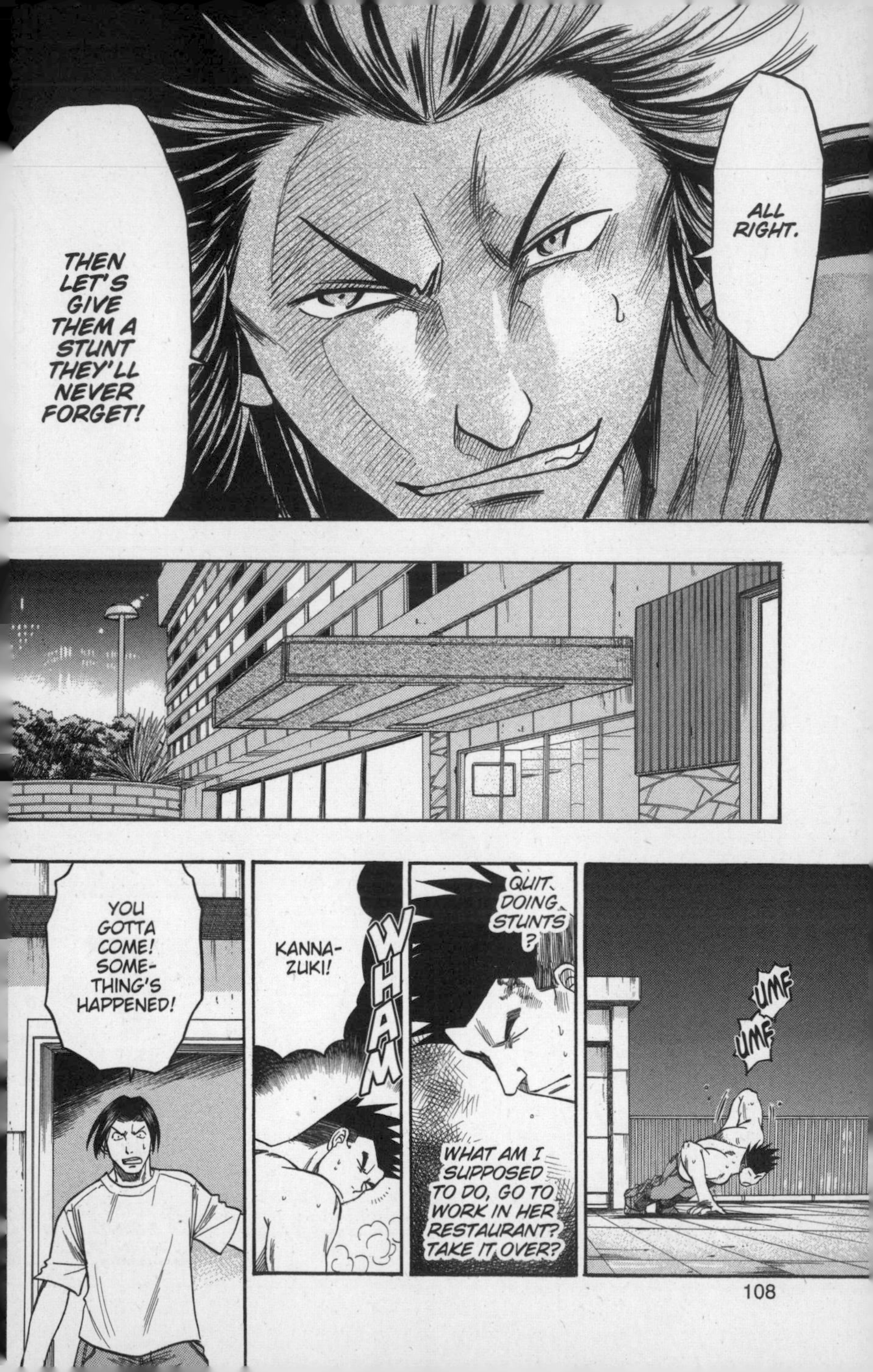
ALL RIGHT.
THEN LET'S GIVE THEM A STUNT THEY'LL NEVER FORGET!
UMF
UMF
QUIT DOING STUNTS?
WHAT AM I SUPPOSED TO DO, GO TO WORK IN HER RESTAURANT? TAKE IT OVER?
WHAM
KANNA-ZUKI!
YOU GOTTA COME! SOME-THING'S HAPPENED!

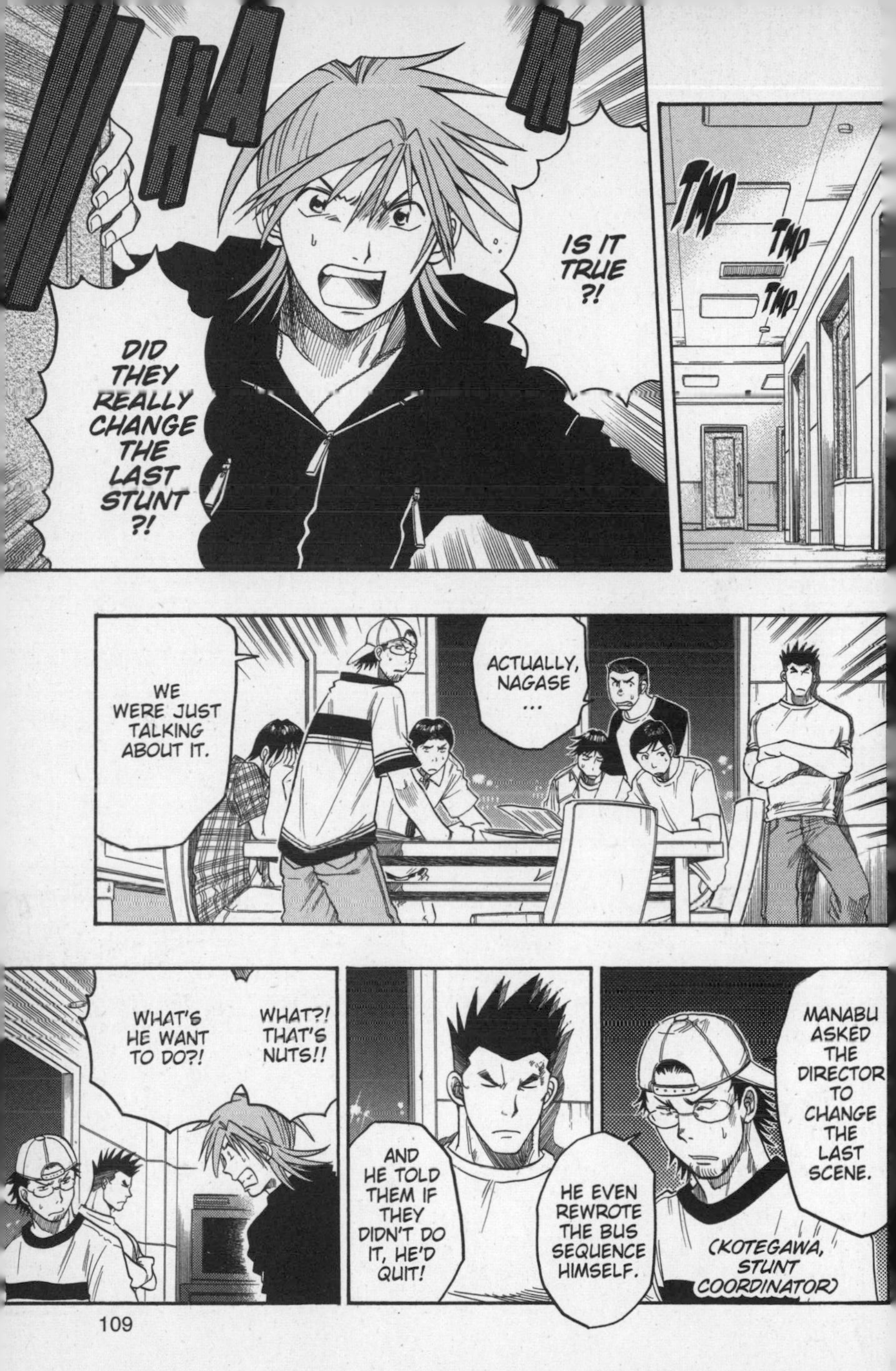
TMP
TMP
TMP
IS IT TRUE?!
DID THEY REALLY CHANGE THE LAST STUNT?!
ACTUALLY, NAGASE...
WE WERE JUST TALKING ABOUT IT.
MANABU ASKED THE DIRECTOR TO CHANGE THE LAST SCENE.
(KOTEGAWA, STUNT COORDINATOR)
HE EVEN REWROTE THE BUS SEQUENCE HIMSELF.
AND HE TOLD THEM IF THEY DIDN'T DO IT, HE'D QUIT!
WHAT?! THAT'S NUTS!!
WHAT'S HE WANT TO DO?!

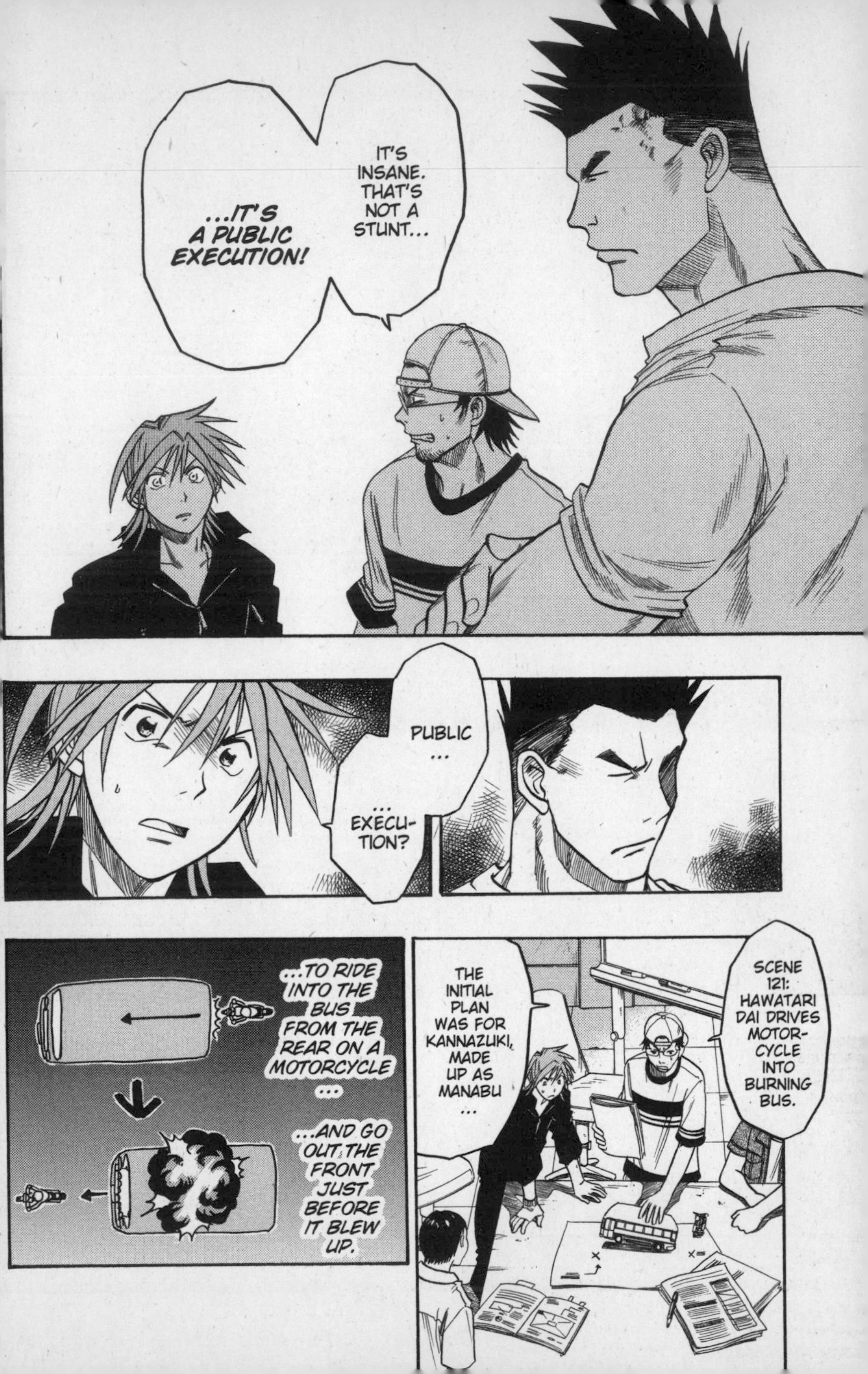
IT'S INSANE. THAT'S NOT A STUNT...
...IT'S A PUBLIC EXECUTION!
PUBLIC...
...EXECUTION?
SCENE 121: HAWATARI DAI DRIVES MOTORCYCLE INTO BURNING BUS.
THE INITIAL PLAN WAS FOR KANNAZUKI, MADE UP AS MANABU...
...TO RIDE INTO THE BUS FROM THE REAR ON A MOTORCYCLE...
...AND GO OUT THE FRONT JUST BEFORE IT BLEW UP.

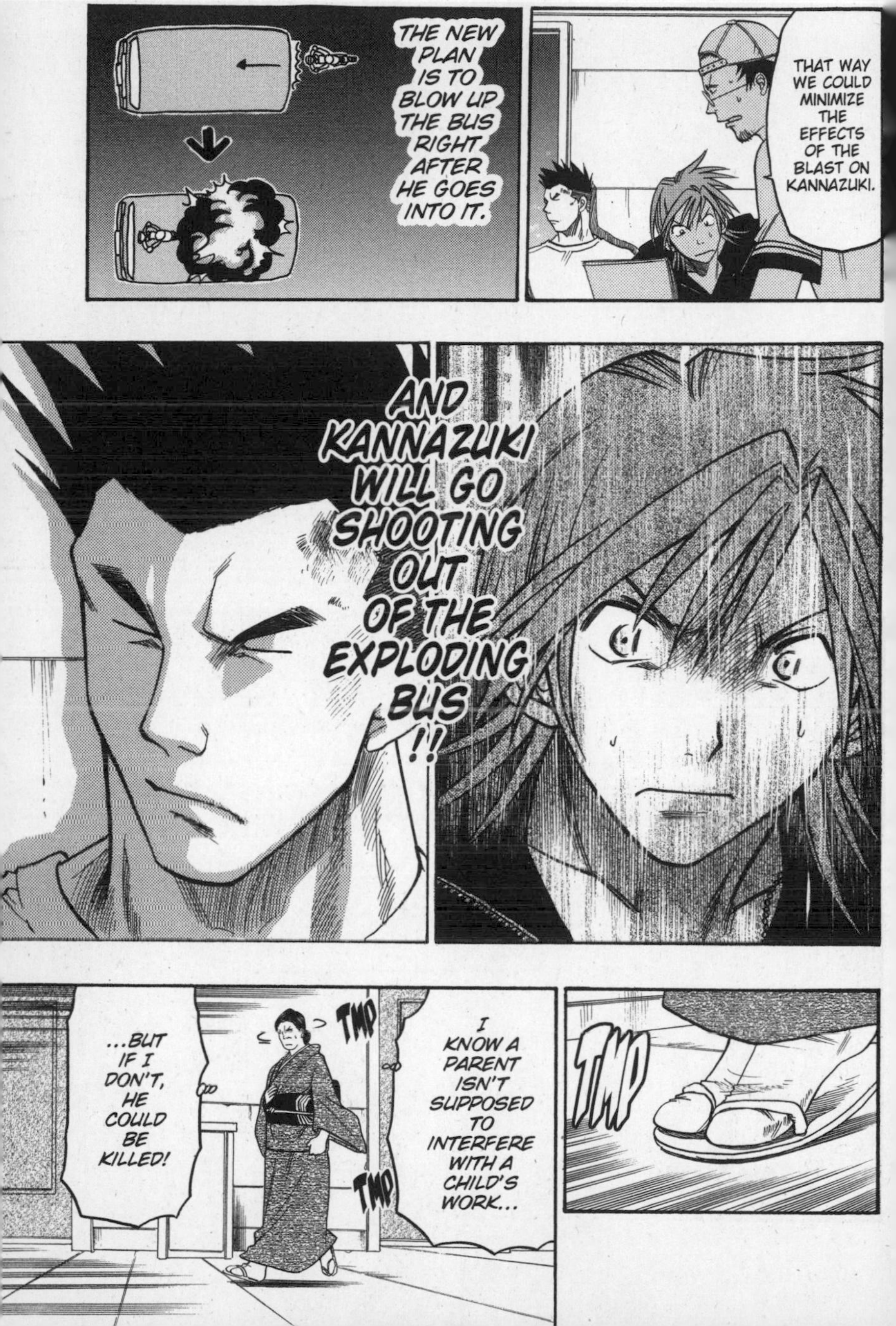
THAT WAY WE COULD MINIMIZE THE EFFECTS OF THE BLAST ON KANNAZUKI.
THE NEW PLAN IS TO BLOW UP THE BUS RIGHT AFTER HE GOES INTO IT.
AND KANNAZUKI WILL GO SHOOTING OUT OF THE EXPLODING BUS !!
TMP
I KNOW A PARENT ISN'T SUPPOSED TO INTERFERE WITH A CHILD'S WORK...
TMP
TMP
...BUT IF I DON'T, HE COULD BE KILLED!

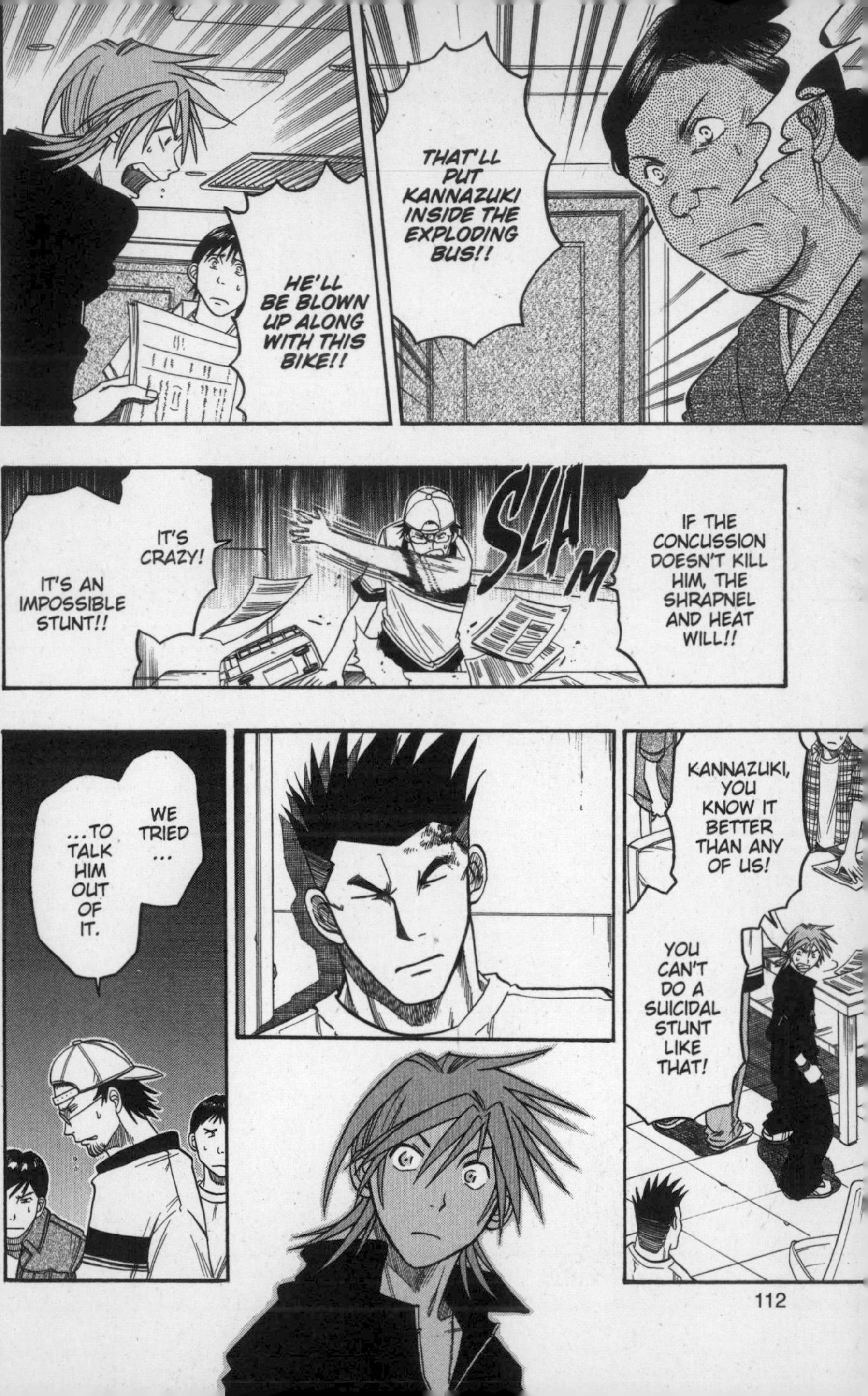
THAT'LL PUT KANNAZUKI INSIDE THE EXPLODING BUS!!
HE'LL BE BLOWN UP ALONG WITH THIS BIKE!!
IF THE CONCUSSION DOESN'T KILL HIM, THE SHRAPNEL AND HEAT WILL!!
SLAM
IT'S CRAZY!
IT'S AN IMPOSSIBLE STUNT!!
KANNAZUKI, YOU KNOW IT BETTER THAN ANY OF US!
YOU CAN'T DO A SUICIDAL STUNT LIKE THAT!
WE TRIED...
...TO TALK HIM OUT OF IT.

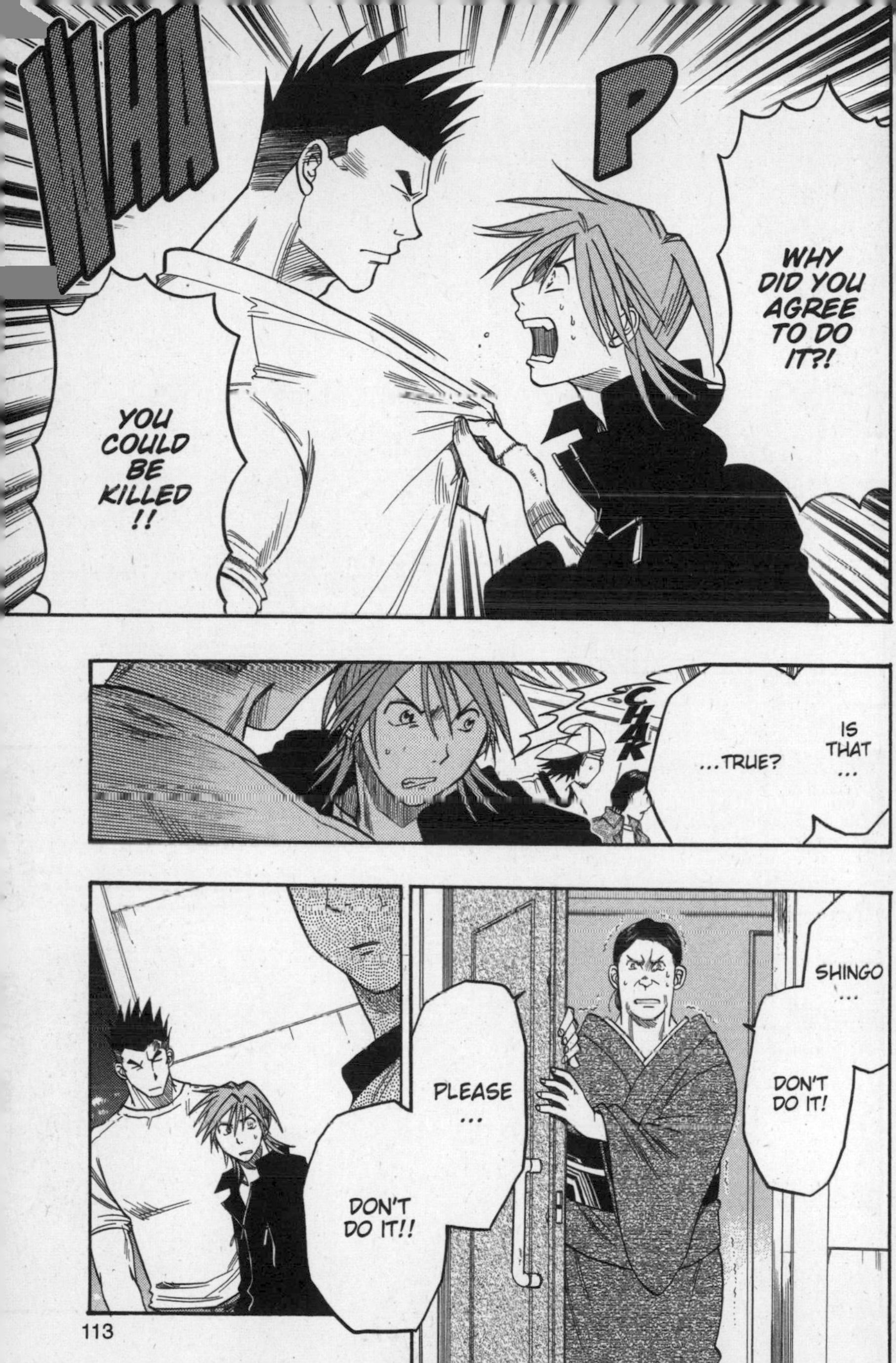
WHAP
WHY DID YOU AGREE TO DO IT?!
YOU COULD BE KILLED!!
CHAK
IS THAT ...
...TRUE?
SHINGO ...
DON'T DO IT!
PLEASE ...
DON'T DO IT!!

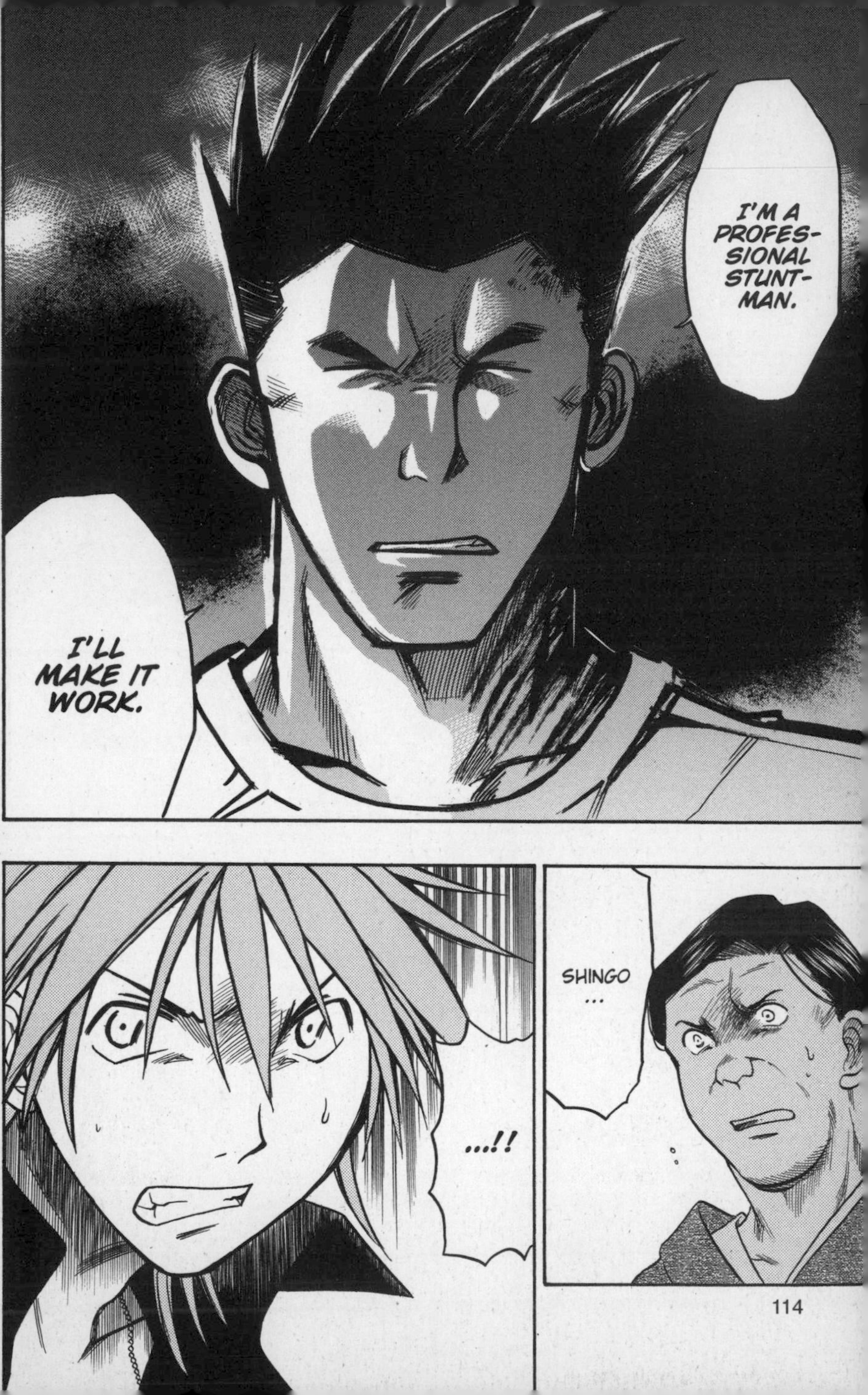
I'M A PROFES-SIONAL STUNT-MAN.
I'LL MAKE IT WORK.
SHINGO ...
...!!

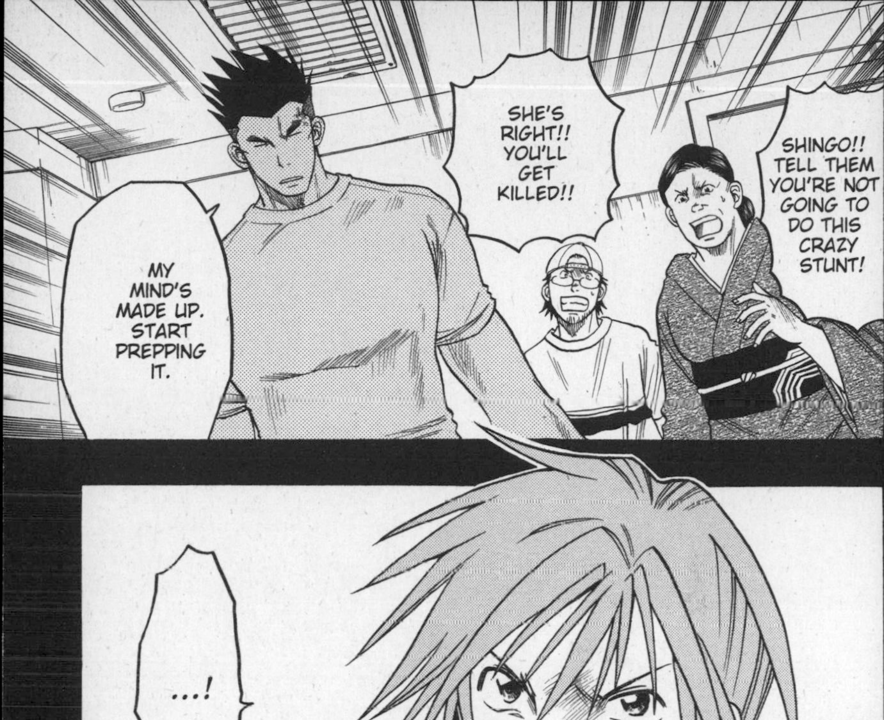
SHINGO!! TELL THEM YOU'RE NOT GOING TO DO THIS CRAZY STUNT!
SHE'S RIGHT!! YOU'LL GET KILLED!!
MY MIND'S MADE UP. START PREPPING IT.
...!

Scene 53:

The Last Action Hero (Part 4)

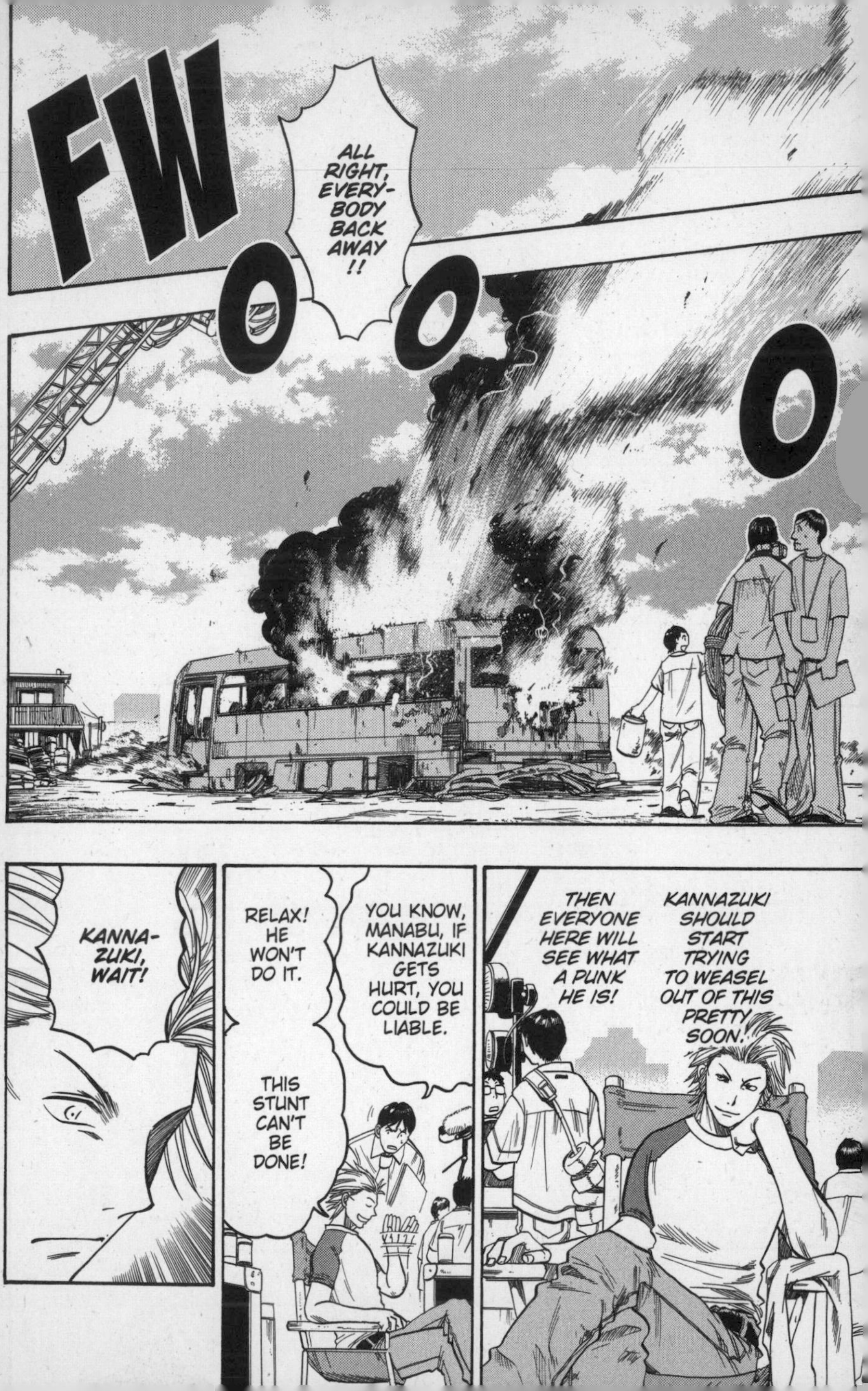
FWOOOO
ALL RIGHT, EVERYBODY BACK AWAY!!
KANNAZUKI SHOULD START TRYING TO WEASEL OUT OF THIS PRETTY SOON.
THEN EVERYONE HERE WILL SEE WHAT A PUNK HE IS!
YOU KNOW, MANABU, IF KANNAZUKI GETS HURT, YOU COULD BE LIABLE.
RELAX! HE WON'T DO IT.
THIS STUNT CAN'T BE DONE!
KANNAZUKI, WAIT!

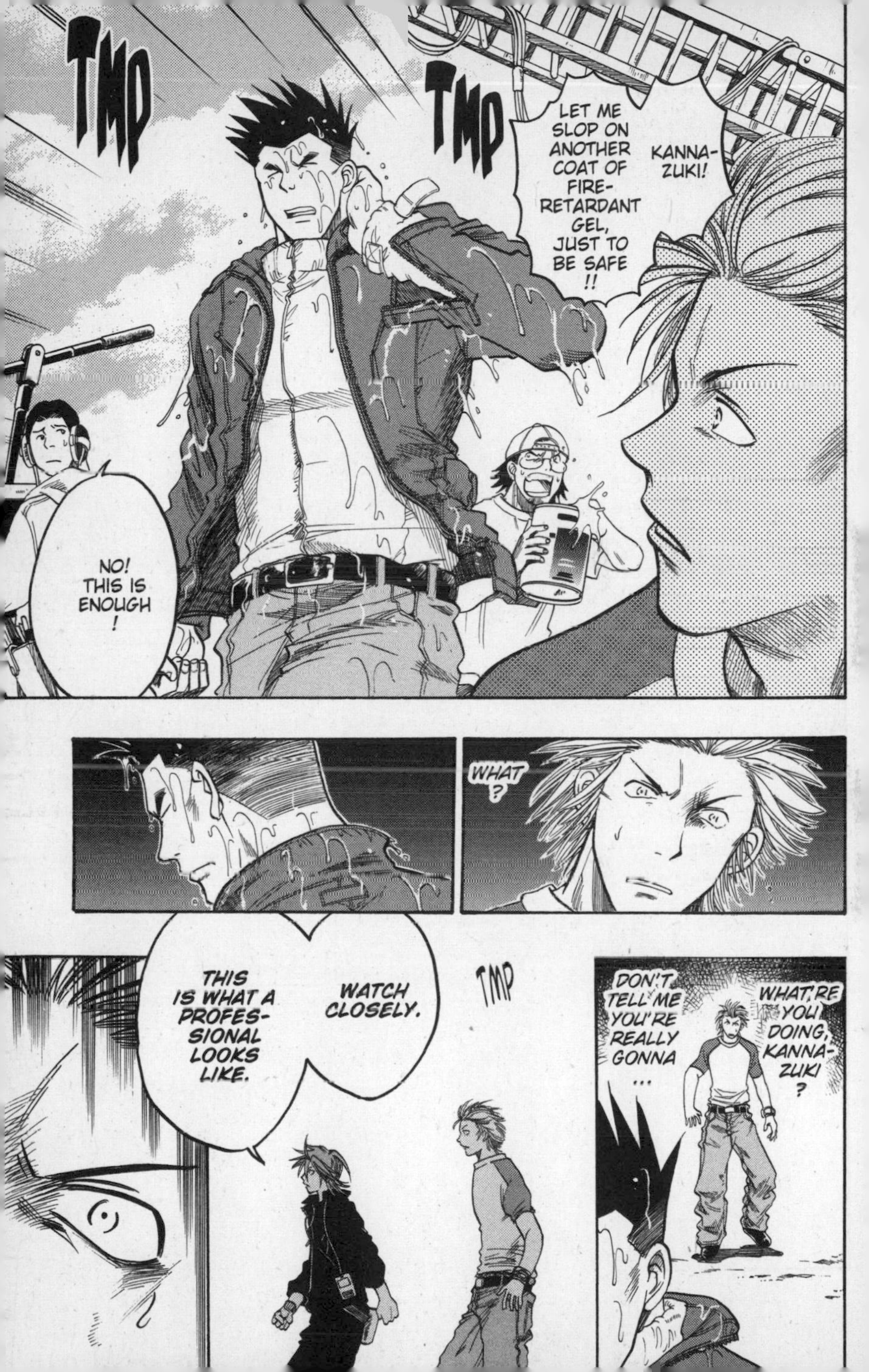
KANNA-ZUKI!
LET ME SLOP ON ANOTHER COAT OF FIRE-RETARDANT GEL, JUST TO BE SAFE!!
TMP
TMP
NO! THIS IS ENOUGH!
WHAT?
WHAT'RE YOU DOING, KANNA-ZUKI?
DON'T TELL ME YOU'RE REALLY GONNA...
TMP
WATCH CLOSELY.
THIS IS WHAT A PROFES-SIONAL LOOKS LIKE.

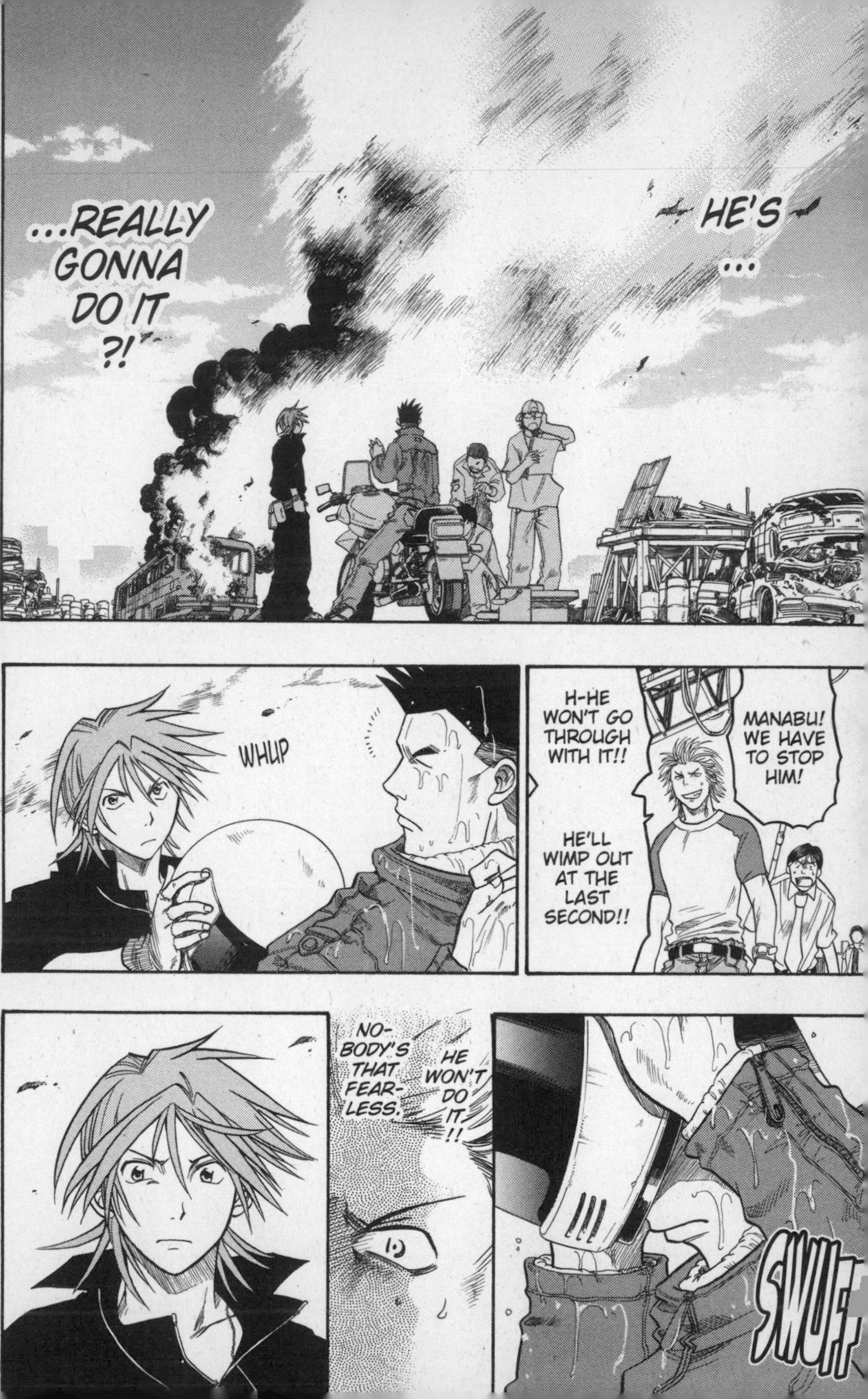
HE'S ...
...REALLY GONNA DO IT ?!
MANABU! WE HAVE TO STOP HIM!
H-HE WON'T GO THROUGH WITH IT!!
HE'LL WIMP OUT AT THE LAST SECOND!!
WHUP
SWUFF
HE WON'T DO IT!!
NO-BODY'S THAT FEAR-LESS.

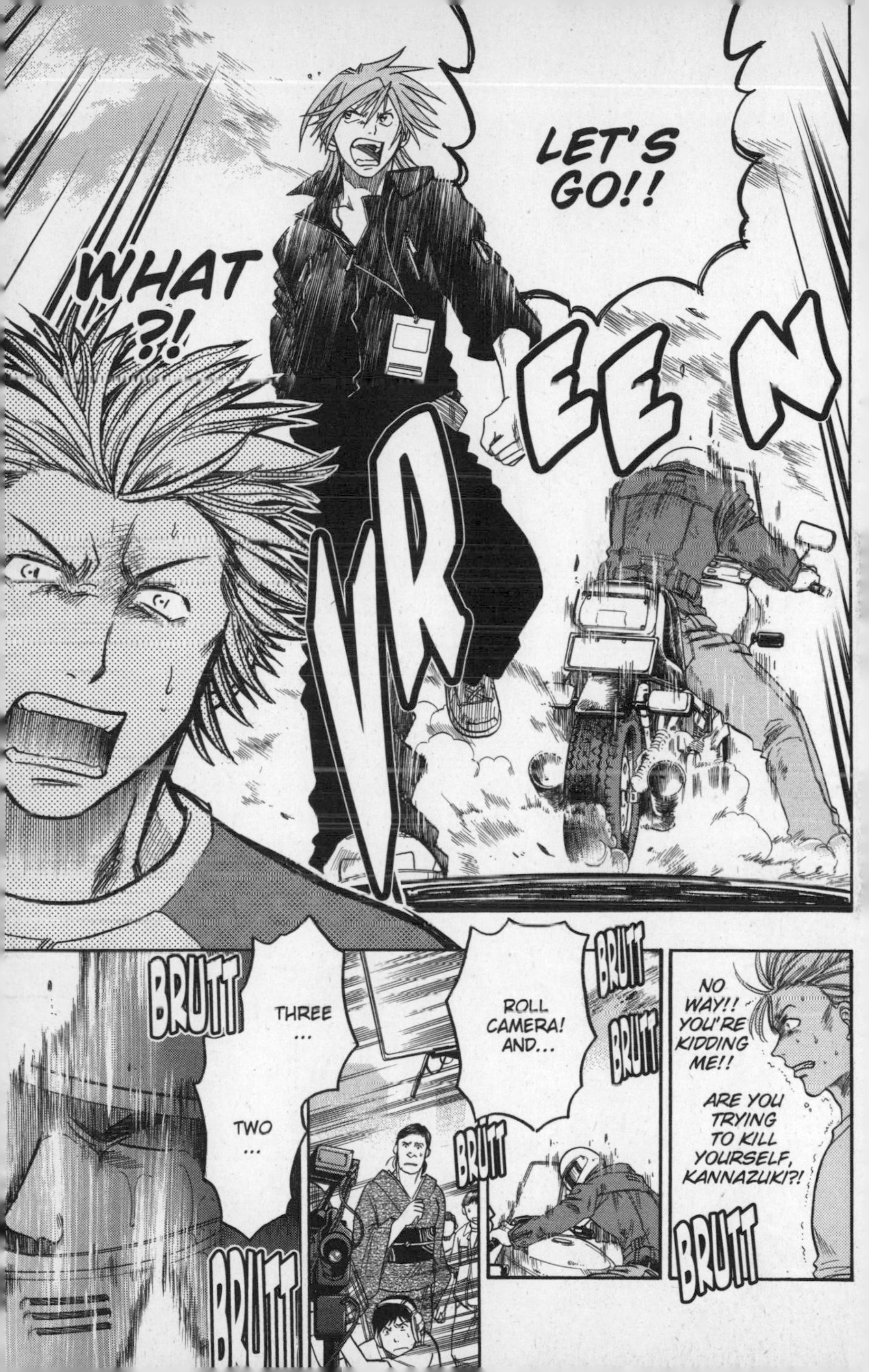
LET'S GO!!
VREEN
WHAT ?!
NO WAY!! YOU'RE KIDDING ME!!
ARE YOU TRYING TO KILL YOURSELF, KANNAZUKI?!
BRUTT
BRUTT
BRUTT
ROLL CAMERA! AND...
BRUTT
BRUTT
...
THREE ...
TWO ...
BRUTT

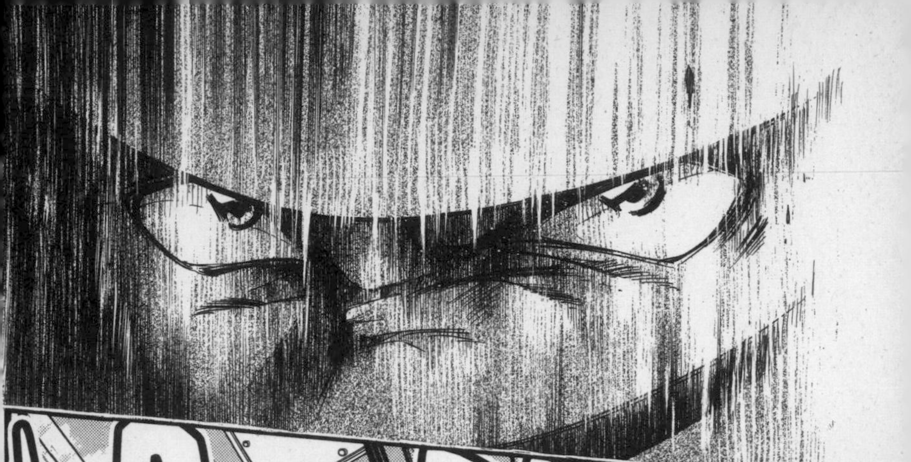

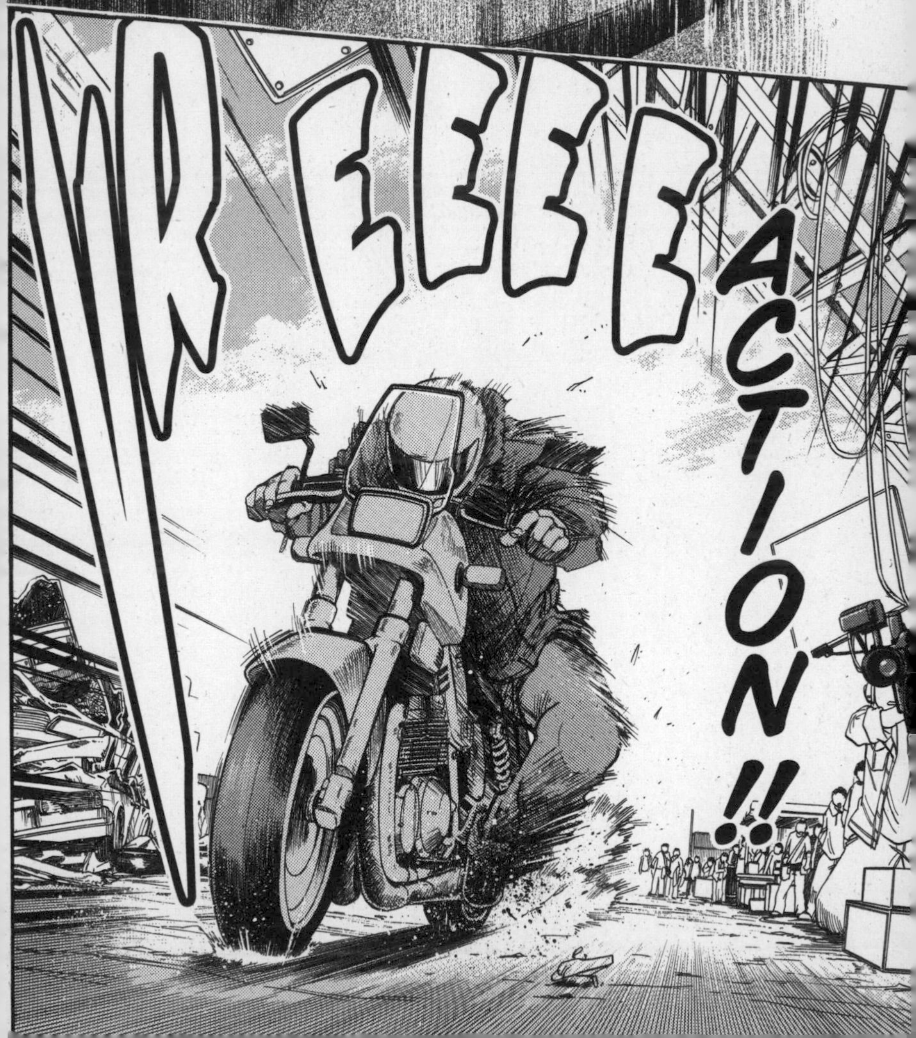
VREEEE
ACTION!!

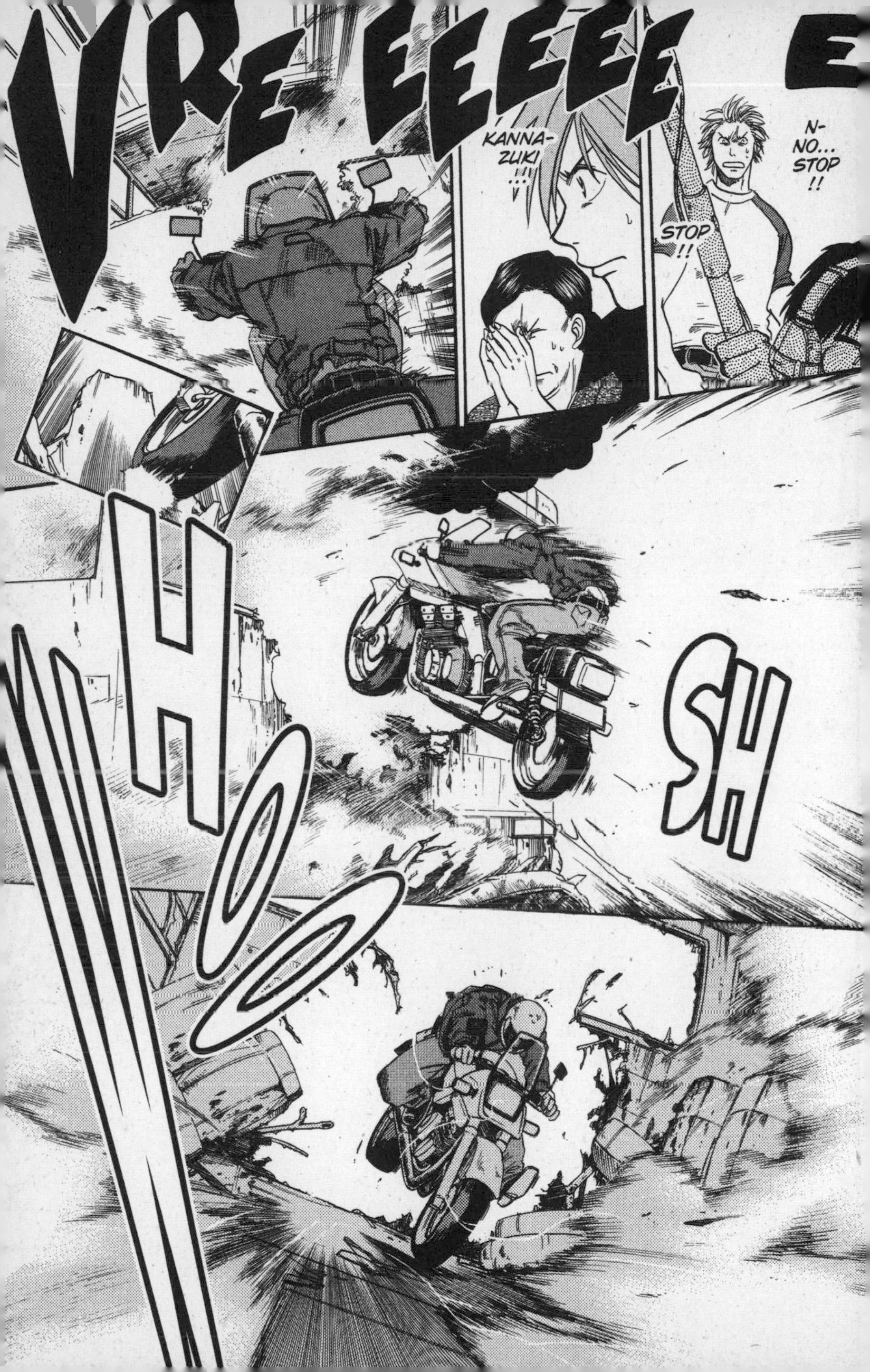
VREEEEEE E
N-NO... STOP!!
STOP!!
KANNAZUKI...!!
WHOOOSH

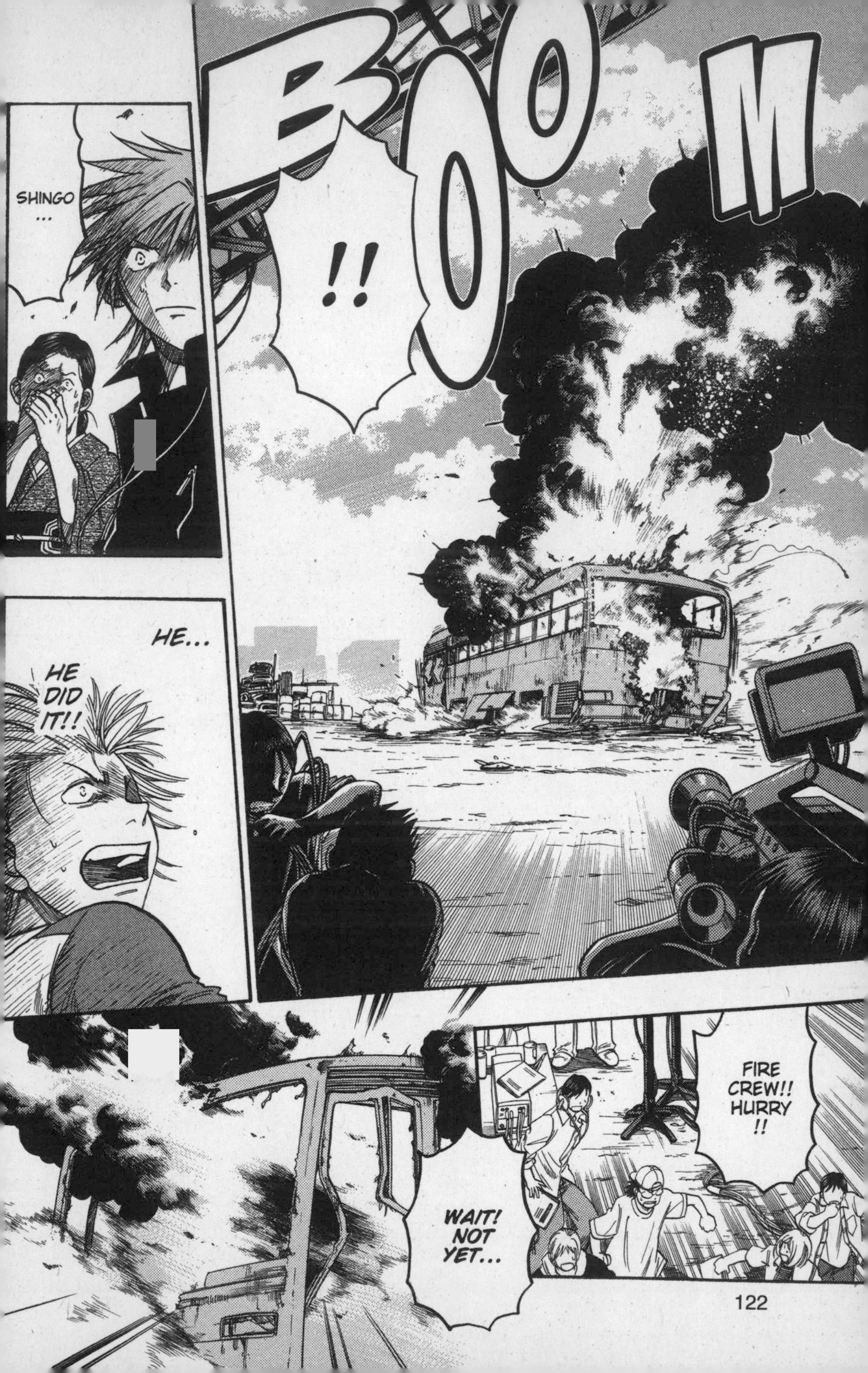
BOOOM
!!
SHINGO ...
HE...
HE DID IT!!
FIRE CREW!! HURRY !!
WAIT! NOT YET...

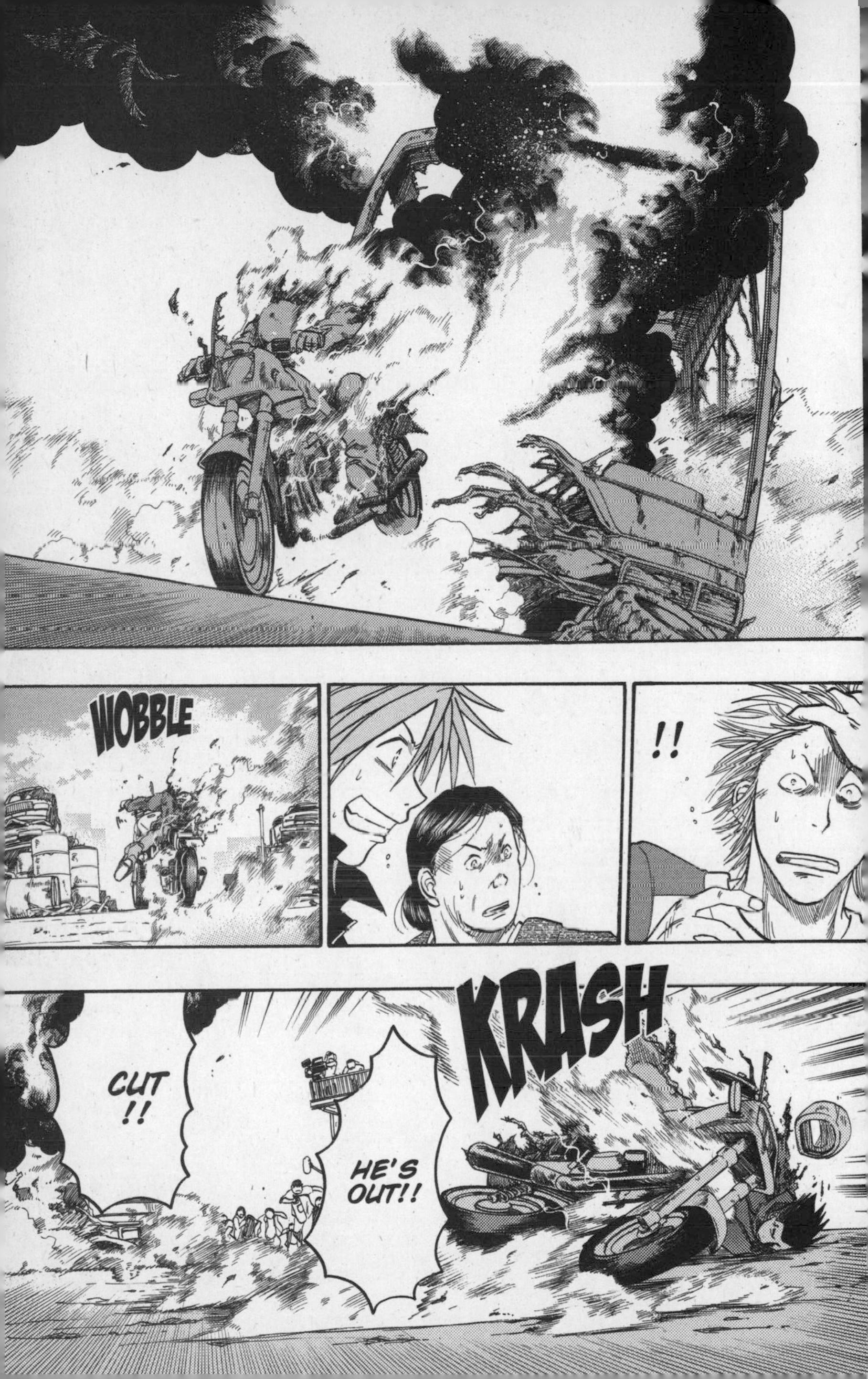
!!
WOBBLE
KRASH
HE'S OUT!!
CUT!!

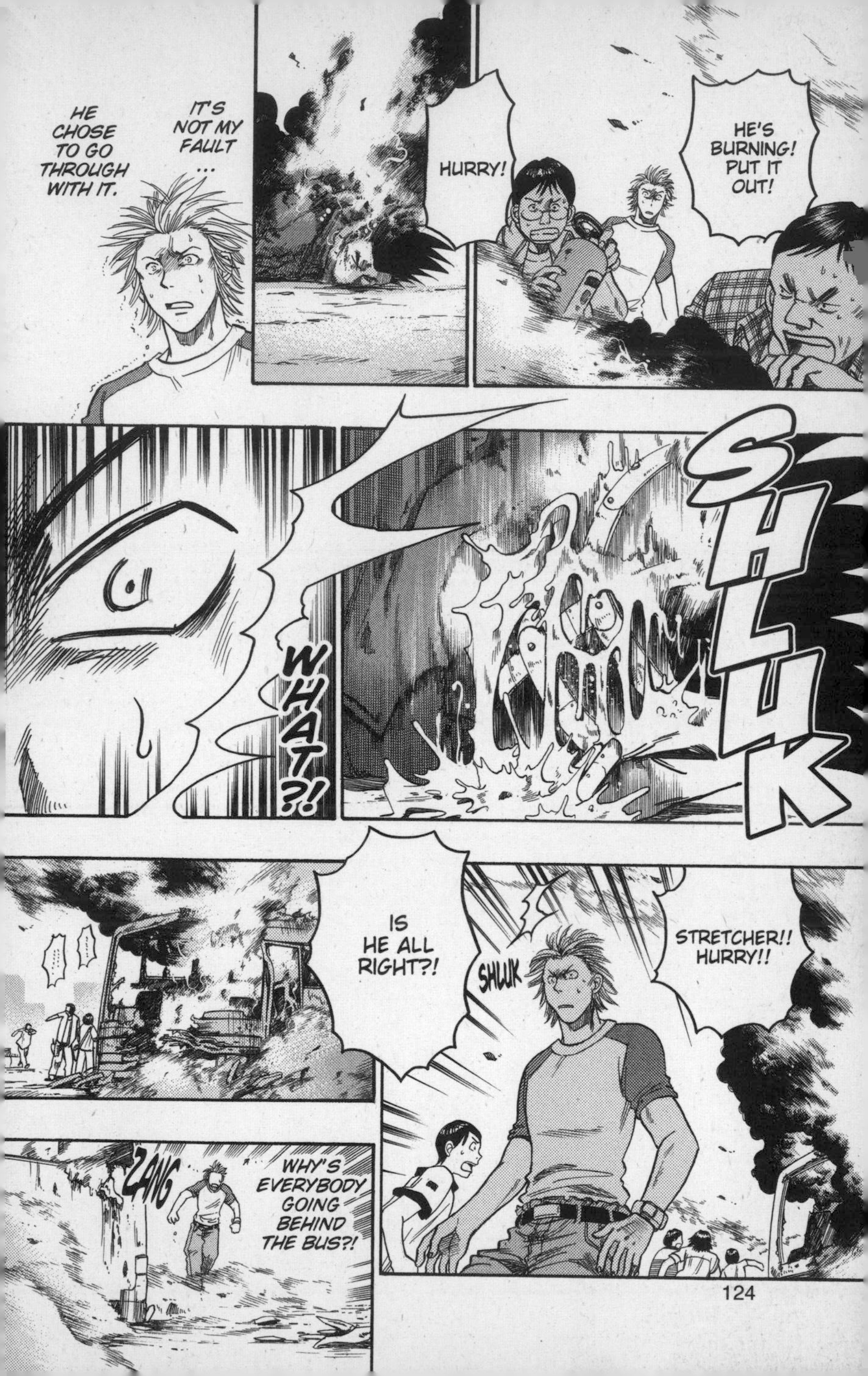
HE'S BURNING! PUT IT OUT!
HURRY!
IT'S NOT MY FAULT ...
HE CHOSE TO GO THROUGH WITH IT.
SHLUK
WHAT?!
STRETCHER!! HURRY!!
IS HE ALL RIGHT?!
SHLUK
WHY'S EVERYBODY GOING BEHIND THE BUS?!
ZANG

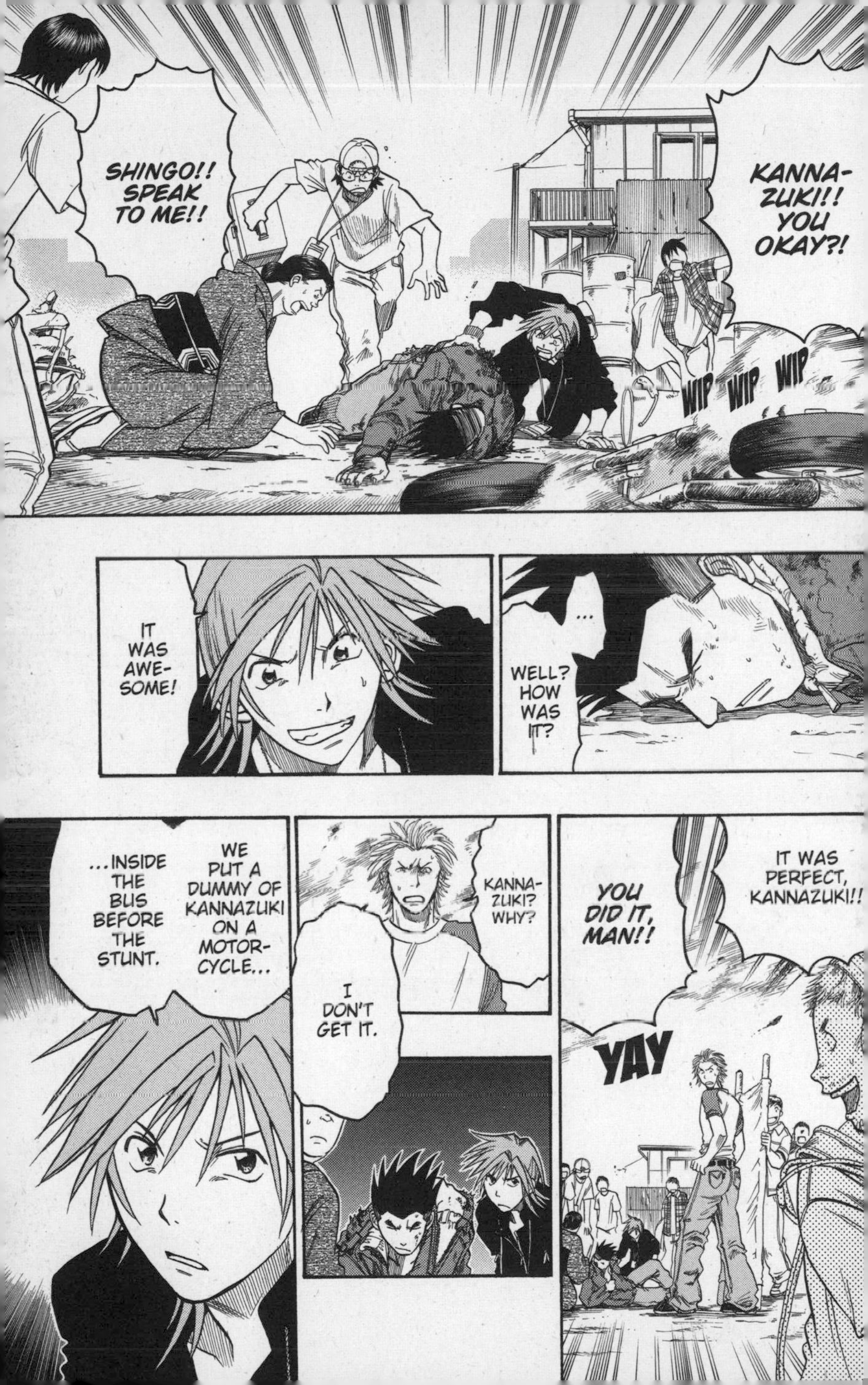
KANNA-ZUKI!! YOU OKAY?!
SHINGO!! SPEAK TO ME!!
WIP WIP WIP
...
WELL? HOW WAS IT?
IT WAS AWE-SOME!
IT WAS PERFECT, KANNAZUKI!!
YOU DID IT, MAN!!
YAY
KANNA-ZUKI? WHY?
I DON'T GET IT.
WE PUT A DUMMY OF KANNAZUKI ON A MOTOR-CYCLE...
...INSIDE THE BUS BEFORE THE STUNT.

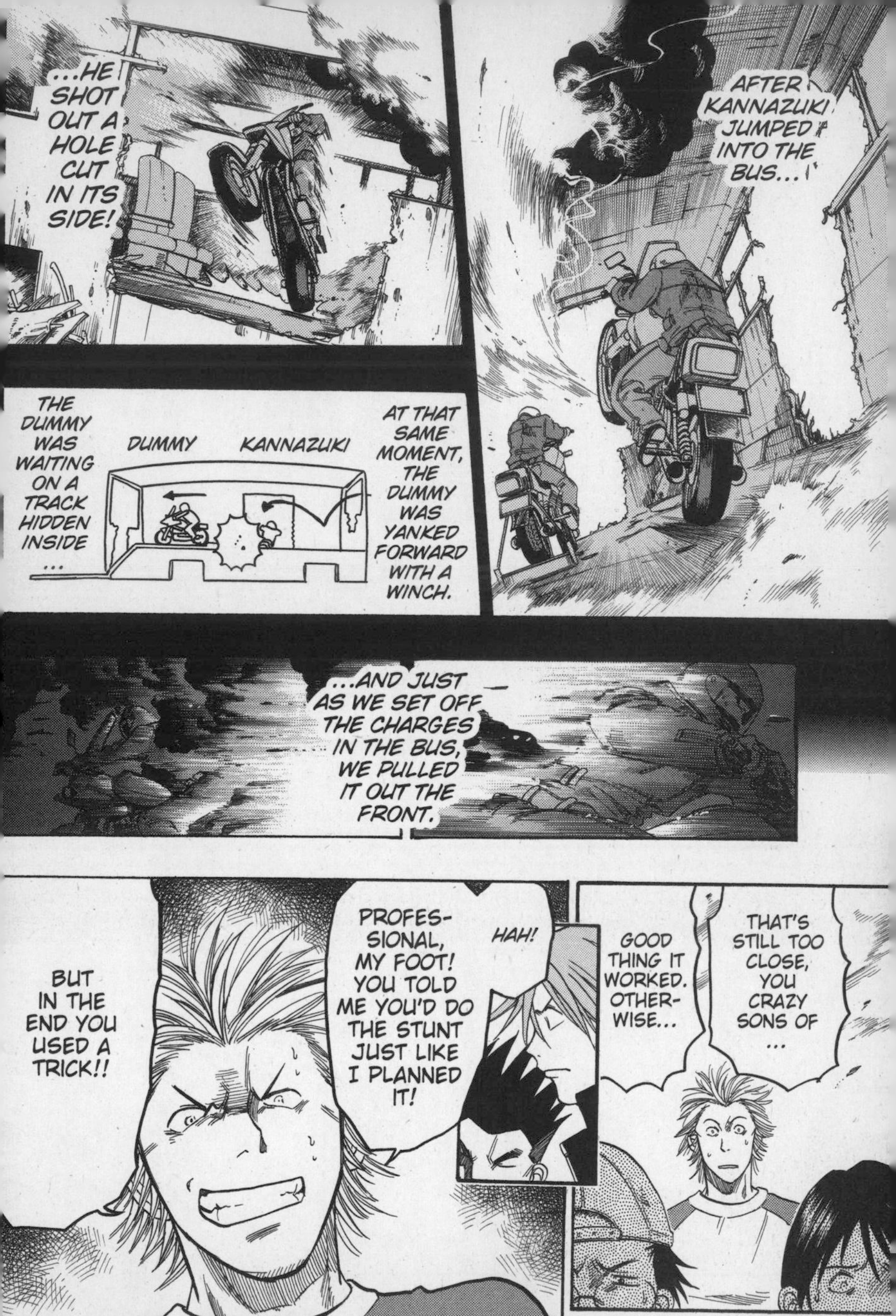
AFTER KANNAZUKI JUMPED INTO THE BUS...
...HE SHOT OUT A HOLE CUT IN ITS SIDE!
AT THAT SAME MOMENT, THE DUMMY WAS YANKED FORWARD WITH A WINCH.
KANNAZUKI
DUMMY
THE DUMMY WAS WAITING ON A TRACK HIDDEN INSIDE...
...AND JUST AS WE SET OFF THE CHARGES IN THE BUS, WE PULLED IT OUT THE FRONT.
THAT'S STILL TOO CLOSE, YOU CRAZY SONS OF...
GOOD THING IT WORKED. OTHERWISE...
HAH!
PROFESSIONAL, MY FOOT! YOU TOLD ME YOU'D DO THE STUNT JUST LIKE I PLANNED IT!
BUT IN THE END YOU USED A TRICK!!

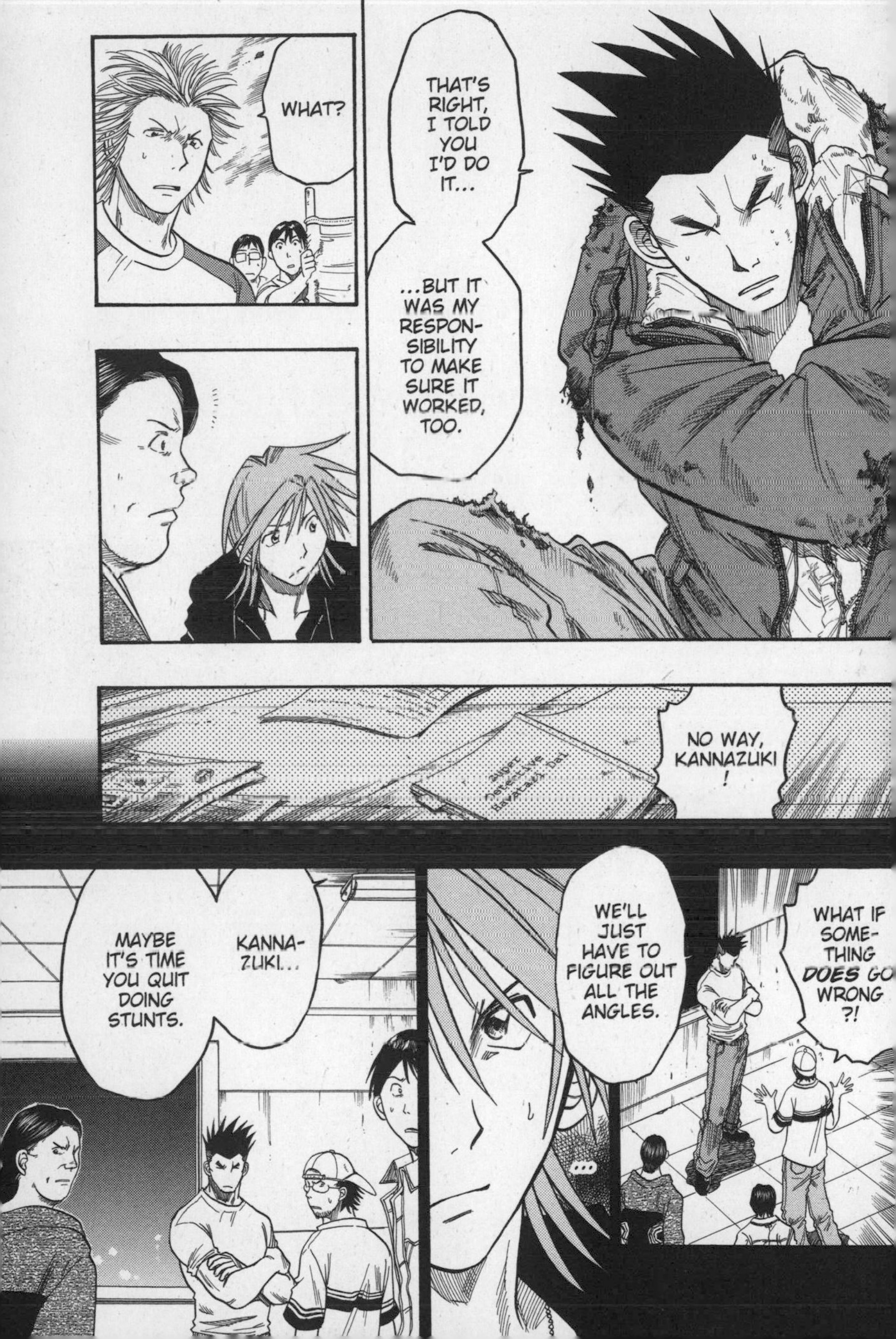
THAT'S RIGHT, I TOLD YOU I'D DO IT...
...BUT IT WAS MY RESPONSIBILITY TO MAKE SURE IT WORKED, TOO.
WHAT?
NO WAY, KANNAZUKI!
WHAT IF SOMETHING **DOES** GO WRONG?!
...
WE'LL JUST HAVE TO FIGURE OUT ALL THE ANGLES.
KANNAZUKI...
MAYBE IT'S TIME YOU QUIT DOING STUNTS.

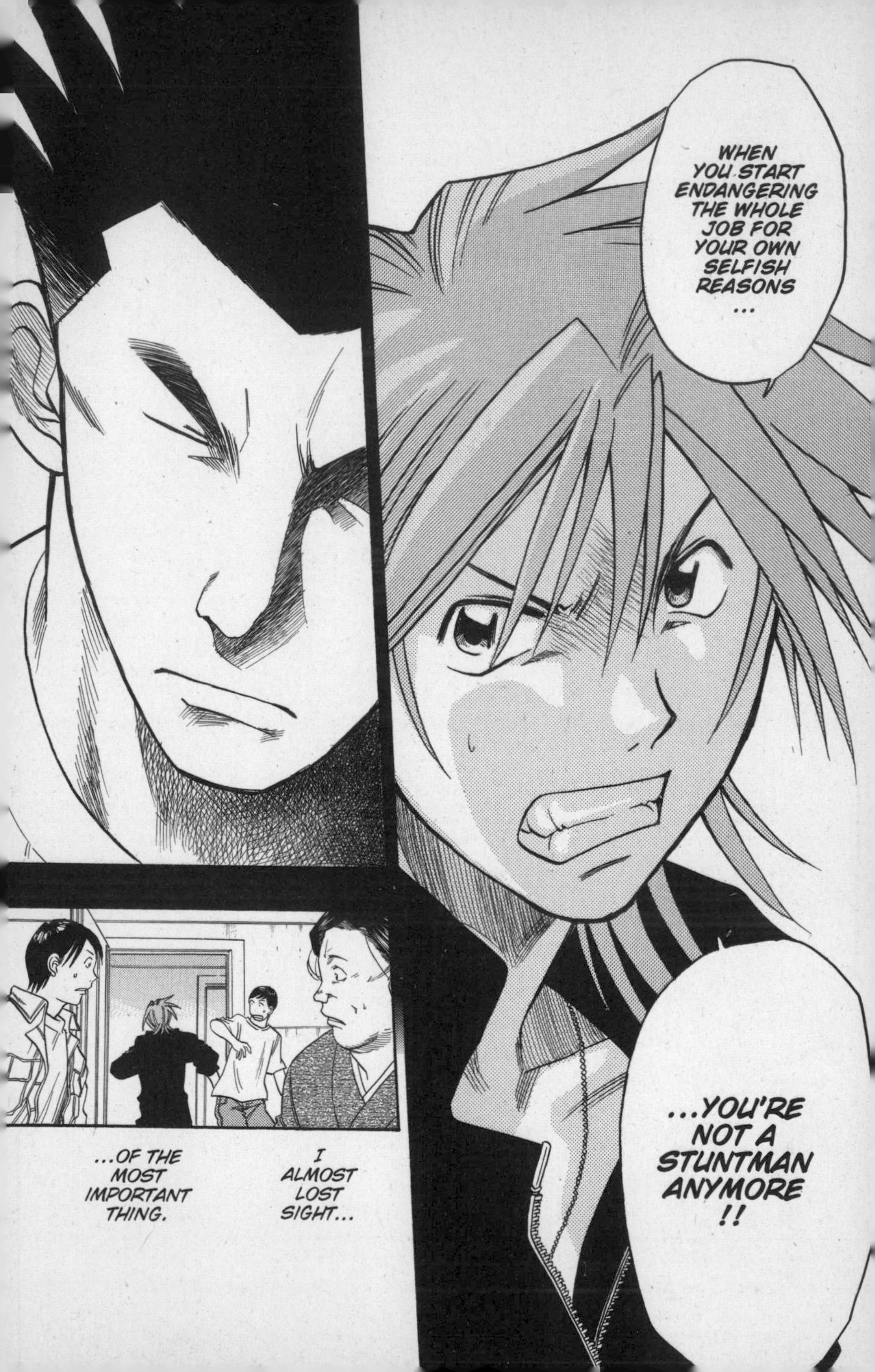
WHEN YOU START ENDANGERING THE WHOLE JOB FOR YOUR OWN SELFISH REASONS ...
...YOU'RE NOT A STUNTMAN ANYMORE !!
I ALMOST LOST SIGHT...
...OF THE MOST IMPORTANT THING.

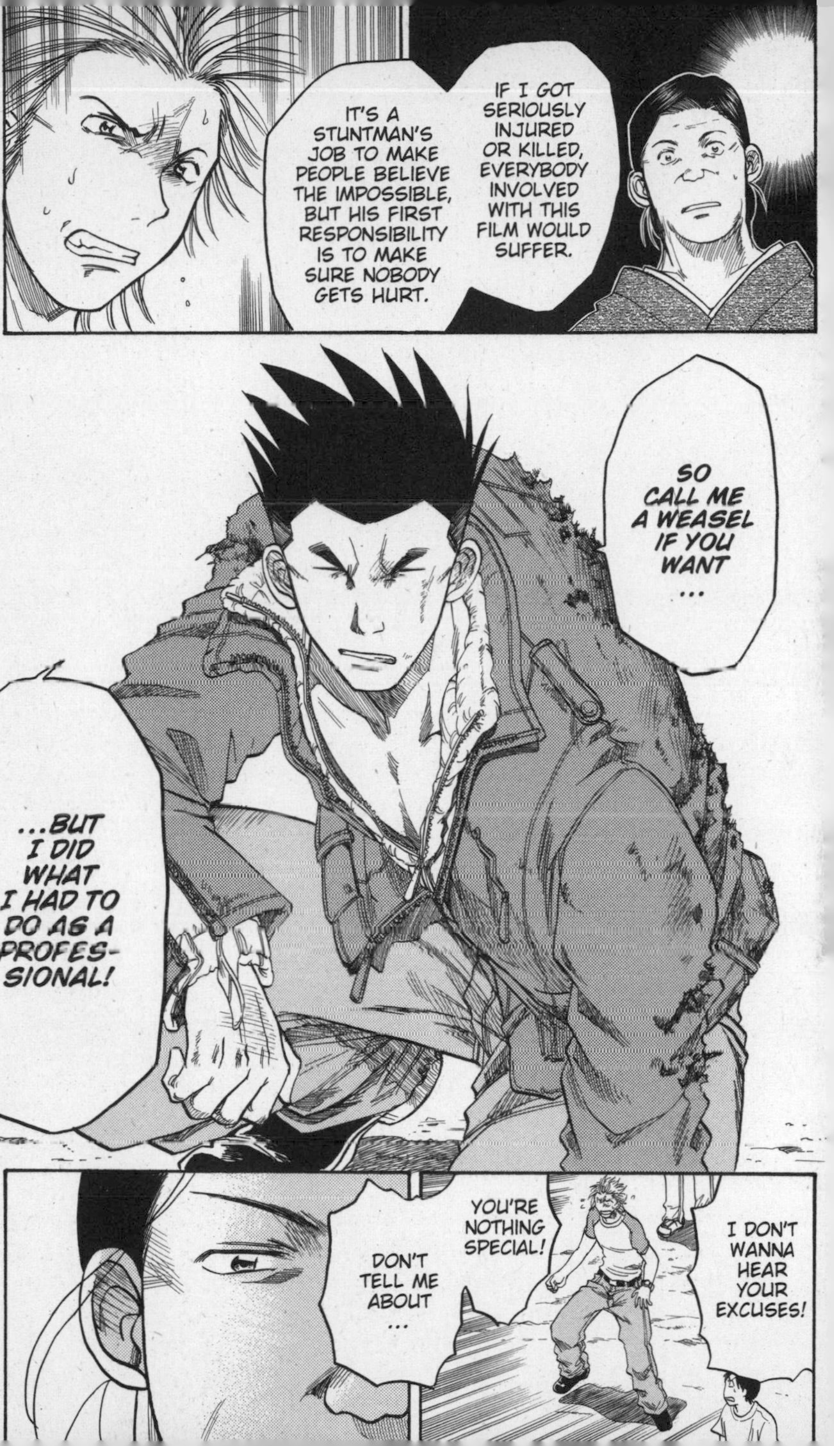
IF I GOT SERIOUSLY INJURED OR KILLED, EVERYBODY INVOLVED WITH THIS FILM WOULD SUFFER.
IT'S A STUNTMAN'S JOB TO MAKE PEOPLE BELIEVE THE IMPOSSIBLE, BUT HIS FIRST RESPONSIBILITY IS TO MAKE SURE NOBODY GETS HURT.
SO CALL ME A WEASEL IF YOU WANT ...
...BUT I DID WHAT I HAD TO DO AS A PROFES-SIONAL!
I DON'T WANNA HEAR YOUR EXCUSES!
YOU'RE NOTHING SPECIAL!
DON'T TELL ME ABOUT ...

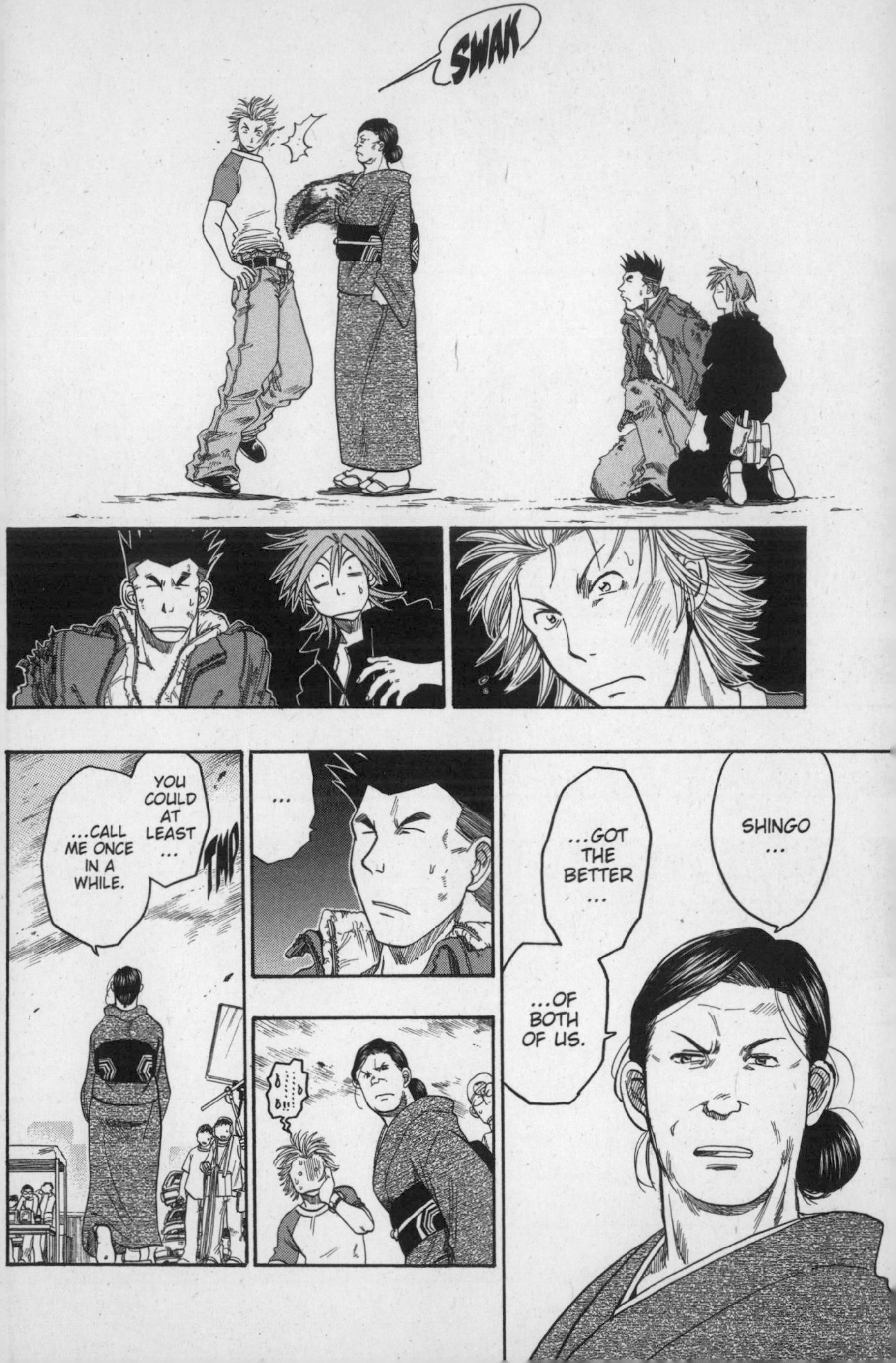
SWAK
SHINGO ...
...GOT THE BETTER ...
...OF BOTH OF US.
...
YOU COULD AT LEAST ...
...CALL ME ONCE IN A WHILE.
TMP

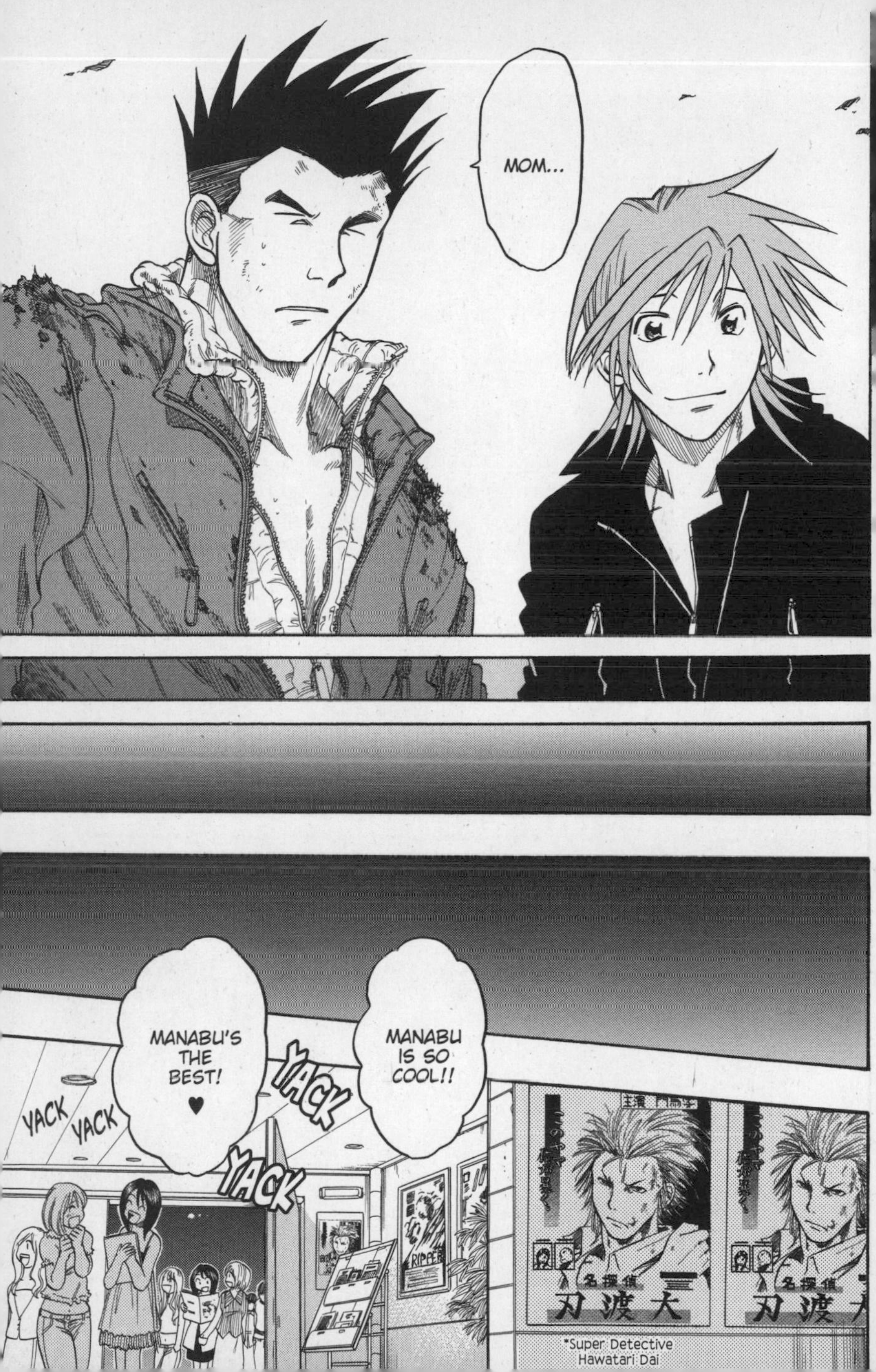
MOM...
MANABU IS SO COOL!!
YACK
MANABU'S THE BEST! ♥
YACK YACK
YACK
名探偵
刃渡大
名探偵
刃渡
RIPPER
*Super Detective Hawatari Dai

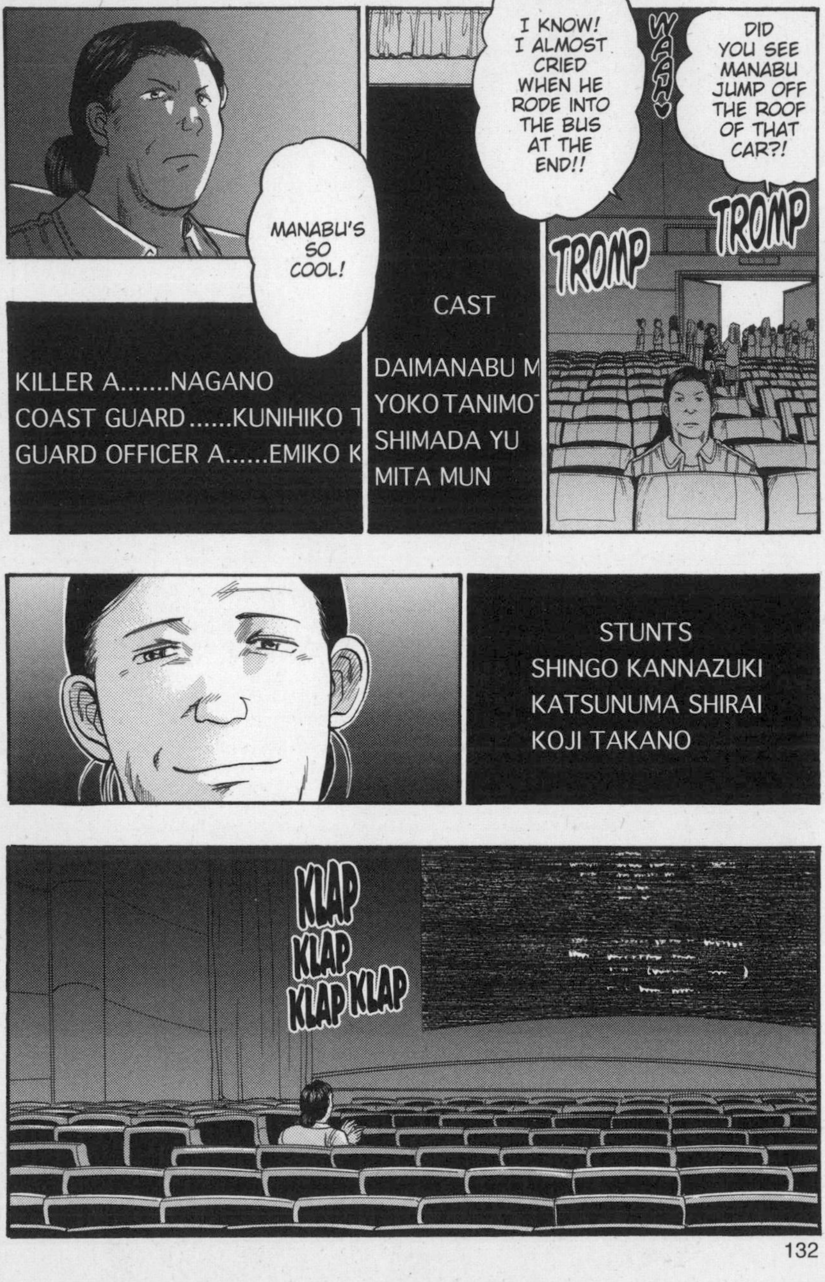
DID YOU SEE MANABU JUMP OFF THE ROOF OF THAT CAR?!
WAAH♥
I KNOW! I ALMOST CRIED WHEN HE RODE INTO THE BUS AT THE END!!
TROMP
TROMP
CAST
DAIMANABU M
YOKO TANIMOT
SHIMADA YU
MITA MUN
MANABU'S SO COOL!
KILLER A.......NAGANO
COAST GUARD......KUNIHIKO T
GUARD OFFICER A......EMIKO K
STUNTS
SHINGO KANNAZUKI
KATSUNUMA SHIRAI
KOJI TAKANO
KLAP
KLAP
KLAP KLAP

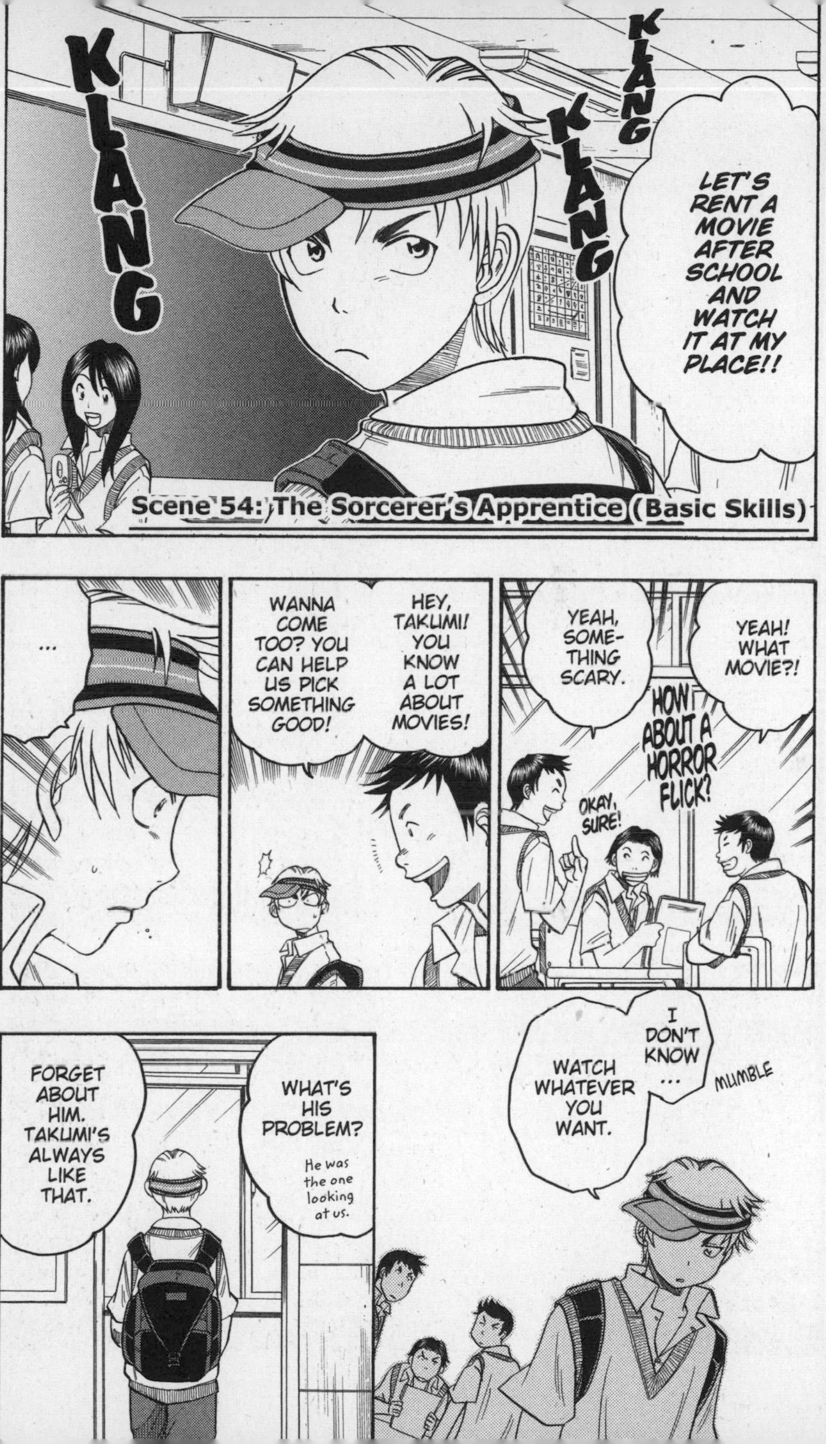
KLANG
KLANG
KLANG
LET'S RENT A MOVIE AFTER SCHOOL AND WATCH IT AT MY PLACE!!
Scene 54: The Sorcerer's Apprentice (Basic Skills)
YEAH! WHAT MOVIE?!
YEAH, SOMETHING SCARY.
HOW ABOUT A HORROR FLICK?
OKAY, SURE!
HEY, TAKUMI! YOU KNOW A LOT ABOUT MOVIES!
WANNA COME TOO? YOU CAN HELP US PICK SOMETHING GOOD!
...
I DON'T KNOW...
MUMBLE
WATCH WHATEVER YOU WANT.
WHAT'S HIS PROBLEM?
He was the one looking at us.
FORGET ABOUT HIM. TAKUMI'S ALWAYS LIKE THAT.

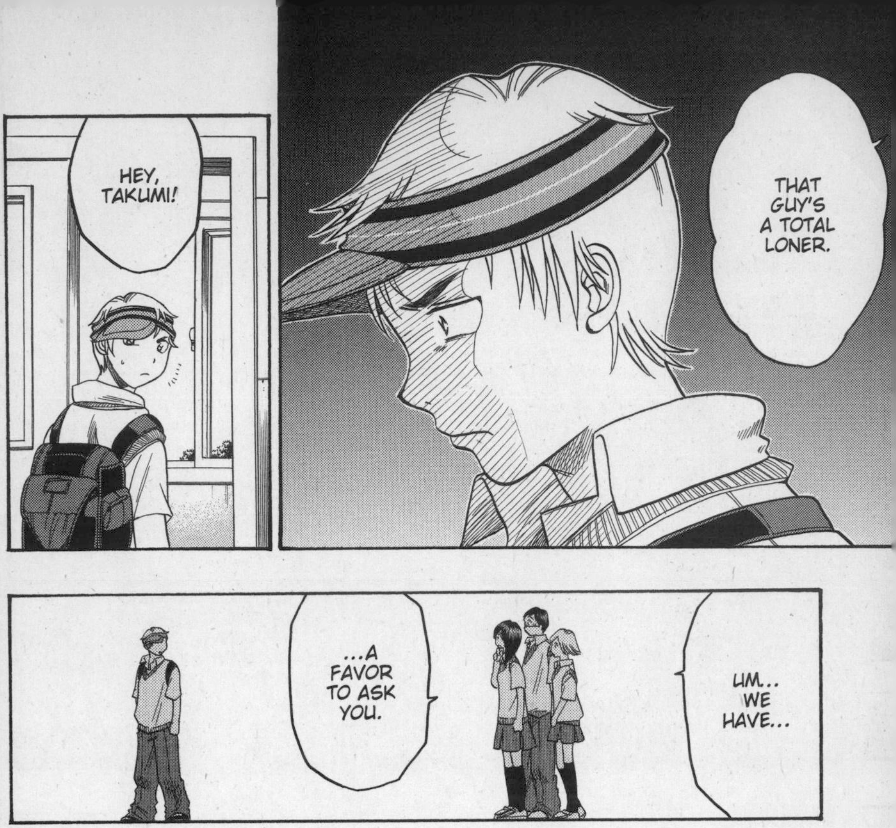
THAT GUY'S A TOTAL LONER.
HEY, TAKUMI!
UM... WE HAVE...
...A FAVOR TO ASK YOU.

Scene 54:

The Sorcerer's Apprentice (Basic Skills)

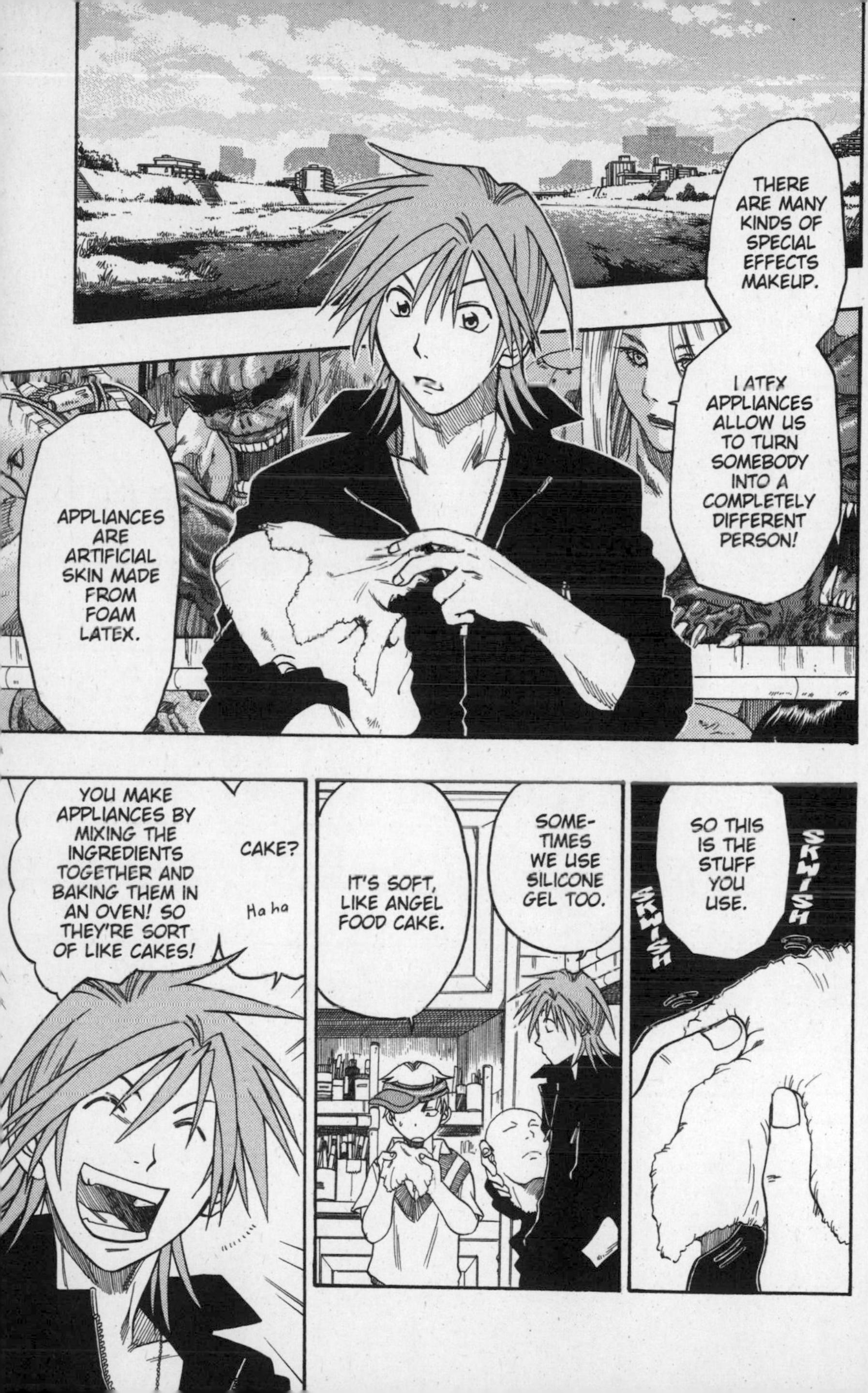
THERE ARE MANY KINDS OF SPECIAL EFFECTS MAKEUP.
LATEX APPLIANCES ALLOW US TO TURN SOMEBODY INTO A COMPLETELY DIFFERENT PERSON!
APPLIANCES ARE ARTIFICIAL SKIN MADE FROM FOAM LATEX.
SO THIS IS THE STUFF YOU USE.
SKWISH
SKWISH
SOME-TIMES WE USE SILICONE GEL TOO.
IT'S SOFT, LIKE ANGEL FOOD CAKE.
CAKE?
YOU MAKE APPLIANCES BY MIXING THE INGREDIENTS TOGETHER AND BAKING THEM IN AN OVEN! SO THEY'RE SORT OF LIKE CAKES!
Ha ha

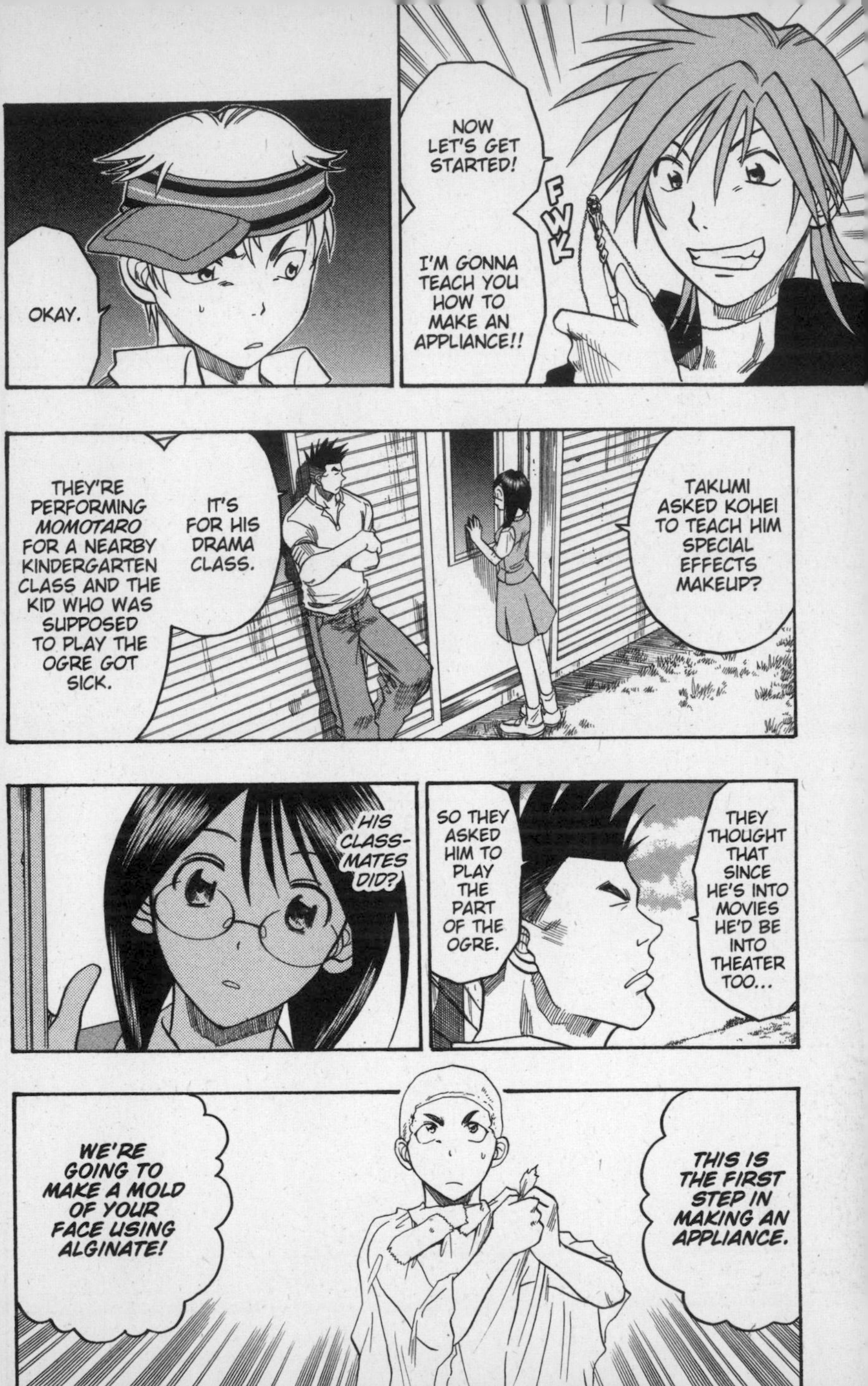
NOW LET'S GET STARTED!
FWK
I'M GONNA TEACH YOU HOW TO MAKE AN APPLIANCE!!
OKAY.
TAKUMI ASKED KOHEI TO TEACH HIM SPECIAL EFFECTS MAKEUP?
IT'S FOR HIS DRAMA CLASS.
THEY'RE PERFORMING *MOMOTARO* FOR A NEARBY KINDERGARTEN CLASS AND THE KID WHO WAS SUPPOSED TO PLAY THE OGRE GOT SICK.
THEY THOUGHT THAT SINCE HE'S INTO MOVIES HE'D BE INTO THEATER TOO...
SO THEY ASKED HIM TO PLAY THE PART OF THE OGRE.
HIS CLASSMATES DID?
THIS IS THE FIRST STEP IN MAKING AN APPLIANCE.
WE'RE GOING TO MAKE A MOLD OF YOUR FACE USING ALGINATE!

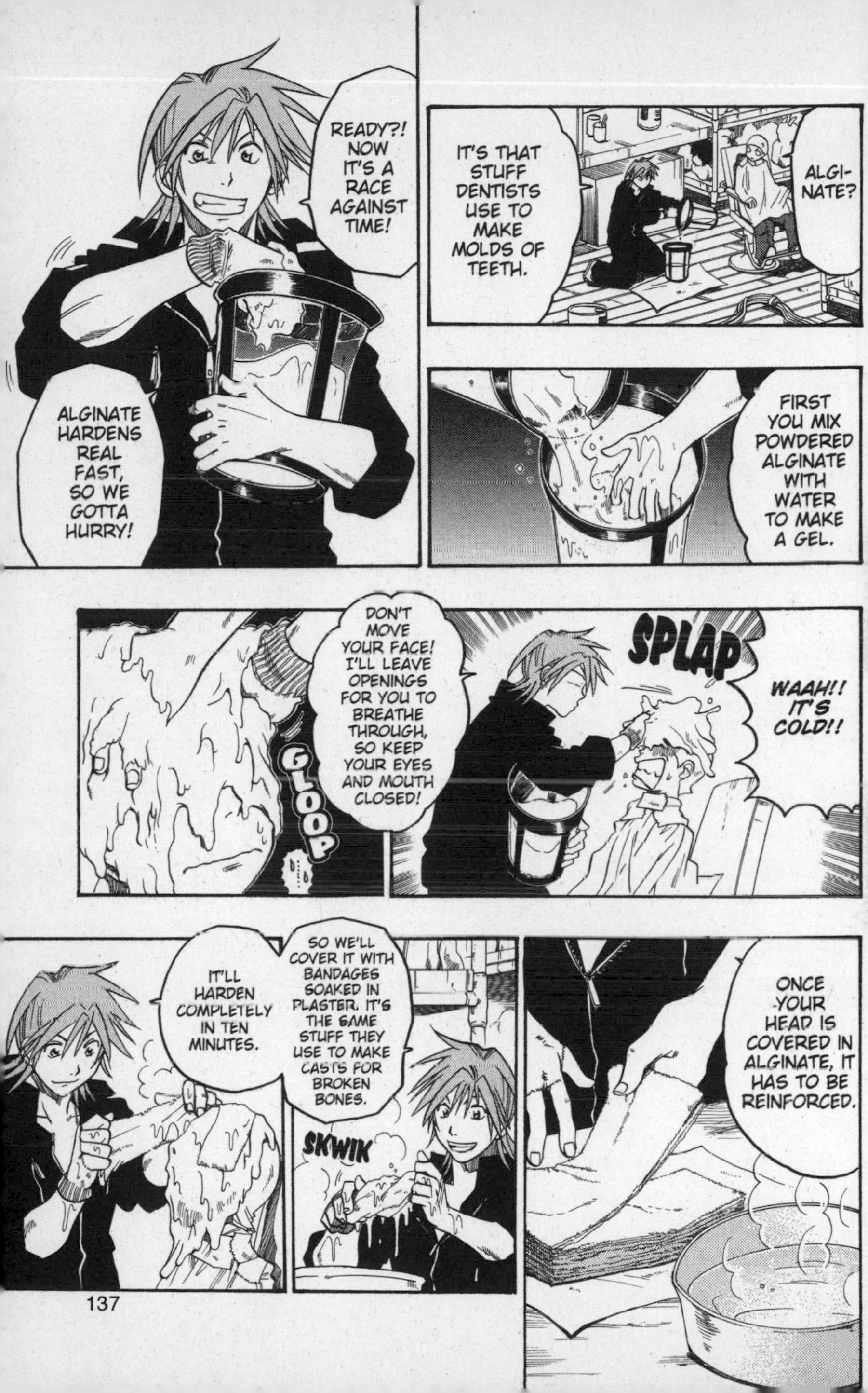
ALGI-NATE?
IT'S THAT STUFF DENTISTS USE TO MAKE MOLDS OF TEETH.
FIRST YOU MIX POWDERED ALGINATE WITH WATER TO MAKE A GEL.
READY?! NOW IT'S A RACE AGAINST TIME!
ALGINATE HARDENS REAL FAST, SO WE GOTTA HURRY!
SPLAP
WAAH!! IT'S COLD!!
DON'T MOVE YOUR FACE! I'LL LEAVE OPENINGS FOR YOU TO BREATHE THROUGH, SO KEEP YOUR EYES AND MOUTH CLOSED!
GLOOP
ONCE YOUR HEAD IS COVERED IN ALGINATE, IT HAS TO BE REINFORCED.
SO WE'LL COVER IT WITH BANDAGES SOAKED IN PLASTER. IT'S THE SAME STUFF THEY USE TO MAKE CASTS FOR BROKEN BONES.
SKWIK
IT'LL HARDEN COMPLETELY IN TEN MINUTES.

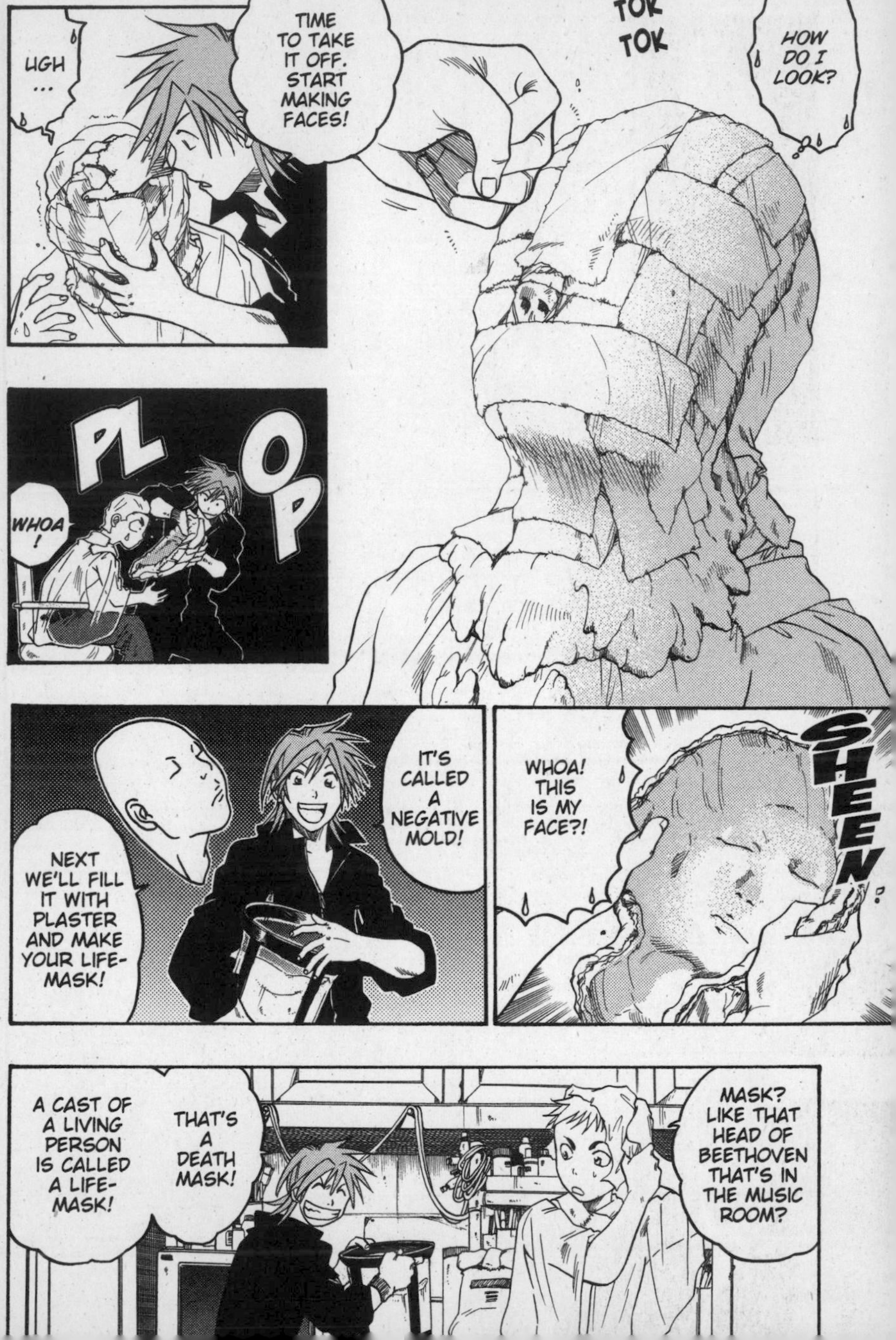
TOK TOK
HOW DO I LOOK?
TIME TO TAKE IT OFF. START MAKING FACES!
UGH ...
PLOP
WHOA!
SHEEN
WHOA! THIS IS MY FACE?!
IT'S CALLED A NEGATIVE MOLD!
NEXT WE'LL FILL IT WITH PLASTER AND MAKE YOUR LIFE-MASK!
MASK? LIKE THAT HEAD OF BEETHOVEN THAT'S IN THE MUSIC ROOM?
THAT'S A DEATH MASK!
A CAST OF A LIVING PERSON IS CALLED A LIFE-MASK!

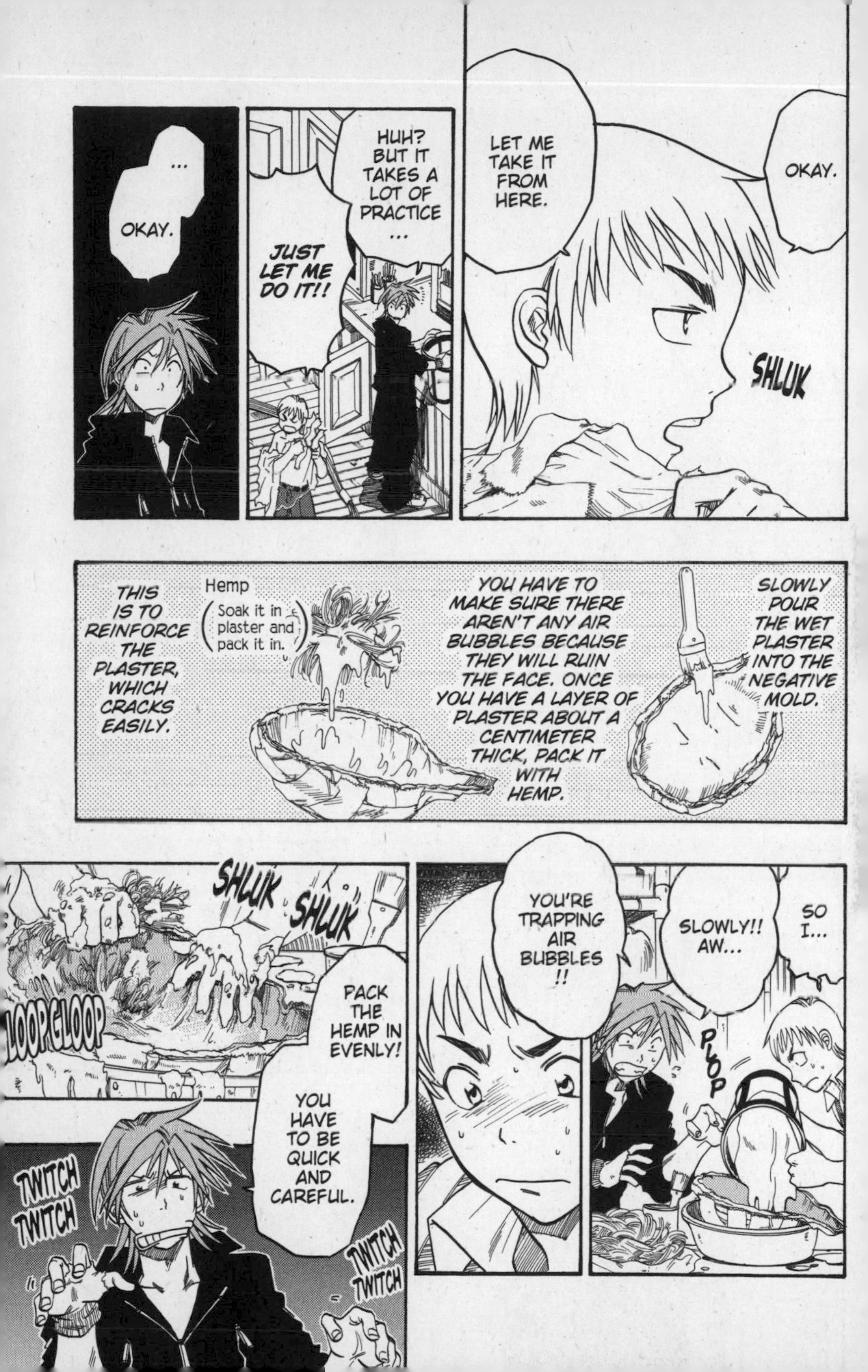
OKAY.
LET ME TAKE IT FROM HERE.
SHLUK
HUH? BUT IT TAKES A LOT OF PRACTICE ...
JUST LET ME DO IT!!
... OKAY.
SLOWLY POUR THE WET PLASTER INTO THE NEGATIVE MOLD.
YOU HAVE TO MAKE SURE THERE AREN'T ANY AIR BUBBLES BECAUSE THEY WILL RUIN THE FACE. ONCE YOU HAVE A LAYER OF PLASTER ABOUT A CENTIMETER THICK, PACK IT WITH HEMP.
Hemp
(Soak it in plaster and pack it in.)
THIS IS TO REINFORCE THE PLASTER, WHICH CRACKS EASILY.
SO I...
SLOWLY!! AW...
YOU'RE TRAPPING AIR BUBBLES !!
PLOP
SHLUK
SHLUK
PACK THE HEMP IN EVENLY!
LOOP GLOOP
YOU HAVE TO BE QUICK AND CAREFUL.
TWITCH TWITCH
TWITCH TWITCH

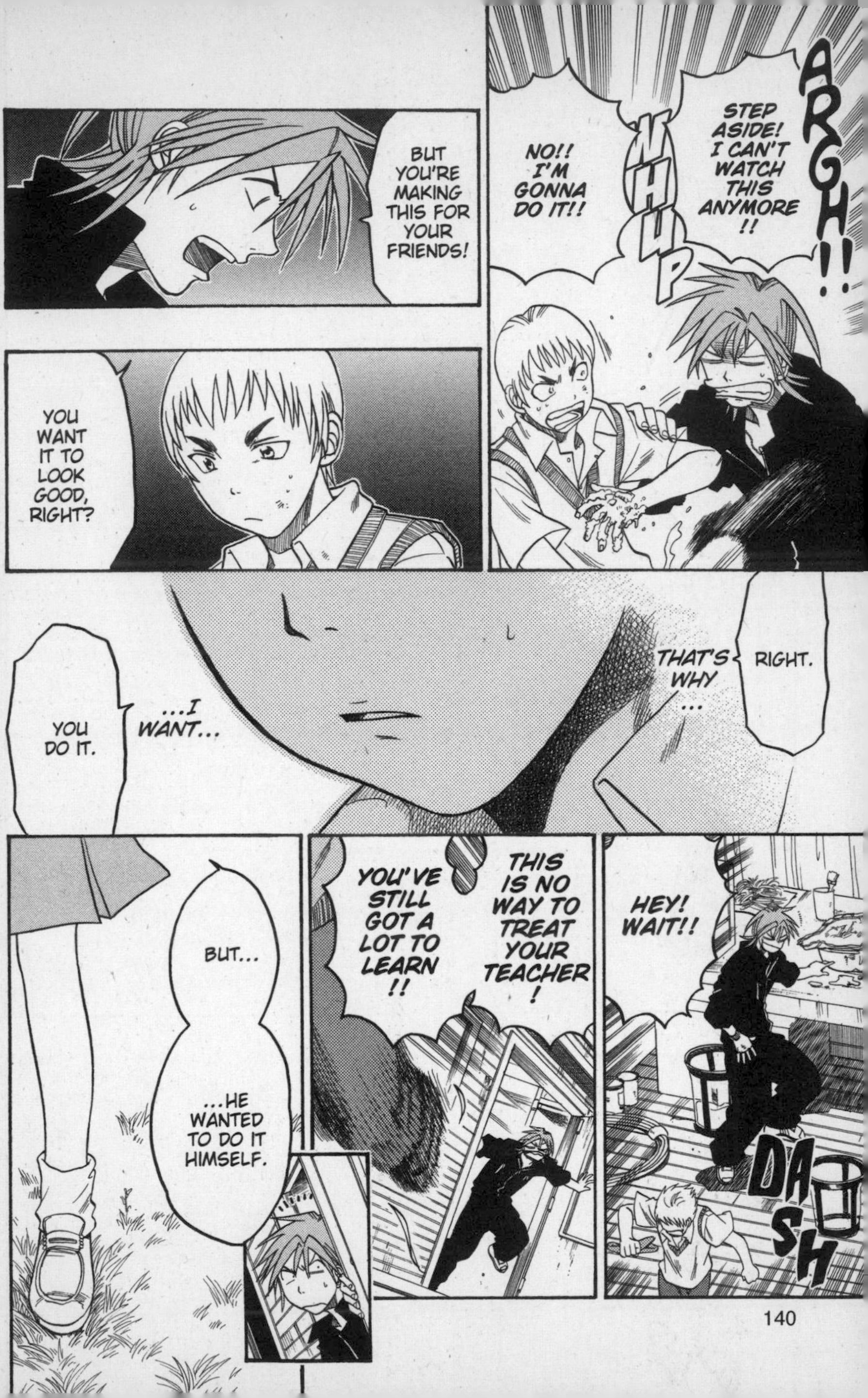
ARGH!!
STEP ASIDE! I CAN'T WATCH THIS ANYMORE!!
NHUP
NO!! I'M GONNA DO IT!!
BUT YOU'RE MAKING THIS FOR YOUR FRIENDS!
YOU WANT IT TO LOOK GOOD, RIGHT?
RIGHT.
THAT'S WHY...
...I WANT...
YOU DO IT.
HEY! WAIT!!
DASH
THIS IS NO WAY TO TREAT YOUR TEACHER!
YOU'VE STILL GOT A LOT TO LEARN!!
BUT...
...HE WANTED TO DO IT HIMSELF.

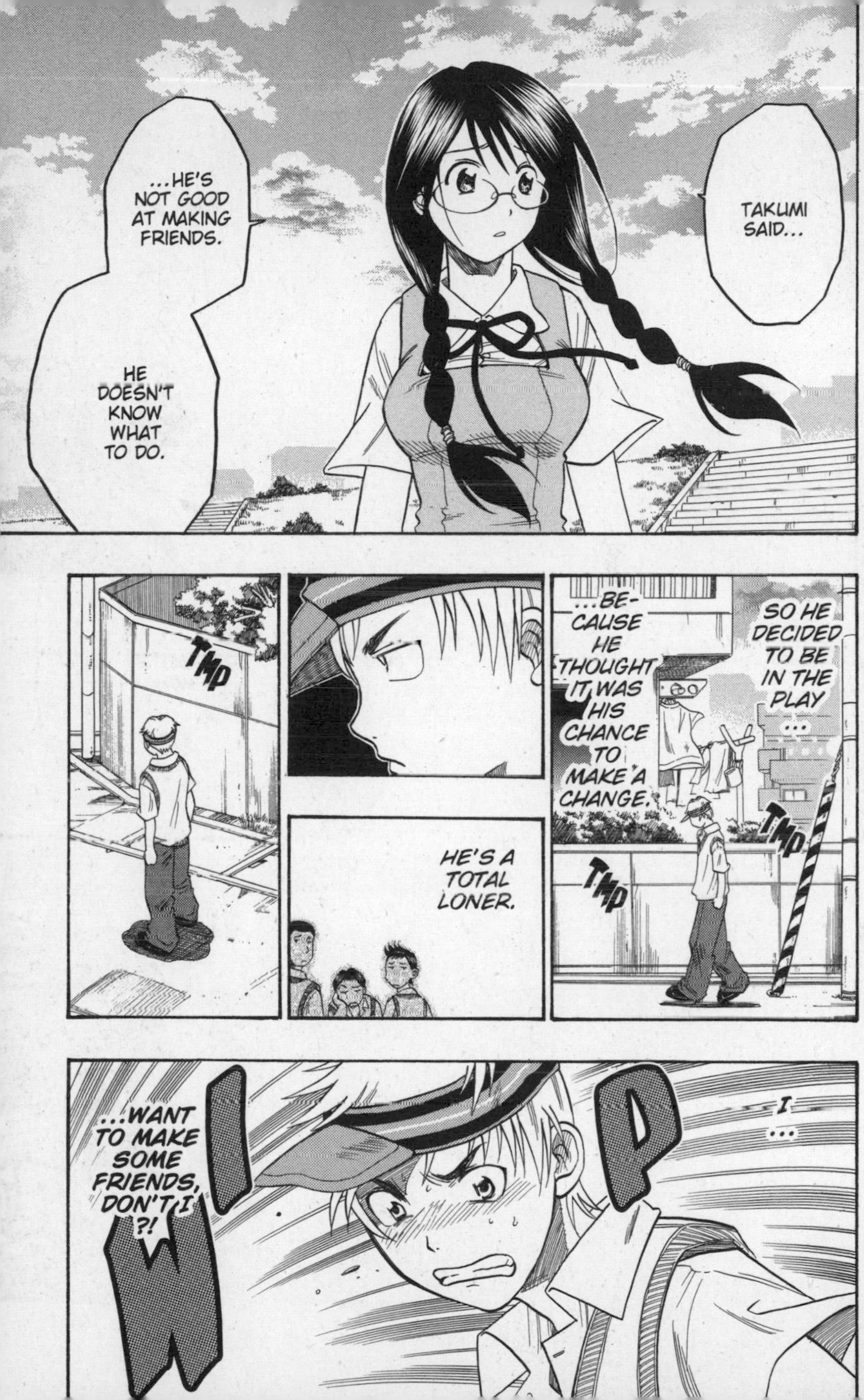
TAKUMI SAID...
...HE'S NOT GOOD AT MAKING FRIENDS.
HE DOESN'T KNOW WHAT TO DO.
SO HE DECIDED TO BE IN THE PLAY...
...BE-CAUSE HE THOUGHT IT WAS HIS CHANCE TO MAKE A CHANGE.
TMP
TMP
HE'S A TOTAL LONER.
TMP
I...
...WANT TO MAKE SOME FRIENDS, DON'T I?!

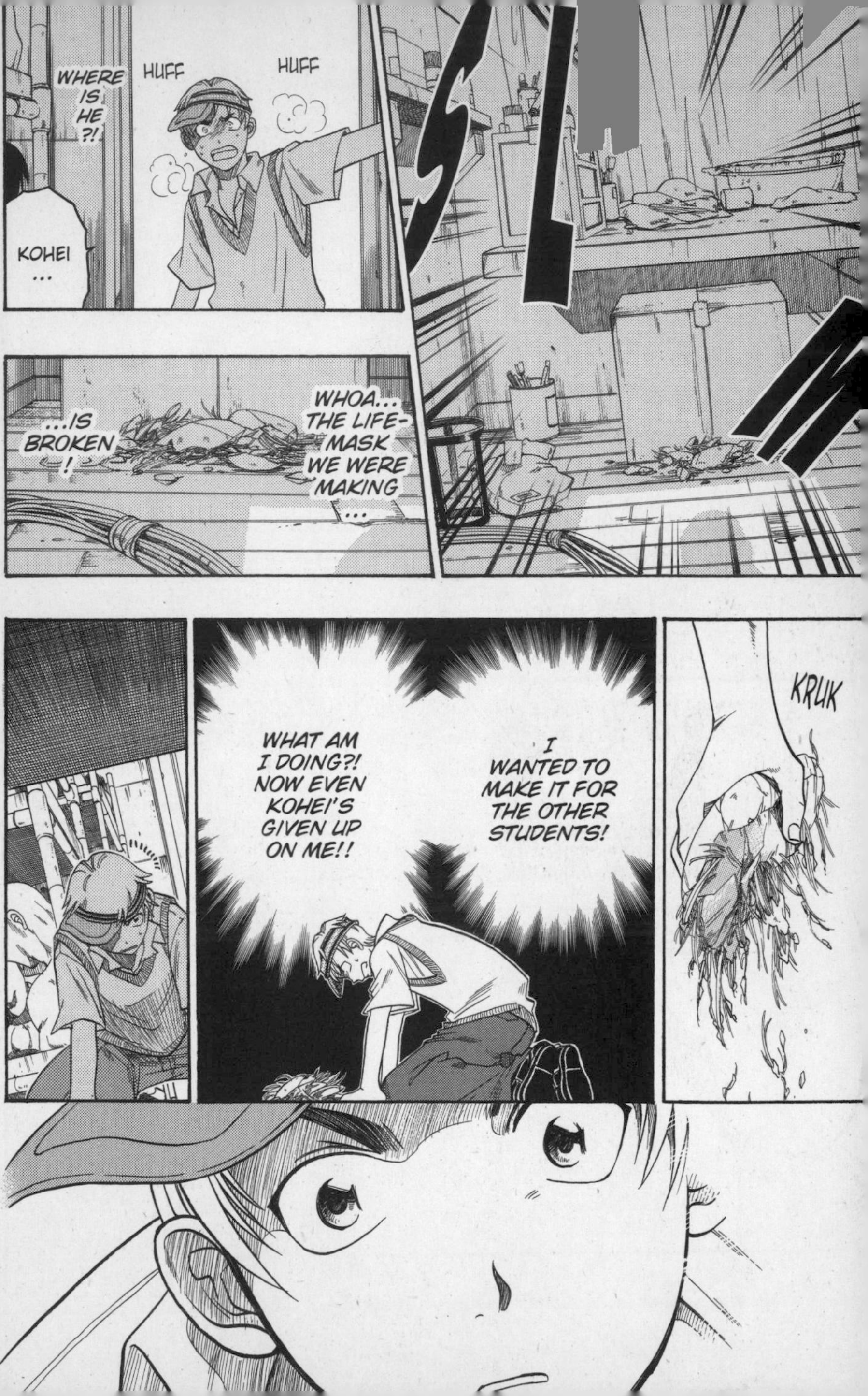
SL
M
HUFF
HUFF
WHERE IS HE ?!
KOHEI ...
WHOA... THE LIFE-MASK WE WERE MAKING ...
...IS BROKEN !
KRUK
I WANTED TO MAKE IT FOR THE OTHER STUDENTS!
WHAT AM I DOING?! NOW EVEN KOHEI'S GIVEN UP ON ME!!

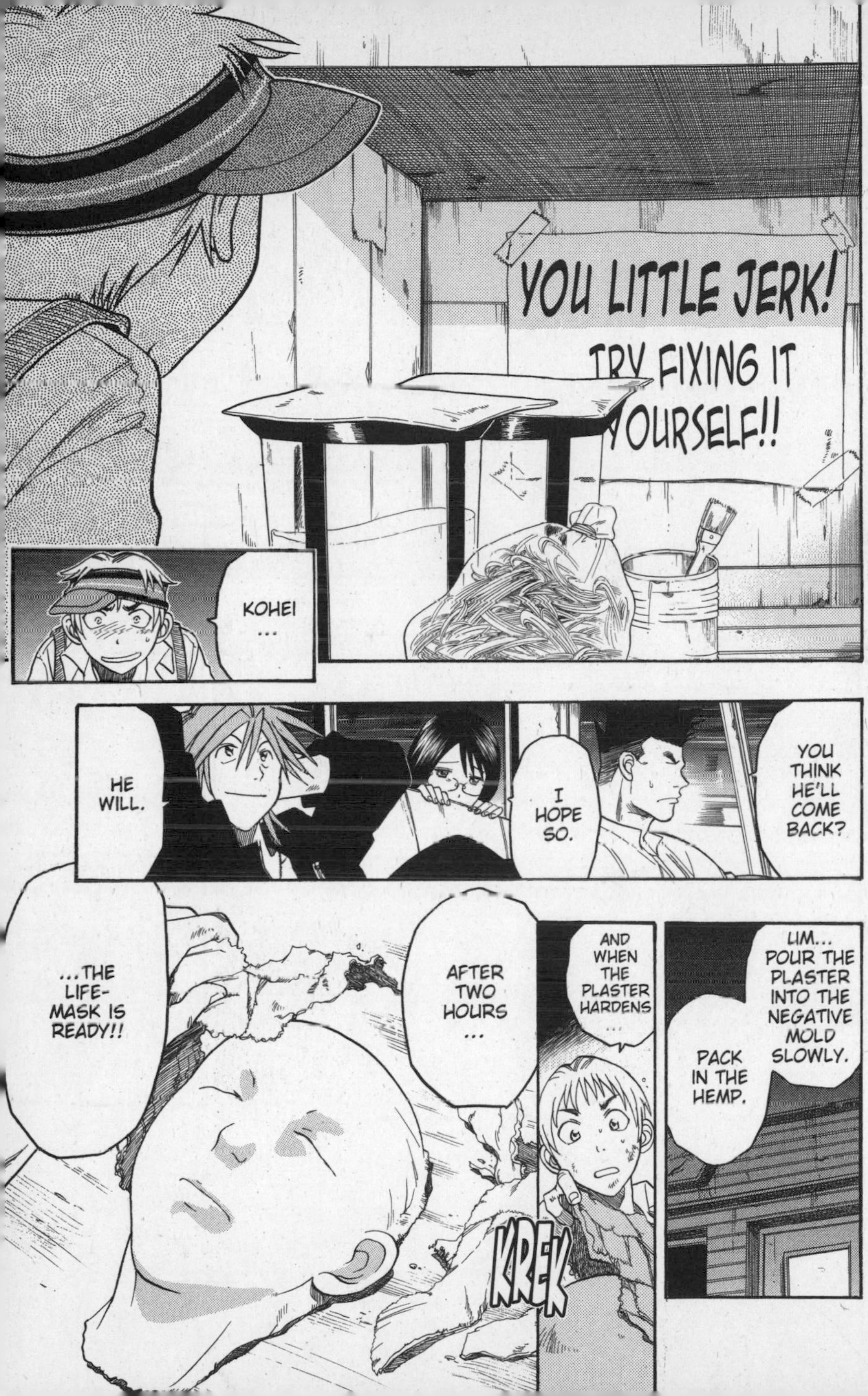
YOU LITTLE JERK!
TRY FIXING IT YOURSELF!!
KOHEI ...
YOU THINK HE'LL COME BACK?
I HOPE SO.
HE WILL.
LIM... POUR THE PLASTER INTO THE NEGATIVE MOLD SLOWLY.
PACK IN THE HEMP.
AND WHEN THE PLASTER HARDENS ...
AFTER TWO HOURS ...
KREK
...THE LIFE-MASK IS READY!!

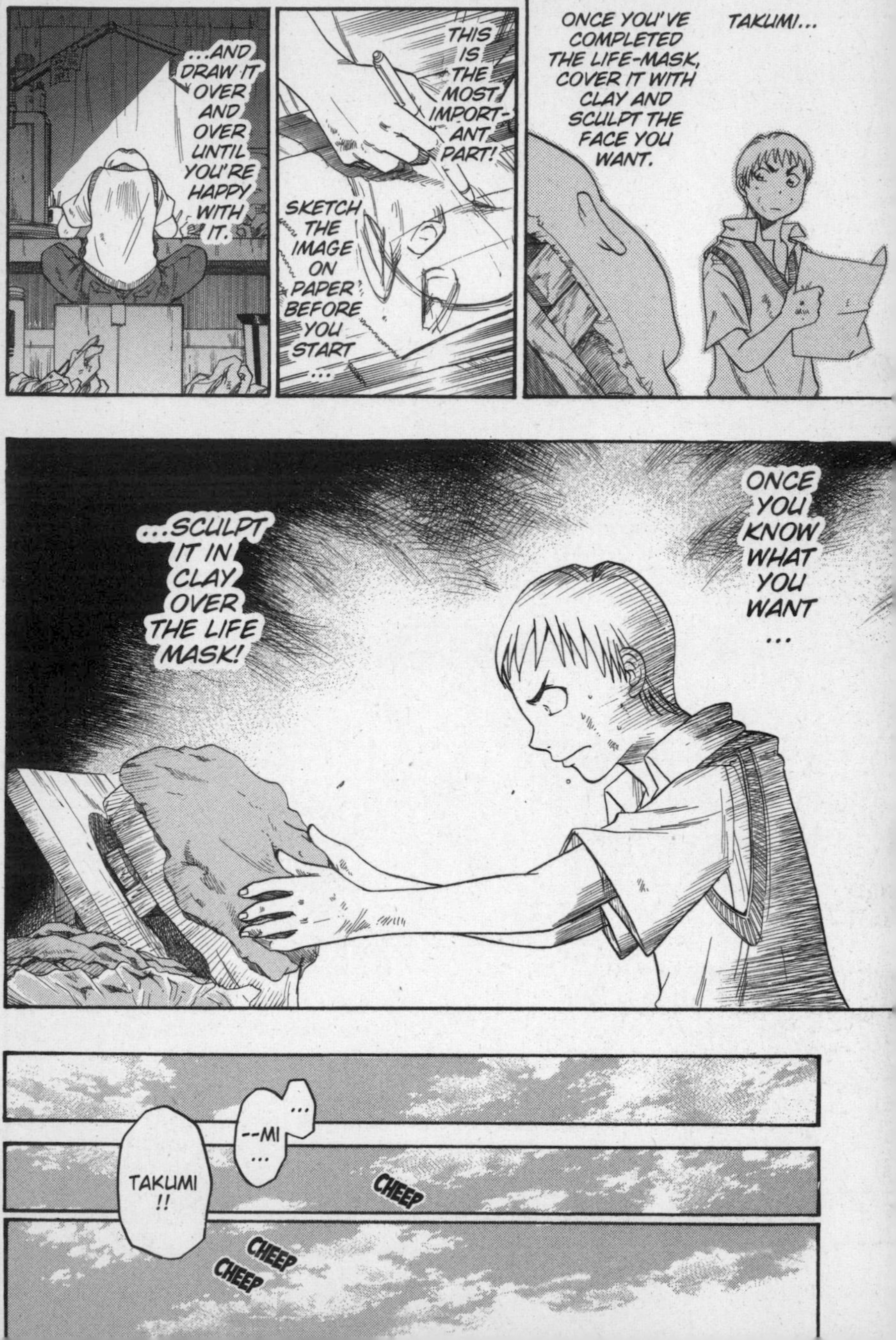
TAKUMI...
ONCE YOU'VE COMPLETED THE LIFE-MASK, COVER IT WITH CLAY AND SCULPT THE FACE YOU WANT.
THIS IS THE MOST IMPORTANT PART!
SKETCH THE IMAGE ON PAPER BEFORE YOU START...
...AND DRAW IT OVER AND OVER UNTIL YOU'RE HAPPY WITH IT.
ONCE YOU KNOW WHAT YOU WANT...
...SCULPT IT IN CLAY OVER THE LIFE MASK!
...
--MI...
CHEEP
TAKUMI!!
CHEEP
CHEEP

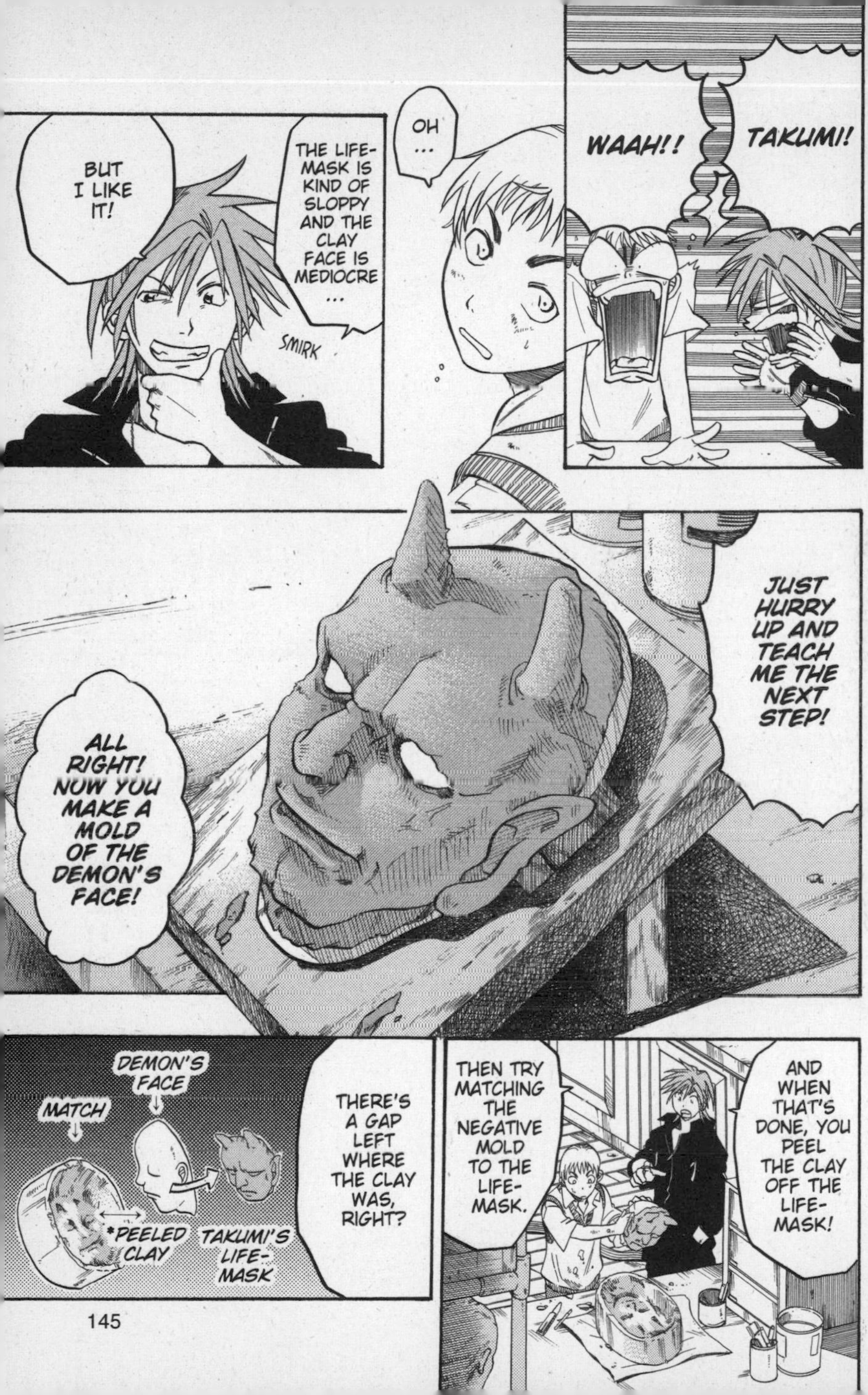
TAKUMI!
WAAH!!
OH ...
THE LIFE-MASK IS KIND OF SLOPPY AND THE CLAY FACE IS MEDIOCRE ...
SMIRK
BUT I LIKE IT!
JUST HURRY UP AND TEACH ME THE NEXT STEP!
ALL RIGHT! NOW YOU MAKE A MOLD OF THE DEMON'S FACE!
AND WHEN THAT'S DONE, YOU PEEL THE CLAY OFF THE LIFE-MASK!
THEN TRY MATCHING THE NEGATIVE MOLD TO THE LIFE-MASK.
THERE'S A GAP LEFT WHERE THE CLAY WAS, RIGHT?
DEMON'S FACE
MATCH
*PEELED CLAY
TAKUMI'S LIFE-MASK

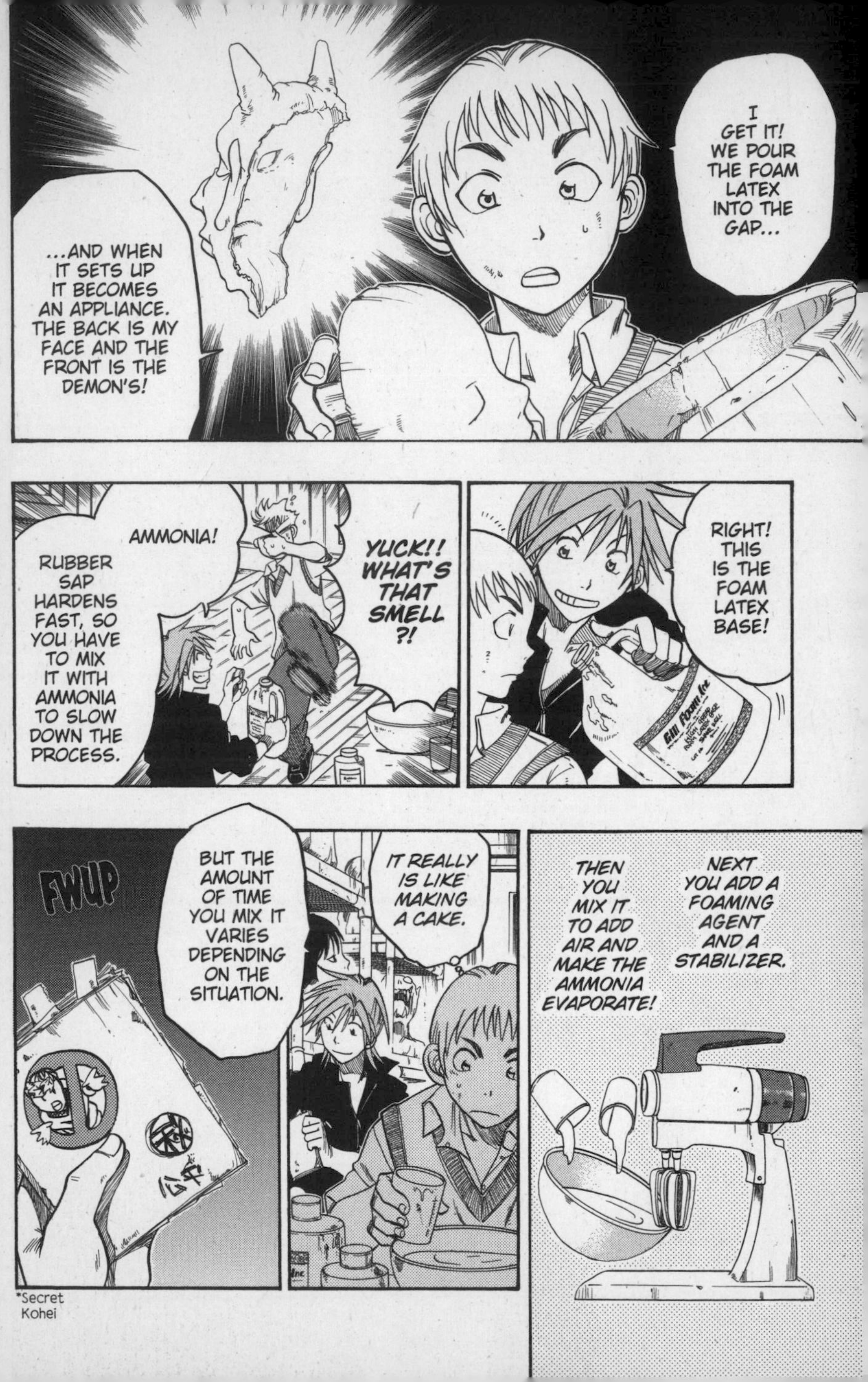
I GET IT! WE POUR THE FOAM LATEX INTO THE GAP...
...AND WHEN IT SETS UP IT BECOMES AN APPLIANCE. THE BACK IS MY FACE AND THE FRONT IS THE DEMON'S!
RIGHT! THIS IS THE FOAM LATEX BASE!
YUCK!! WHAT'S THAT SMELL?!
AMMONIA!
RUBBER SAP HARDENS FAST, SO YOU HAVE TO MIX IT WITH AMMONIA TO SLOW DOWN THE PROCESS.
NEXT YOU ADD A FOAMING AGENT AND A STABILIZER.
THEN YOU MIX IT TO ADD AIR AND MAKE THE AMMONIA EVAPORATE!
IT REALLY IS LIKE MAKING A CAKE.
BUT THE AMOUNT OF TIME YOU MIX IT VARIES DEPENDING ON THE SITUATION.
FWUP

*Secret Kohei

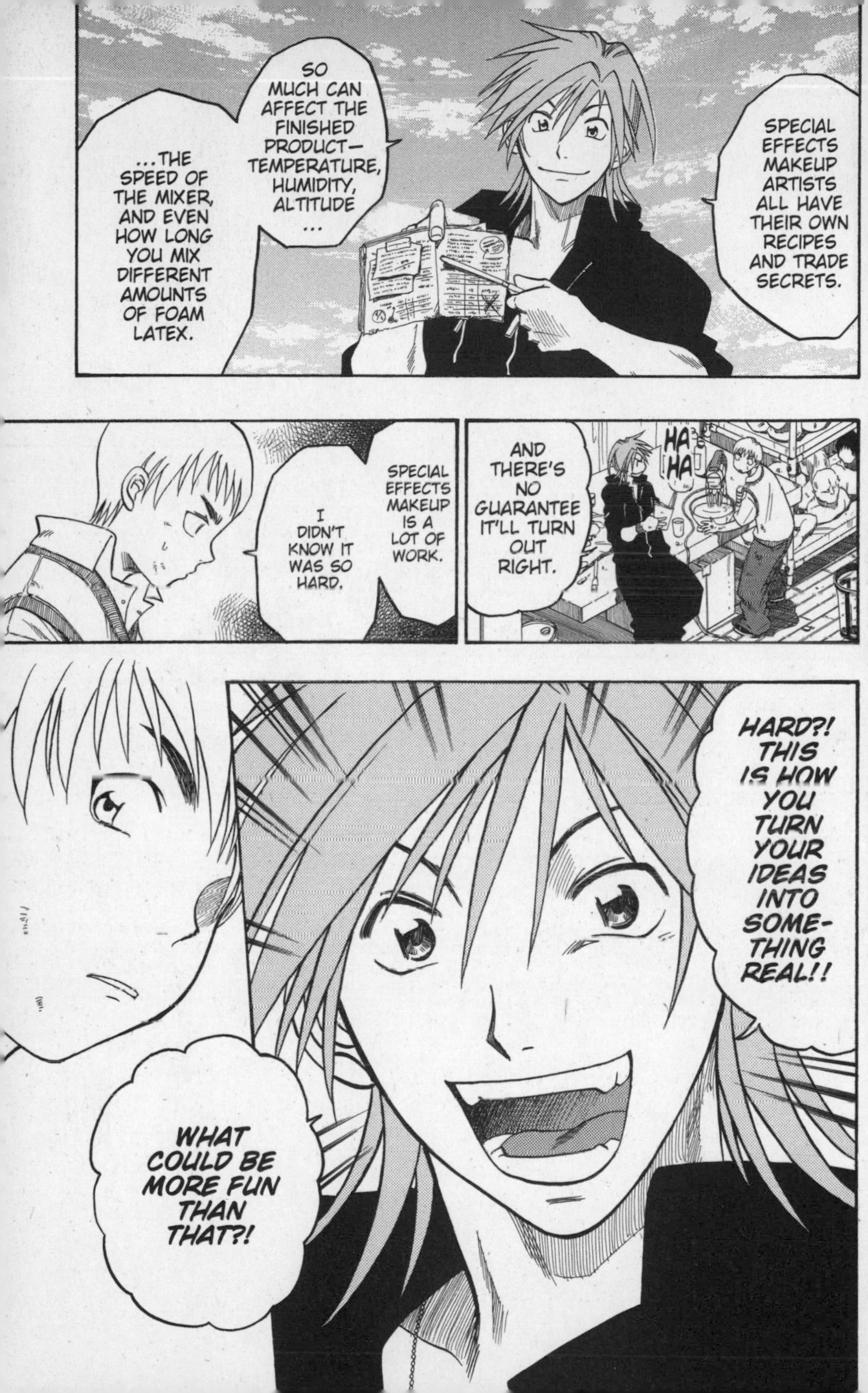
SPECIAL EFFECTS MAKEUP ARTISTS ALL HAVE THEIR OWN RECIPES AND TRADE SECRETS.
SO MUCH CAN AFFECT THE FINISHED PRODUCT—TEMPERATURE, HUMIDITY, ALTITUDE...
...THE SPEED OF THE MIXER, AND EVEN HOW LONG YOU MIX DIFFERENT AMOUNTS OF FOAM LATEX.
HA HA
AND THERE'S NO GUARANTEE IT'LL TURN OUT RIGHT.
SPECIAL EFFECTS MAKEUP IS A LOT OF WORK.
I DIDN'T KNOW IT WAS SO HARD.
HARD?! THIS IS HOW YOU TURN YOUR IDEAS INTO SOMETHING REAL!!
WHAT COULD BE MORE FUN THAN THAT?!

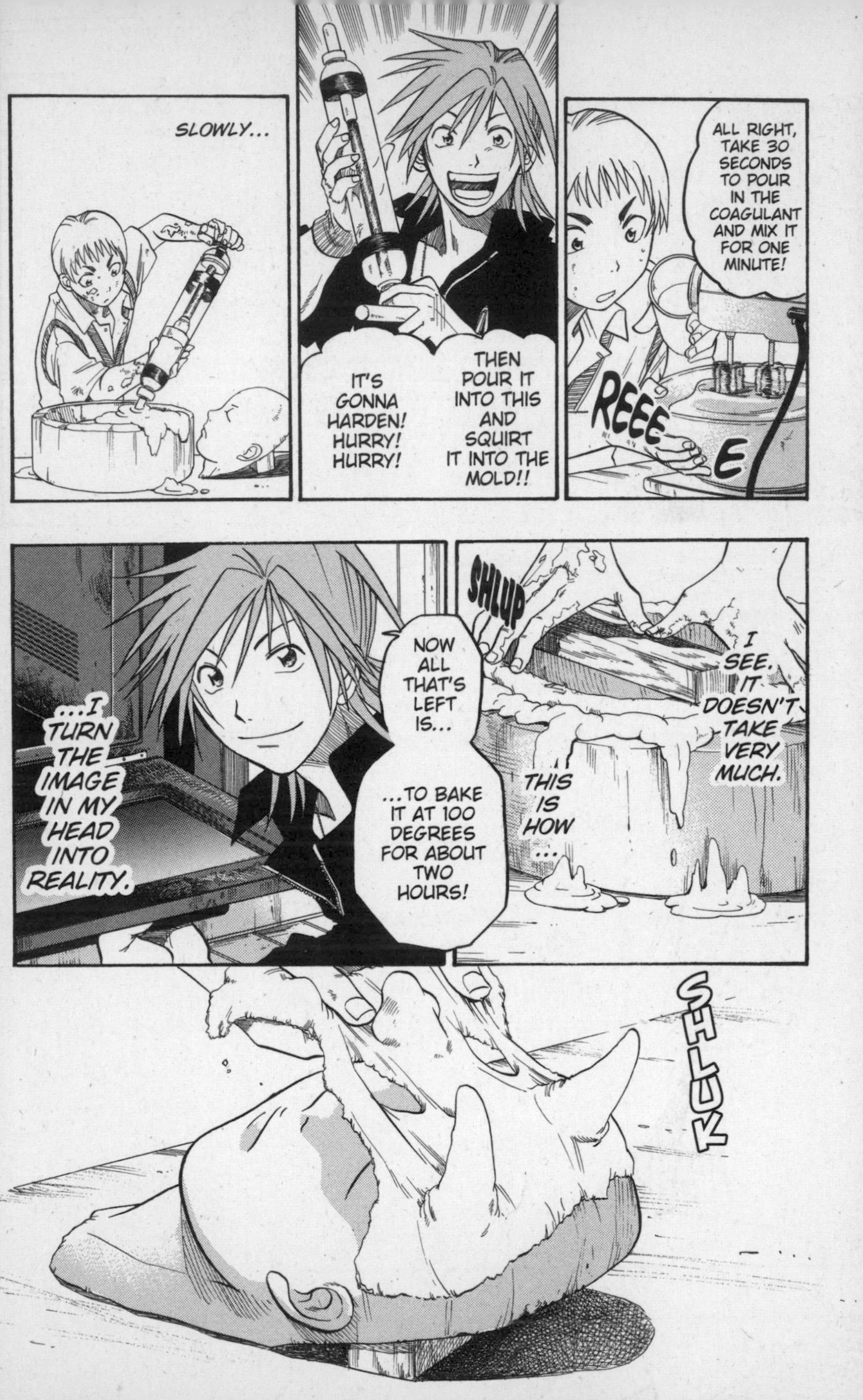
ALL RIGHT, TAKE 30 SECONDS TO POUR IN THE COAGULANT AND MIX IT FOR ONE MINUTE!
REEEE
THEN POUR IT INTO THIS AND SQUIRT IT INTO THE MOLD!!
IT'S GONNA HARDEN! HURRY! HURRY!
SLOWLY...
SHLUP
I SEE. IT DOESN'T TAKE VERY MUCH.
THIS IS HOW...
NOW ALL THAT'S LEFT IS...
...TO BAKE IT AT 100 DEGREES FOR ABOUT TWO HOURS!
...I TURN THE IMAGE IN MY HEAD INTO REALITY.
SHLUK

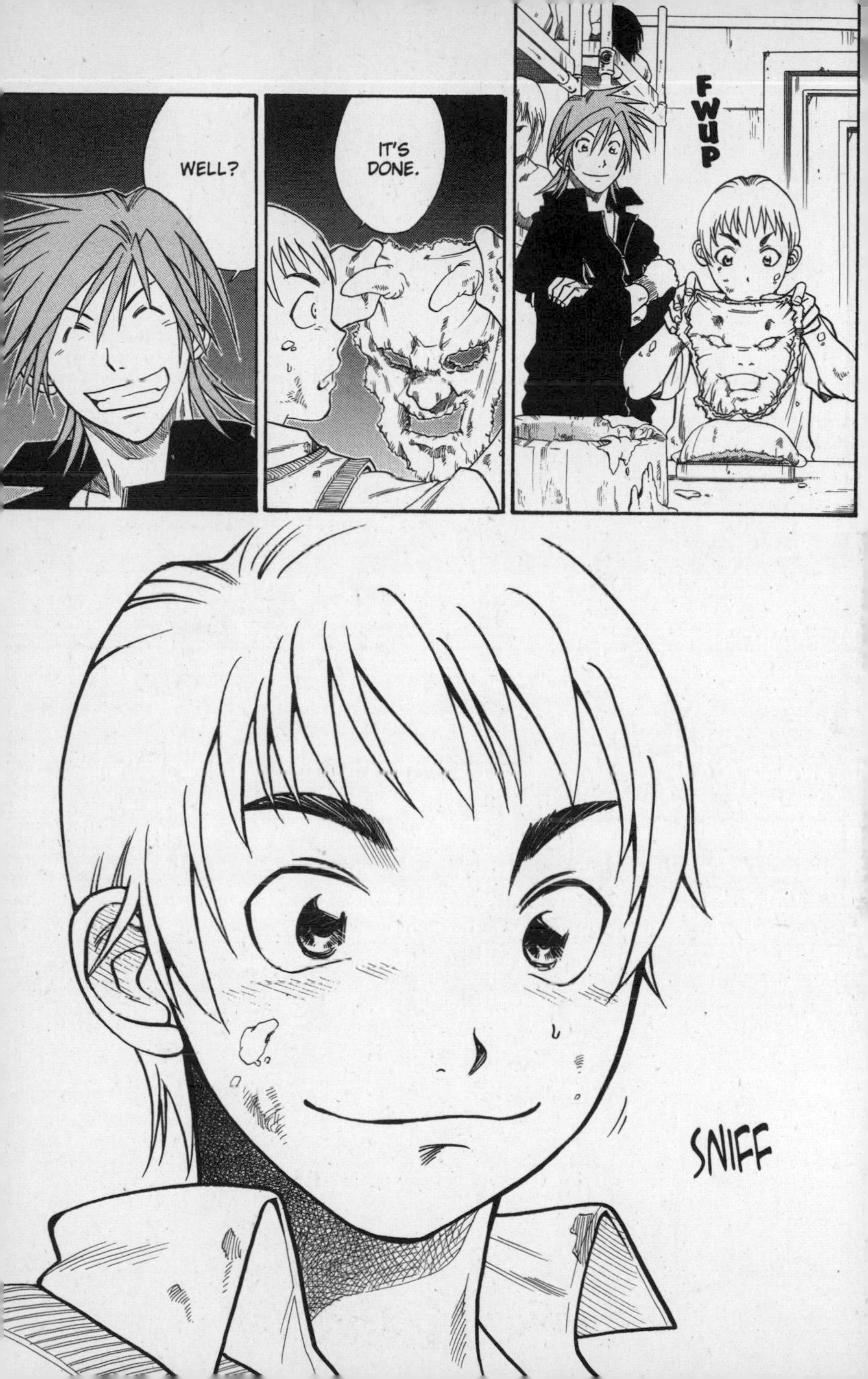
FWUP
IT'S DONE.
WELL?
SNIFF

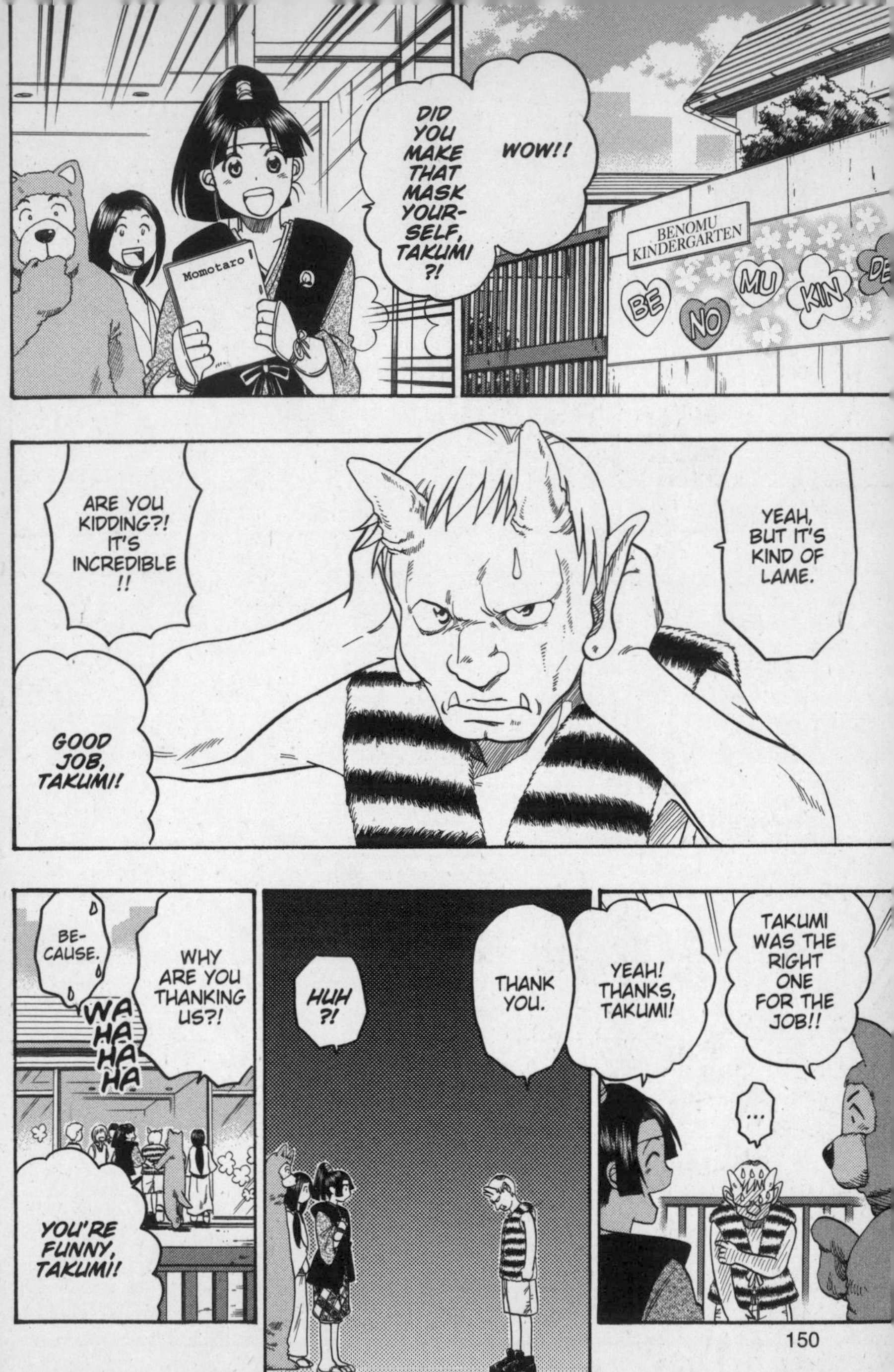
BENOMU KINDERGARTEN
BE NO MU KIN
WOW!!
DID YOU MAKE THAT MASK YOURSELF, TAKUMI?!
Momotaro
YEAH, BUT IT'S KIND OF LAME.
ARE YOU KIDDING?! IT'S INCREDIBLE!!
GOOD JOB, TAKUMI!
TAKUMI WAS THE RIGHT ONE FOR THE JOB!!
YEAH! THANKS, TAKUMI!
...
THANK YOU.
HUH?!
WHY ARE YOU THANKING US?!
BE-CAUSE.
WA HA HA HA
YOU'RE FUNNY, TAKUMI!

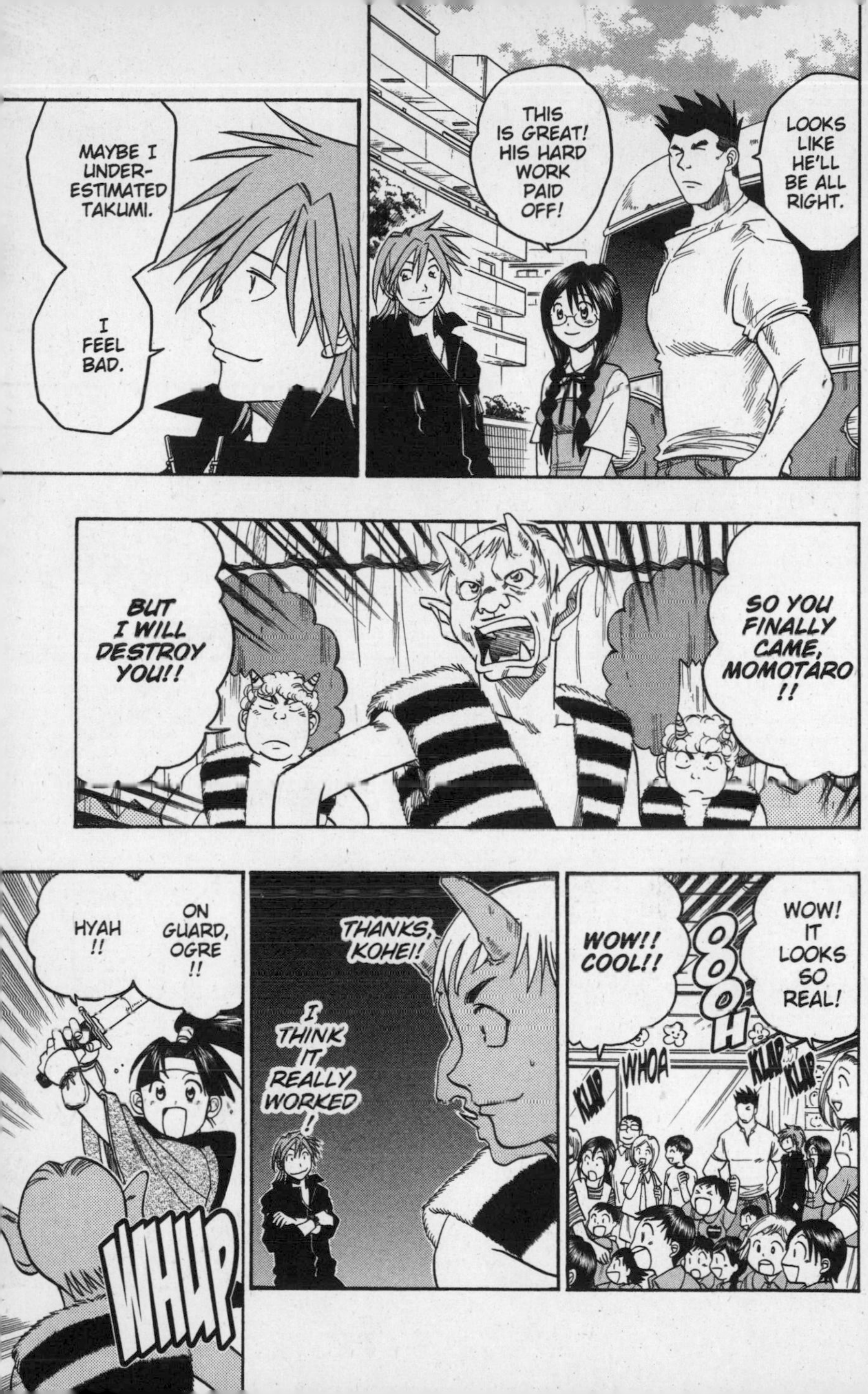
LOOKS LIKE HE'LL BE ALL RIGHT.
THIS IS GREAT! HIS HARD WORK PAID OFF!
MAYBE I UNDER-ESTIMATED TAKUMI.
I FEEL BAD.
SO YOU FINALLY CAME, MOMOTARO!!
BUT I WILL DESTROY YOU!!
WOW! IT LOOKS SO REAL!
OOOH
WOW!! COOL!!
KLAP KLAP KLAP
WHOA
KLAP
THANKS, KOHEI!
I THINK IT REALLY WORKED!
ON GUARD, OGRE!!
HYAH!!
WHUP

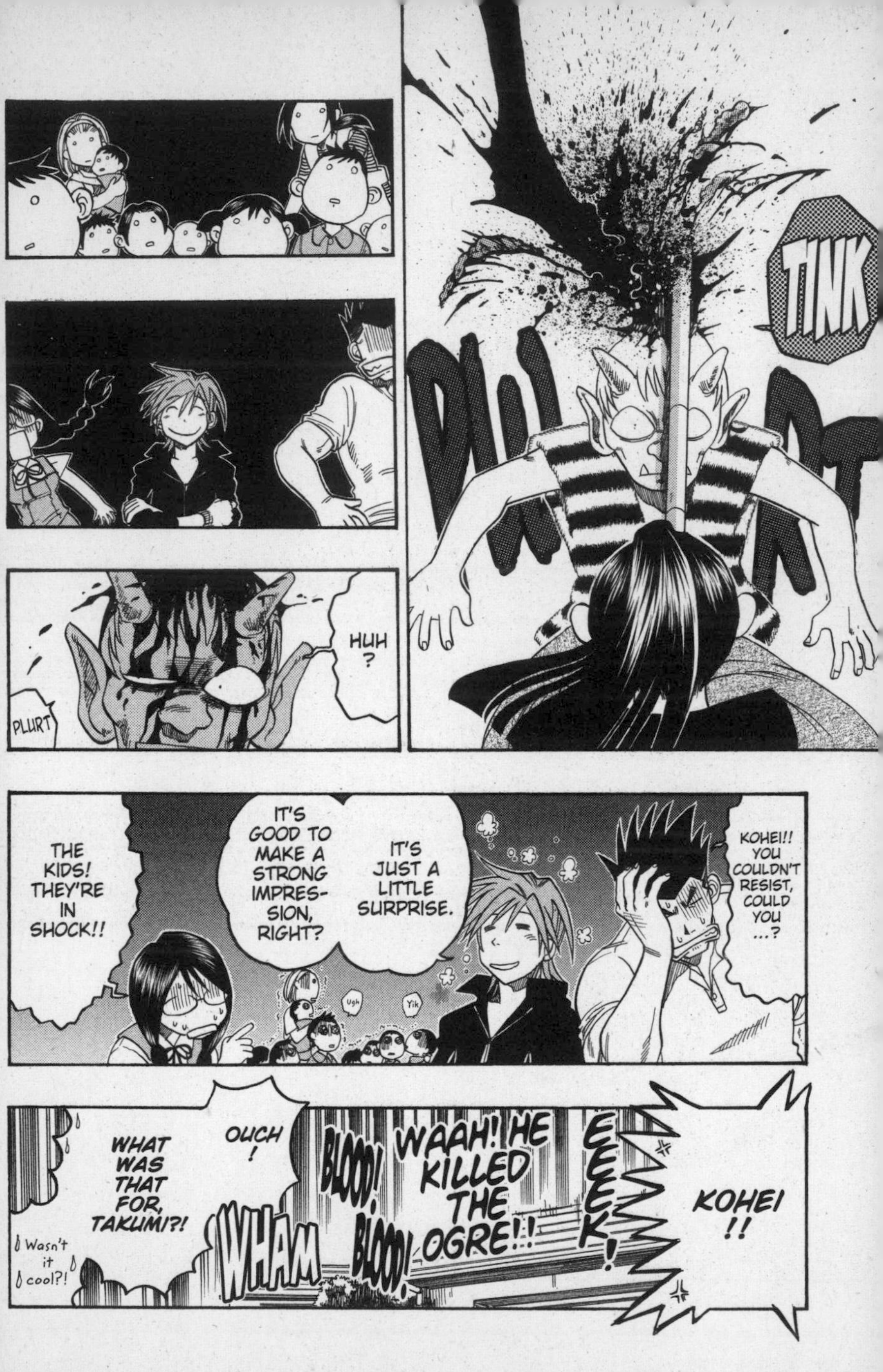
TINK
HUH?
PLURT
KOHEI!! YOU COULDN'T RESIST, COULD YOU ...?
IT'S JUST A LITTLE SURPRISE.
IT'S GOOD TO MAKE A STRONG IMPRESSION, RIGHT?
THE KIDS! THEY'RE IN SHOCK!!
Yik
Ugh
KOHEI!!
EEEEK!
WAAH! HE KILLED THE OGRE!!
BLOOD! BLOOD!
WHAM
OUCH!
WHAT WAS THAT FOR, TAKUMI?!
Wasn't it cool?!

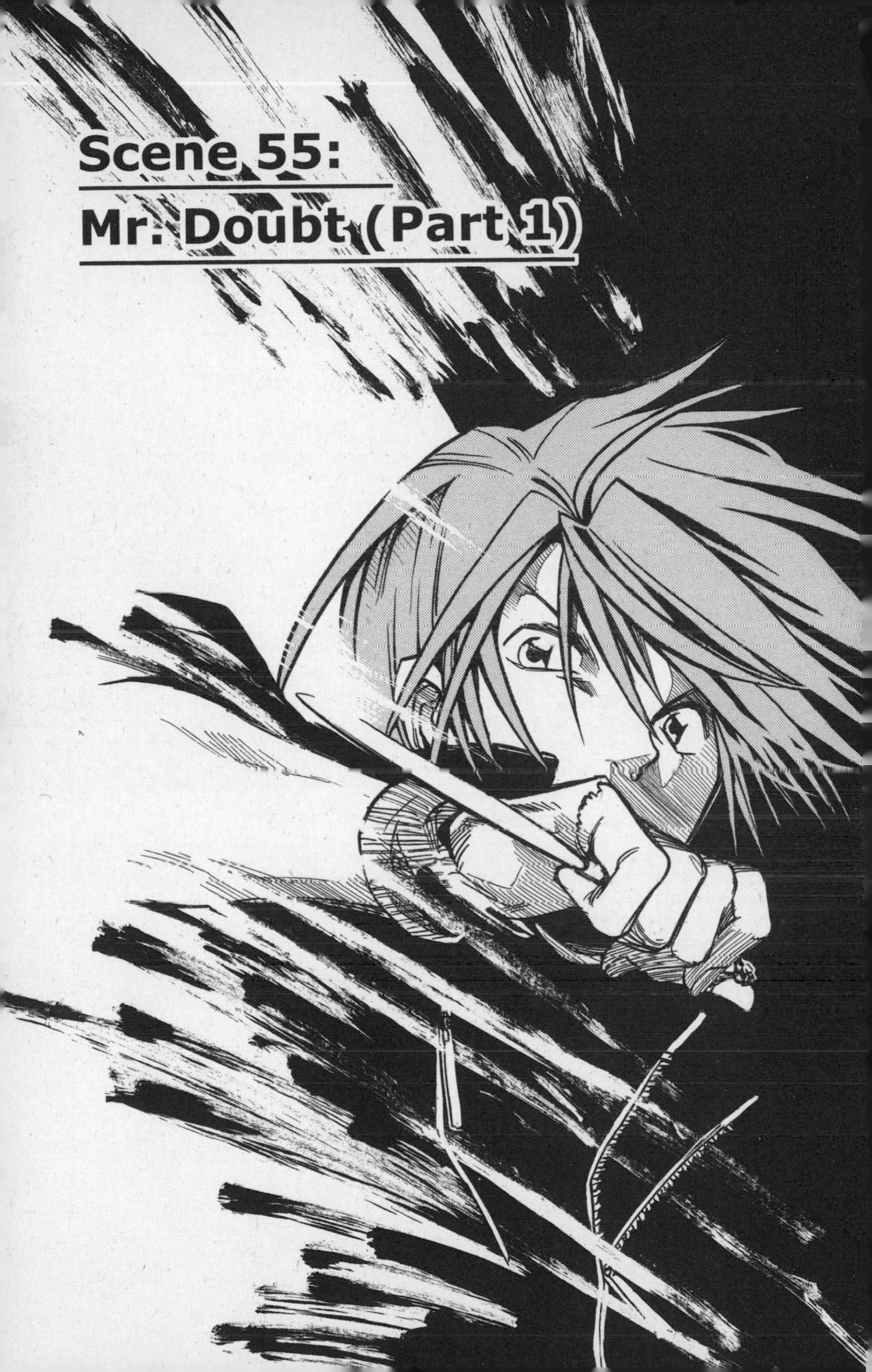
Scene 55:
Mr. Doubt (Part 1)

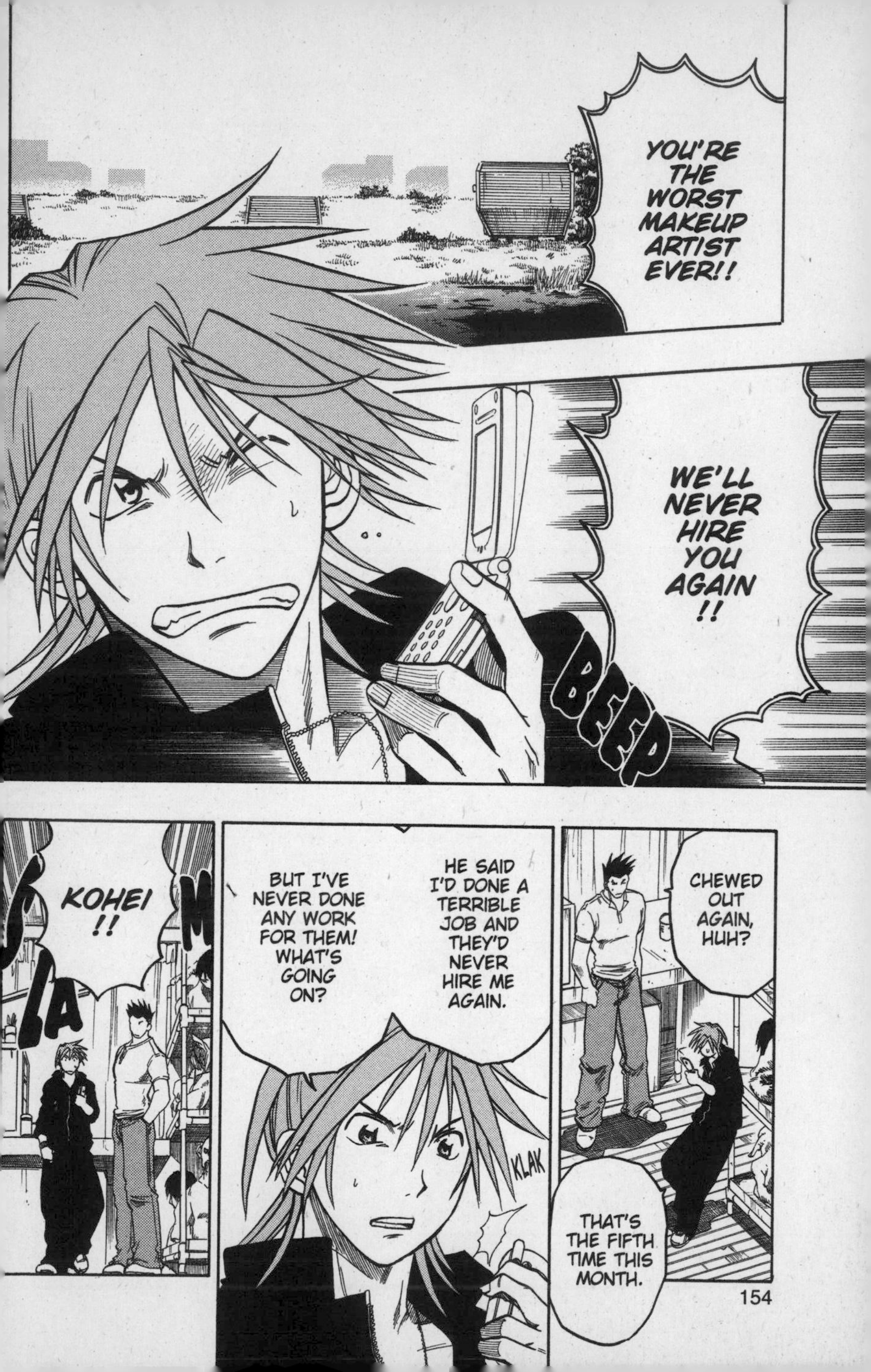
YOU'RE THE WORST MAKEUP ARTIST EVER!!
WE'LL NEVER HIRE YOU AGAIN!!
BEEP
CHEWED OUT AGAIN, HUH?
THAT'S THE FIFTH TIME THIS MONTH.
HE SAID I'D DONE A TERRIBLE JOB AND THEY'D NEVER HIRE ME AGAIN.
BUT I'VE NEVER DONE ANY WORK FOR THEM! WHAT'S GOING ON?
KLAK
KOHEI!!

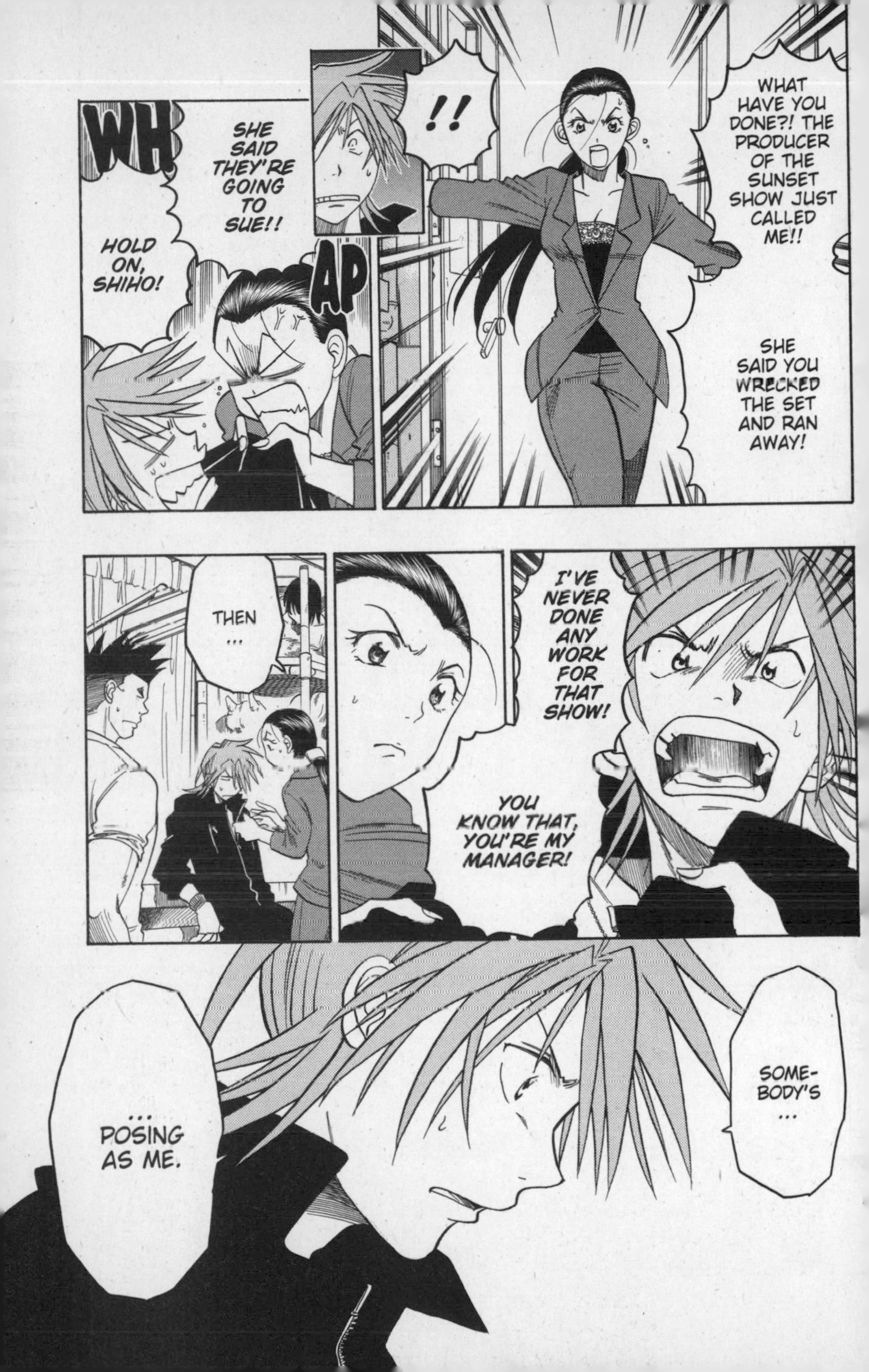
WHAT HAVE YOU DONE?! THE PRODUCER OF THE SUNSET SHOW JUST CALLED ME!!
SHE SAID YOU WRECKED THE SET AND RAN AWAY!
!!
SHE SAID THEY'RE GOING TO SUE!!
WH
AP
HOLD ON, SHIHO!
I'VE NEVER DONE ANY WORK FOR THAT SHOW!
YOU KNOW THAT, YOU'RE MY MANAGER!
THEN ...
SOME-BODY'S ...
... POSING AS ME.

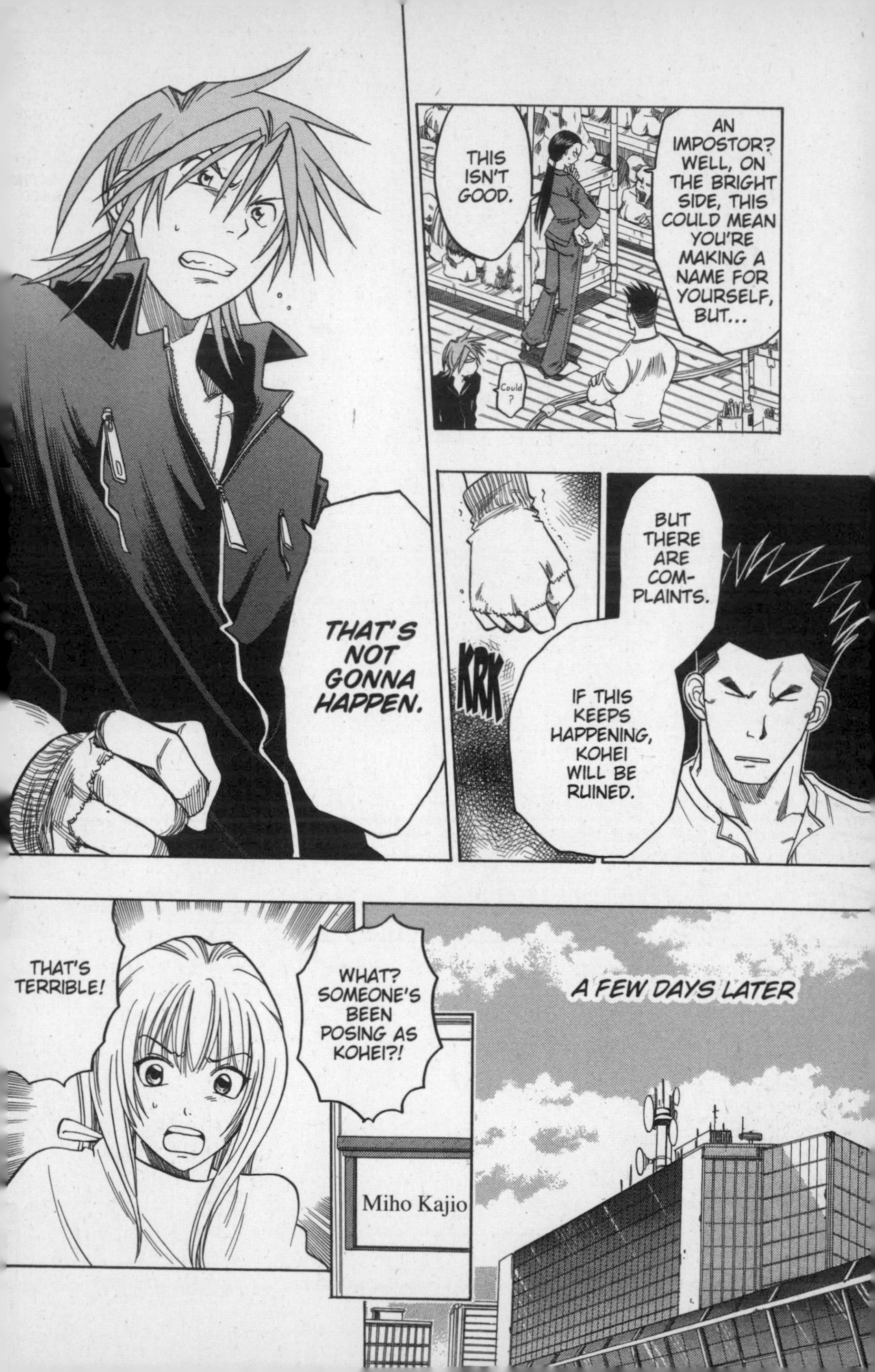
AN IMPOSTOR? WELL, ON THE BRIGHT SIDE, THIS COULD MEAN YOU'RE MAKING A NAME FOR YOURSELF, BUT...
THIS ISN'T GOOD.
Could ?
BUT THERE ARE COM-PLAINTS.
IF THIS KEEPS HAPPENING, KOHEI WILL BE RUINED.
KRK
THAT'S NOT GONNA HAPPEN.
A FEW DAYS LATER
Miho Kajio
WHAT? SOMEONE'S BEEN POSING AS KOHEI?!
THAT'S TERRIBLE!

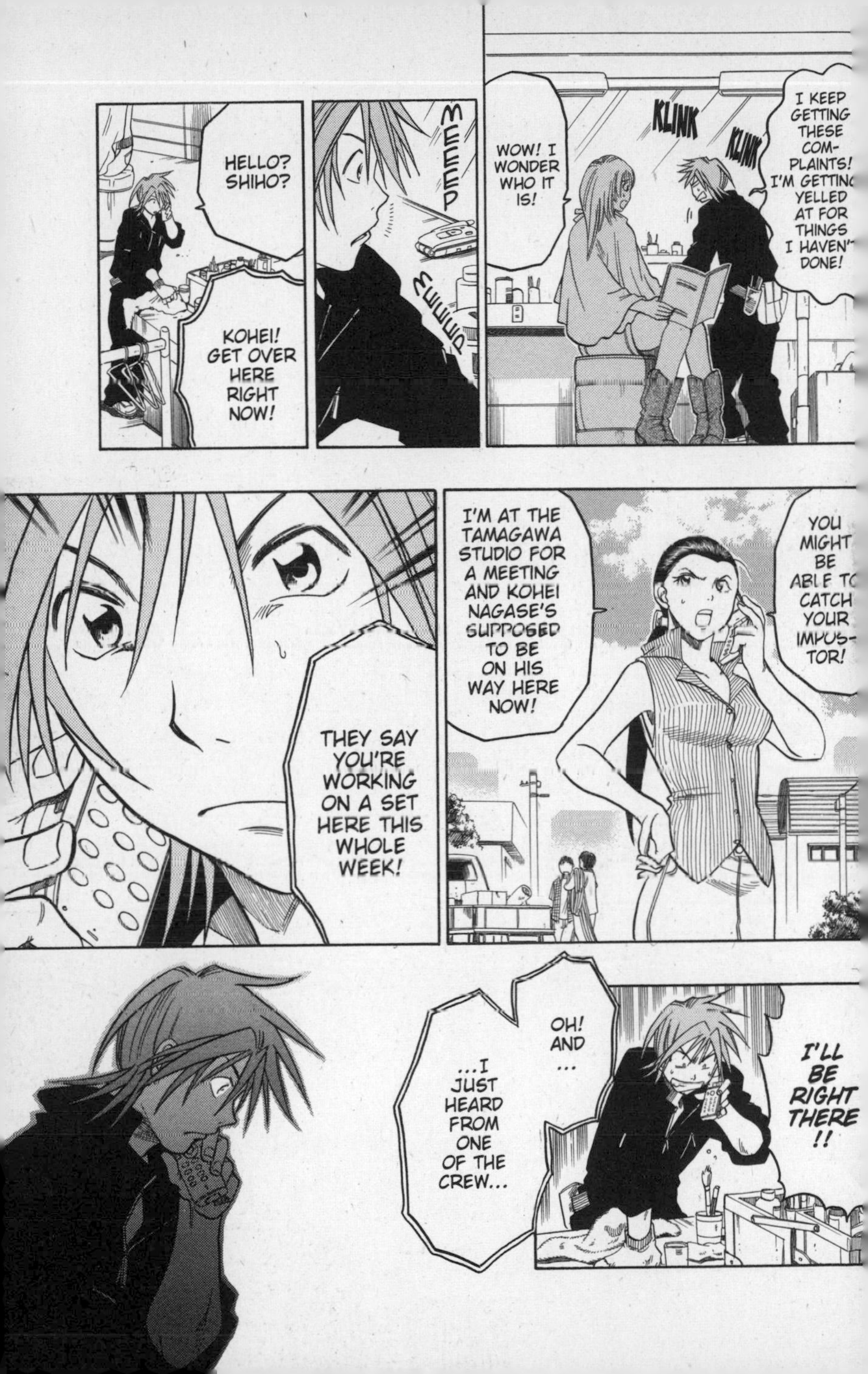
I KEEP GETTING THESE COM-PLAINTS! I'M GETTING YELLED AT FOR THINGS I HAVEN'T DONE!
KLINK
KLINK
WOW! I WONDER WHO IT IS!
MEEEP
HELLO? SHIHO?
KOHEI! GET OVER HERE RIGHT NOW!
YOU MIGHT BE ABLE TO CATCH YOUR IMPOS-TOR!
I'M AT THE TAMAGAWA STUDIO FOR A MEETING AND KOHEI NAGASE'S SUPPOSED TO BE ON HIS WAY HERE NOW!
THEY SAY YOU'RE WORKING ON A SET HERE THIS WHOLE WEEK!
I'LL BE RIGHT THERE!!
OH! AND ...
...I JUST HEARD FROM ONE OF THE CREW...

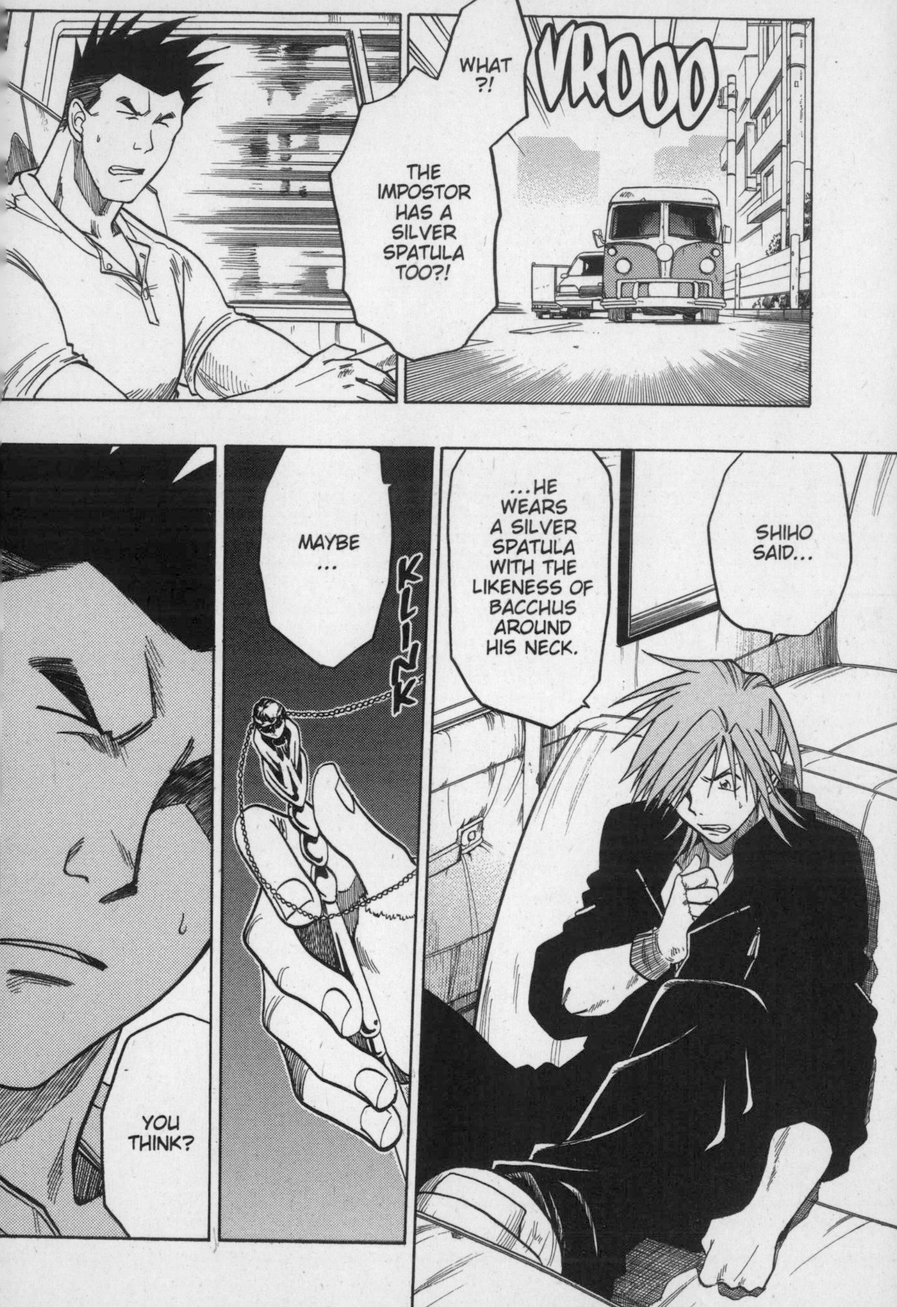
VROOO
WHAT ?!
THE IMPOSTOR HAS A SILVER SPATULA TOO?!
SHIHO SAID...
...HE WEARS A SILVER SPATULA WITH THE LIKENESS OF BACCHUS AROUND HIS NECK.
MAYBE ...
KLINK
YOU THINK?

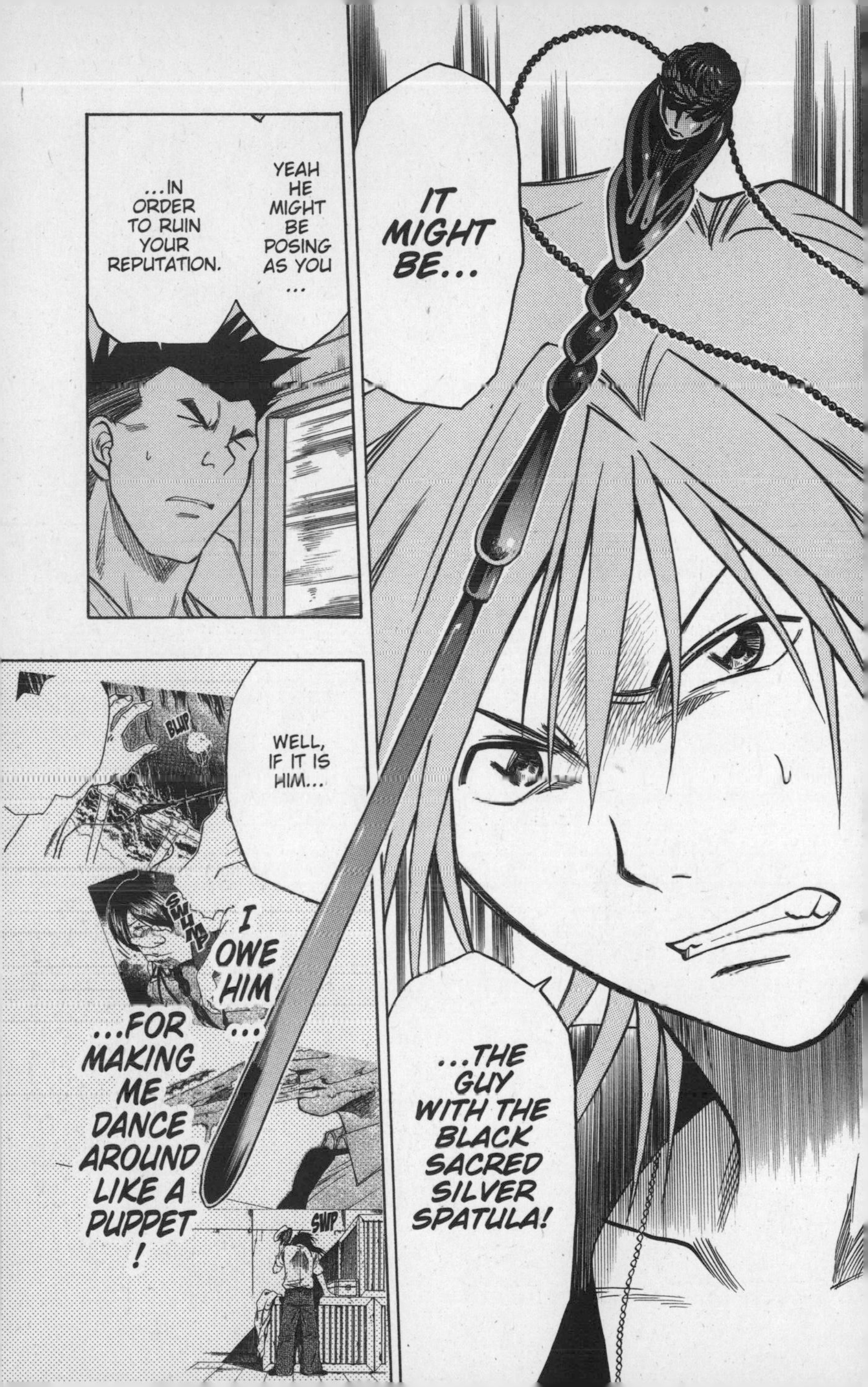
YEAH HE MIGHT BE POSING AS YOU...
...IN ORDER TO RUIN YOUR REPUTATION.
IT MIGHT BE...
...THE GUY WITH THE BLACK SACRED SILVER SPATULA!
WELL, IF IT IS HIM...
BLIP
SWUMP
I OWE HIM...
...FOR MAKING ME DANCE AROUND LIKE A PUPPET!
SWP

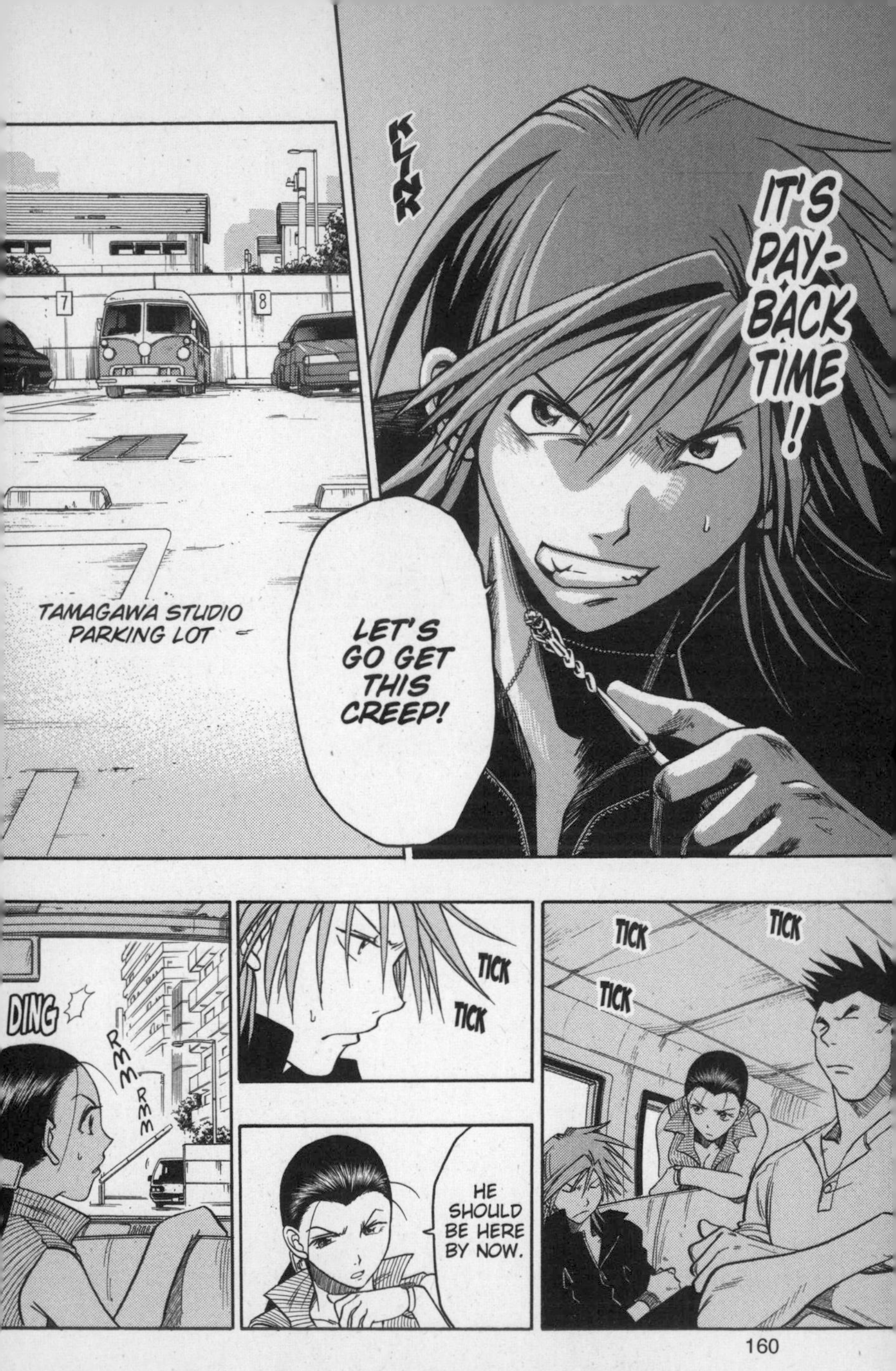
KLINK
IT'S PAY-BACK TIME!
LET'S GO GET THIS CREEP!
TAMAGAWA STUDIO PARKING LOT
TICK
TICK
TICK
TICK
TICK
HE SHOULD BE HERE BY NOW.
DING
RMM RMM RMM

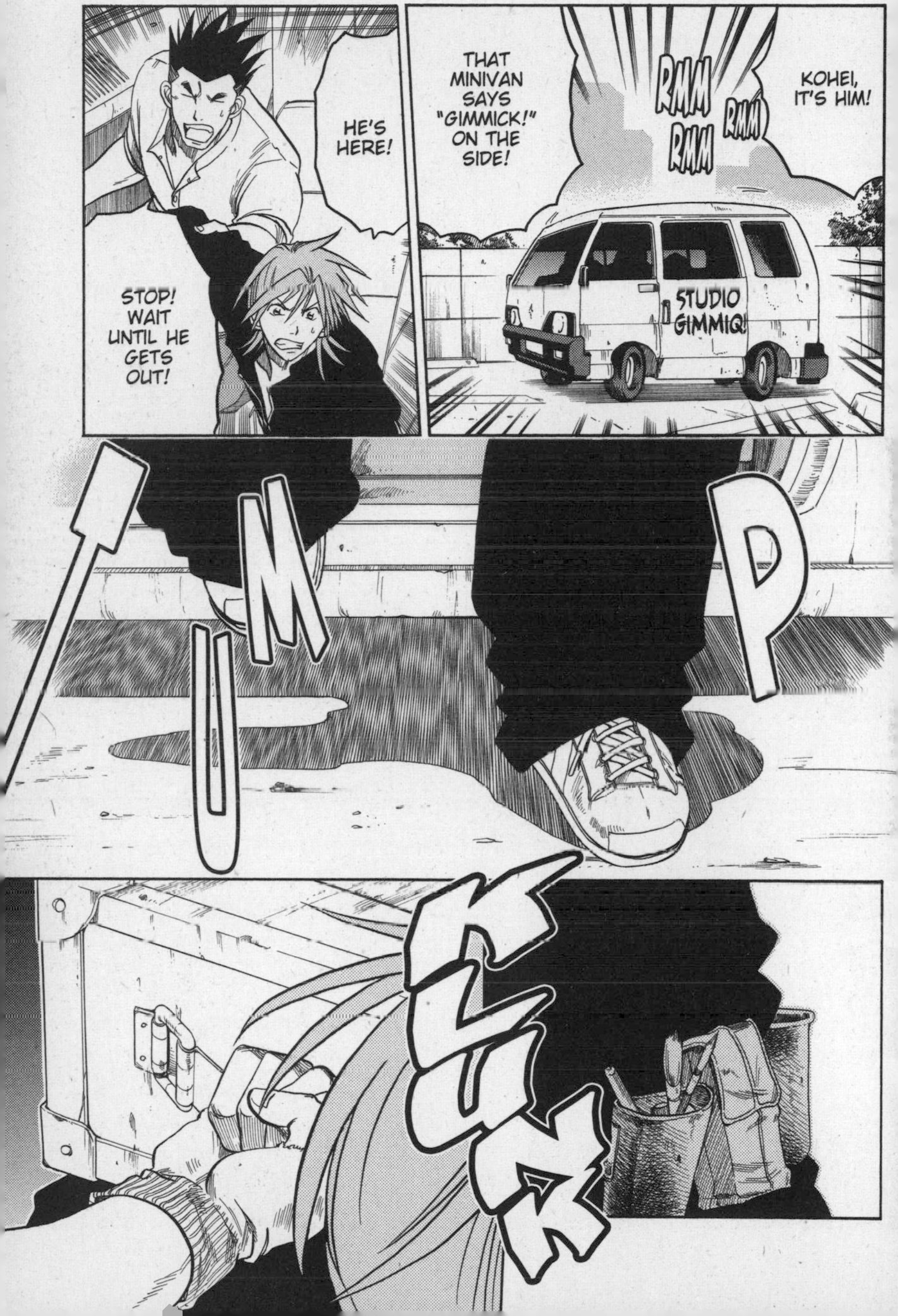
KOHEI, IT'S HIM!
RMM RMM RMM
THAT MINIVAN SAYS "GIMMICK!" ON THE SIDE!
STUDIO GIMMIQ
HE'S HERE!
STOP! WAIT UNTIL HE GETS OUT!
JUMP

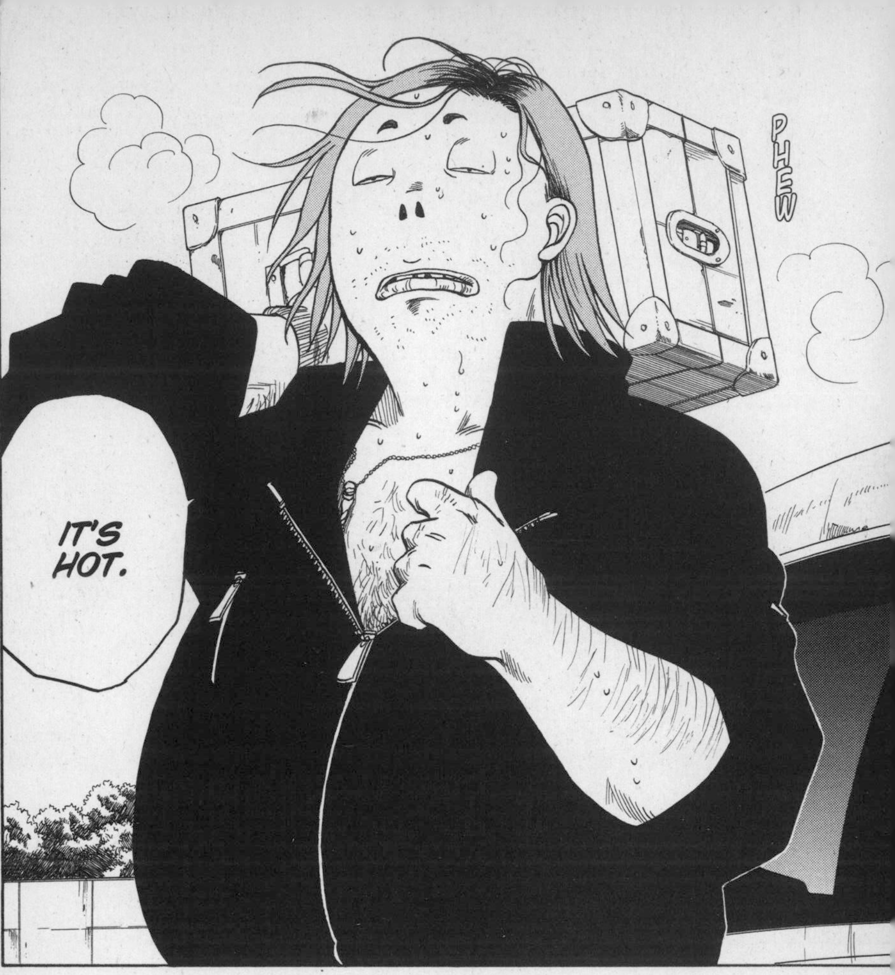
PHEW
IT'S HOT.
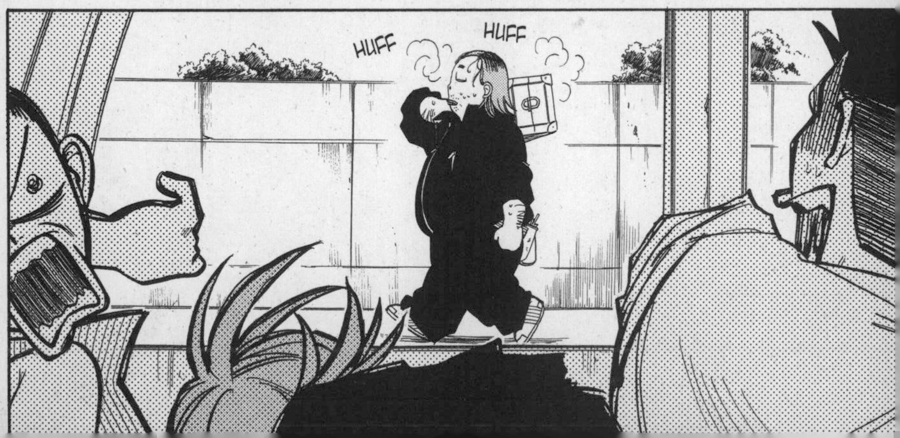
HUFF
HUFF

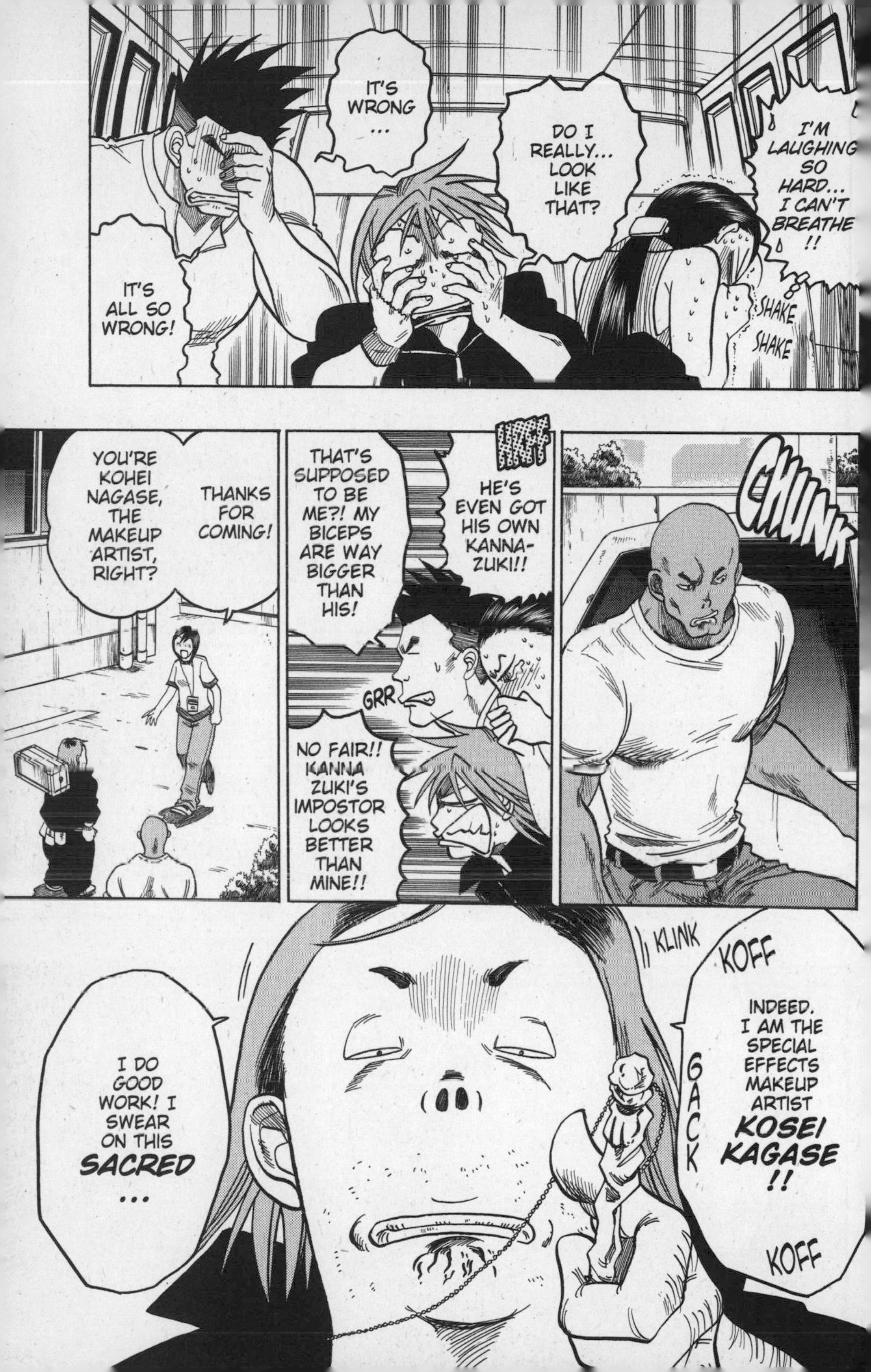
I'M LAUGHING SO HARD... I CAN'T BREATHE!!
SHAKE
SHAKE
DO I REALLY... LOOK LIKE THAT?
IT'S WRONG...
IT'S ALL SO WRONG!
CHUNK
HE'S EVEN GOT HIS OWN KANNA-ZUKI!!
THAT'S SUPPOSED TO BE ME?! MY BICEPS ARE WAY BIGGER THAN HIS!
GRR
NO FAIR!! KANNA ZUKI'S IMPOSTOR LOOKS BETTER THAN MINE!!
THANKS FOR COMING!
YOU'RE KOHEI NAGASE, THE MAKEUP ARTIST, RIGHT?
KLINK
KOFF
INDEED. I AM THE SPECIAL EFFECTS MAKEUP ARTIST **KOSEI KAGASE**!!
GACK
KOFF
I DO GOOD WORK! I SWEAR ON THIS **SACRED**...

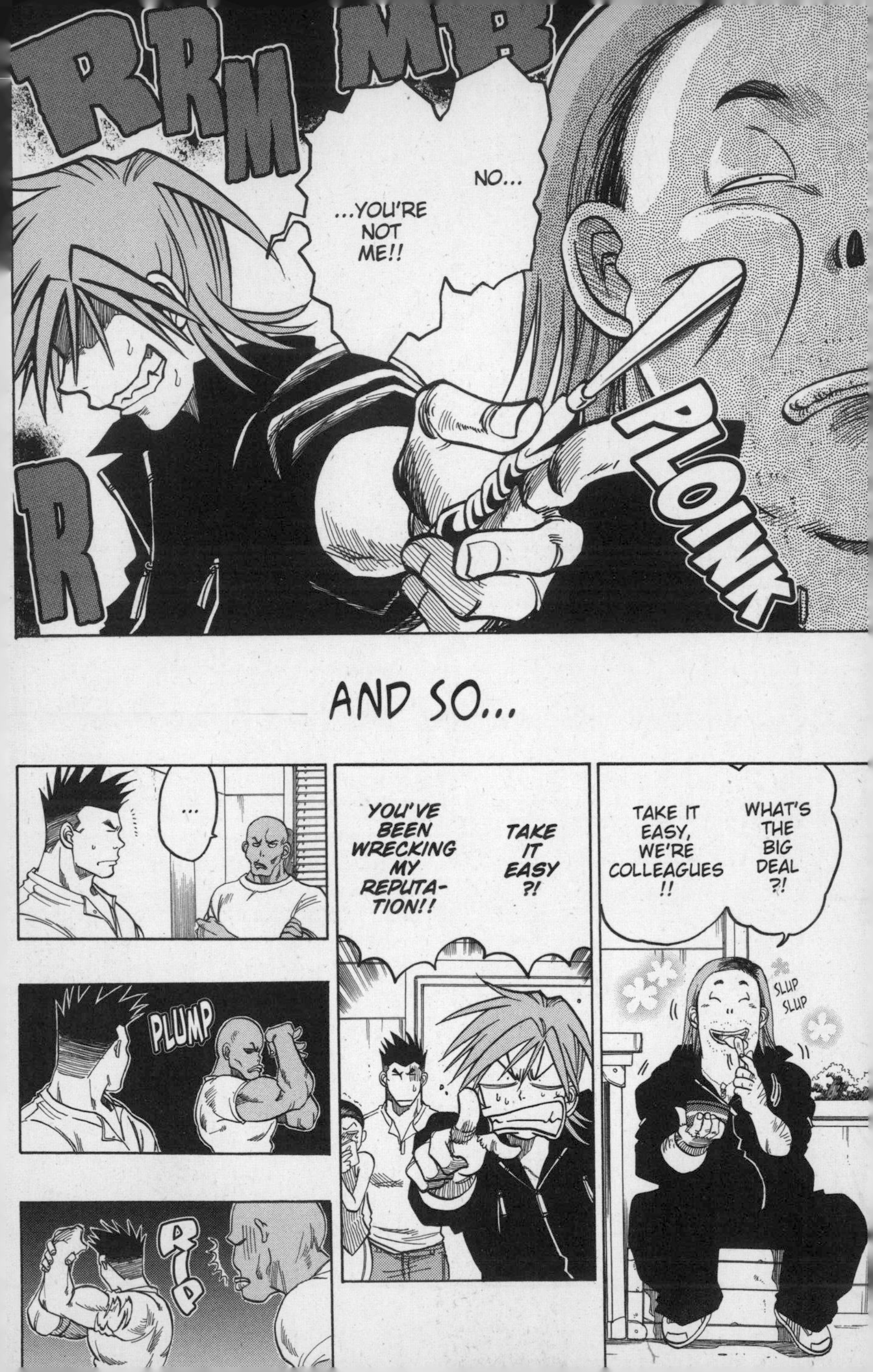

RRRMMB
NO...
...YOU'RE NOT ME!!
PLOINK
R
AND SO...
WHAT'S THE BIG DEAL ?!
TAKE IT EASY, WE'RE COLLEAGUES !!
SLUP SLUP
TAKE IT EASY ?!
YOU'VE BEEN WRECKING MY REPUTATION!!
...
PLUMP
RIP

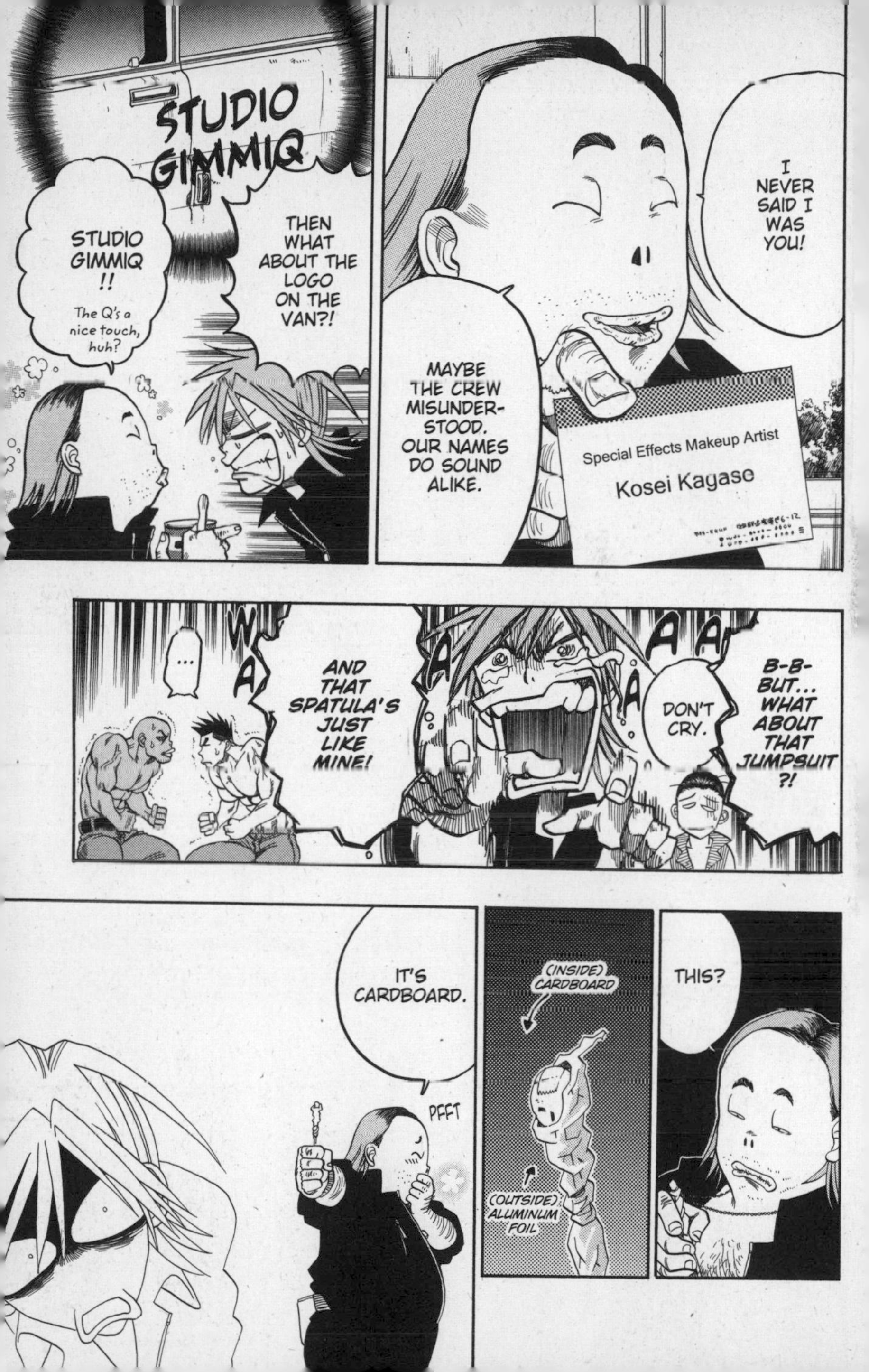
I NEVER SAID I WAS YOU!
MAYBE THE CREW MISUNDERSTOOD. OUR NAMES DO SOUND ALIKE.
Special Effects Makeup Artist
Kosei Kagaso
STUDIO GIMMIQ
THEN WHAT ABOUT THE LOGO ON THE VAN?!
STUDIO GIMMIQ!!
The Q's a nice touch, huh?
B-B-BUT... WHAT ABOUT THAT JUMPSUIT?!
DON'T CRY.
WAAAAA
AND THAT SPATULA'S JUST LIKE MINE!
...
THIS?
(INSIDE) CARDBOARD
(OUTSIDE) ALUMINUM FOIL
IT'S CARDBOARD.
PFFT

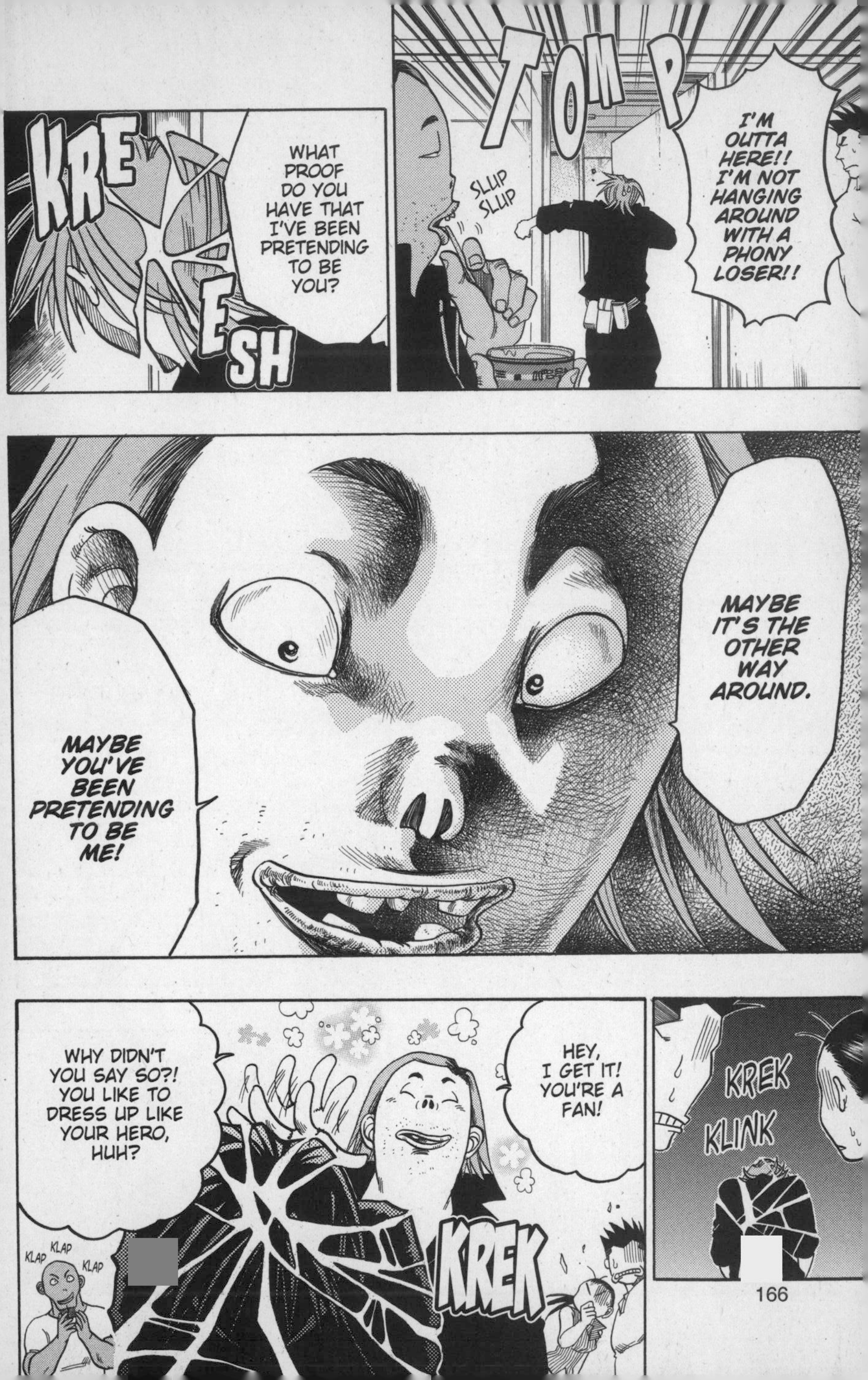
I'M OUTTA HERE!! I'M NOT HANGING AROUND WITH A PHONY LOSER!!
TOMP
SLUP SLUP
WHAT PROOF DO YOU HAVE THAT I'VE BEEN PRETENDING TO BE YOU?
KREESH
MAYBE IT'S THE OTHER WAY AROUND.
MAYBE YOU'VE BEEN PRETENDING TO BE ME!
KREK
KLINK
HEY, I GET IT! YOU'RE A FAN!
WHY DIDN'T YOU SAY SO?! YOU LIKE TO DRESS UP LIKE YOUR HERO, HUH?
KREK
KLAP
KLAP
KLAP

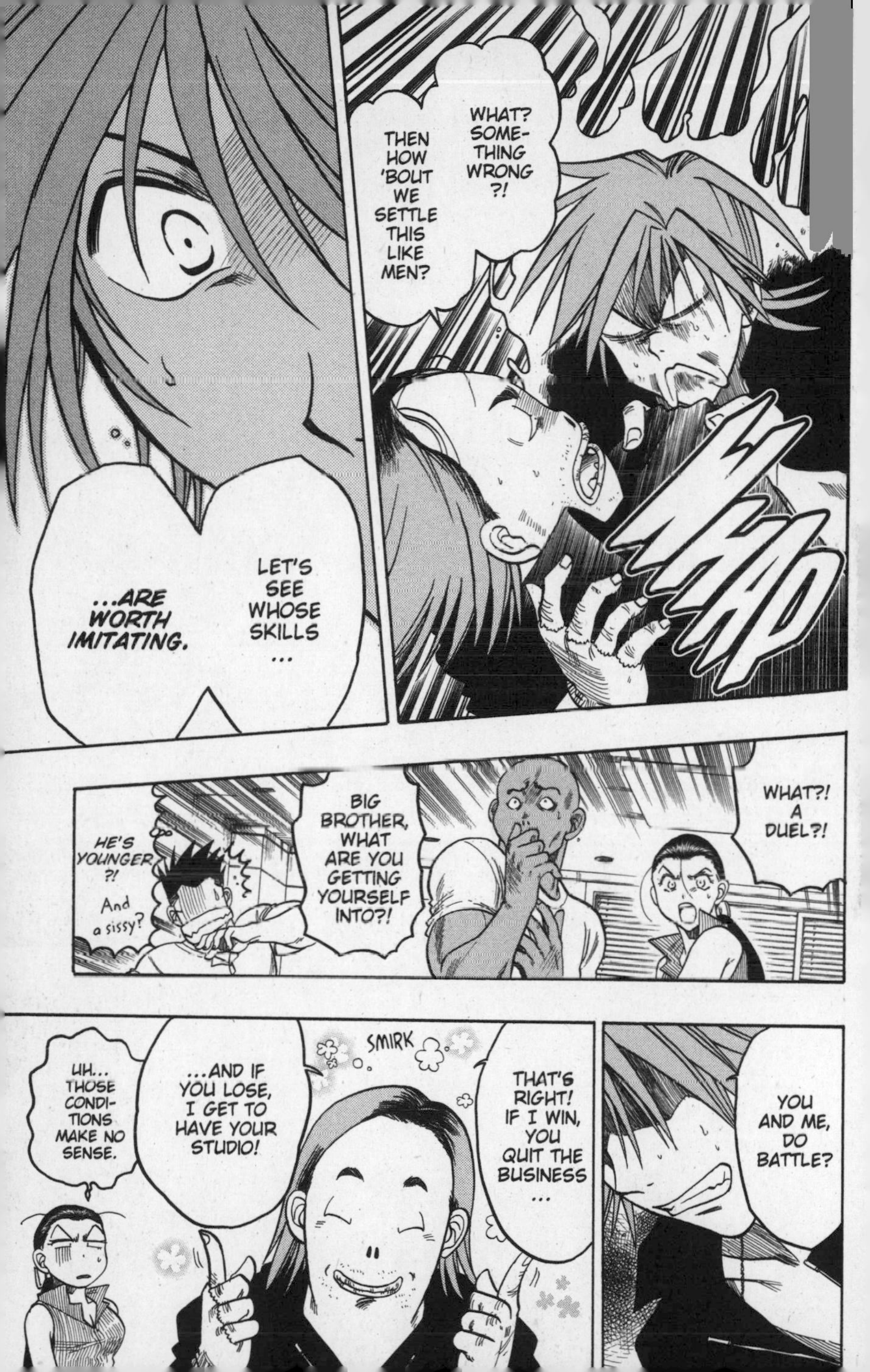
WHAT? SOMETHING WRONG?!
THEN HOW 'BOUT WE SETTLE THIS LIKE MEN?
WHAP
LET'S SEE WHOSE SKILLS...
...ARE WORTH IMITATING.
WHAT?! A DUEL?!
BIG BROTHER, WHAT ARE YOU GETTING YOURSELF INTO?!
HE'S YOUNGER?!
And a sissy?
YOU AND ME, DO BATTLE?
THAT'S RIGHT! IF I WIN, YOU QUIT THE BUSINESS...
SMIRK
...AND IF YOU LOSE, I GET TO HAVE YOUR STUDIO!
UH... THOSE CONDITIONS MAKE NO SENSE.

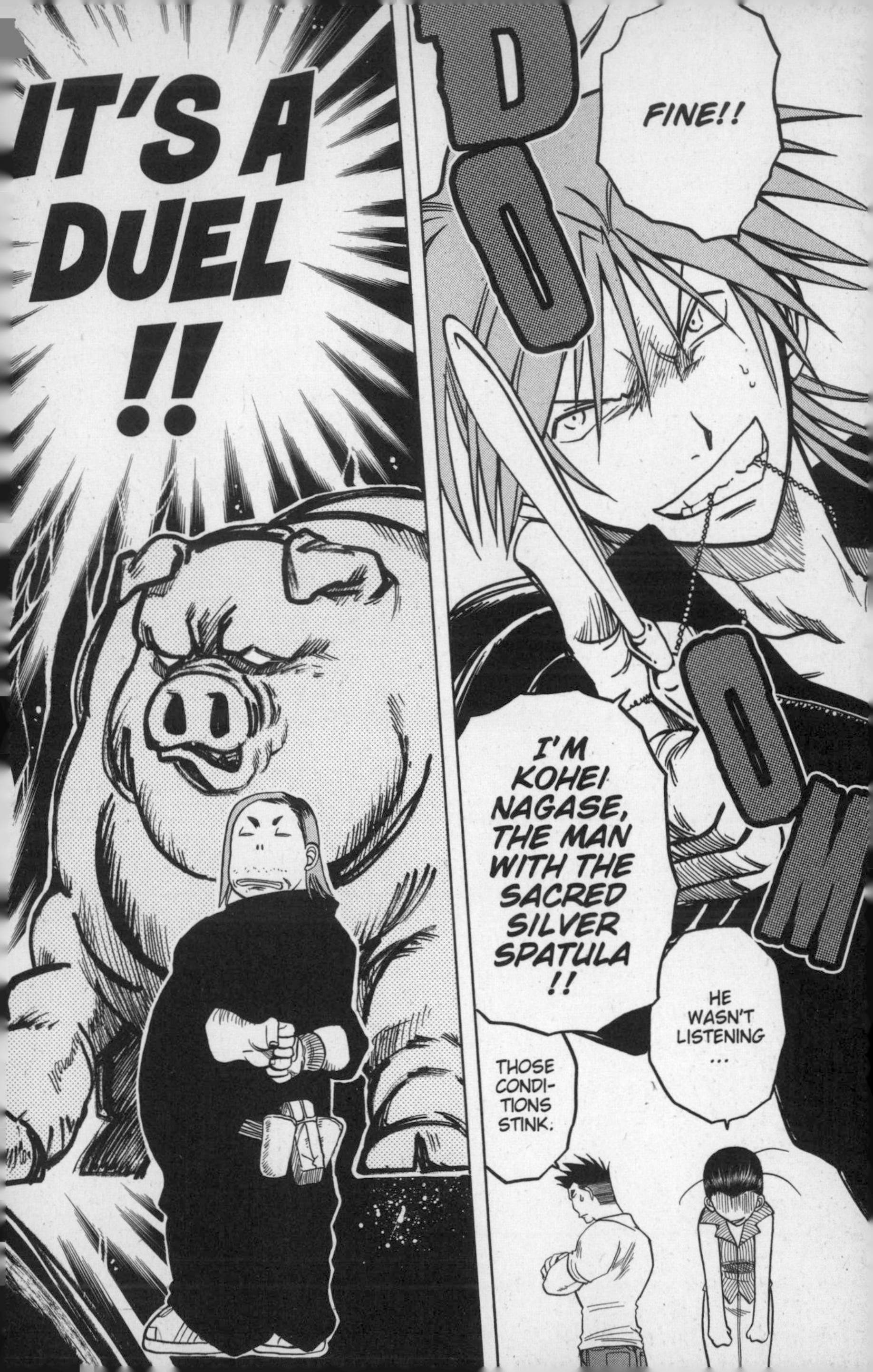
FINE!!
DOOM
I'M KOHEI NAGASE, THE MAN WITH THE SACRED SILVER SPATULA!!
HE WASN'T LISTENING...
THOSE CONDITIONS STINK.
IT'S A DUEL!!

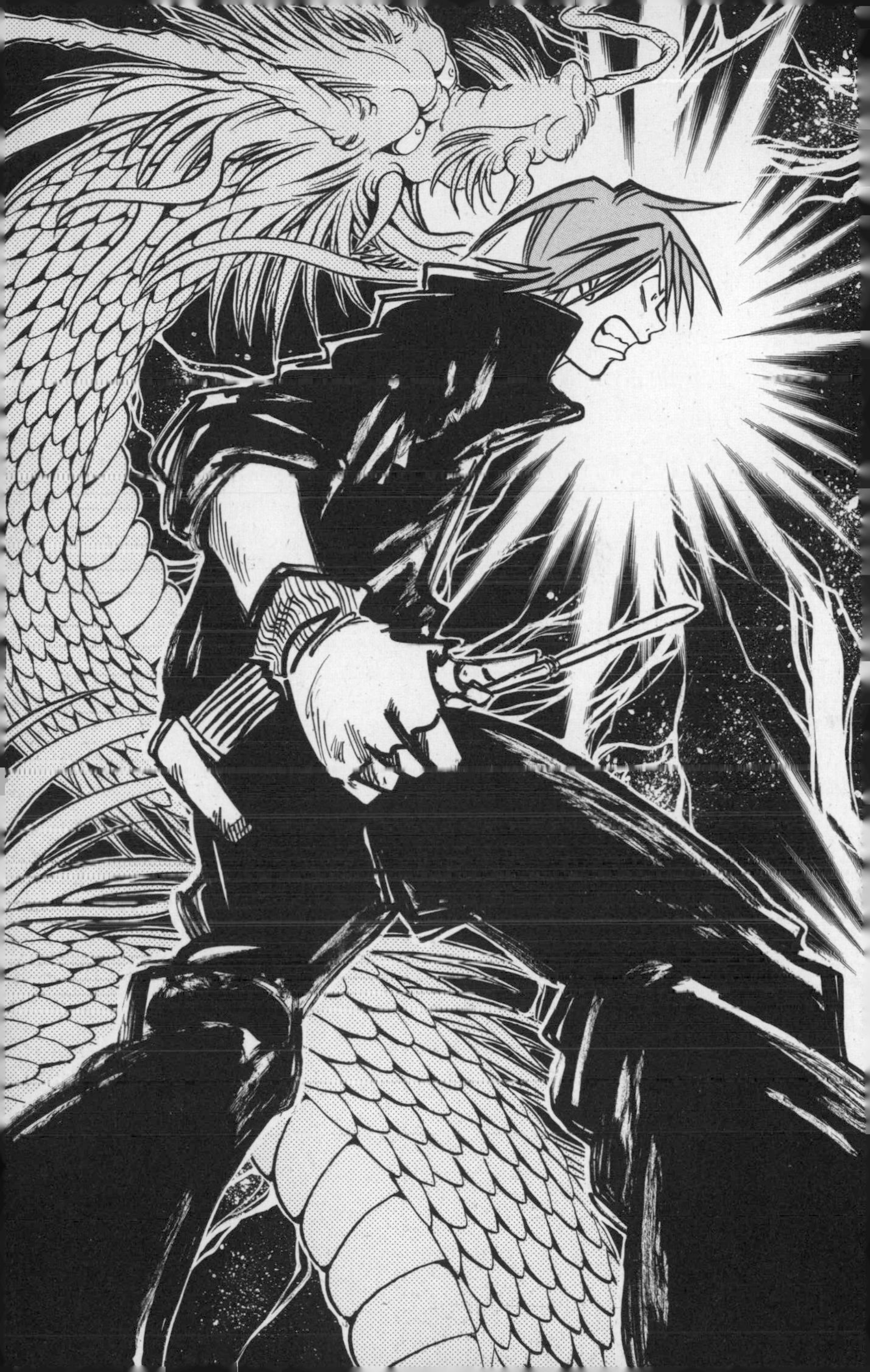

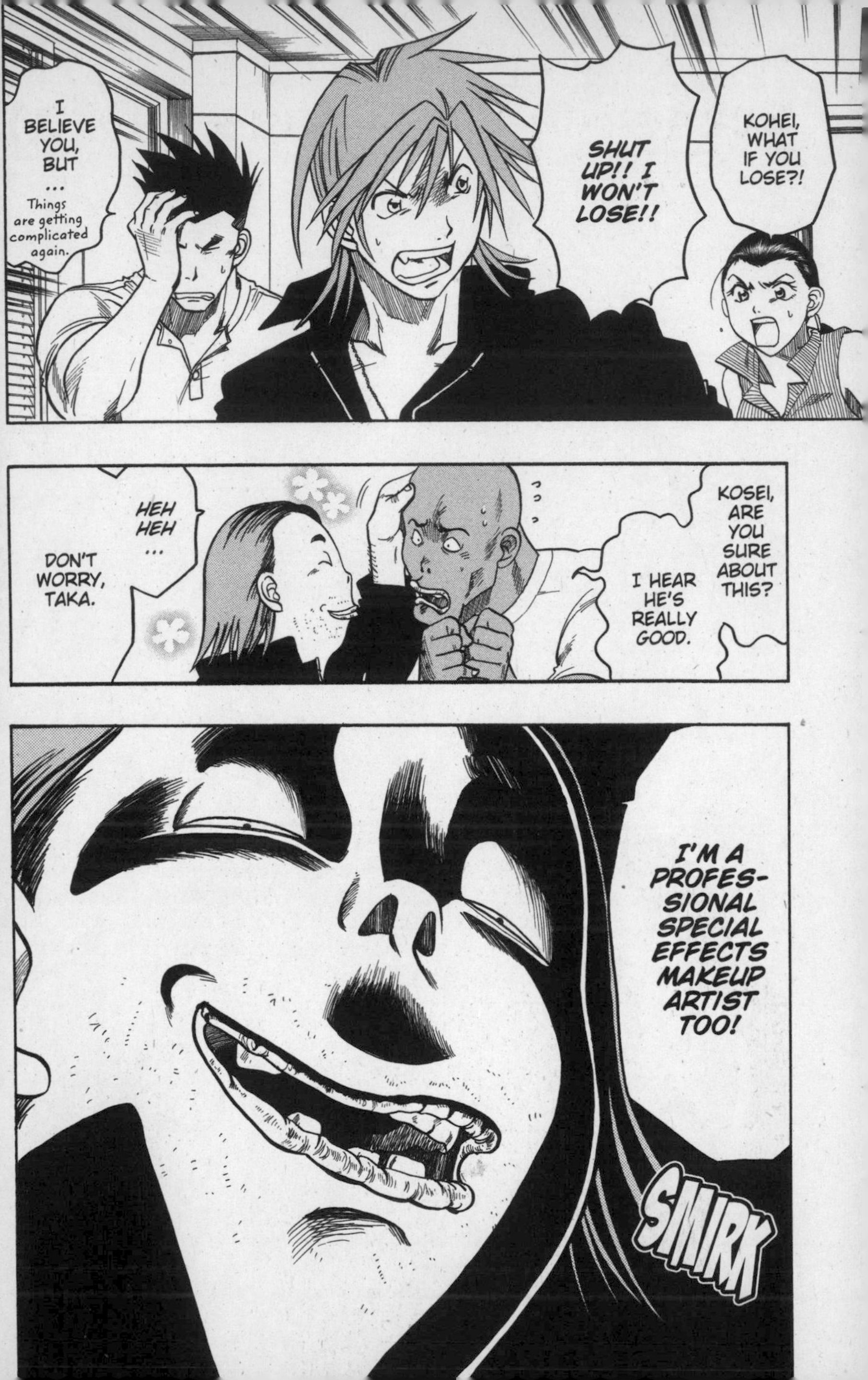
KOHEI, WHAT IF YOU LOSE?!
SHUT UP!! I WON'T LOSE!!
I BELIEVE YOU, BUT ...
Things are getting complicated again.
KOSEI, ARE YOU SURE ABOUT THIS?
I HEAR HE'S REALLY GOOD.
HEH HEH ...
DON'T WORRY, TAKA.
I'M A PROFES-SIONAL SPECIAL EFFECTS MAKEUP ARTIST TOO!
SMIRK

Scene 56: Mr. Doubt (Part 2)

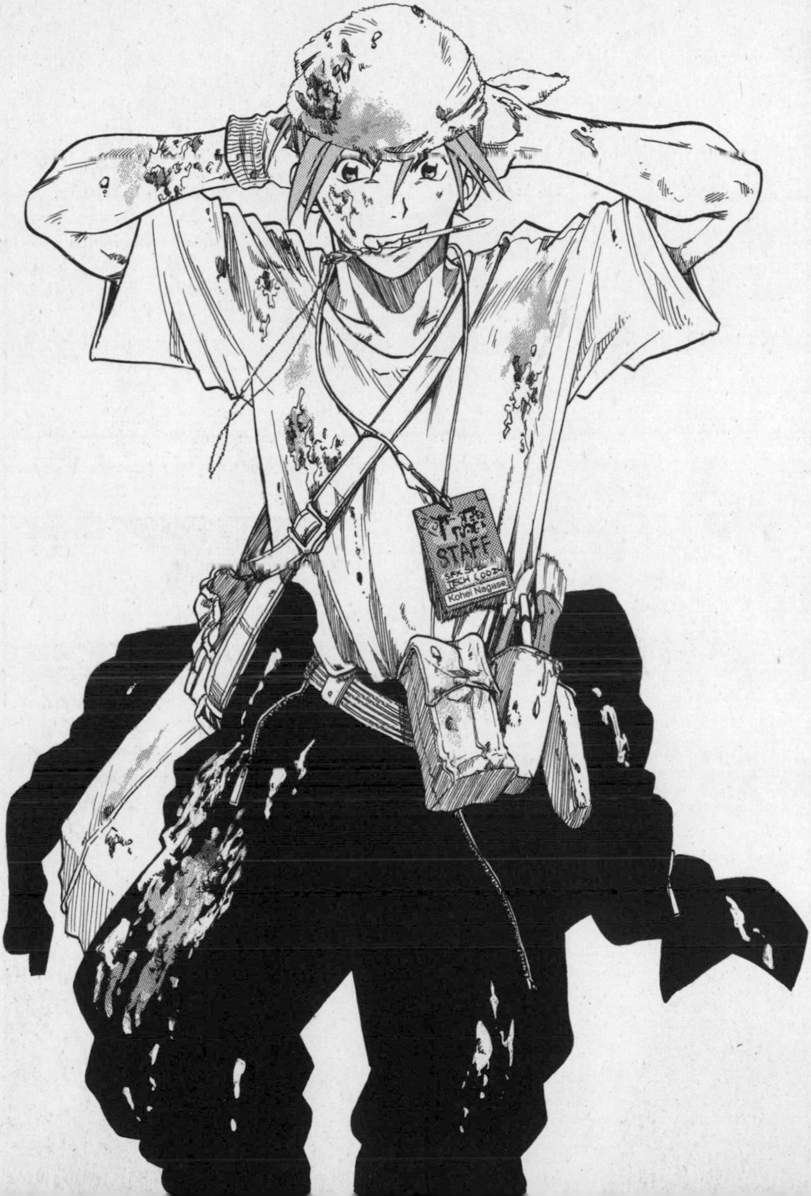
STAFF
Kohei Nagase

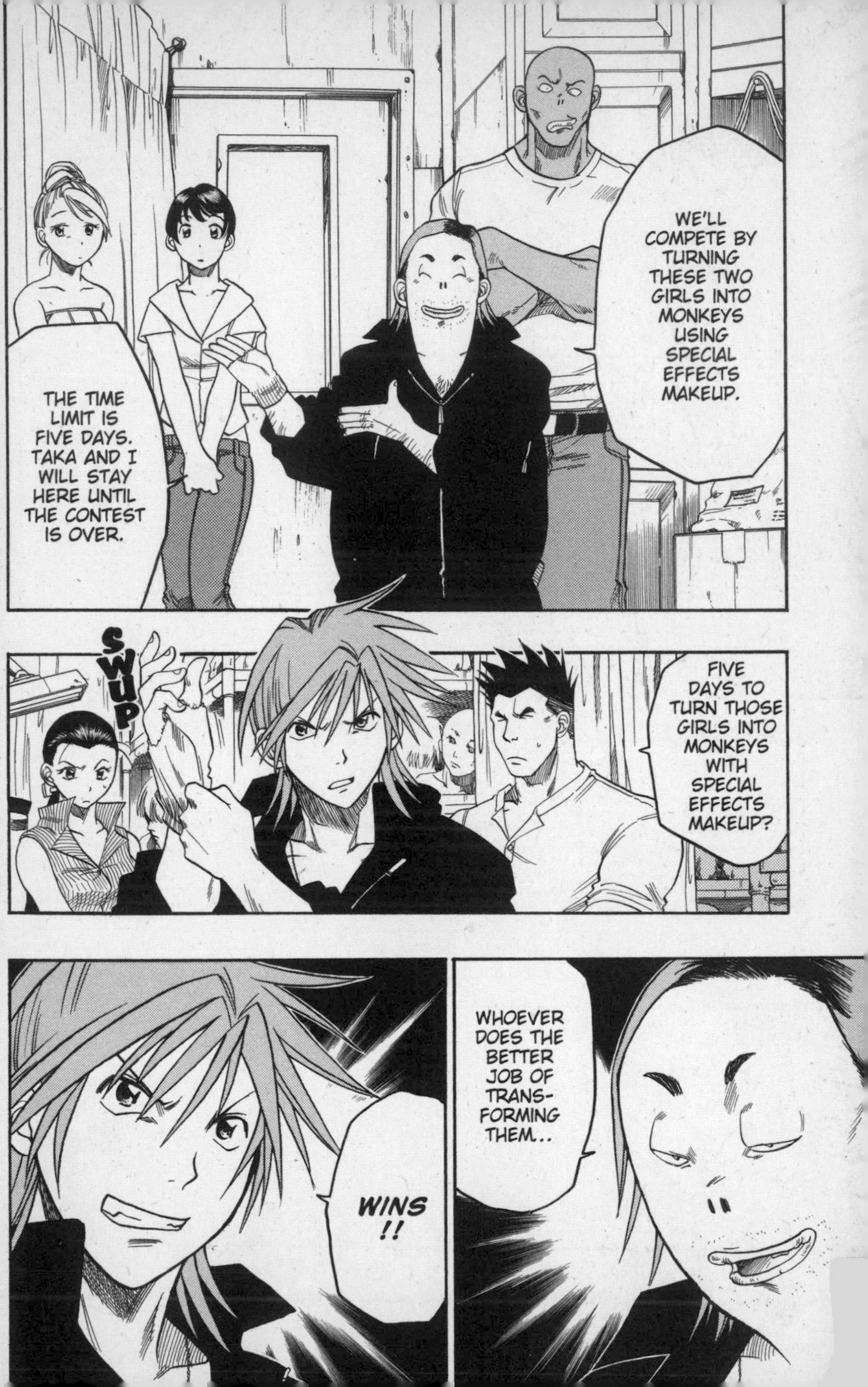
WE'LL COMPETE BY TURNING THESE TWO GIRLS INTO MONKEYS USING SPECIAL EFFECTS MAKEUP.
THE TIME LIMIT IS FIVE DAYS. TAKA AND I WILL STAY HERE UNTIL THE CONTEST IS OVER.
FIVE DAYS TO TURN THOSE GIRLS INTO MONKEYS WITH SPECIAL EFFECTS MAKEUP?
SWUP
WHOEVER DOES THE BETTER JOB OF TRANS-FORMING THEM..
WINS !!

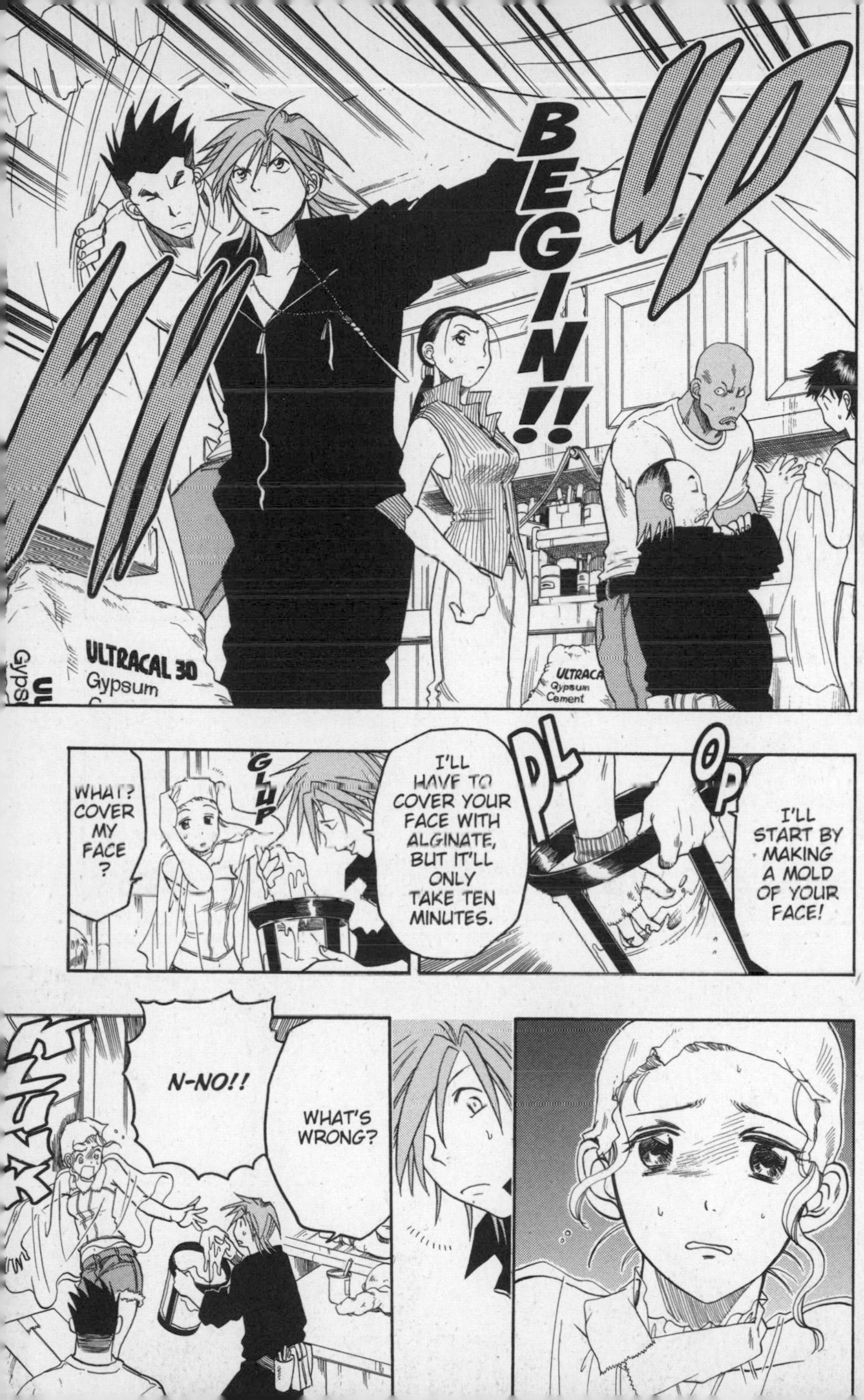
BEGIN!!
ULTRACAL 30
Gypsum
ULTRACAL
Gypsum
Cement
I'LL START BY MAKING A MOLD OF YOUR FACE!
DLOP
I'LL HAVE TO COVER YOUR FACE WITH ALGINATE, BUT IT'LL ONLY TAKE TEN MINUTES.
GLUP
WHAT? COVER MY FACE?
N-NO!!
WHAT'S WRONG?

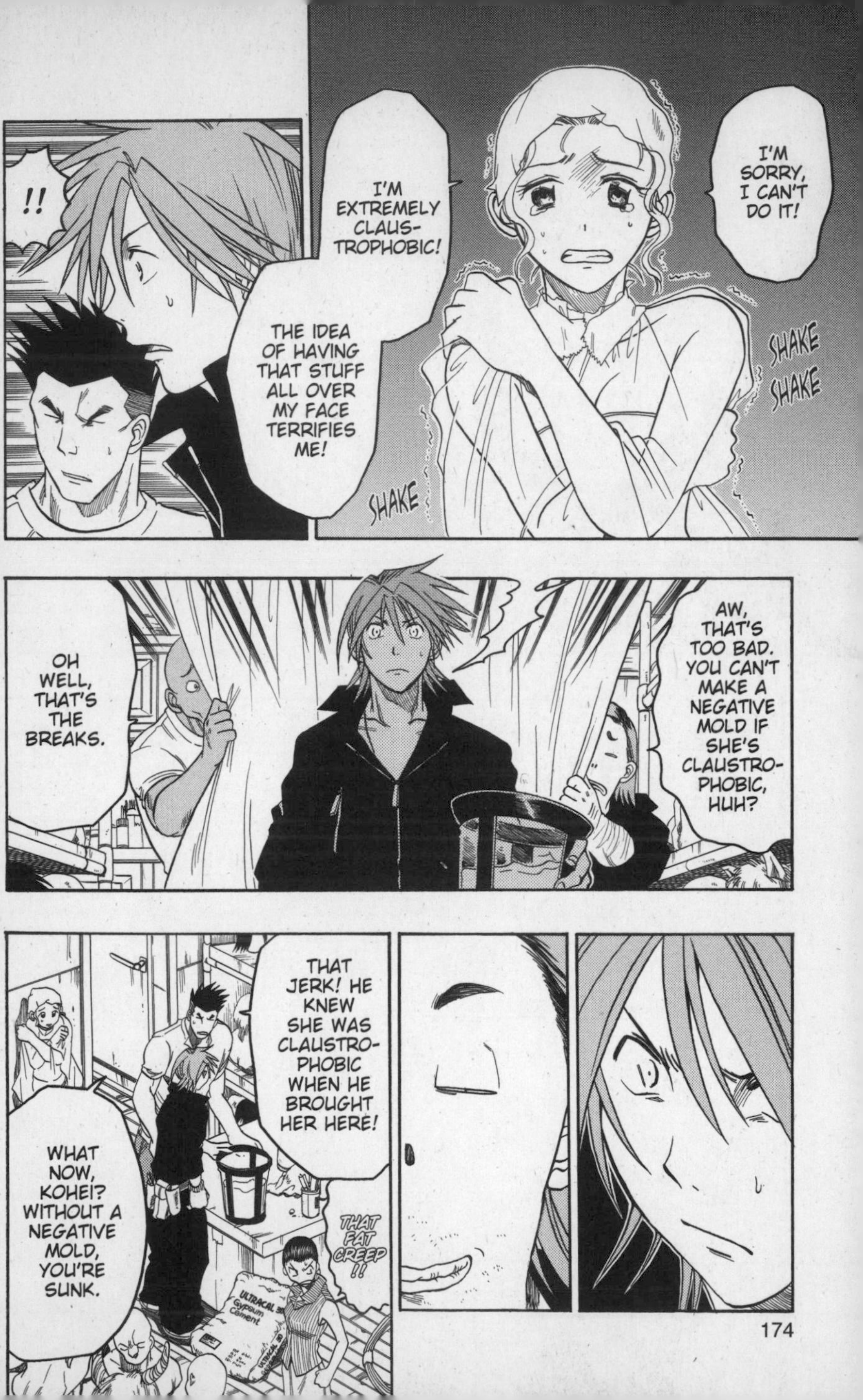
I'M SORRY, I CAN'T DO IT!
I'M EXTREMELY CLAUS-TROPHOBIC!
THE IDEA OF HAVING THAT STUFF ALL OVER MY FACE TERRIFIES ME!
SHAKE SHAKE
SHAKE
!!
AW, THAT'S TOO BAD. YOU CAN'T MAKE A NEGATIVE MOLD IF SHE'S CLAUSTRO-PHOBIC, HUH?
OH WELL, THAT'S THE BREAKS.
THAT JERK! HE KNEW SHE WAS CLAUSTRO-PHOBIC WHEN HE BROUGHT HER HERE!
THAT FAT CREEP!!
WHAT NOW, KOHEI? WITHOUT A NEGATIVE MOLD, YOU'RE SUNK.
ULTRACAL 30 Gypsum Cement

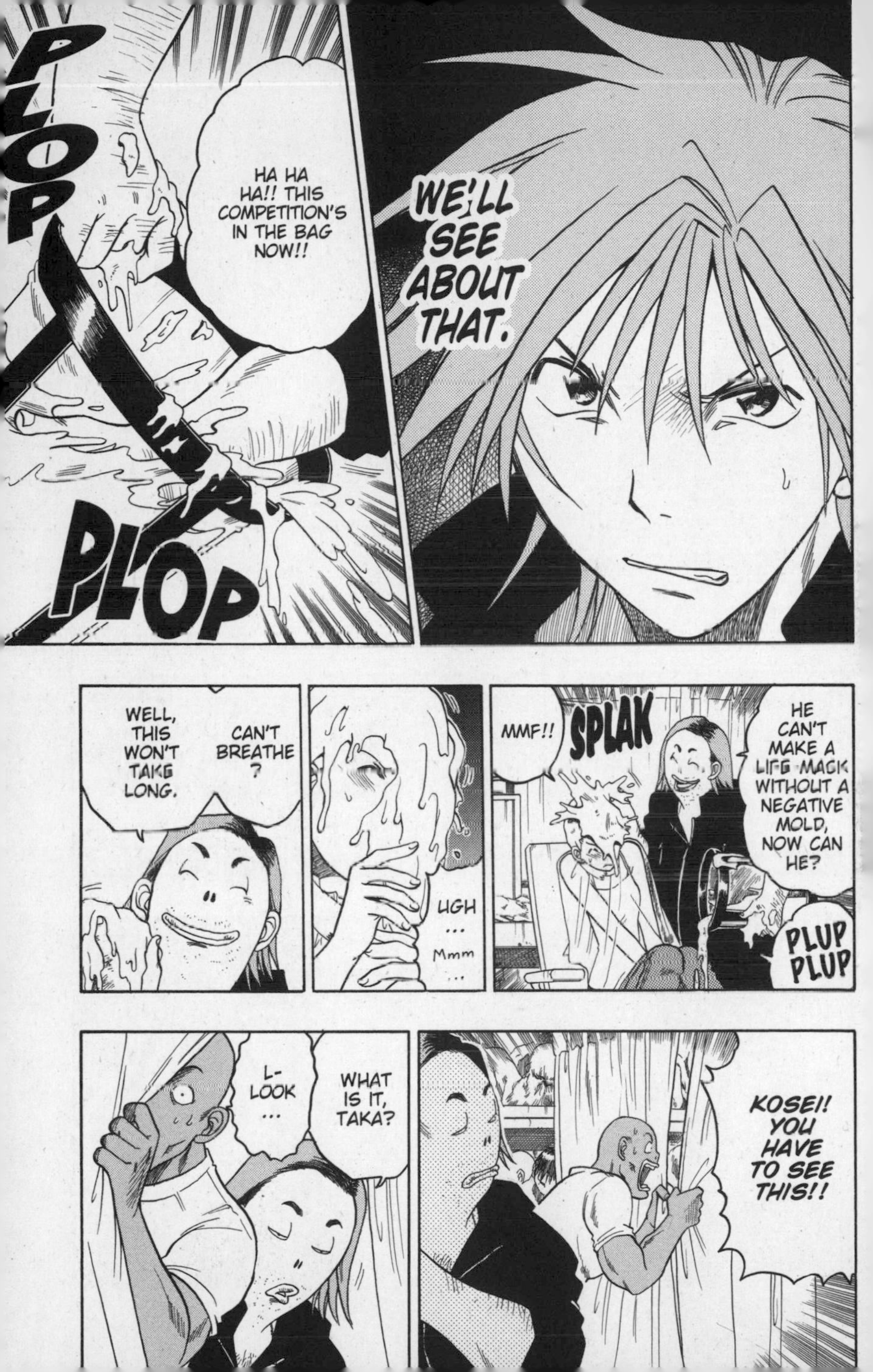
WE'LL SEE ABOUT THAT.
HA HA HA!! THIS COMPETITION'S IN THE BAG NOW!!
PLOP
PLOP
HE CAN'T MAKE A LIFE MASK WITHOUT A NEGATIVE MOLD, NOW CAN HE?
SPLAK
MMF!!
PLUP PLUP
UGH ...
Mmm ...
CAN'T BREATHE?
WELL, THIS WON'T TAKE LONG.
KOSEI! YOU HAVE TO SEE THIS!!
WHAT IS IT, TAKA?
L-LOOK ...

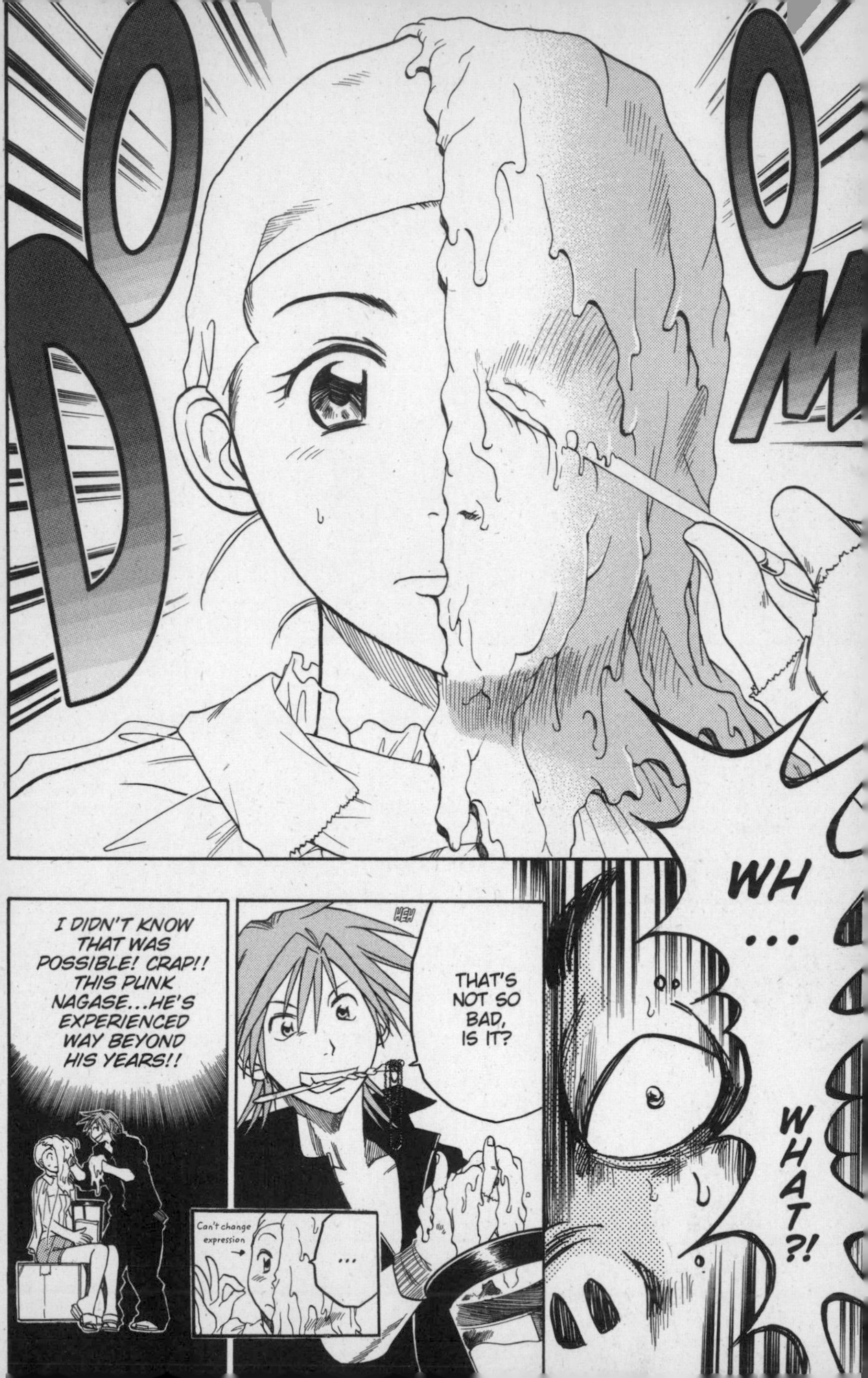
DOOM
WH...
WHAT?!
HEH
THAT'S NOT SO BAD, IS IT?
Can't change expression
...
I DIDN'T KNOW THAT WAS POSSIBLE! CRAP!! THIS PUNK NAGASE...HE'S EXPERIENCED WAY BEYOND HIS YEARS!!

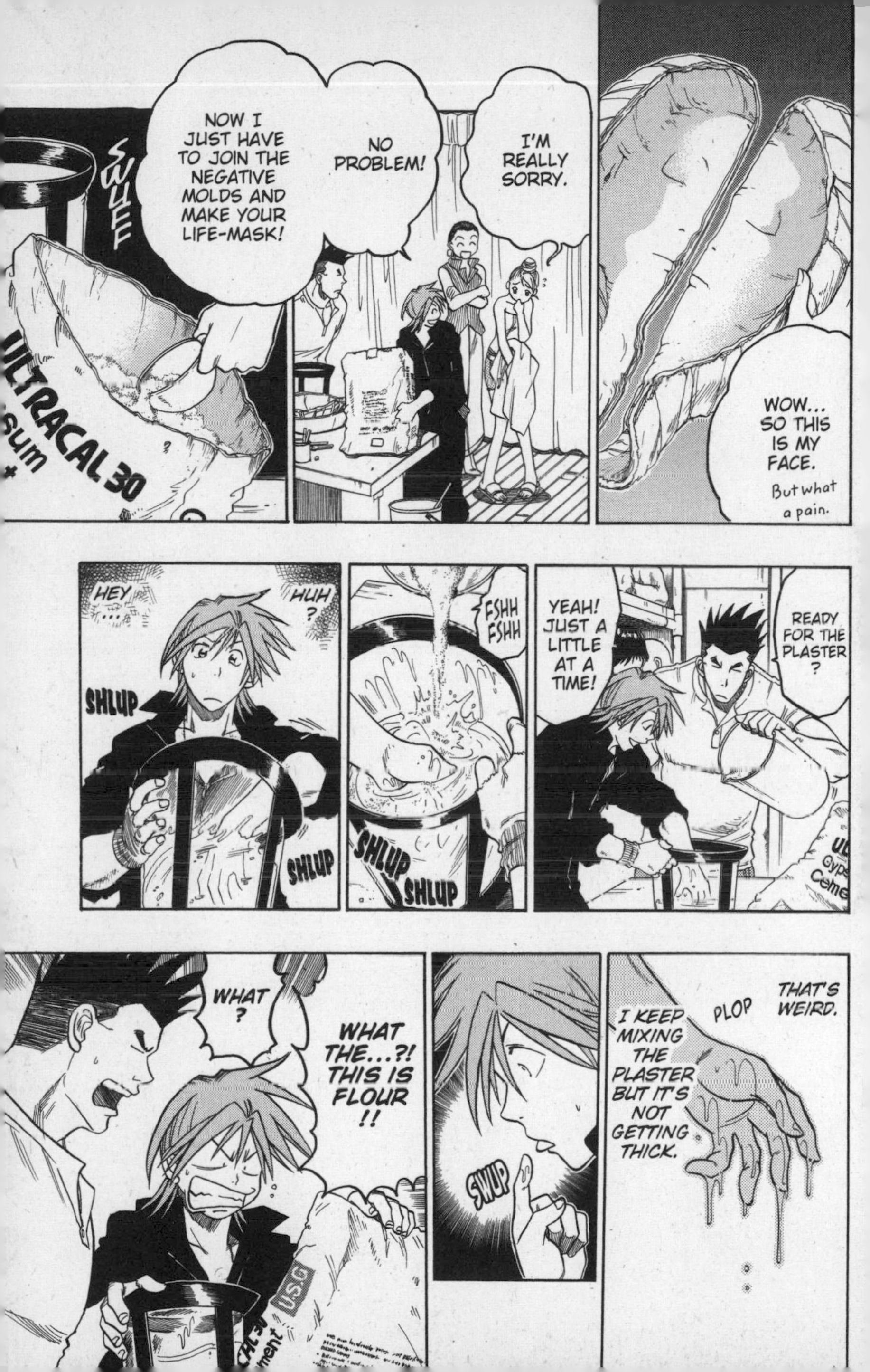
WOW... SO THIS IS MY FACE.
But what a pain.
I'M REALLY SORRY.
NO PROBLEM!
NOW I JUST HAVE TO JOIN THE NEGATIVE MOLDS AND MAKE YOUR LIFE-MASK!
SWUFF
ULTRACAL 30
READY FOR THE PLASTER?
YEAH! JUST A LITTLE AT A TIME!
FSHH FSHH
SHLUP
SHLUP
HUH?
HEY...
SHLUP
SHLUP
THAT'S WEIRD.
PLOP
I KEEP MIXING THE PLASTER BUT IT'S NOT GETTING THICK.
SWUP
WHAT?
WHAT THE...?! THIS IS FLOUR!!
USG

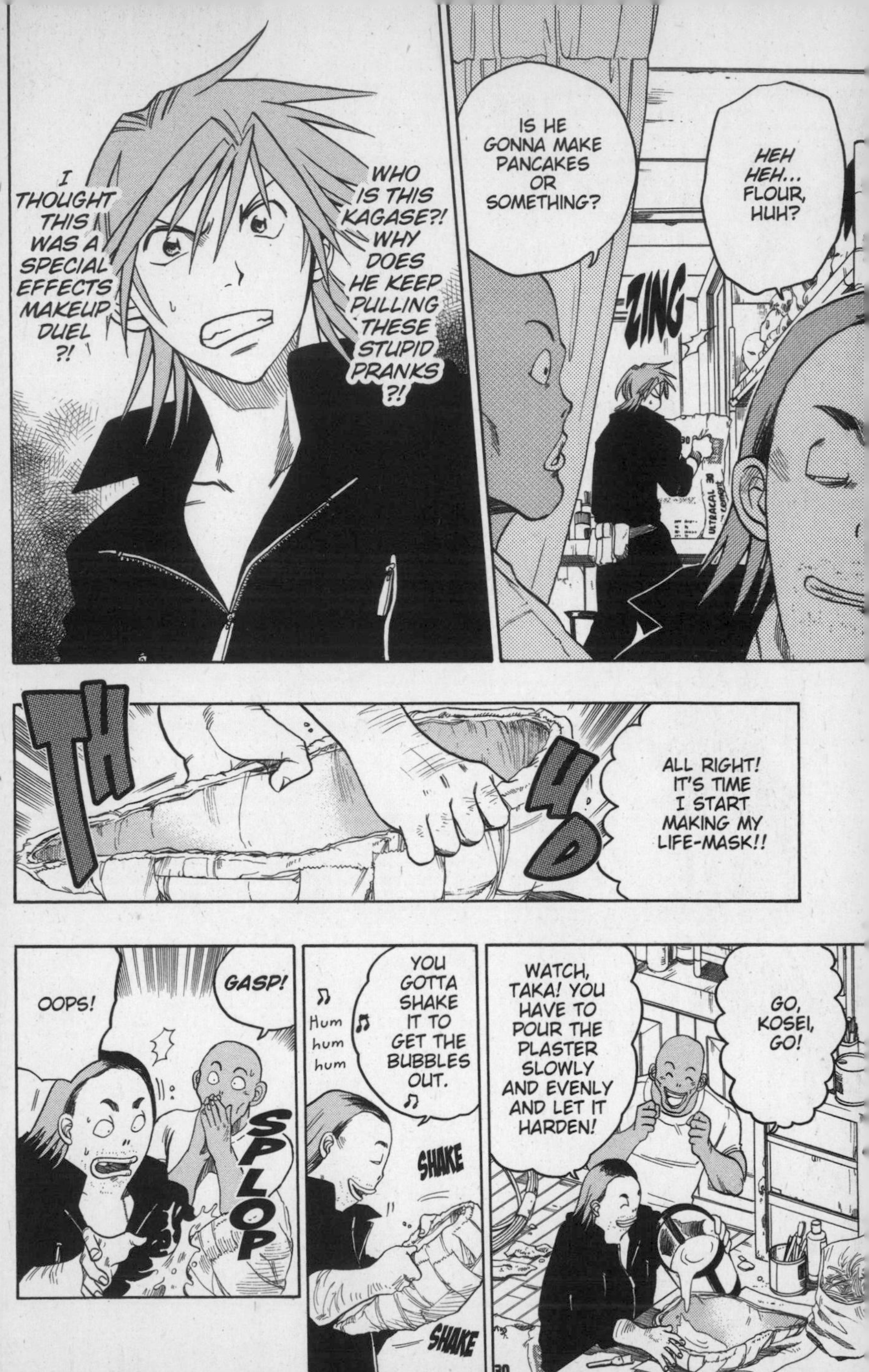
HEH HEH... FLOUR, HUH?
IS HE GONNA MAKE PANCAKES OR SOMETHING?
ZING
WHO IS THIS KAGASE?! WHY DOES HE KEEP PULLING THESE STUPID PRANKS?!
I THOUGHT THIS WAS A SPECIAL EFFECTS MAKEUP DUEL?!
ALL RIGHT! IT'S TIME I START MAKING MY LIFE-MASK!!
THUD
GO, KOSEI, GO!
WATCH, TAKA! YOU HAVE TO POUR THE PLASTER SLOWLY AND EVENLY AND LET IT HARDEN!
YOU GOTTA SHAKE IT TO GET THE BUBBLES OUT.
Hum hum hum
SHAKE
SHAKE
GASP!
SPLOP
OOPS!

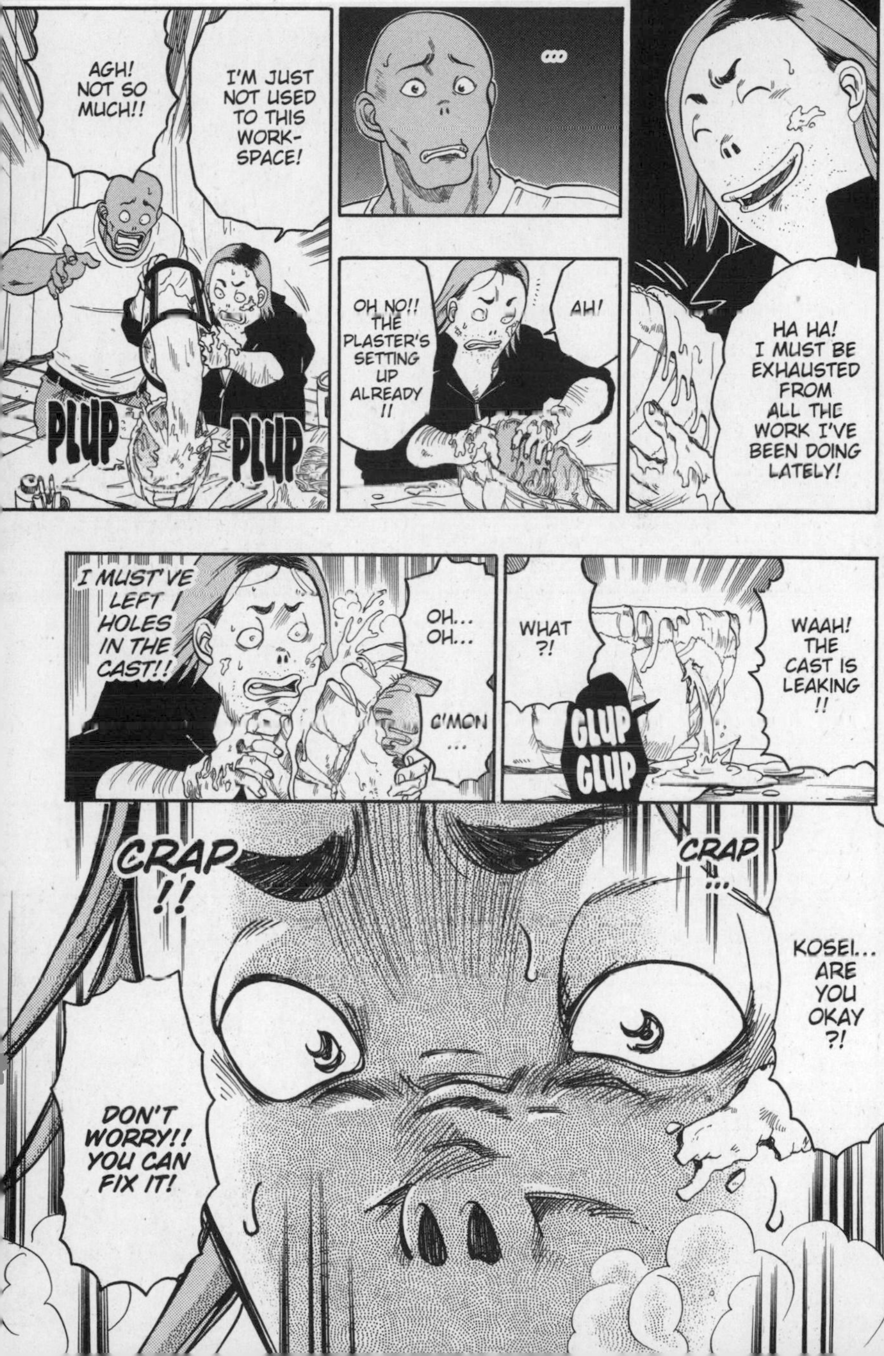
HA HA! I MUST BE EXHAUSTED FROM ALL THE WORK I'VE BEEN DOING LATELY!
...
AH!
OH NO!! THE PLASTER'S SETTING UP ALREADY!!
I'M JUST NOT USED TO THIS WORK-SPACE!
AGH! NOT SO MUCH!!
PLUP
PLUP
WAAH! THE CAST IS LEAKING!!
WHAT?!
GLUP GLUP
OH... OH...
C'MON...
I MUST'VE LEFT HOLES IN THE CAST!!
CRAP...
KOSEI... ARE YOU OKAY?!
CRAP!!
DON'T WORRY!! YOU CAN FIX IT!

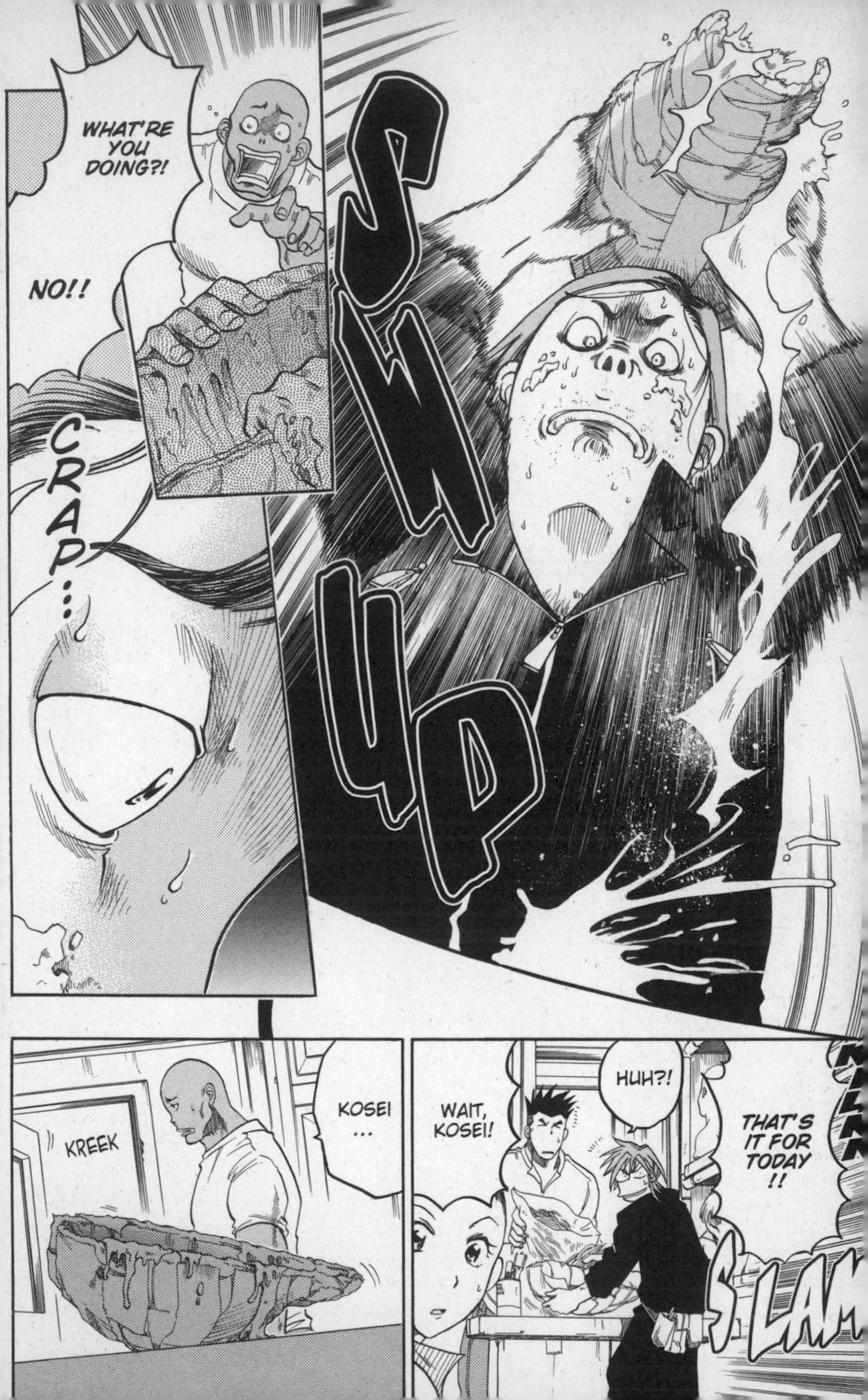
SHUP
WHAT'RE YOU DOING?!
NO!!
CRAP...
SLAM
THAT'S IT FOR TODAY!!
HUH?!
WAIT, KOSEI!
KOSEI ...
KREEK

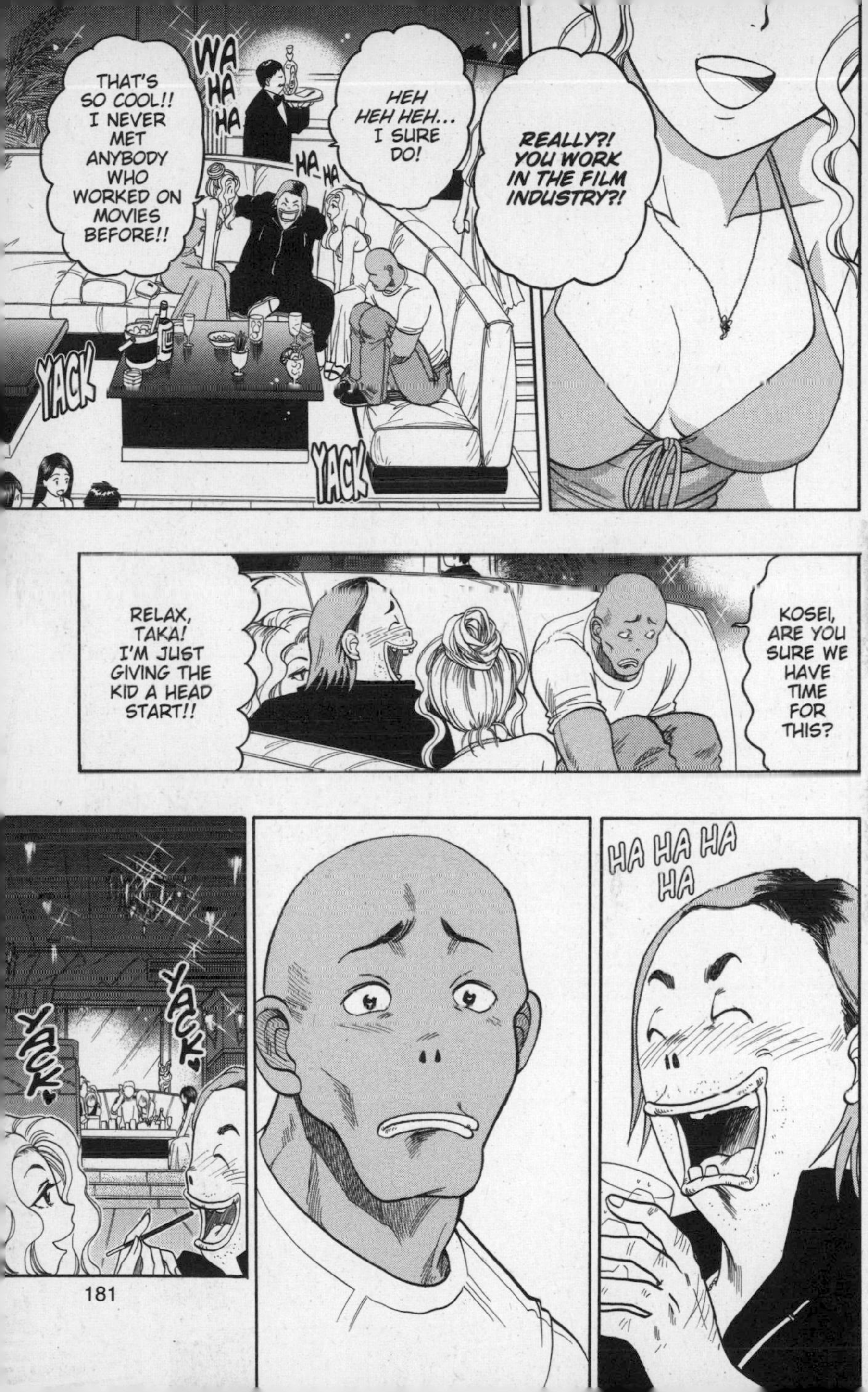
REALLY?! YOU WORK IN THE FILM INDUSTRY?!
HEH HEH HEH... I SURE DO!
WA HA HA
HA HA
THAT'S SO COOL!! I NEVER MET ANYBODY WHO WORKED ON MOVIES BEFORE!!
YACK
YACK
KOSEI, ARE YOU SURE WE HAVE TIME FOR THIS?
RELAX, TAKA! I'M JUST GIVING THE KID A HEAD START!!
HA HA HA HA
YACK
YACK

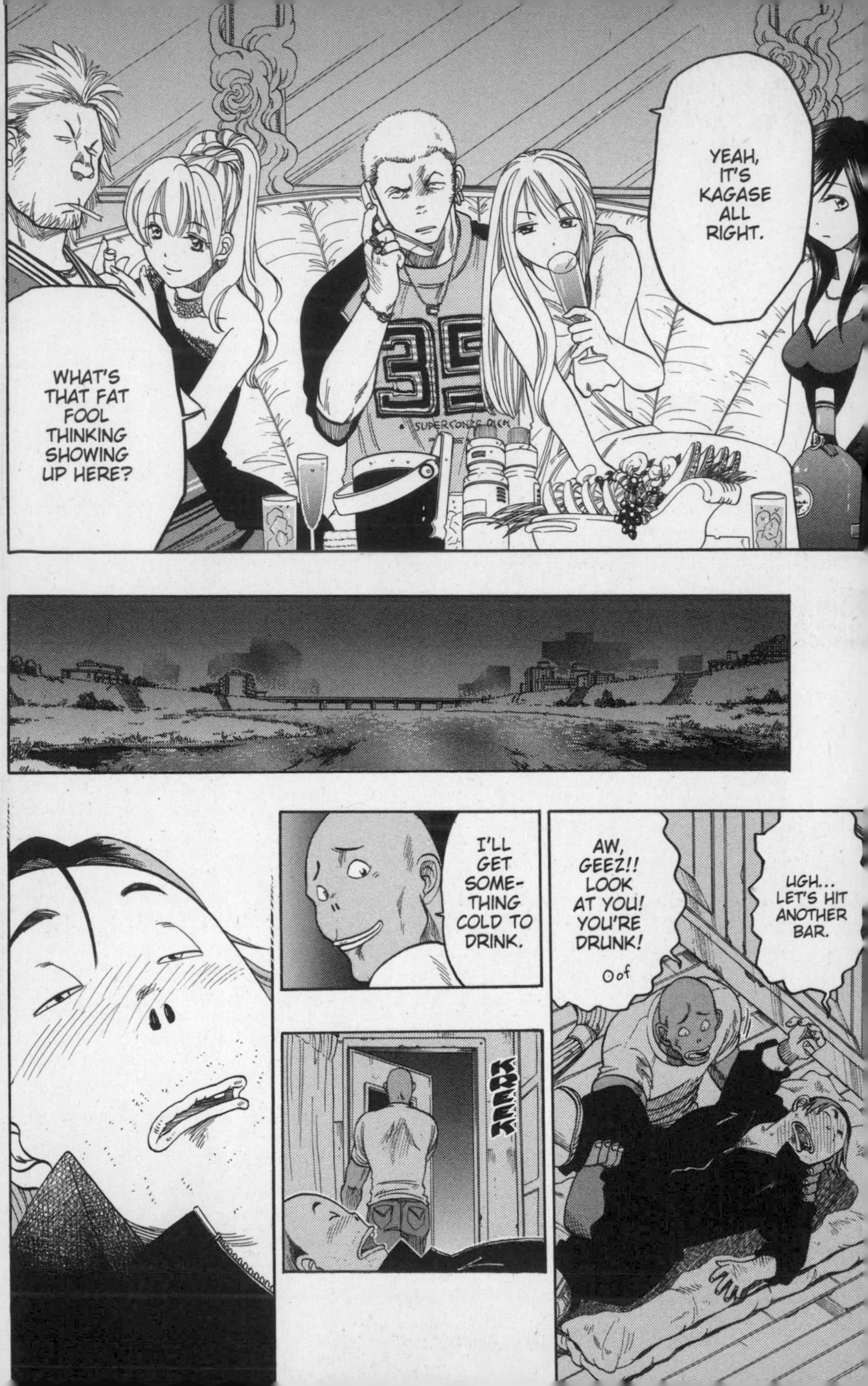
YEAH, IT'S KAGASE ALL RIGHT.
WHAT'S THAT FAT FOOL THINKING SHOWING UP HERE?
UGH... LET'S HIT ANOTHER BAR.
AW, GEEZ!! LOOK AT YOU! YOU'RE DRUNK!
Oof
I'LL GET SOME-THING COLD TO DRINK.
KREEK

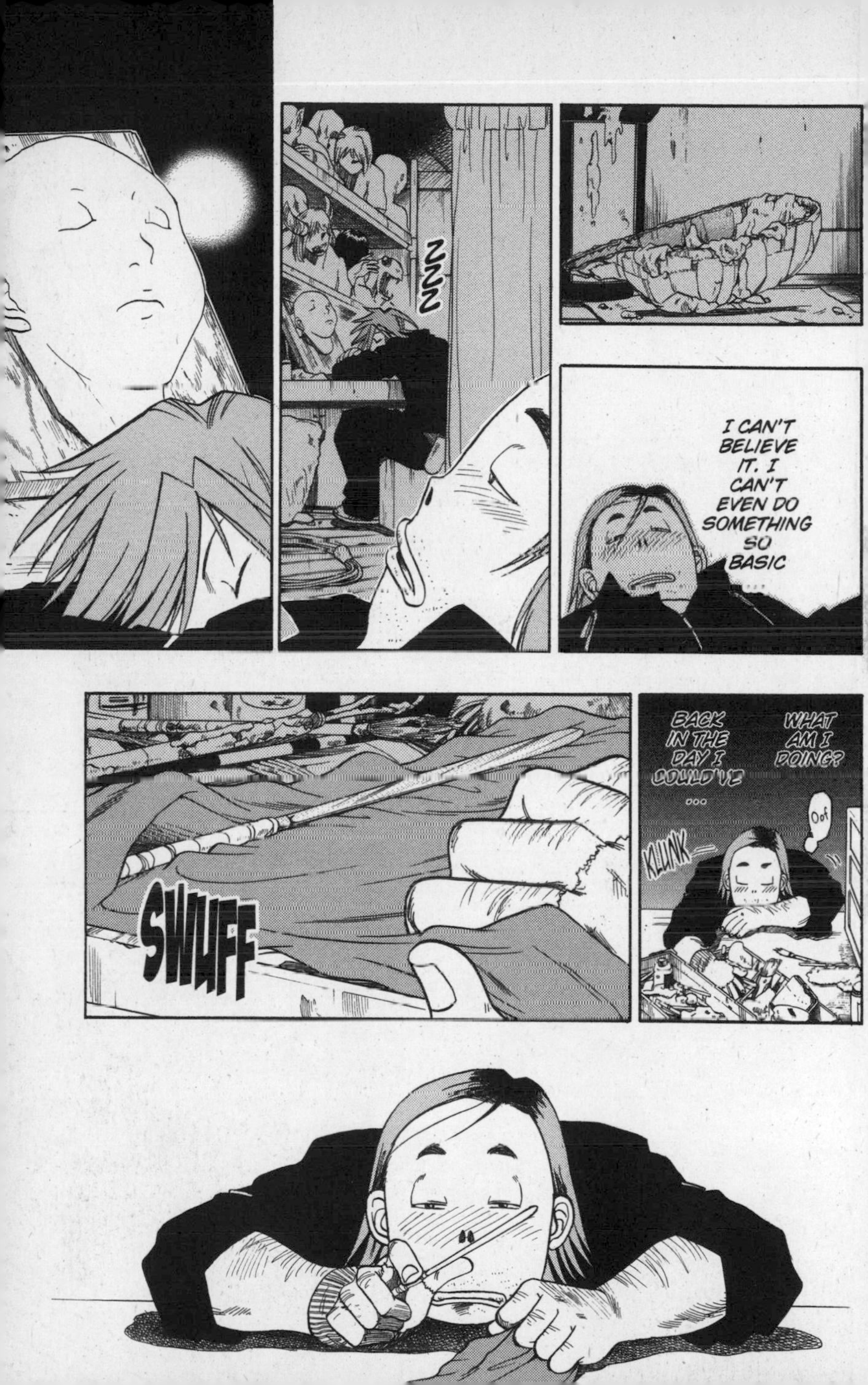
I CAN'T BELIEVE IT. I CAN'T EVEN DO SOMETHING SO BASIC ...
ZZZZ
WHAT AM I DOING?
BACK IN THE DAY I COULD'VE ...
Oof
KLUNK
SWUFF

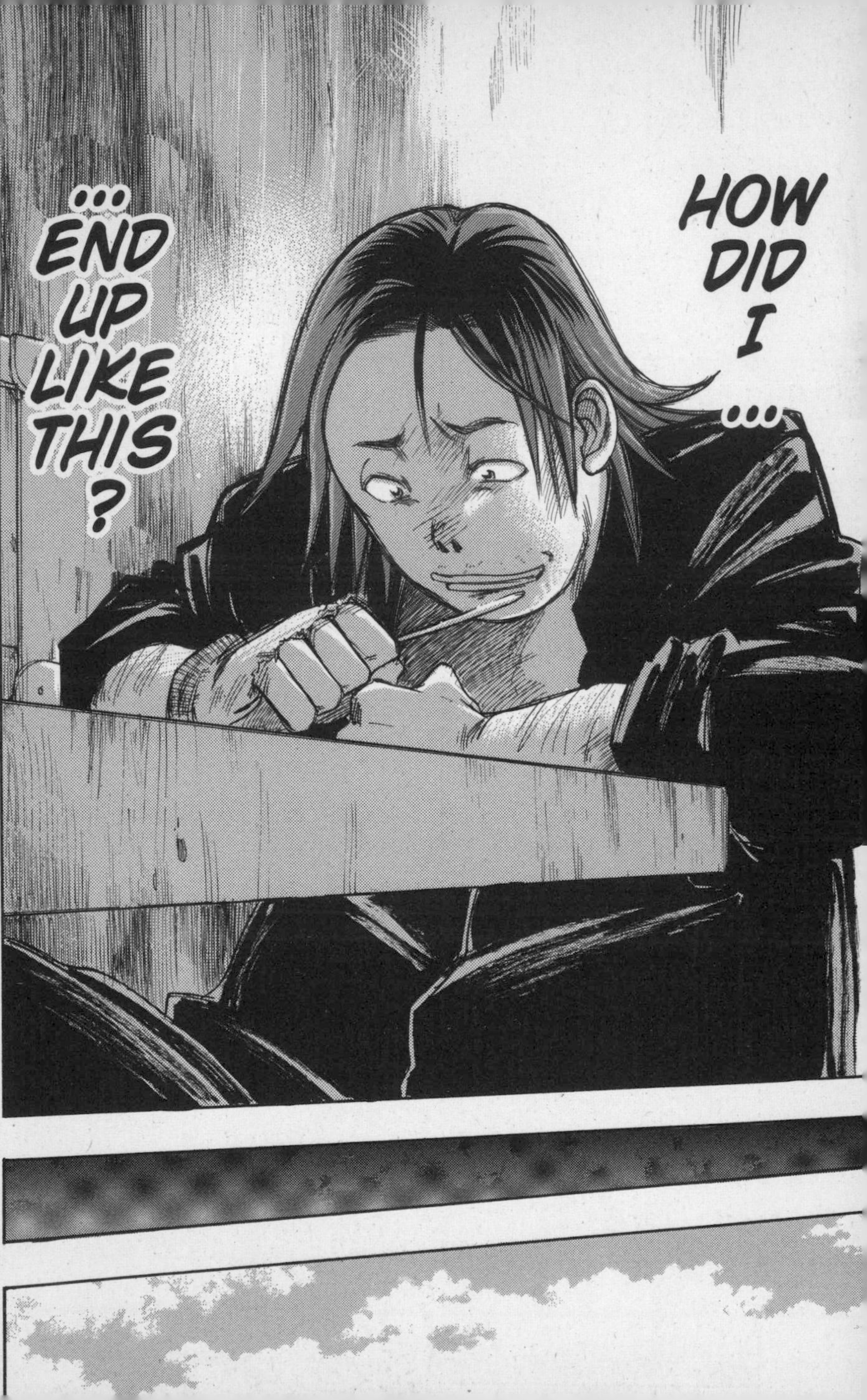
HOW DID I ...
...END UP LIKE THIS ?

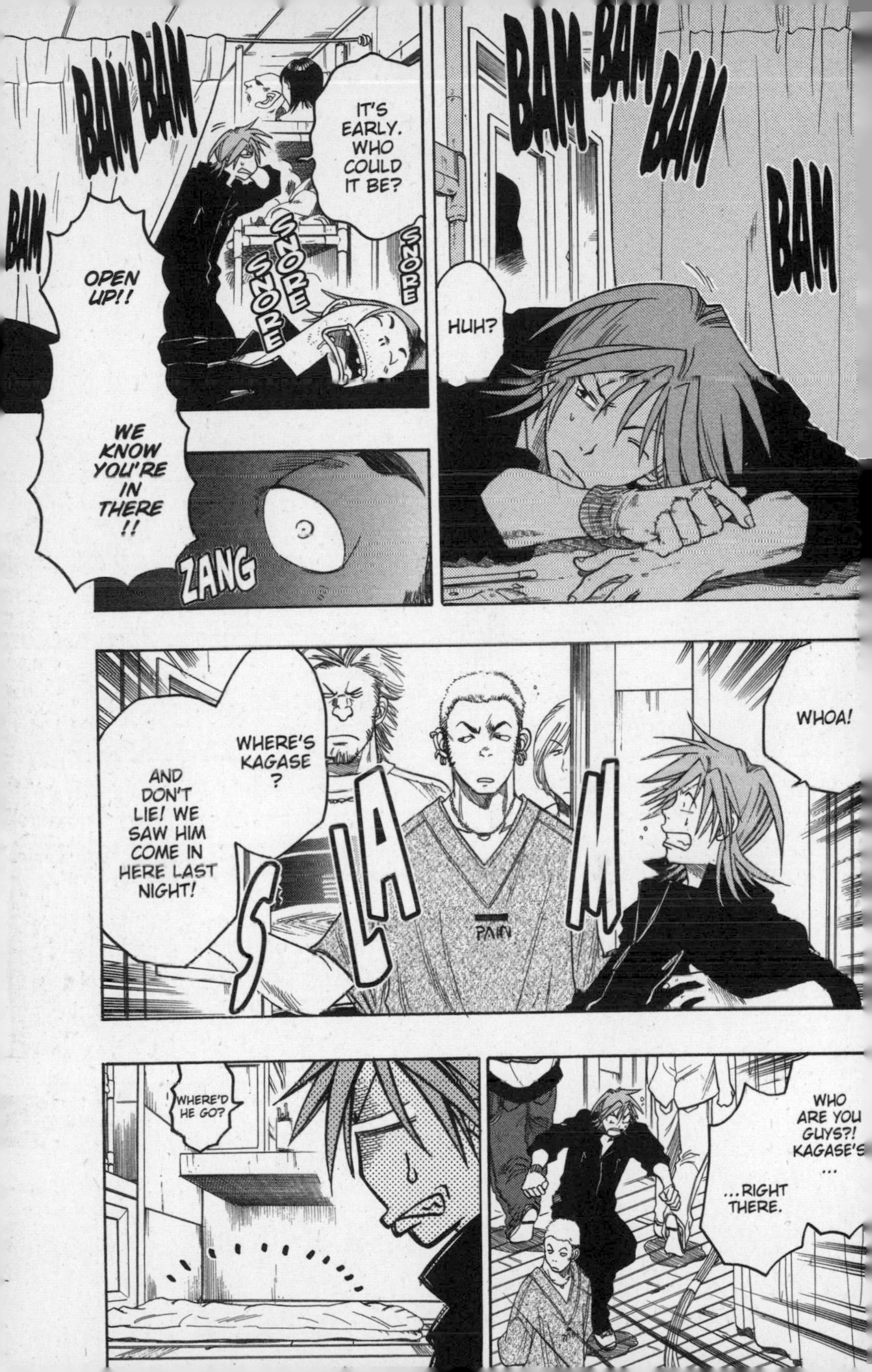
BAM BAM BAM BAM
BAM
HUH?
BAM BAM
BAM
OPEN UP!!
WE KNOW YOU'RE IN THERE!!
IT'S EARLY. WHO COULD IT BE?
SNORE
SNORE
SNORE
ZANG
WHOA!
SLAM
WHERE'S KAGASE?
AND DON'T LIE! WE SAW HIM COME IN HERE LAST NIGHT!
WHO ARE YOU GUYS?! KAGASE'S ...
...RIGHT THERE.
WHERE'D HE GO?
....

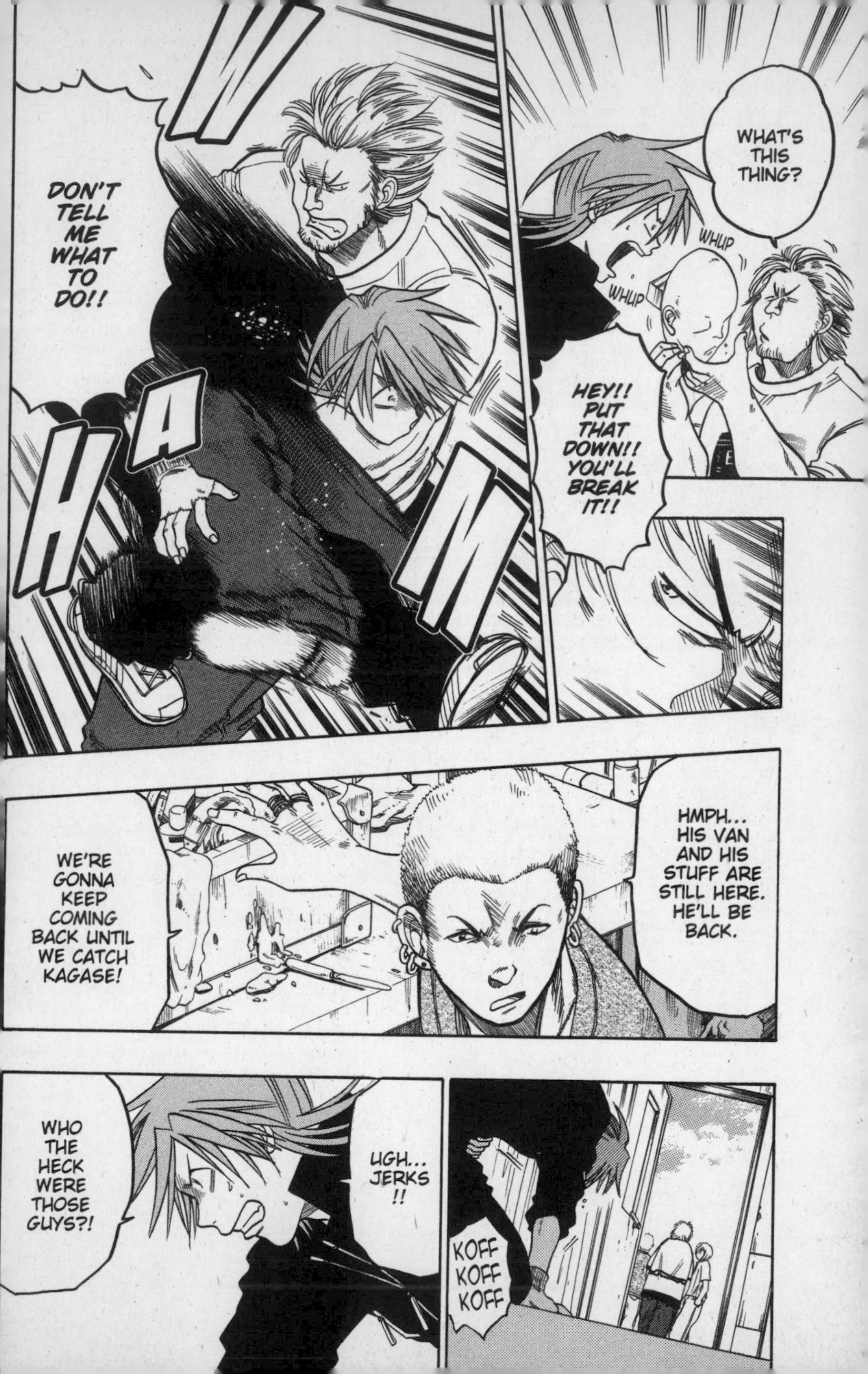
WHAT'S THIS THING?
WHUP
WHUP
HEY!! PUT THAT DOWN!! YOU'LL BREAK IT!!
DON'T TELL ME WHAT TO DO!!
WHAM
HMPH... HIS VAN AND HIS STUFF ARE STILL HERE. HE'LL BE BACK.
WE'RE GONNA KEEP COMING BACK UNTIL WE CATCH KAGASE!
KOFF KOFF KOFF
UGH... JERKS!!
WHO THE HECK WERE THOSE GUYS?!

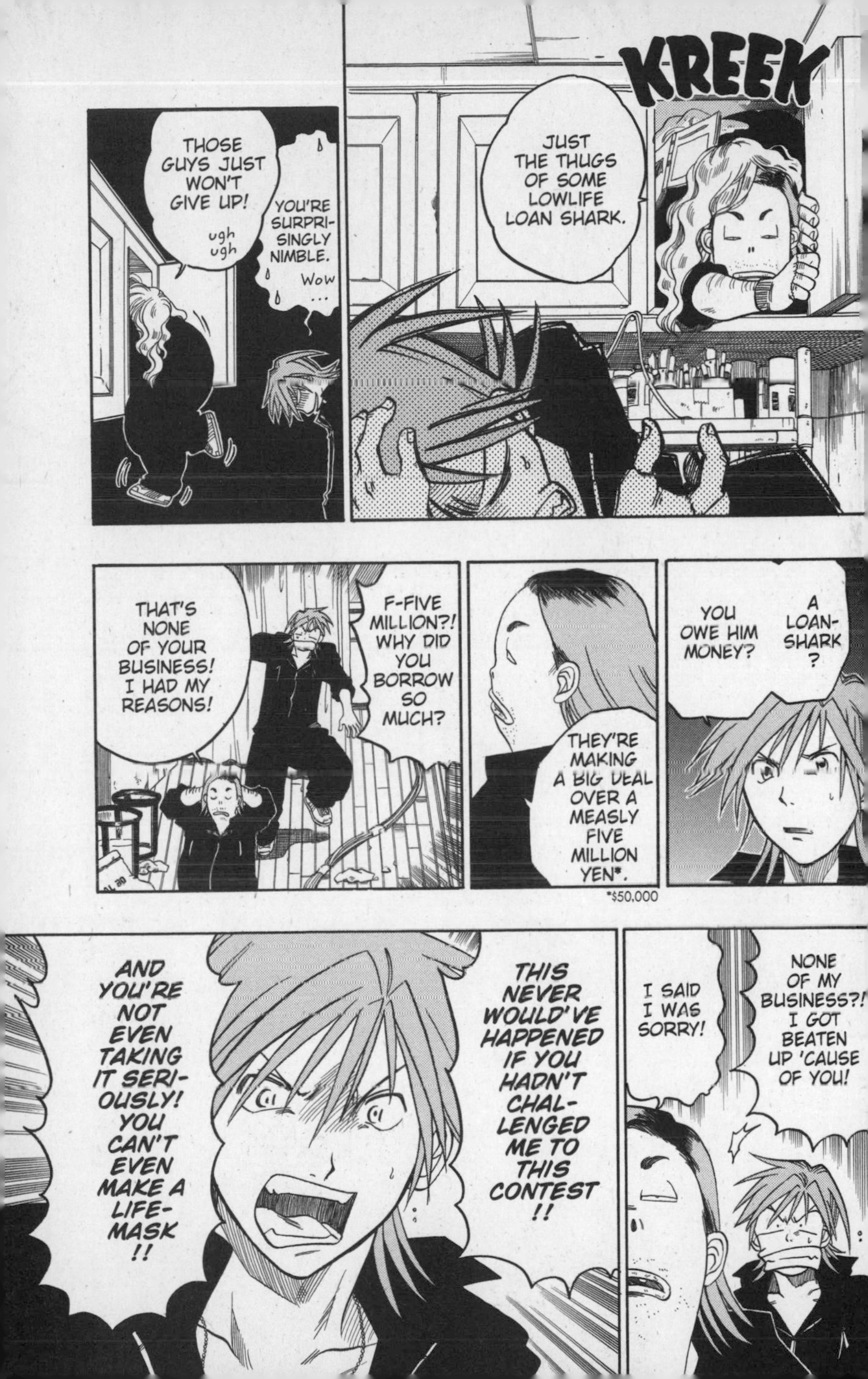
KREEK
JUST THE THUGS OF SOME LOWLIFE LOAN SHARK.
YOU'RE SURPRI-SINGLY NIMBLE.
Wow ...
THOSE GUYS JUST WON'T GIVE UP!
ugh ugh
A LOAN-SHARK?
YOU OWE HIM MONEY?
THEY'RE MAKING A BIG DEAL OVER A MEASLY FIVE MILLION YEN*.
F-FIVE MILLION?! WHY DID YOU BORROW SO MUCH?
THAT'S NONE OF YOUR BUSINESS! I HAD MY REASONS!
*$50,000
NONE OF MY BUSINESS?! I GOT BEATEN UP 'CAUSE OF YOU!
I SAID I WAS SORRY!
THIS NEVER WOULD'VE HAPPENED IF YOU HADN'T CHAL-LENGED ME TO THIS CONTEST!!
AND YOU'RE NOT EVEN TAKING IT SERI-OUSLY! YOU CAN'T EVEN MAKE A LIFE-MASK!!

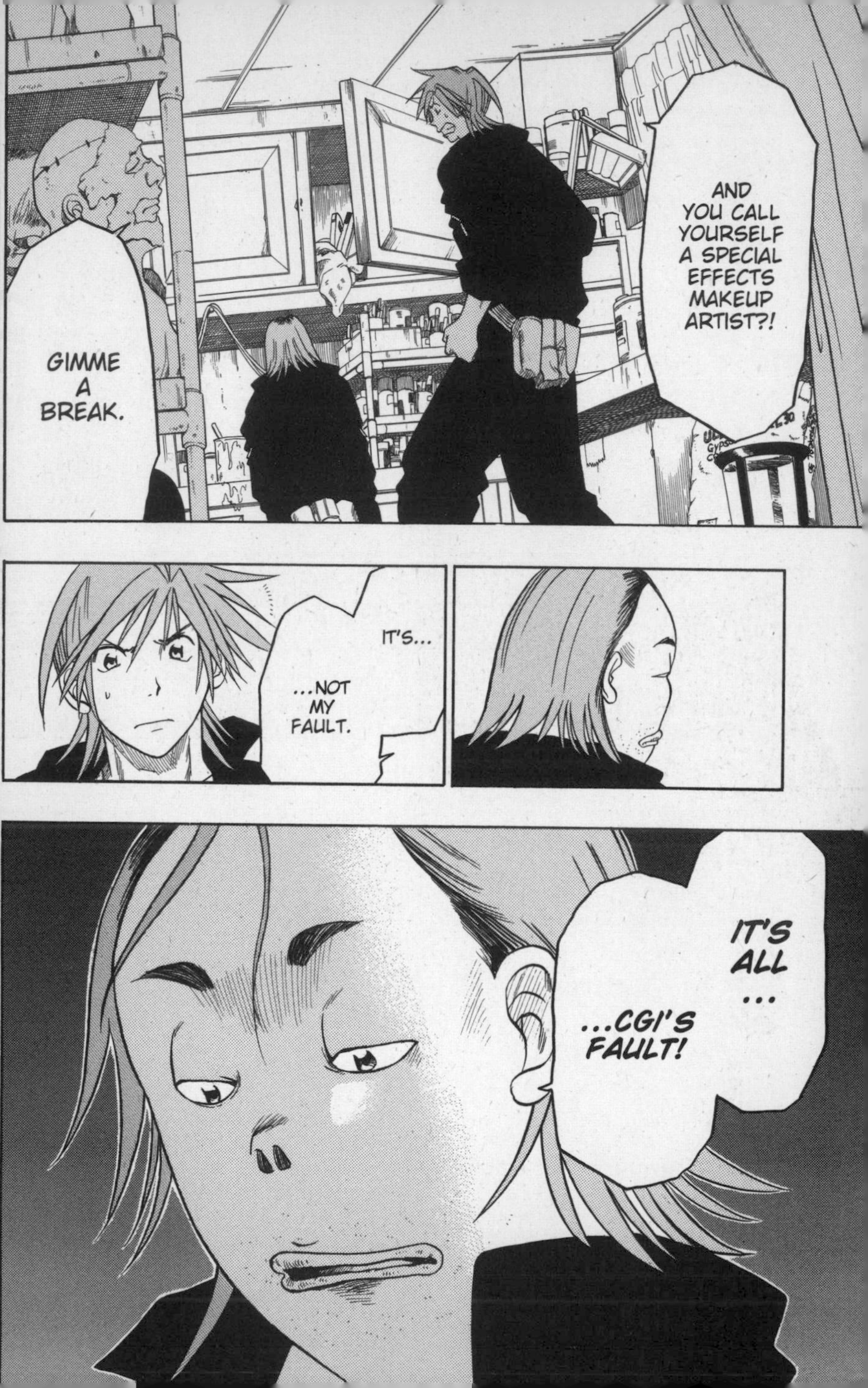
AND YOU CALL YOURSELF A SPECIAL EFFECTS MAKEUP ARTIST?!
GIMME A BREAK.
IT'S...
...NOT MY FAULT.
IT'S ALL...
...CGI'S FAULT!

Scene 57: Mr. Doubt (Part 3)

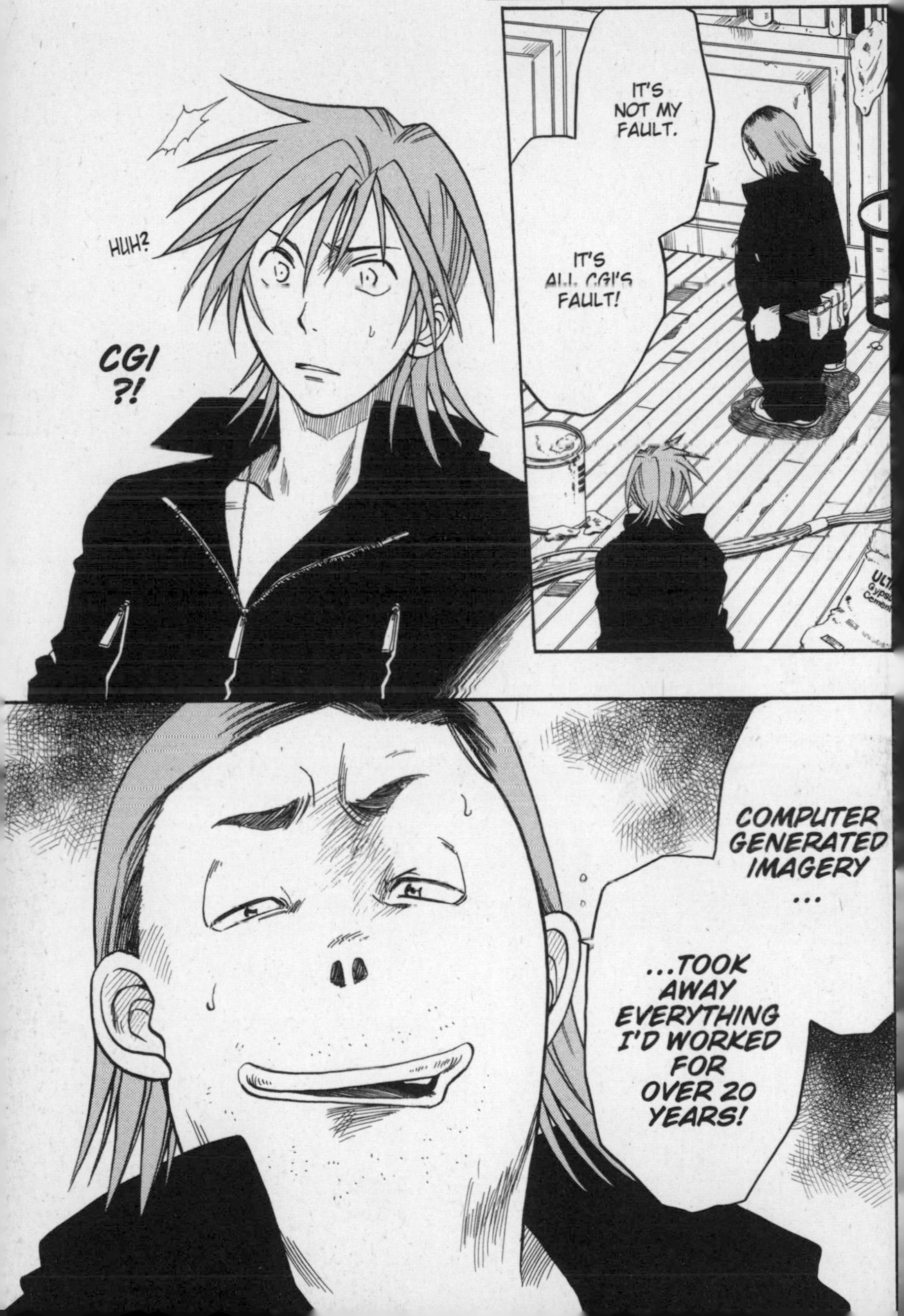
IT'S NOT MY FAULT.
IT'S ALL CGI'S FAULT!
HUH?
CGI ?!
COMPUTER GENERATED IMAGERY ...
...TOOK AWAY EVERYTHING I'D WORKED FOR OVER 20 YEARS!

Scene 57: Mr. Doubt (Part 3)

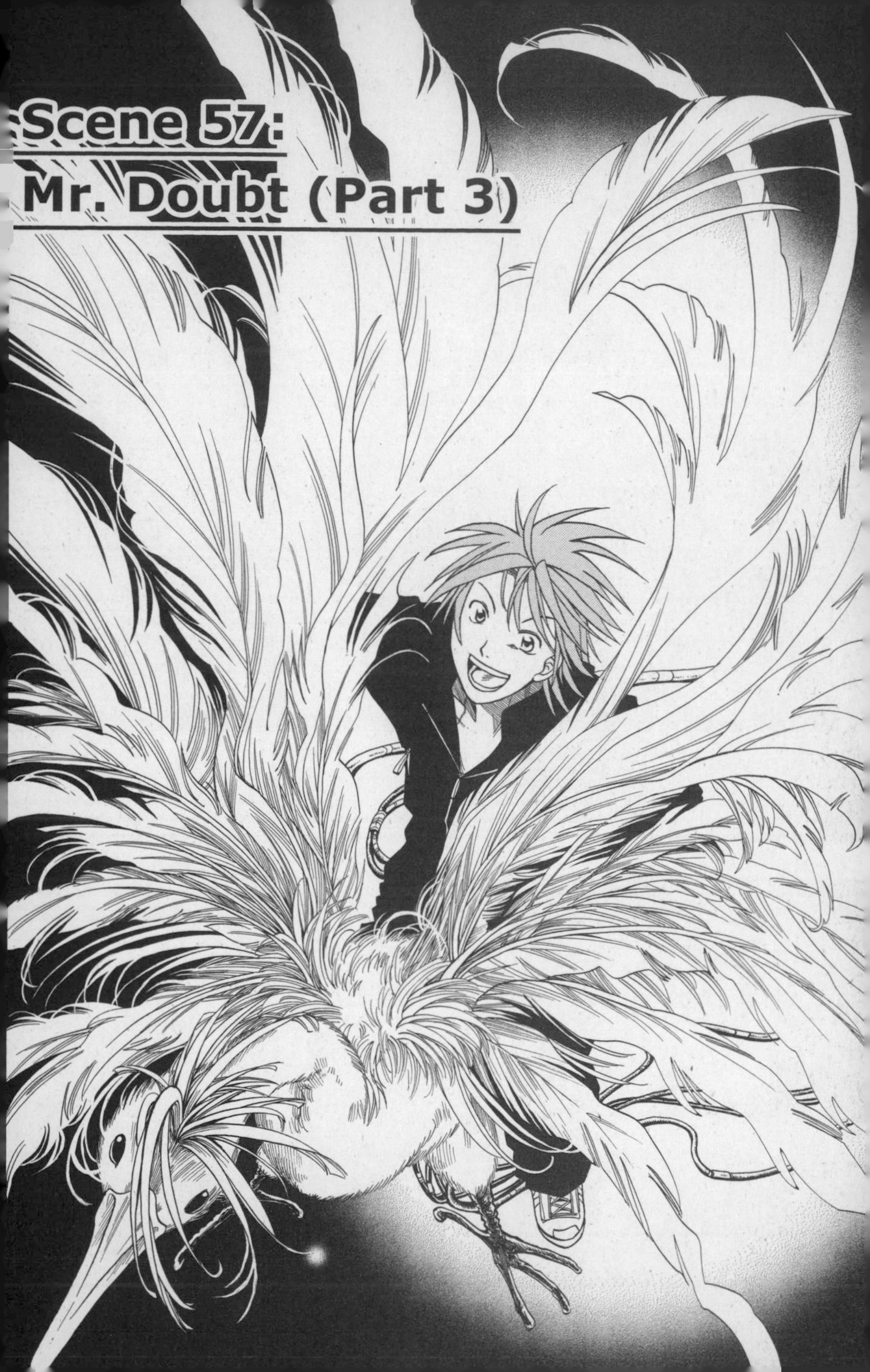

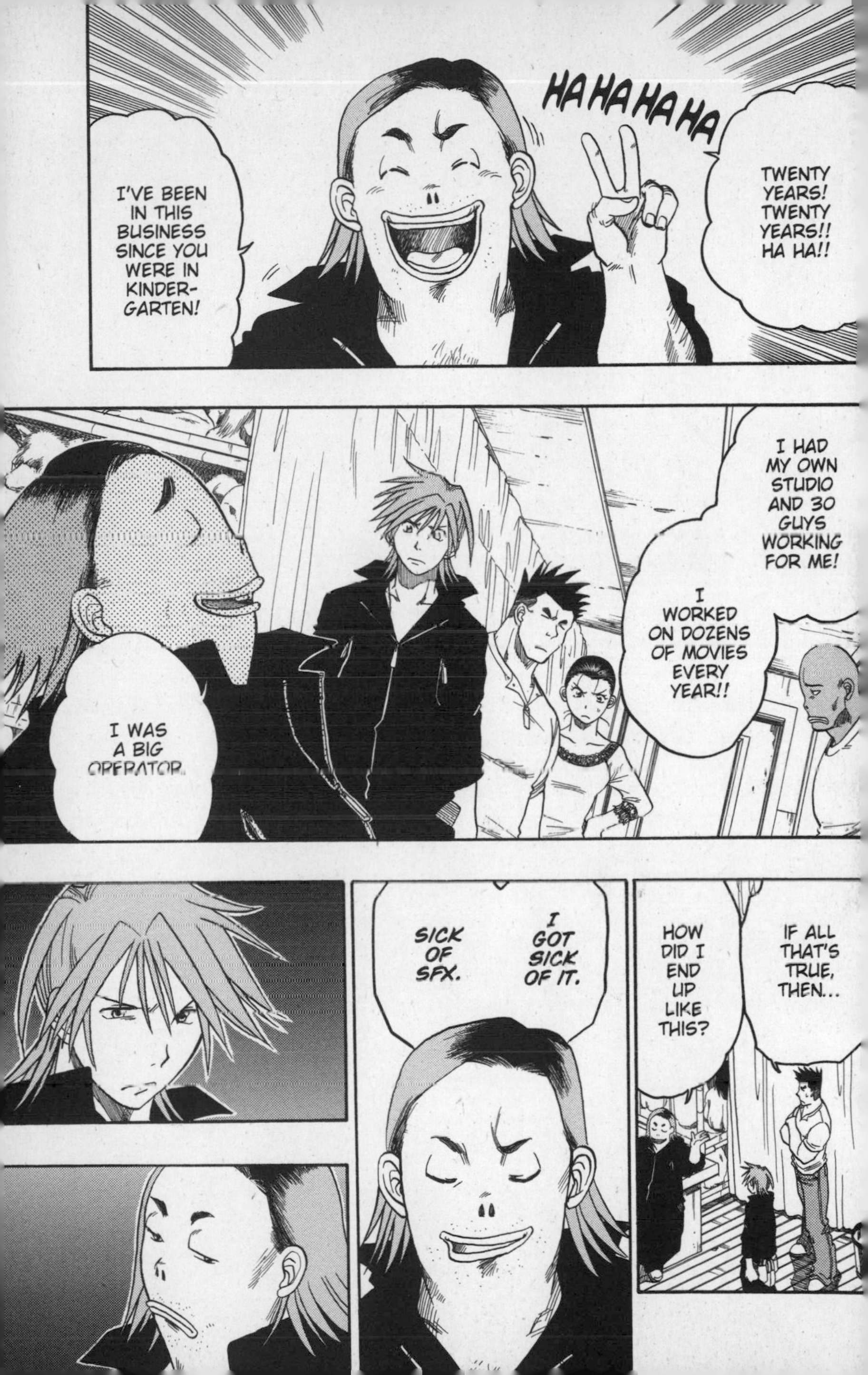
HA HA HA HA
TWENTY YEARS! TWENTY YEARS!! HA HA!!
I'VE BEEN IN THIS BUSINESS SINCE YOU WERE IN KINDER-GARTEN!
I HAD MY OWN STUDIO AND 30 GUYS WORKING FOR ME!
I WORKED ON DOZENS OF MOVIES EVERY YEAR!!
I WAS A BIG OPERATOR.
IF ALL THAT'S TRUE, THEN...
HOW DID I END UP LIKE THIS?
I GOT SICK OF IT.
SICK OF SFX.

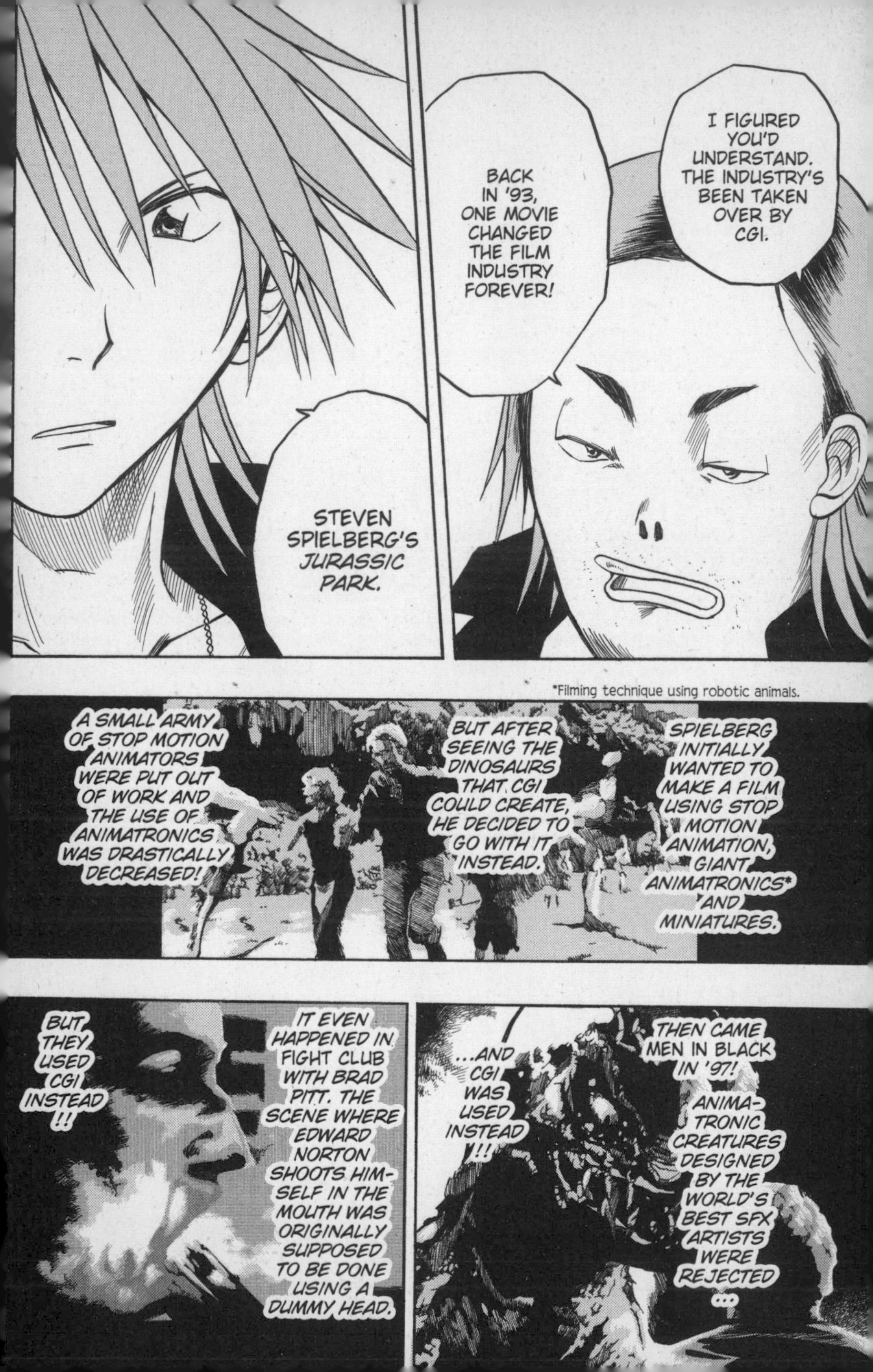
I FIGURED YOU'D UNDERSTAND. THE INDUSTRY'S BEEN TAKEN OVER BY CGI.
BACK IN '93, ONE MOVIE CHANGED THE FILM INDUSTRY FOREVER!
STEVEN SPIELBERG'S JURASSIC PARK.
*Filming technique using robotic animals.
SPIELBERG INITIALLY WANTED TO MAKE A FILM USING STOP MOTION ANIMATION, GIANT ANIMATRONICS* AND MINIATURES.
BUT AFTER SEEING THE DINOSAURS THAT CGI COULD CREATE, HE DECIDED TO GO WITH IT INSTEAD.
A SMALL ARMY OF STOP MOTION ANIMATORS WERE PUT OUT OF WORK AND THE USE OF ANIMATRONICS WAS DRASTICALLY DECREASED!
THEN CAME MEN IN BLACK IN '97!
ANIMA-TRONIC CREATURES DESIGNED BY THE WORLD'S BEST SFX ARTISTS WERE REJECTED...
...AND CGI WAS USED INSTEAD!!
IT EVEN HAPPENED IN FIGHT CLUB WITH BRAD PITT. THE SCENE WHERE EDWARD NORTON SHOOTS HIM-SELF IN THE MOUTH WAS ORIGINALLY SUPPOSED TO BE DONE USING A DUMMY HEAD.
BUT THEY USED CGI INSTEAD!!

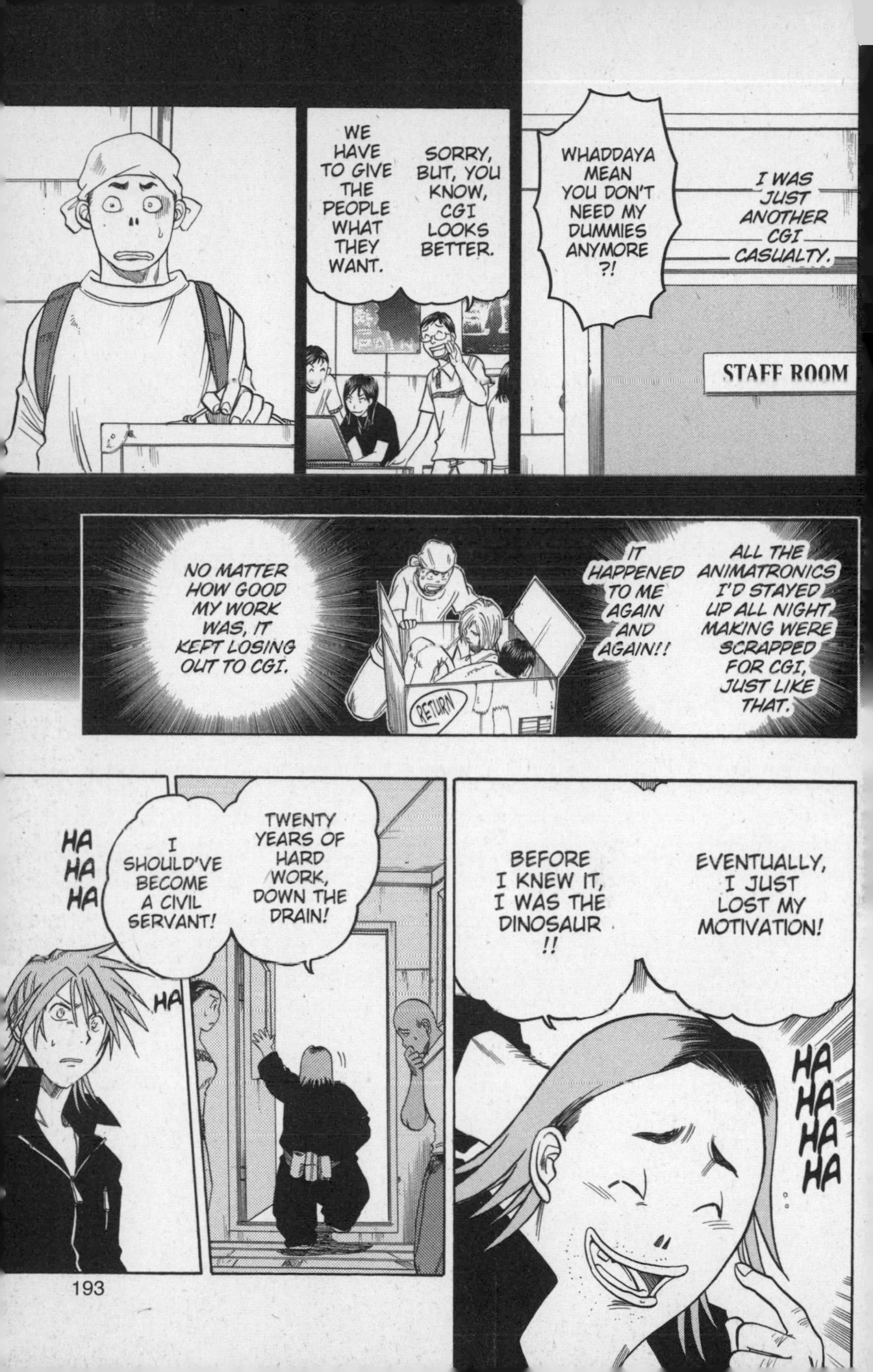
I WAS JUST ANOTHER CGI CASUALTY.
WHADDAYA MEAN YOU DON'T NEED MY DUMMIES ANYMORE?!
STAFF ROOM
SORRY, BUT, YOU KNOW, CGI LOOKS BETTER.
WE HAVE TO GIVE THE PEOPLE WHAT THEY WANT.
ALL THE ANIMATRONICS I'D STAYED UP ALL NIGHT MAKING WERE SCRAPPED FOR CGI, JUST LIKE THAT.
IT HAPPENED TO ME AGAIN AND AGAIN!!
NO MATTER HOW GOOD MY WORK WAS, IT KEPT LOSING OUT TO CGI.
RETURN
EVENTUALLY, I JUST LOST MY MOTIVATION!
BEFORE I KNEW IT, I WAS THE DINOSAUR!!
HA HA HA HA
TWENTY YEARS OF HARD WORK, DOWN THE DRAIN!
I SHOULD'VE BECOME A CIVIL SERVANT!
HA HA HA
HA

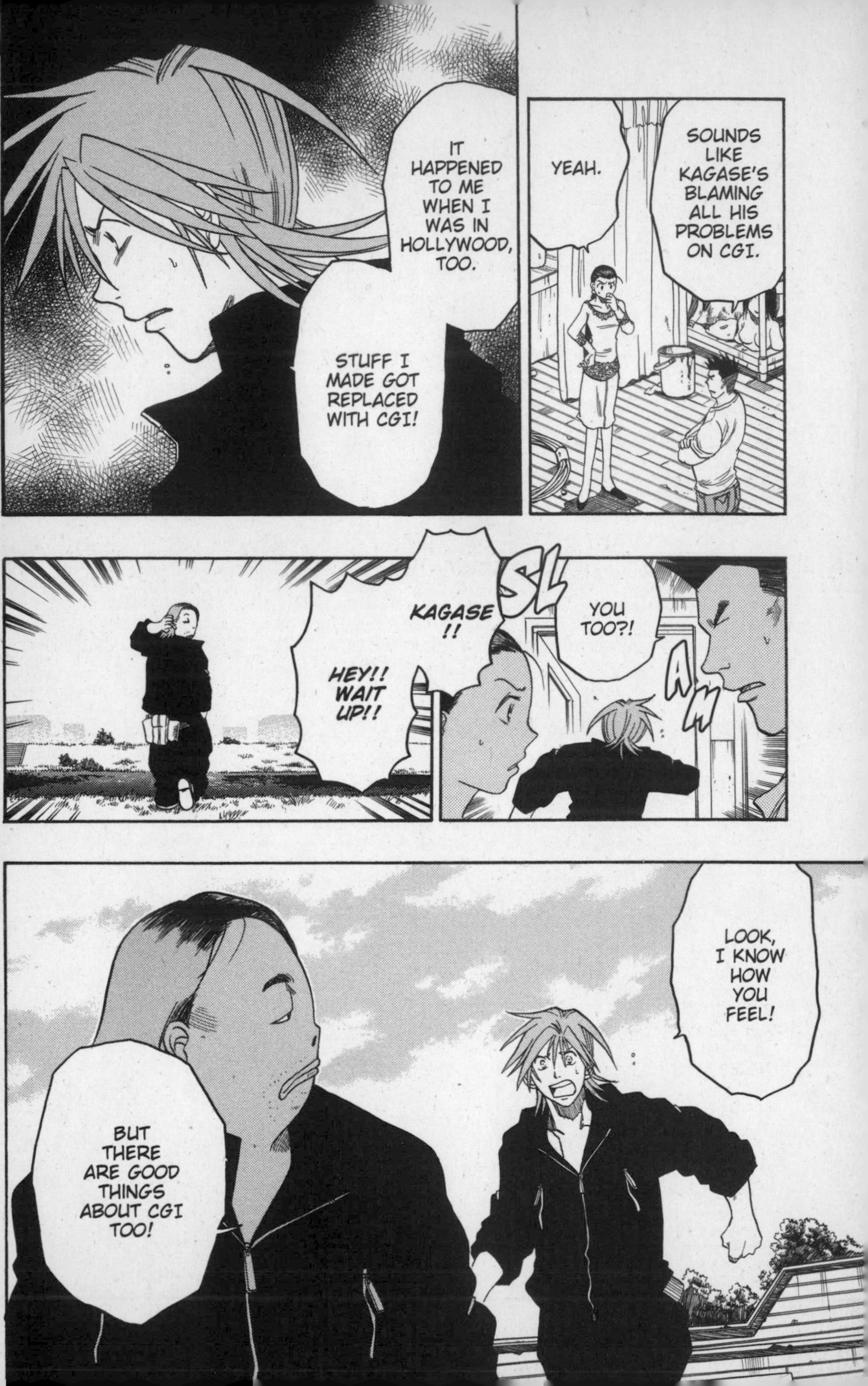
SOUNDS LIKE KAGASE'S BLAMING ALL HIS PROBLEMS ON CGI.
YEAH.
IT HAPPENED TO ME WHEN I WAS IN HOLLYWOOD, TOO.
STUFF I MADE GOT REPLACED WITH CGI!
YOU TOO?!
SL
AM
KAGASE!!
HEY!! WAIT UP!!
LOOK, I KNOW HOW YOU FEEL!
BUT THERE ARE GOOD THINGS ABOUT CGI TOO!

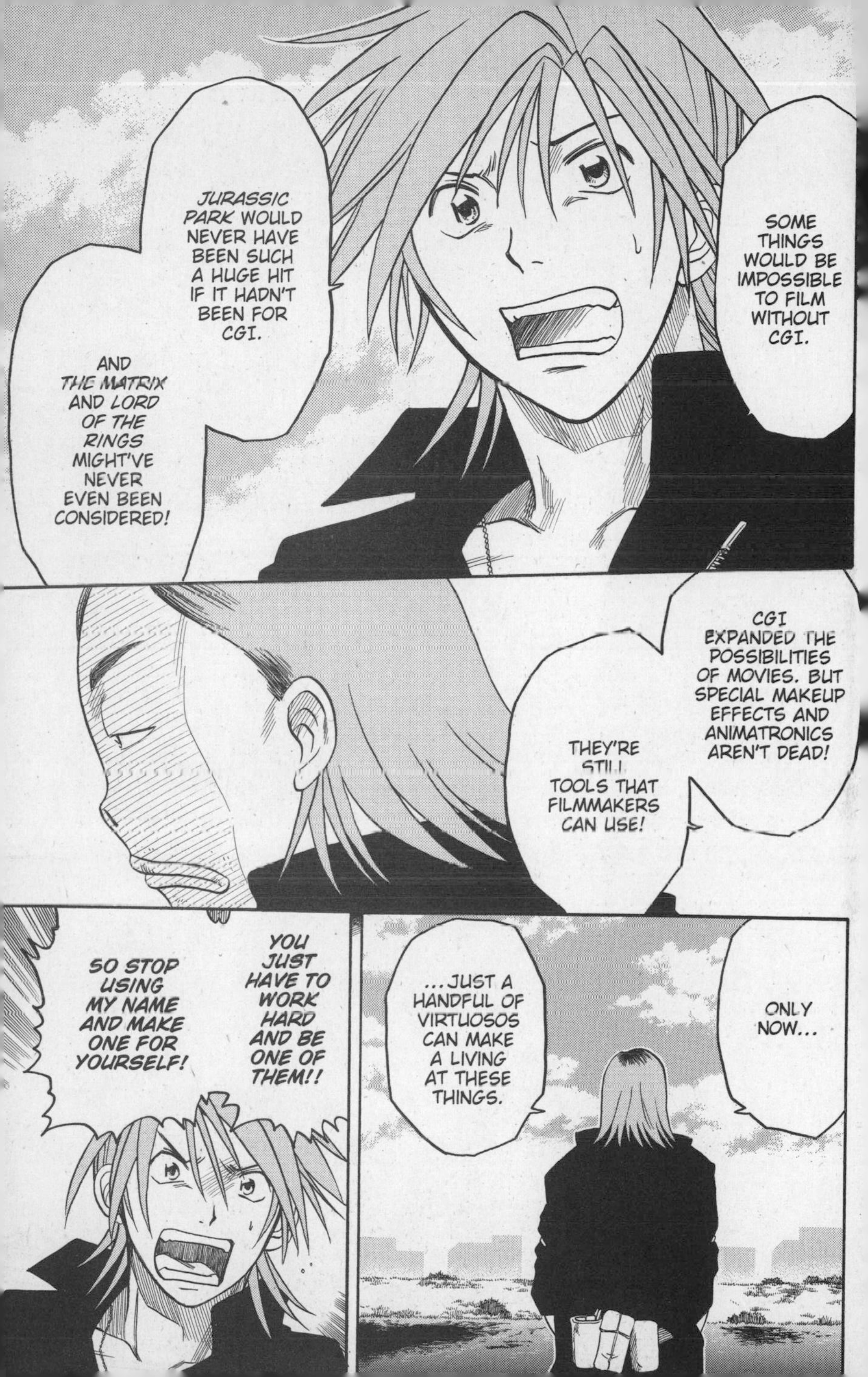
SOME THINGS WOULD BE IMPOSSIBLE TO FILM WITHOUT CGI.
JURASSIC PARK WOULD NEVER HAVE BEEN SUCH A HUGE HIT IF IT HADN'T BEEN FOR CGI.
AND *THE MATRIX* AND *LORD OF THE RINGS* MIGHT'VE NEVER EVEN BEEN CONSIDERED!
CGI EXPANDED THE POSSIBILITIES OF MOVIES. BUT SPECIAL MAKEUP EFFECTS AND ANIMATRONICS AREN'T DEAD!
THEY'RE STILL TOOLS THAT FILMMAKERS CAN USE!
ONLY NOW...
...JUST A HANDFUL OF VIRTUOSOS CAN MAKE A LIVING AT THESE THINGS.
YOU JUST HAVE TO WORK HARD AND BE ONE OF THEM!!
SO STOP USING MY NAME AND MAKE ONE FOR YOURSELF!

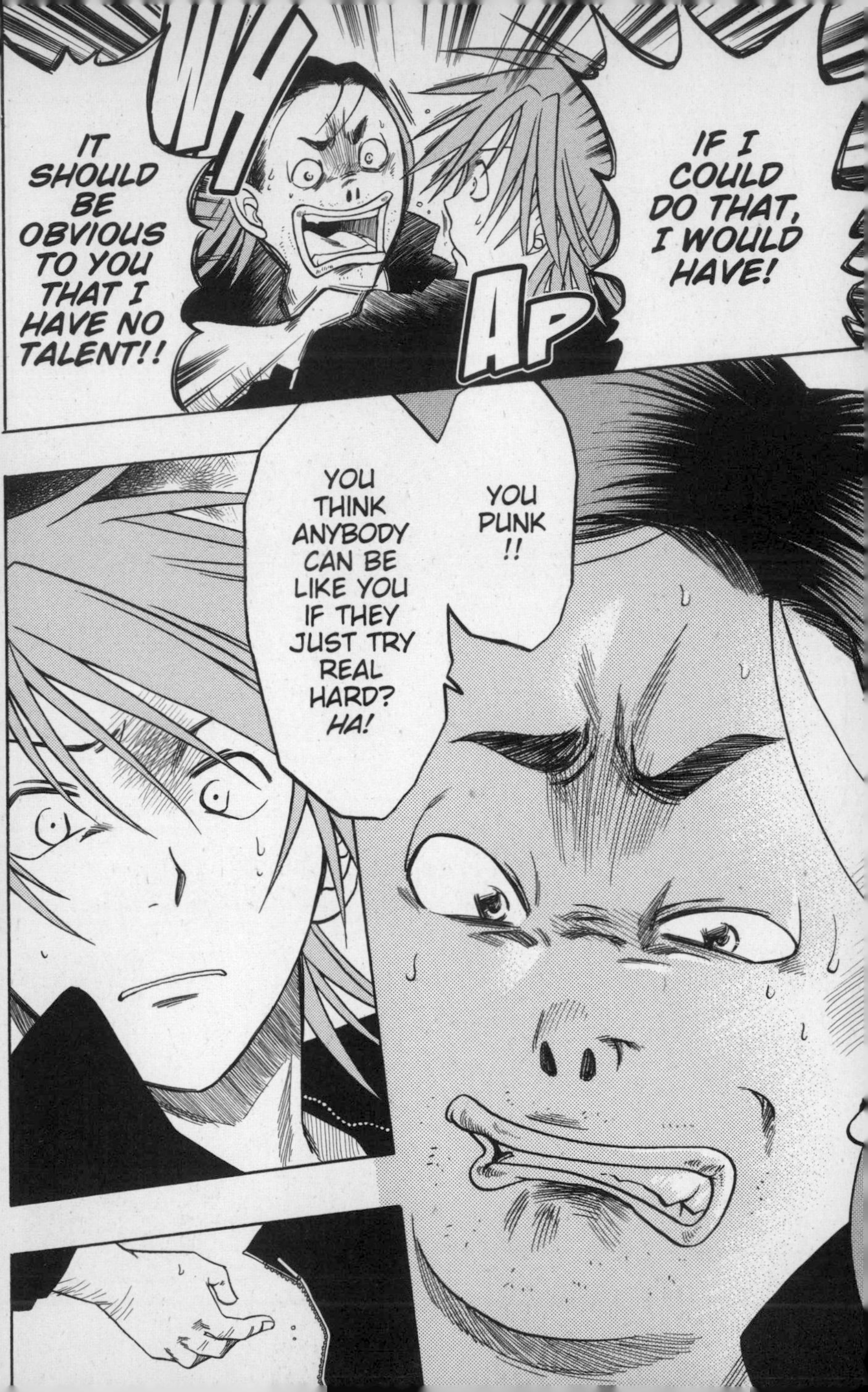
IF I COULD DO THAT, I WOULD HAVE!
WHAP
IT SHOULD BE OBVIOUS TO YOU THAT I HAVE NO TALENT!!
YOU PUNK!!
YOU THINK ANYBODY CAN BE LIKE YOU IF THEY JUST TRY REAL HARD? HA!

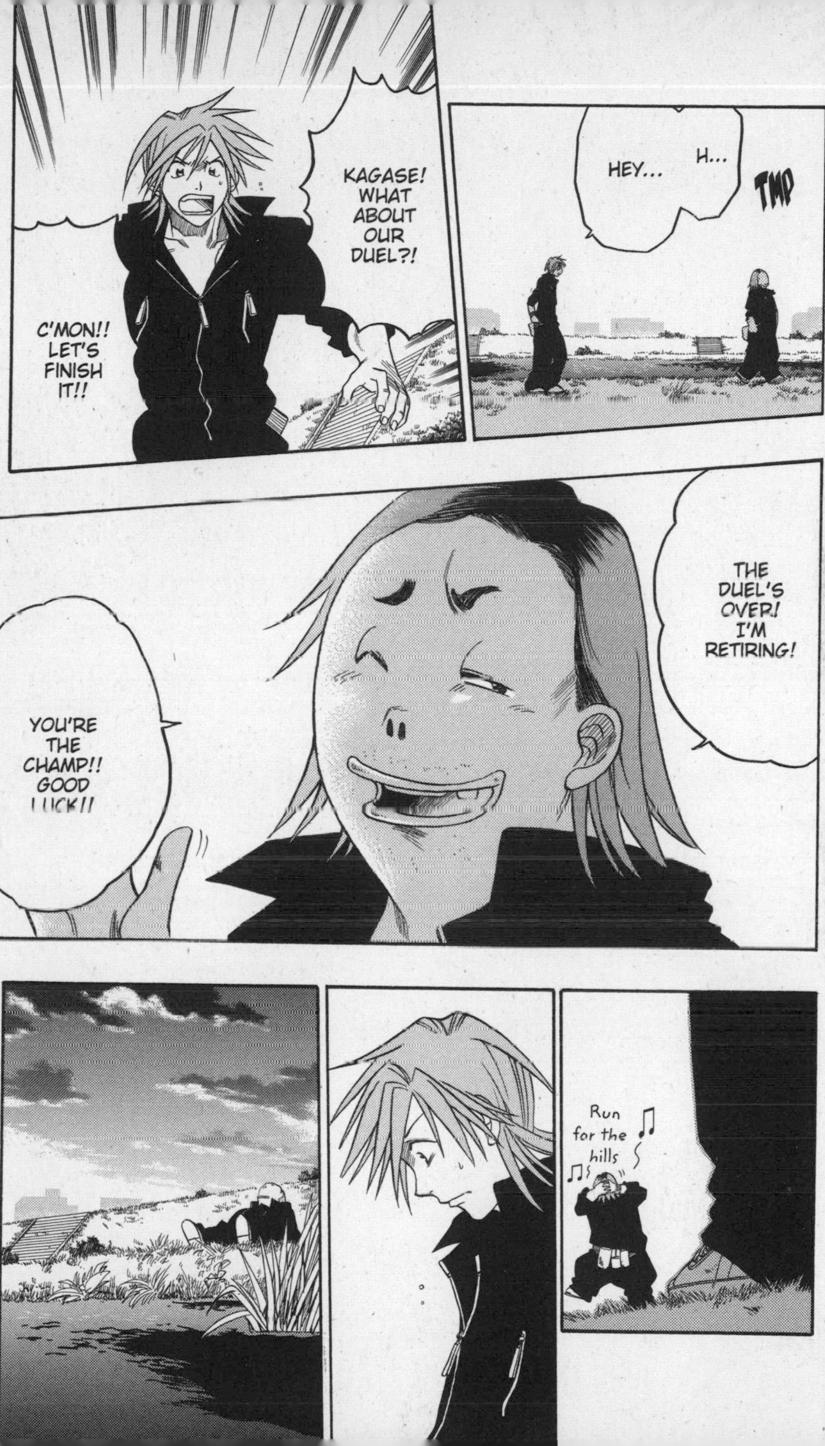
H...
HEY...
TMP
KAGASE! WHAT ABOUT OUR DUEL?!
C'MON!! LET'S FINISH IT!!
THE DUEL'S OVER! I'M RETIRING!
YOU'RE THE CHAMP!! GOOD LUCK!!
Run for the hills

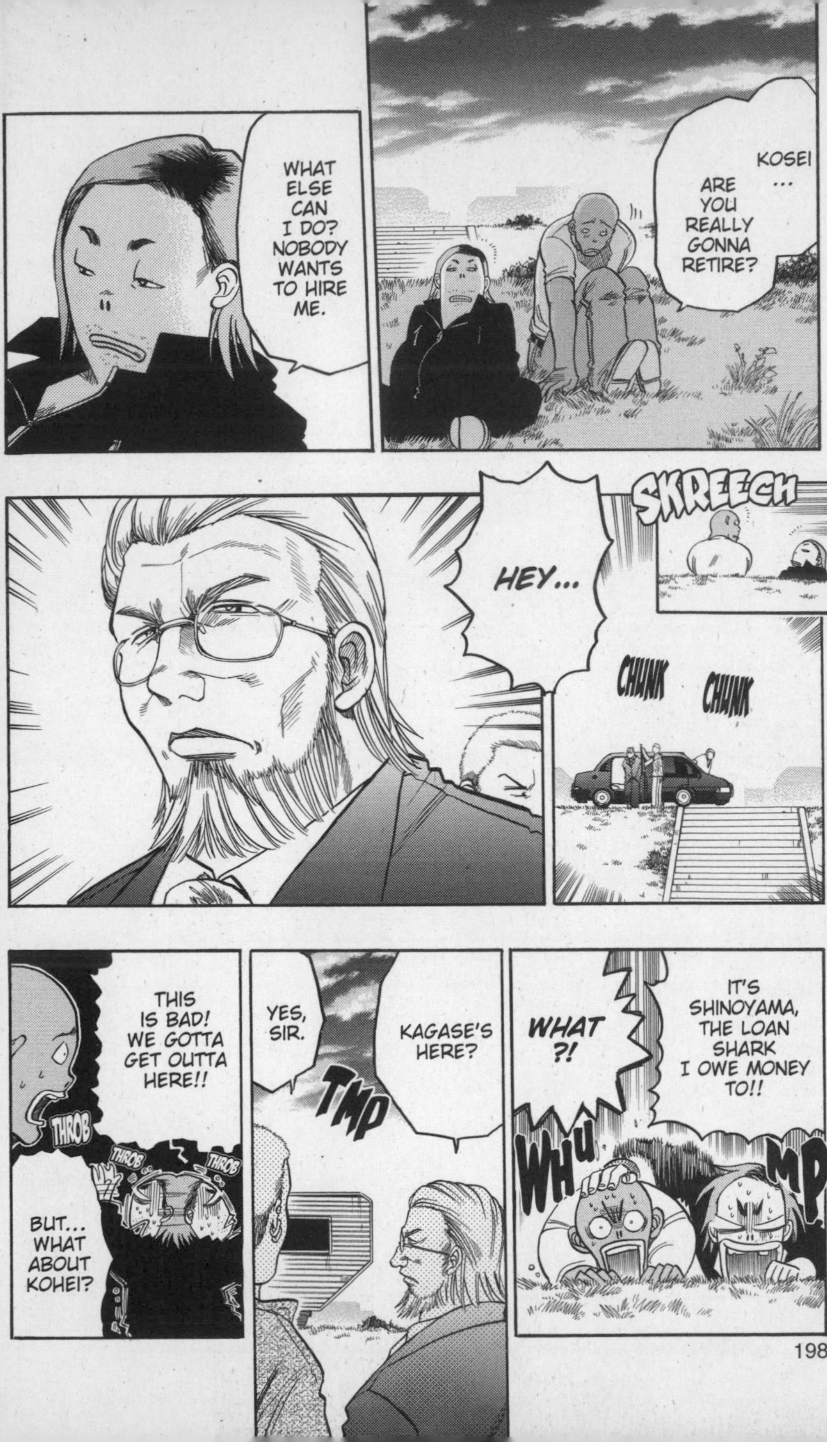

KOSEI ... ARE YOU REALLY GONNA RETIRE?
WHAT ELSE CAN I DO? NOBODY WANTS TO HIRE ME.
SKREECH
CHUNK
CHUNK
HEY...
IT'S SHINOYAMA, THE LOAN SHARK I OWE MONEY TO!!
WHAT?!
WHUMP
KAGASE'S HERE?
YES, SIR.
TMP
THIS IS BAD! WE GOTTA GET OUTTA HERE!!
THROB
THROB
THROB
BUT... WHAT ABOUT KOHEI?

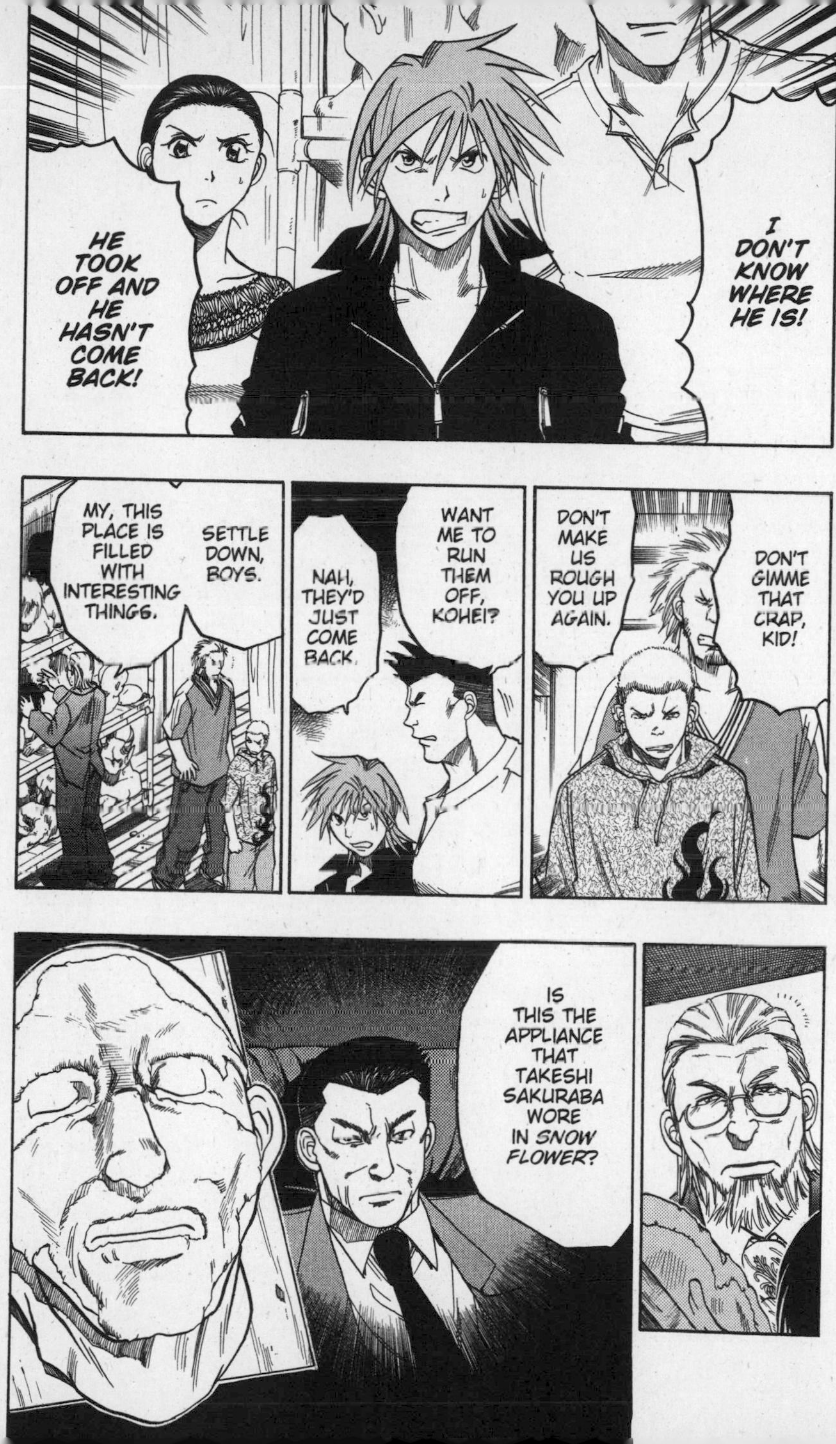
I DON'T KNOW WHERE HE IS!
HE TOOK OFF AND HE HASN'T COME BACK!
DON'T GIMME THAT CRAP, KID!
DON'T MAKE US ROUGH YOU UP AGAIN.
WANT ME TO RUN THEM OFF, KOHEI?
NAH, THEY'D JUST COME BACK.
SETTLE DOWN, BOYS.
MY, THIS PLACE IS FILLED WITH INTERESTING THINGS.
IS THIS THE APPLIANCE THAT TAKESHI SAKURABA WORE IN *SNOW FLOWER*?

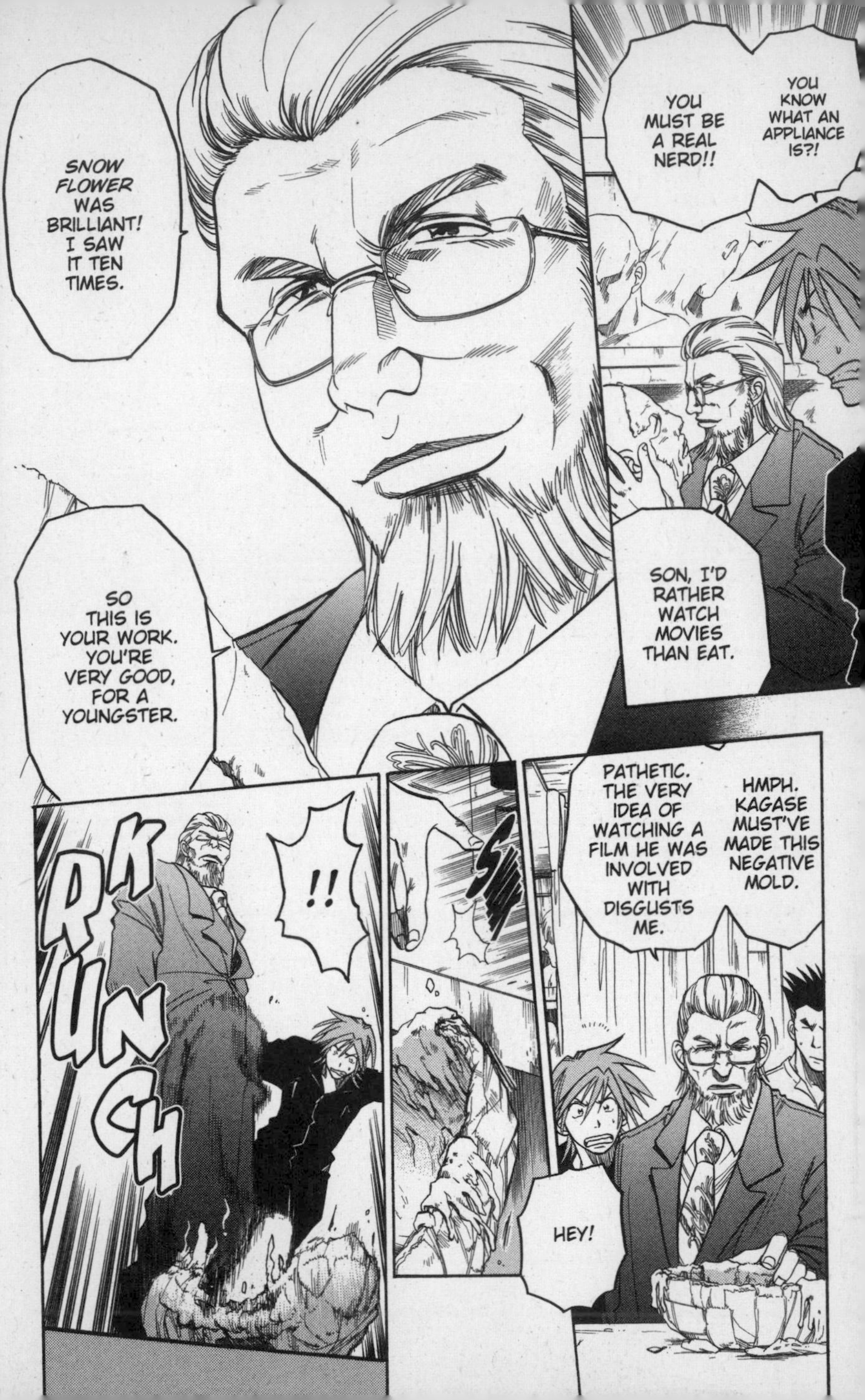
YOU KNOW WHAT AN APPLIANCE IS?!
YOU MUST BE A REAL NERD!!
SON, I'D RATHER WATCH MOVIES THAN EAT.
SNOW FLOWER WAS BRILLIANT! I SAW IT TEN TIMES.
SO THIS IS YOUR WORK. YOU'RE VERY GOOD, FOR A YOUNGSTER.
HMPH. KAGASE MUST'VE MADE THIS NEGATIVE MOLD.
PATHETIC. THE VERY IDEA OF WATCHING A FILM HE WAS INVOLVED WITH DISGUSTS ME.
HEY!
!!
KRUNCH

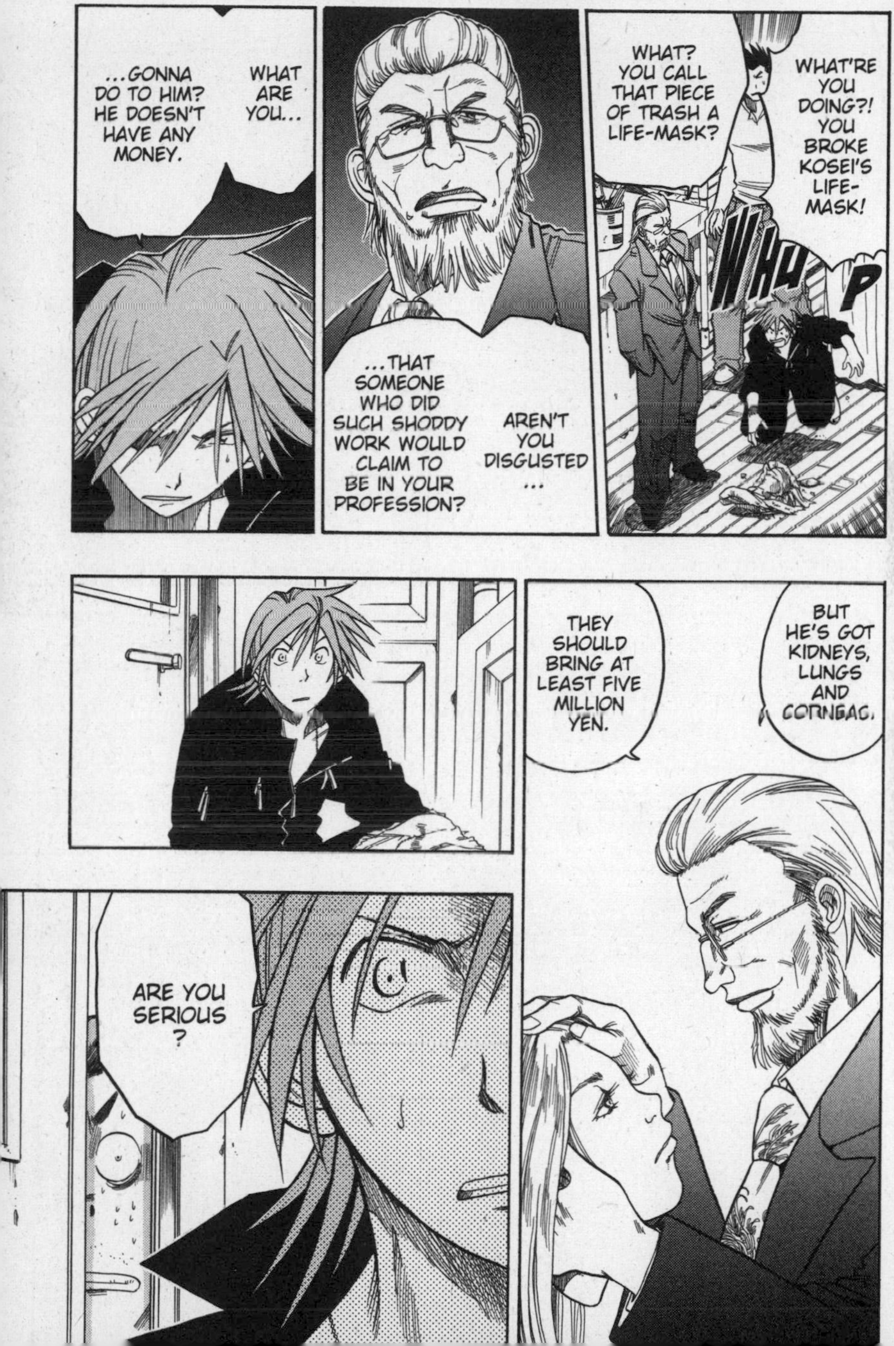
WHAT'RE YOU DOING?! YOU BROKE KOSEI'S LIFE-MASK!
WHAT? YOU CALL THAT PIECE OF TRASH A LIFE-MASK?
WHU P
AREN'T YOU DISGUSTED ...
...THAT SOMEONE WHO DID SUCH SHODDY WORK WOULD CLAIM TO BE IN YOUR PROFESSION?
WHAT ARE YOU...
...GONNA DO TO HIM? HE DOESN'T HAVE ANY MONEY.
BUT HE'S GOT KIDNEYS, LUNGS AND CORNEAS.
THEY SHOULD BRING AT LEAST FIVE MILLION YEN.
ARE YOU SERIOUS ?

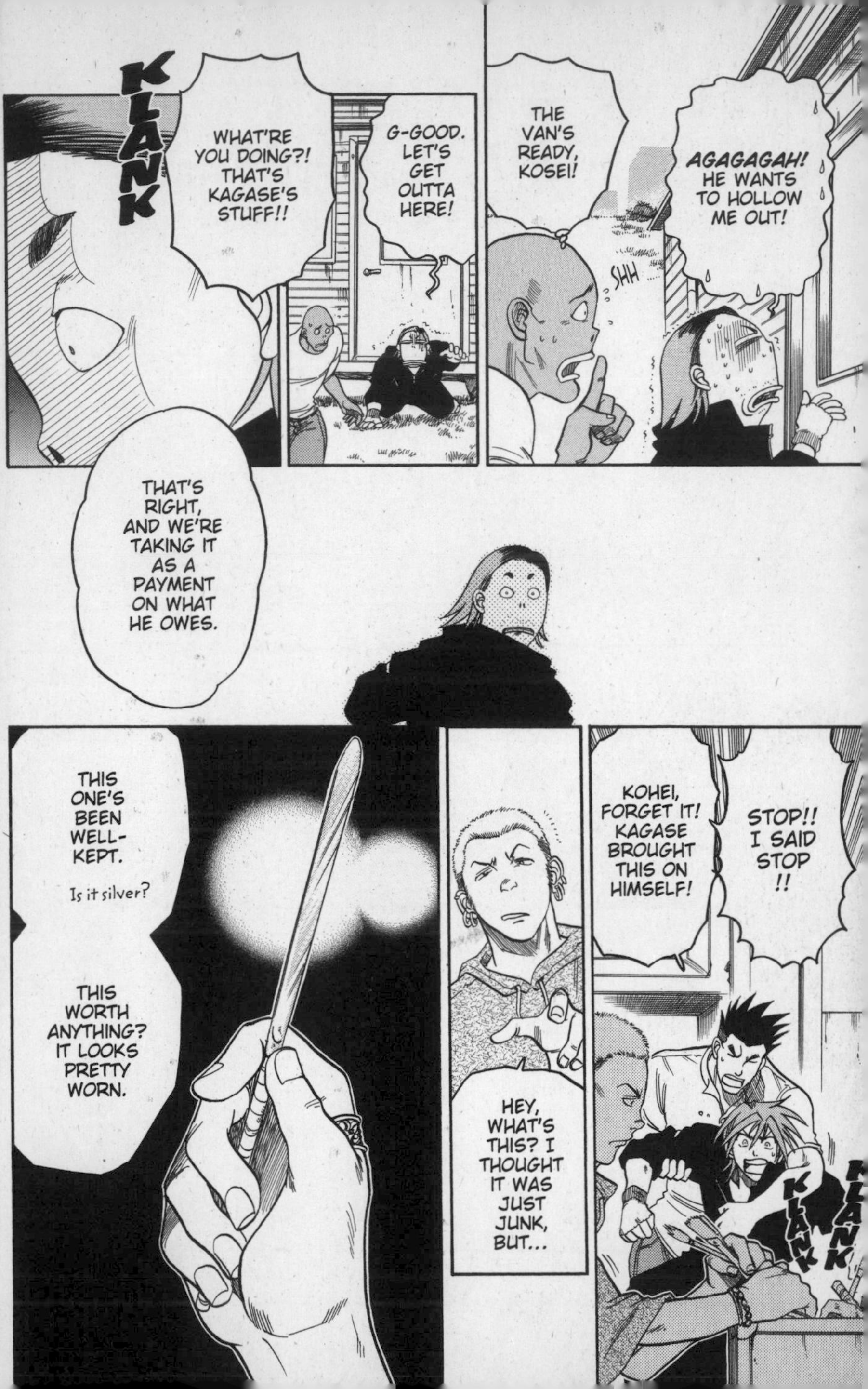
AGAGAGAH! HE WANTS TO HOLLOW ME OUT!
THE VAN'S READY, KOSEI!
SHH
G-GOOD. LET'S GET OUTTA HERE!
WHAT'RE YOU DOING?! THAT'S KAGASE'S STUFF!!
KLANK
THAT'S RIGHT, AND WE'RE TAKING IT AS A PAYMENT ON WHAT HE OWES.
STOP!! I SAID STOP!!
KOHEI, FORGET IT! KAGASE BROUGHT THIS ON HIMSELF!
KLANK
KLANK
HEY, WHAT'S THIS? I THOUGHT IT WAS JUST JUNK, BUT...
THIS ONE'S BEEN WELL-KEPT.
Is it silver?
THIS WORTH ANYTHING? IT LOOKS PRETTY WORN.

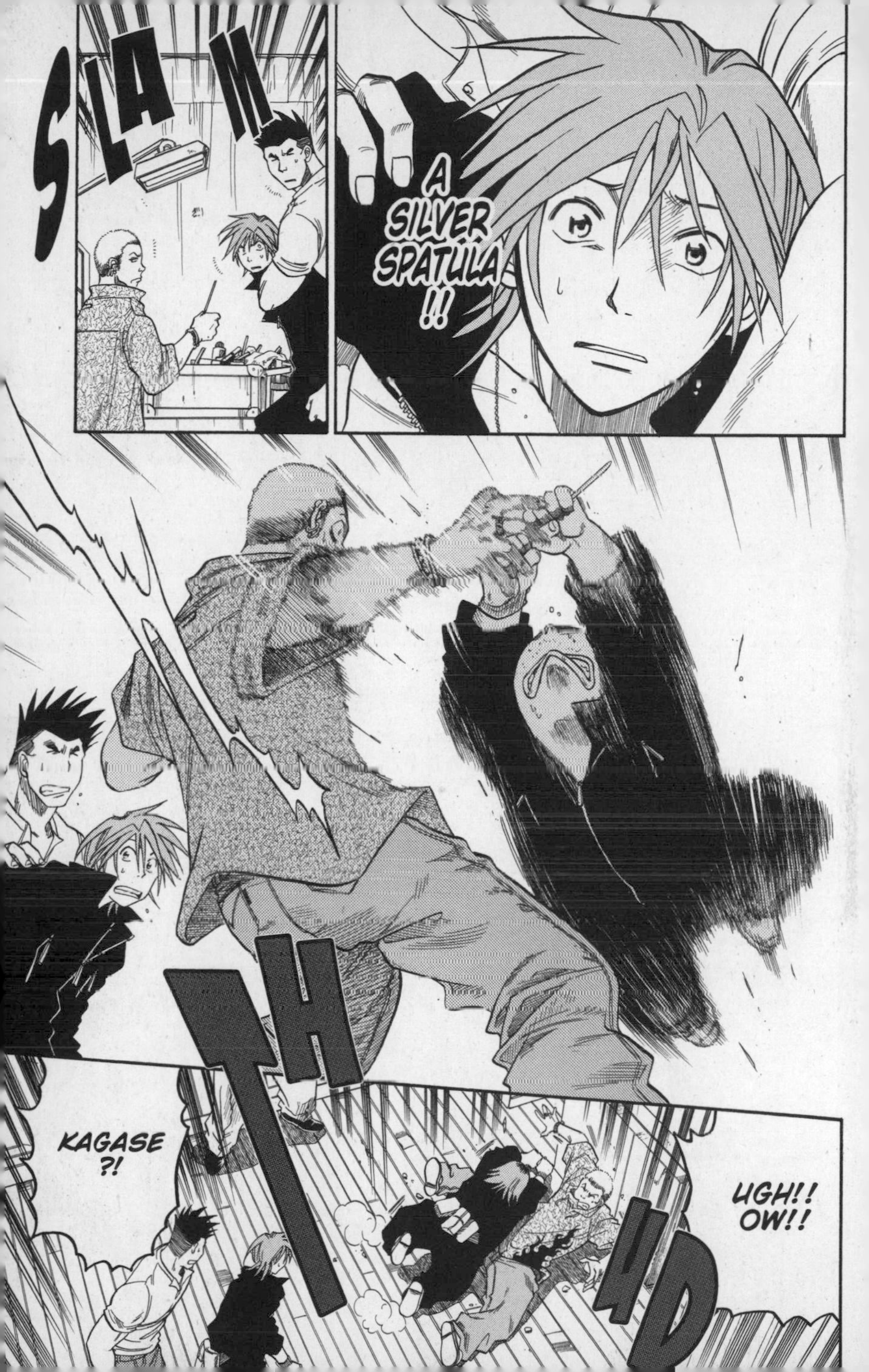
A SILVER SPATULA!!
SLAM
UGH!! OW!!
THUD
KAGASE ?!

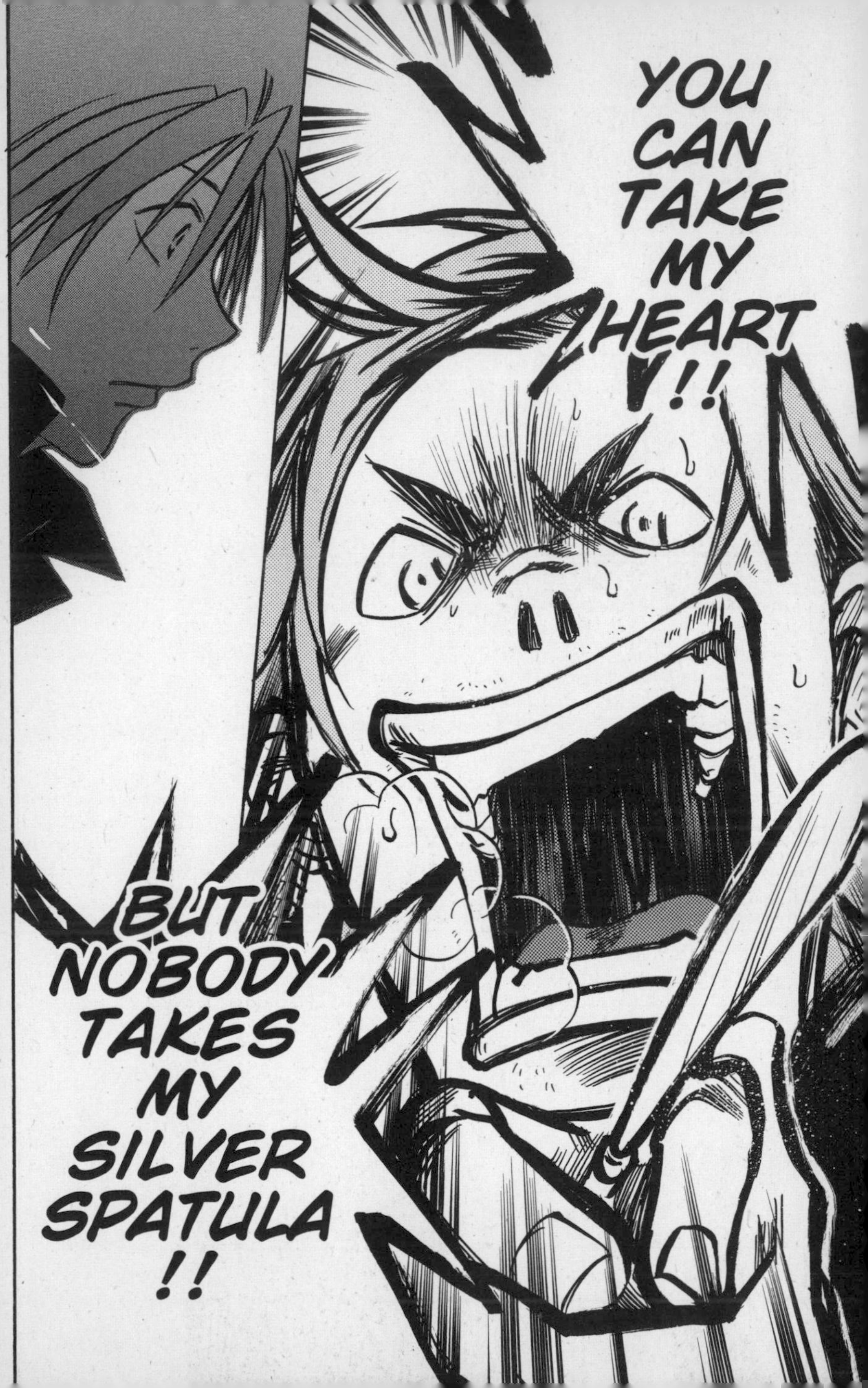
YOU CAN TAKE MY HEART!!
BUT NOBODY TAKES MY SILVER SPATULA!!

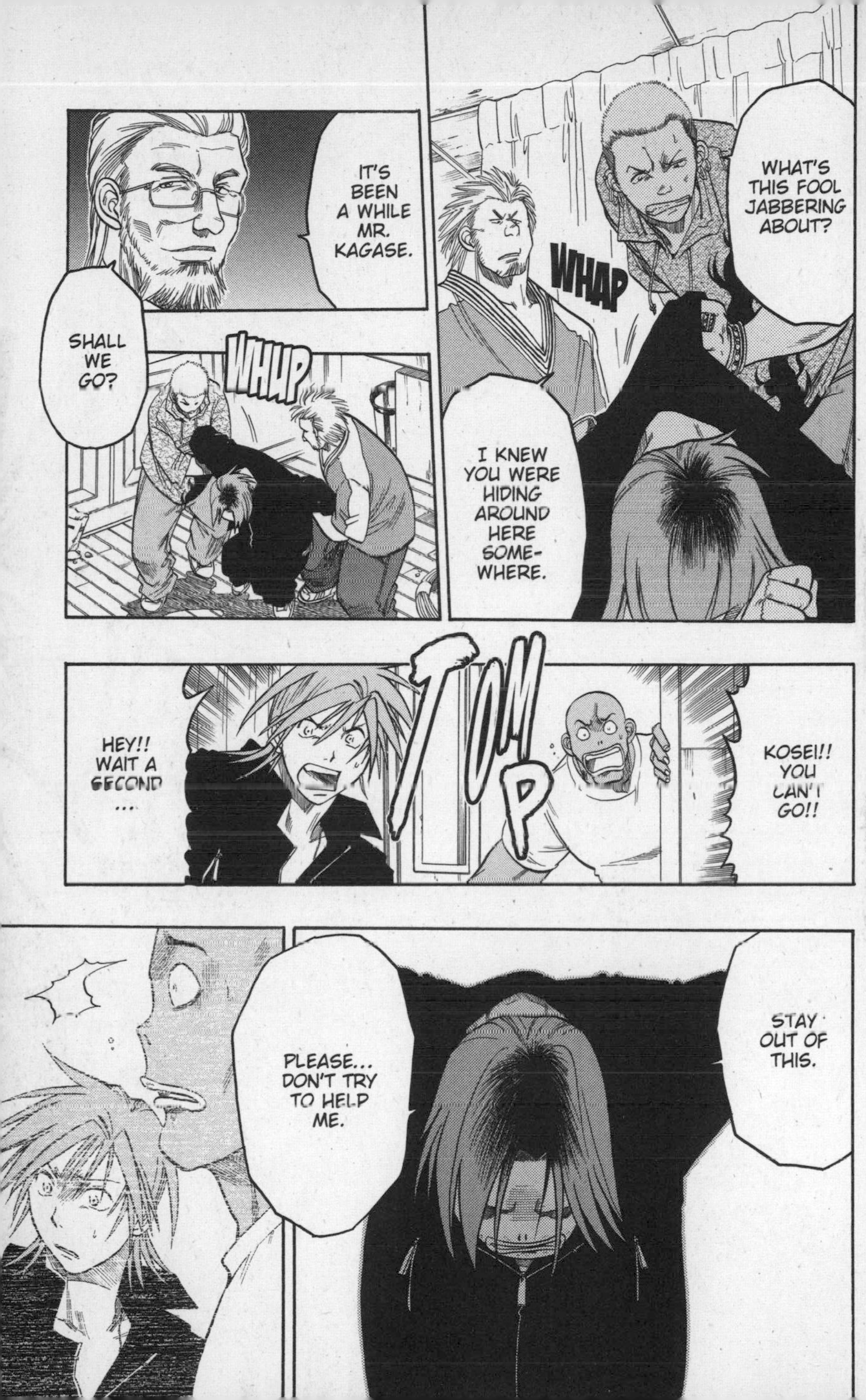
WHAT'S THIS FOOL JABBERING ABOUT?
WHAP
I KNEW YOU WERE HIDING AROUND HERE SOMEWHERE.
IT'S BEEN A WHILE MR. KAGASE.
SHALL WE GO?
WHUP
KOSEI!! YOU CAN'T GO!!
TOMP
HEY!! WAIT A SECOND ...
STAY OUT OF THIS.
PLEASE... DON'T TRY TO HELP ME.

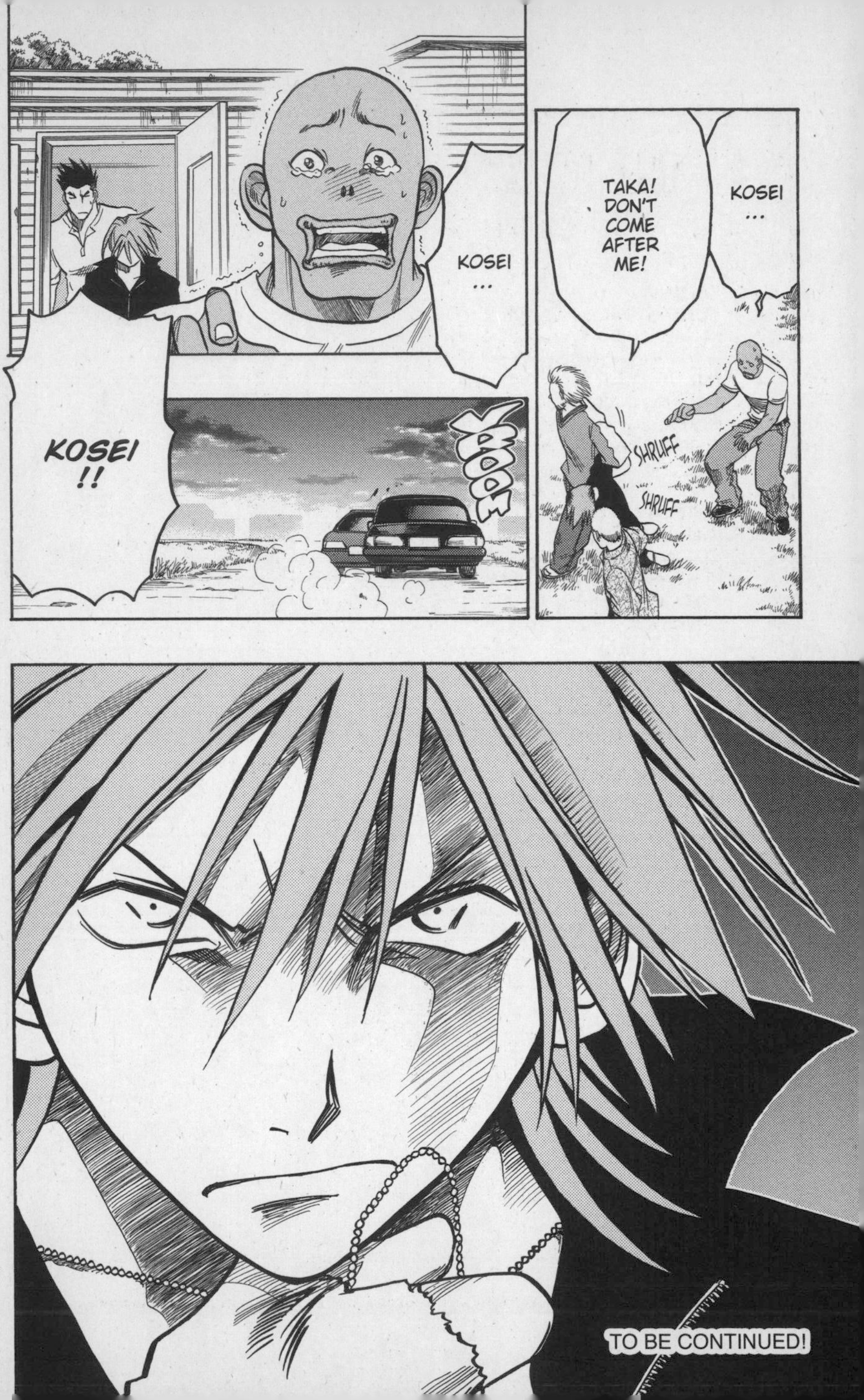
KOSEI ...
TAKA! DON'T COME AFTER ME!
SHRUFF
SHRUFF
KOSEI ...
VROOM
KOSEI !!
TO BE CONTINUED!

THE MAKING OF GIMMICK!
Episode 6   By Youzaburou Kanari

"MONE-Y TRAIN"
"LET'S SHOW WHAT KOHEI'S DAILY LIFE WOULD BE LIKE
IF HE DIDN'T HAVE ANY TO DO WORK FOR A WEEK." THAT
WAS THE INITIAL IDEA SUGGESTED BY MY EDITOR
MR. I-TANI. BUT REREADING THIS STORY NOW, IT SEEMS
TO HAVE VEERED QUITE A LOT FROM THAT ORIGINAL
PREMISE. THEY BUST A GROPER USING SPECIAL MAKEUP
EFFECTS. BY THE WAY, THE GROPER WAS MODELED ON
MR. I-TANI. (JUST HIS FACE, NOT HIS BEHAVIOR!)

"GREAT STUNTMAN"
KANNAZUKI'S A NICE GUY. HE'S AWKWARD AND NOT MUCH
OF A TALKER, BUT HE'S ACTUALLY A REALLY KIND MAN.
I STARTED WONDERING WHY AND I IMAGINED HE MUST'VE
HAD A PAINFUL EXPERIENCE IN THE PAST. HE CAN FEEL
OTHERS' PAIN, MAYBE THAT'S IT.

"SUNRISE BOULEVARD"
DO YOU KNOW WHO SETSUKO HARA IS? SHE WAS ONE
OF JAPAN'S PREMIER PRE- AND POST-WAR ACTRESSES
WHO STARRED IN DOZENS OF FILMS AND WON LOTS OF
AWARDS. HER WORK ON DIRECTOR YASUJIRO OZU'S
BAKUSHU (1951) AND *TOKYO MONOGATARI* (1953) WAS
HIGHLY ACCLAIMED. BUT SHE SUDDENLY DISAPPEARED
FROM THE SCREEN. SHE HASN'T APPEARED IN ANY FILMS
OR ON TELEVISION SINCE. IF ANY ACTRESS CAN BE
CALLED A LEGEND, IT'S SHE. I CAN'T SAY THAT MISUZU
KANZAKI WAS BASED ON SETSUKO HARA, BUT I'D BE
VERY HAPPY IF ANYONE WAS REMINDED OF SETSUKO HARA
WHILE READING THIS STORY.

CONTINUED IN VOLUME 7

THE MAKING OF GIMMICK! CHARACTERS

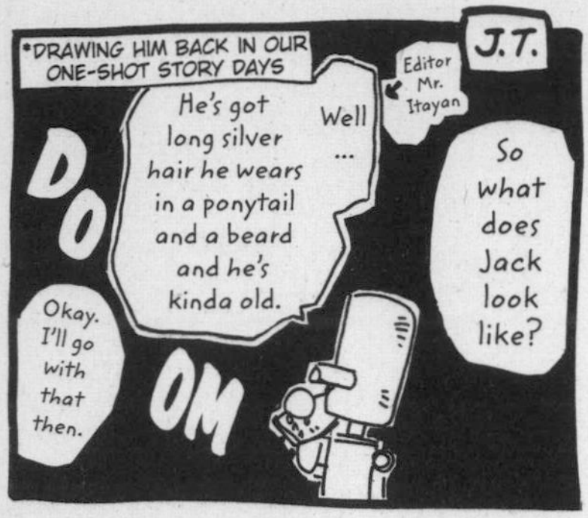
J.T.
*DRAWING HIM BACK IN OUR ONE-SHOT STORY DAYS
So what does Jack look like?
Editor Mr. Itayan
Well ...
He's got long silver hair he wears in a ponytail and a beard and he's kinda old.
DO
OM
Okay. I'll go with that then.

RECENTLY IT OCCURRED TO ME THAT J.T. IS THE ONLY CHARACTER BESIDES KOHEI AND KANNAZUKI THAT STILL SURVIVES FROM OUR ONE-SHOT STORY DAYS. BUT WE NEVER SHOWED HIM FROM THE FRONT EVEN THOUGH I THINK WE'D ALREADY DECIDED WHAT HE WOULD LOOK LIKE.

WHEN I MET RICK BAKER IN L.A. BEFORE THE SERIES BEGAN, I THOUGHT, "HE LOOKS JUST LIKE OUR JACK TAYLOR." I HAD NO PROBLEM COMING UP WITH HIS LOOK AND I REALLY ENJOY DRAWING HIM.

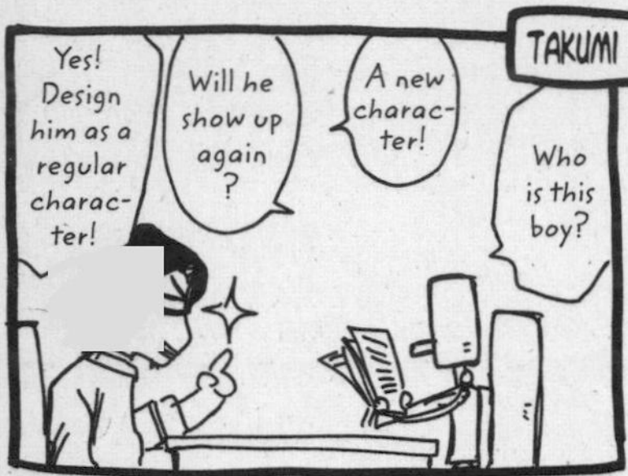
TAKUMI
Who is this boy?
A new character!
Will he show up again?
Yes! Design him as a regular character!

THEY USUALLY GIVE ME SOME WARNING WHEN A CHARACTER IS GOING TO BE RECURRING, BUT TAKUMI CAME OUT OF NOWHERE. I FOUND OUT ABOUT HIM JUST A FEW DAYS BEFORE I STARTED WORKING ON THE SCRIPT. I HAD A HARD TIME DECIDING WHAT HE SHOULD LOOK LIKE. BUT HE DOESN'T REALLY TURN UP THAT OFTEN. (LAUGH)

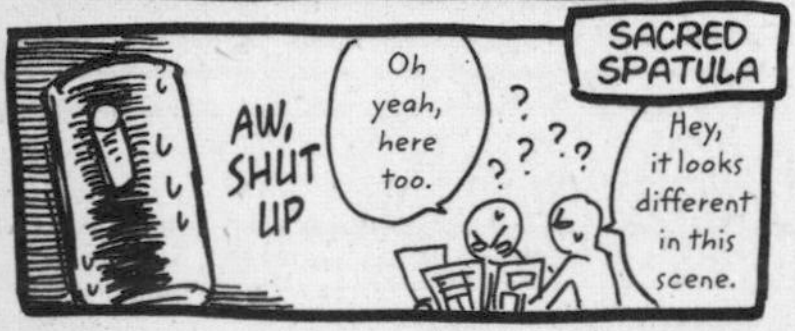
SACRED SPATULA
Hey, it looks different in this scene.
? ? ? ? ?
Oh yeah, here too.
AW, SHUT UP

WE HAD A REAL SACRED SPATULA MADE FOR OUR ONE-YEAR ANNIVERSARY. I HAD A HARD TIME DOING A THREE-DIMENSIONAL DRAWING OF IT. TO THE PERSON WHO MADE IT FOR US, A HUNDRED APOLOGIES. I'M SORRY, I'M SORRY...

GIMMICK! RESEARCH TRIP ANECDOTE

★ TO THE U.S.A.

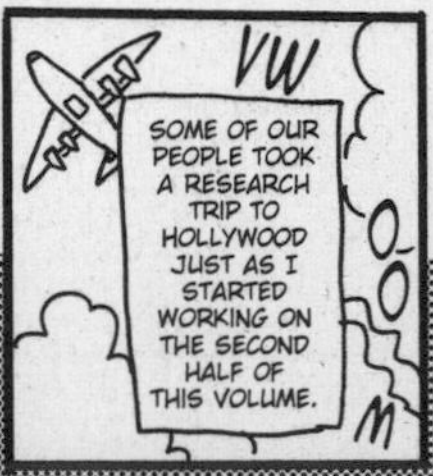
VW
SOME OF OUR PEOPLE TOOK A RESEARCH TRIP TO HOLLYWOOD JUST AS I STARTED WORKING ON THE SECOND HALF OF THIS VOLUME.
OOM

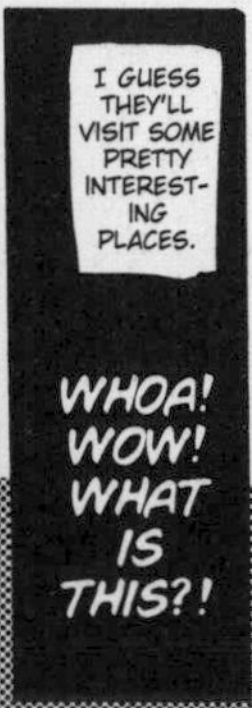
I GUESS THEY'LL VISIT SOME PRETTY INTERESTING PLACES.
WHOA! WOW! WHAT IS THIS?!

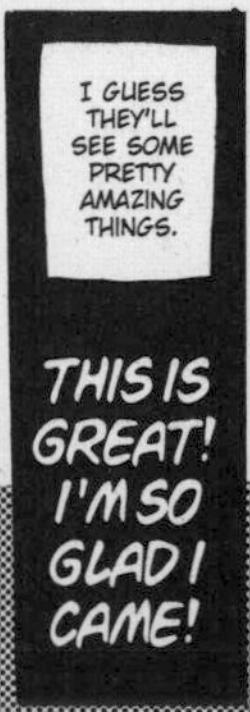
I GUESS THEY'LL SEE SOME PRETTY AMAZING THINGS.
THIS IS GREAT! I'M SO GLAD I CAME!

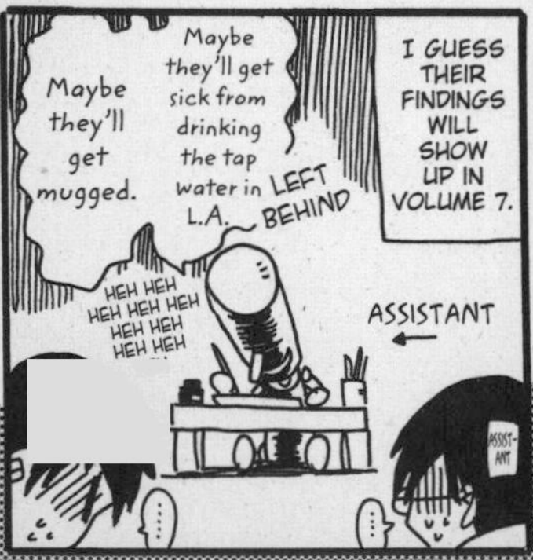
I GUESS THEIR FINDINGS WILL SHOW UP IN VOLUME 7.
Maybe they'll get sick from drinking the tap water in L.A.
LEFT BEHIND
Maybe they'll get mugged.
ASSISTANT
HEH HEH HEH HEH HEH HEH HEH HEH HEH
ASSISTANT
...
...

PATTERN PARTNER

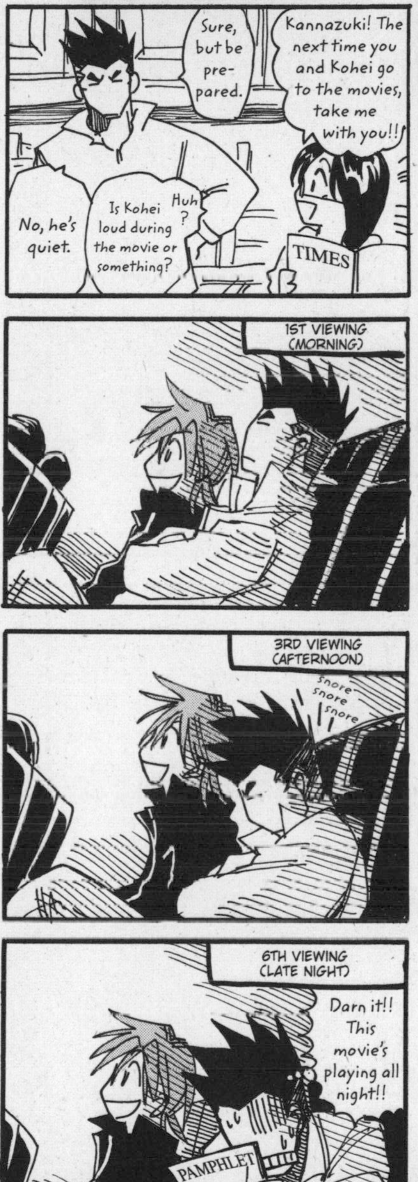
Kannazuki! The next time you and Kohei go to the movies, take me with you!!
Sure, but be pre-pared.
TIMES
Huh?
Is Kohei loud during the movie or something?
No, he's quiet.
1ST VIEWING (MORNING)
3RD VIEWING (AFTERNOON)
snore snore snore
6TH VIEWING (LATE NIGHT)
Darn it!! This movie's playing all night!!
PAMPHLET

OF COURSE HE BUYS THE DVD TOO!!

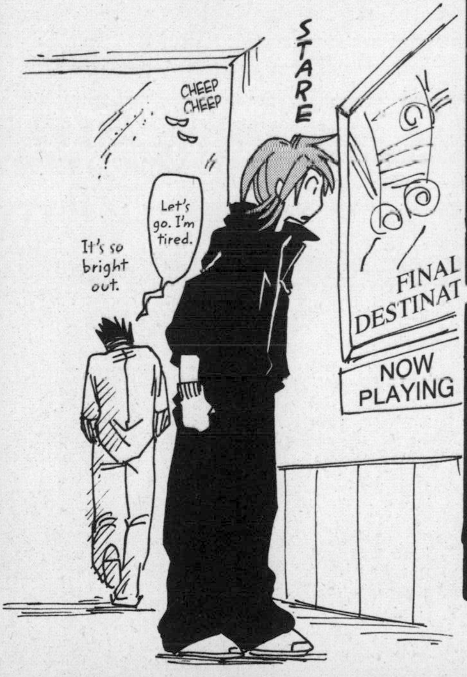
STARE
CHEEP CHEEP
FINAL DESTINAT
NOW PLAYING
Let's go. I'm tired.
It's so bright out.

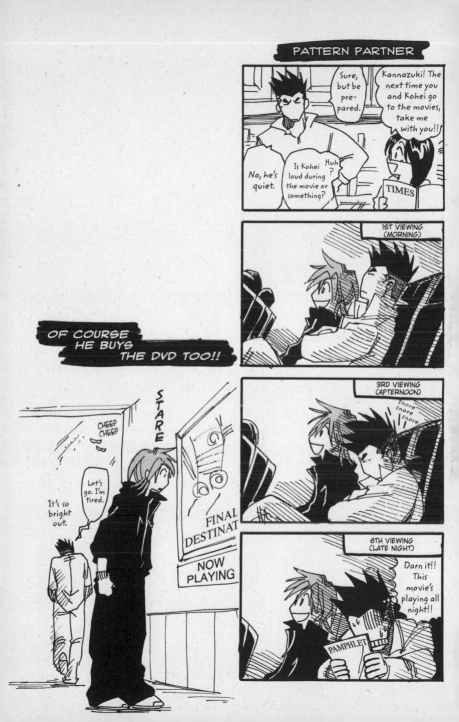

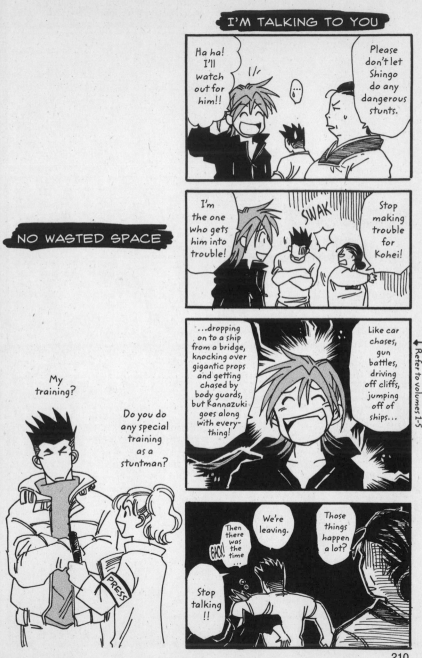

I'M TALKING TO YOU

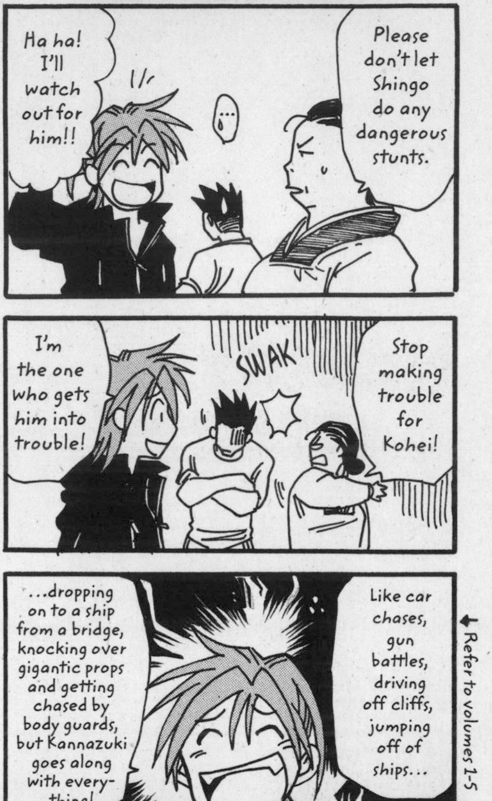
Please don't let Shingo do any dangerous stunts.
...
Ha ha! I'll watch out for him!!
Stop making trouble for Kohei!
SWAK
I'm the one who gets him into trouble!
Like car chases, gun battles, driving off cliffs, jumping off of ships...
...dropping on to a ship from a bridge, knocking over gigantic props and getting chased by body guards, but Kannazuki goes along with every-thing!
Refer to volumes 1-5
Those things happen a lot?
We're leaving.
Then there was the time...
GACK!
Stop talking!!

NO WASTED SPACE

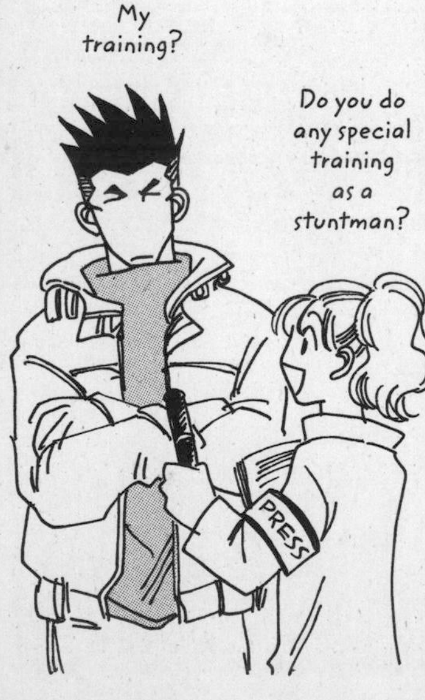
Do you do any special training as a stuntman?
My training?
PRESS

I'M A PRO

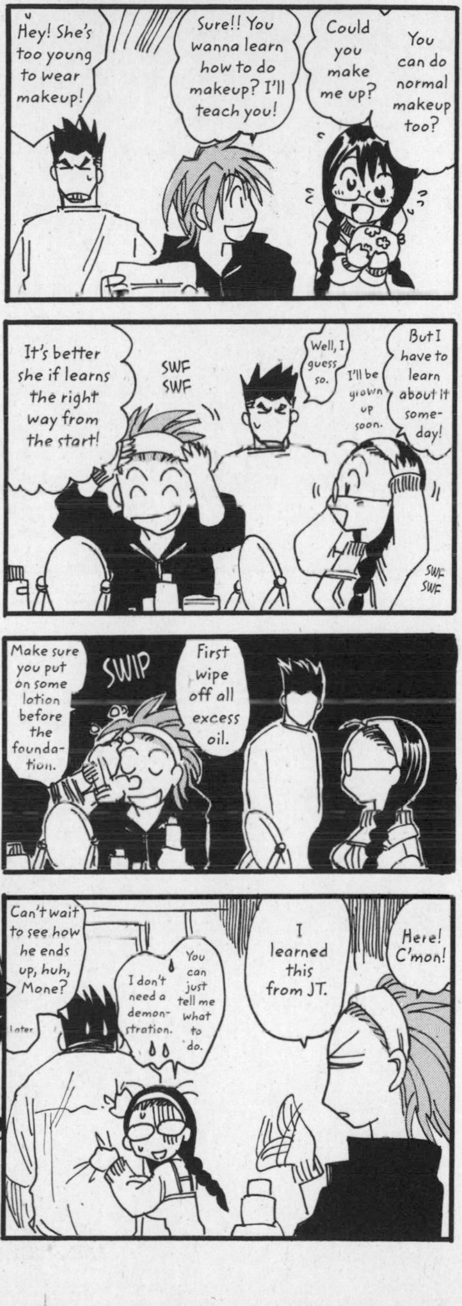
You can do normal makeup too?
Could you make me up?
Sure!! You wanna learn how to do makeup? I'll teach you!
Hey! She's too young to wear makeup!
But I have to learn about it someday!
I'll be grown up soon.
Well, I guess so.
SWF SWF
It's better she if learns the right way from the start!
SWF SWF
First wipe off all excess oil.
SWIP
Make sure you put on some lotion before the foundation.
Here! C'mon!
I learned this from JT.
You can just tell me what to do.
I don't need a demonstration.
Can't wait to see how he ends up, huh, Mone?
Later.

MONE'S FIRST MAKEUP LESSON

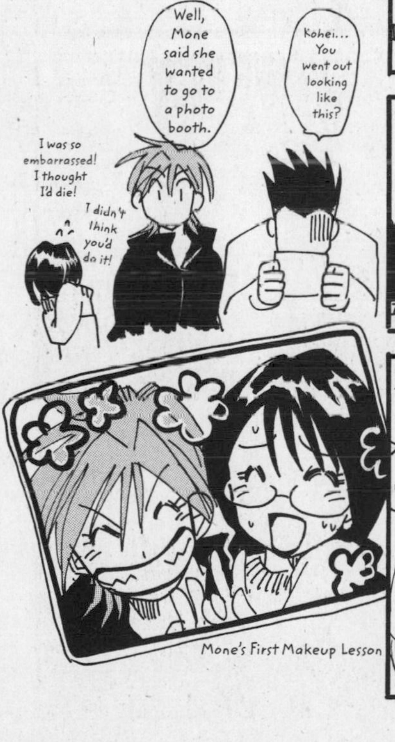
Kohei... You went out looking like this?
Well, Mone said she wanted to go to a photo booth.
I was so embarrassed! I thought I'd die!
I didn't think you'd do it!

Mone's First Makeup Lesson

It's a lot of fun to make even the simplest makeup effects yourself! I recommend everybody try it at least once!

—Kanari

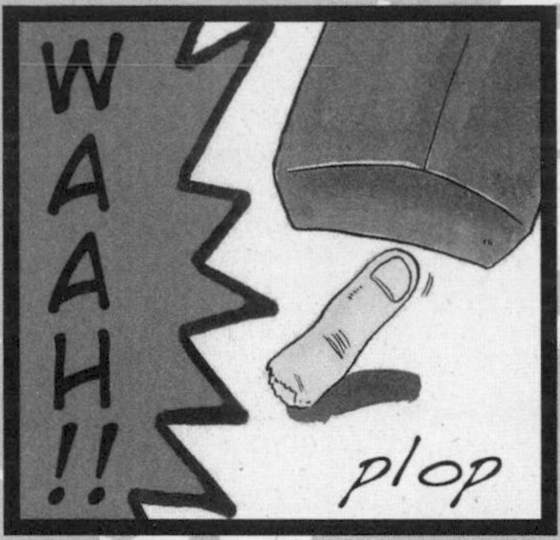
WAAH!!
plop

Somebody actually made a fake finger using the tutorial found in this volume and sent it to us. It was very impressive. I was surprised how real it looked.

—Yabuguchi

GIMMICK!
Vol. 6

Story by Youzaburou Kanari
Art by Kuroko Yabuguchi

English Adaptation/Lance Caselman
Translation/Joe Yamazaki
Touch-up Art & Lettering/Rina Mapa
Design/Amy Martin
Editor/Megan Bates

Editor in Chief, Books/Alvin Lu
Editor in Chief, Magazines/Marc Weidenbaum
VP, Publishing Licensing/Rika Inouye
VP, Sales & Product Marketing/Gonzalo Ferreyra
VP, Creative/Linda Espinosa
Publisher/Hyoe Narita

GIMMICK! © 2005 by Youzaburou Kanari, Kuroko Yabuguchi. All rights reserved.
First published in Japan in 2005 by SHUEISHA Inc., Tokyo. English translation
rights arranged by SHUEISHA Inc. The stories, characters and incidents
mentioned in this publication are entirely fictional.

No portion of this book may be reproduced or transmitted in any form or by any
means without written permission from the copyright holders.

Printed in the U.S.A.

Published by VIZ Media, LLC
P.O. Box 77010
San Francisco, CA 94107

10 9 8 7 6 5 4 3 2 1
First printing, April 2009

www.viz.com

store.viz.com

PARENTAL ADVISORY
GIMMICK! is rated T+ for Older Teen and is recommended for
ages 16 and up. This volume contains strong language, realistic
and fantasy violence, crude humor and adult situations.
ratings.viz.com

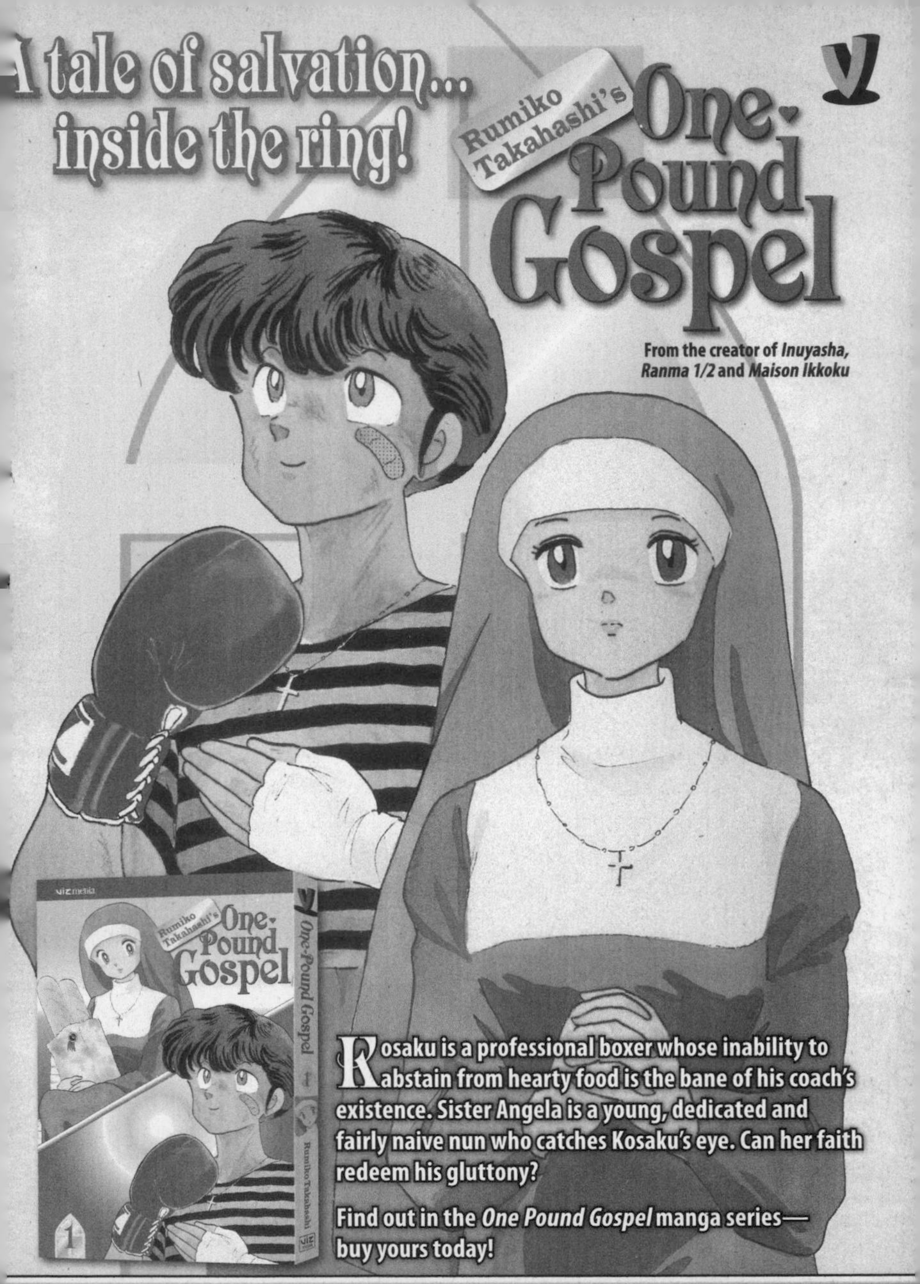
A tale of salvation...
inside the ring!
Rumiko Takahashi's
One-Pound Gospel
From the creator of *Inuyasha, Ranma 1/2* and *Maison Ikkoku*
Kosaku is a professional boxer whose inability to abstain from hearty food is the bane of his coach's existence. Sister Angela is a young, dedicated and fairly naive nun who catches Kosaku's eye. Can her faith redeem his gluttony?
Find out in the *One Pound Gospel* manga series—buy yours today!

A New Twist on
an Old Classic

" Excellent...**intense action** and combat, detailed renderings of inventive super-technology, **unpredictable story line**, surprisingly deep philosophical bent, and **cute heroine.** "

—*Library Journal*

only
$9.95
a volume

The classic series in a new, affordable format!

Relive the adventures of your favorite female cyborg, complete with new features in each volume, including:
• Character bios
• Diagrams
• Comic strips
• An afterword by Yukito Kishiro

Plus, the series appears in the same episodic order as the Japanese version!

The original series and the inspiration for Battle Angel Alita: Last Order -- graphic novels now available!

www.viz.com
store.viz.com

GUNNM © 1991 by YUKITO KISHIRO/SHUEISHA Inc.

LOVE MANGA?
LET US KNOW WHAT YOU THINK!

OUR MANGA SURVEY IS NOW
AVAILABLE ONLINE. PLEASE VISIT:
VIZ.COM/MANGASURVEY

HELP US MAKE THE MANGA
YOU LOVE BETTER!

FULLMETAL ALCHEMIST © Hiromu Arakawa/SQUARE ENIX INUYASHA © 1997 Rumiko TAKAHASHI/Shogakukan Inc.
NAOKI URASAWA'S MONSTER © 1995 Naoki URASAWA Studio Nuts/Shogakukan Inc. ZATCH BELL! © 2001 Makoto RAIKU/Shogakukan Inc.